Being WHITE

Being WHITE

STORIES OF RACE AND RACISM

Karyn D. McKinney

Routledge
New York • London

Published in 2005 by
Routledge
Taylor & Francis Group
270 Madison Avenue
New York, NY 10016
www.routledge-ny.com

Published in Great Britain by
Routledge
Taylor & Francis Group
2 Park Square
Milton Park, Abingdon
Oxon OX14 4RN
www.routledge.co.uk

10 9 8 7 6 5 4 3 2 1

Library of Congress Cataloging-in-Publication Data
McKinney, Karyn D., 1969–
   Being white : stories of race and racism / Karyn D. McKinney.
      p. cm.
   Includes bibliographical references and index.
   ISBN 0-415-93572-5 (hb) — ISBN 0-415-93573-3 (pbk.)
    1. Whites–Race identity–United States. 2. Youth–United States–Attitudes.
3. Race awareness–United States. I. Title.

HT1575.M35 2004
305.809—dc22   2004016459

Dedication
To Amir, Joe, Krista, Mother,
and Daddy, who show me
the forest when I can see only trees.

Contents

Chapter 6

Acknowledgments

Many people deserve my sincere thanks for their support as I have completed this project. First, my gratitude goes to Amir Marvasti for sharing his insights on drafts of this manuscript with me, and for his intellectual and emotional support throughout this process. My sincerest thanks go to him for walking the final arduous mile with me in the preparation of this book. This project would not have been completed without him, and my highest admiration goes to him both as a scholar and a companion. I wish to thank my parents, Roy McKinney, Jr., and Mary McKinney, for making education and intellectual curiosity a priority in our home and for their support at each stage of my career. Special appreciation goes to my father for substantively and technically proofreading and editing this manuscript with prodigious dedication and wisdom. His work as a scholar has been invaluable to this project since its inception. I also thank Krista McKinney, my sister and dearest friend, for her encouragement. She has been a constant source of strength. My sincerest appreciation also goes to Dr. Joe R. Feagin, who offered his substantive insights and technical advice on this project and was particularly supportive in the final stages of completion. Joe has been a model of both academic excellence and high personal standards for me throughout my academic career, and as such has encouraged me to be both a better scholar and human being. I also thank Dr. Lori Bechtel and Dr. Megan Simpson, who have offered their support, advice, and friendship during my work on this book. My appreciation is extended to my editors, Ilene Kalish and Mike Bickerstaff, for their support and encouragement in the publication process. Thanks also to Alexandra Teague, Eric Liddick and Vanessa Gonthier for their diligent copyediting assistance. Finally, I am indebted to each of the young people who so candidly shared the thoughts with me that enabled me to undertake and complete this project. I wish for them increased understanding and peace.

Foreword

Joe R. Feagin

In this fine book Karyn McKinney goes boldly where few scholars have ventured. She is perhaps the first scholar to explore thoroughly how young white Americans of this era think about—or, often, do not think about—their white identities, privileges, and racist society. McKinney probes cleverly and deeply into how young white Americans relate to being white and their evanescent sense of whiteness. While young whites are often portrayed in the mass media as liberal on racial matters, indeed much more so than parents and grandparents, in fact as a group they are racially illiberal. This point is one that McKinney demonstrates empirically and repeatedly throughout her perceptive analysis. Many questions come to mind as one listens to these young white voices, and one is this: "How have so many scholars, pollsters, and commentators missed just how racially conservative many young whites really are?"

Clearly, African Americans and other Americans of color are *not* now the "racial problem" in U.S. society. They never have been, for it is whites who conceived of the ugly material and ideological reality we call "race." Thus, McKinney is part of a long, if thin, line of scholars who have made whites and whiteness the "problem" of U.S. society, one deserving much more in-depth analytical attention than it usually gets. Most in this long line, not surprisingly perhaps, have been scholars of color. It was an African-American sociologist, the scholarly genius and civil rights activist W. E. B. Du Bois, who invented whiteness studies in the early 1900s. So far as I can discover, Du Bois's path-breaking chapter in his 1920 book *Darkwater*, titled "The Souls of White Folk," is the *first* lengthy analysis ever to explore deeply and dissect accurately white identity and whiteness. There Du Bois suggests, among many other insights, that "the discovery of personal whiteness among the world's people is a very modern thing . . . and the [Western] world in a sudden, emotional conversion has discovered that it is white and by that token, wonderful!" Analyzing whiteness incisively, Du Bois examines the white conceit that asserts "title to the universe" and that attempts to make all "children believe that every great soul the world ever saw was a white man's soul." With a biting sense of irony, he later assesses the professed morality of white Christendom about liberty and democracy: "the number of white individuals who are practicing with even reasonable approximation the democracy and unselfishness of Jesus Christ is so small and unimportant as to be fit subject for jest in Sunday supplements."[1]

Much of what McKinney finds fits into Du Bois's pioneering insights about whites' feeling "title to the universe." Using an innovative methodology that secured racial autobiographies from nearly two hundred students in northern and southern universities, McKinney foregrounds and investigates their under-standings of racial matters and their racial experiences and identities. Her sample seems reasonably representative of the country's white youth, and quoted respondents include numerous young women and young men.

A key finding that McKinney offers is how infrequently whites think directly and consciously about whiteness and what it entails. Indeed, in the United States whiteness is so central a social reality, so "normal," that most whites of all ages rarely examine the reality of their white identities and privi-leges. For most whites, including scholars and commentators, even the term "American" seems to conjure up the image of a white person. Indeed, it prob-ably conjures up the image of a white person for most people across the globe. Examine a recent newspaper, magazine, or popular book and you will usually find numerous examples of the words "American" and "Americans" used rou-tinely and unconsciously to mean "white American" and "white Americans." One of my graduate students, Nick Mrozinske, examined all of the articles in sixty-five major English language newspapers for a six-month period. He found there thousands of references to "black Americans" or "African Americans," yet only 46 mentions of "white Americans." And virtually all references to "white Americans" occurred when the writer was also using terms for Americans of color such as "black Americans." It appears that for this country's (mostly white) journalists, as for many ordinary whites, whiteness is an unmentioned centrality, the "elephant in the room" that is called out only when a compara-tive reference is made to racial outgroups.

As McKinney's autobiographies constantly show, racial identity is, almost by definition, invisible when a person occupies the top rung of the racial hierar-chy. There is plenty of empirical evidence—albeit evidence somehow hidden to the reality of most whites—that most major institutions of the United States not only were socially constructed by whites and for whites but are still over-whelmingly dominated by whites. Significantly, most whites, today as in the past, do not see these institutions as white, but rather as "American" and "normal." Rarely do McKinney's students see the major institutions in which they live out their lives for what they indeed are—thoroughly whitewashed institutions cen-trally embedding and constantly reproducing the interests, privileges, and val-ues of white Americans like themselves.

McKinney's accounts indicate that many young whites construct their white-ness in terms of what they are *not*—that is, they are not African Americans or other people of color, whom they often see in more or less negative terms. In these autobiographical accounts, we see considerable white stereotyping—sometimes blatant, sometimes subtle—of Americans of color, as well as considerable criticism of, or resistance to, Americans of color. These substantial levels of stereotyping and racial discomfort do not jibe with recent public opinion surveys in which young whites often appear very liberal on racial issues (for example, on intermarriage). There is a clear suggestion in McKinney's research that young whites appear liberal because they have learned to be *socially correct* to strangers (such as opinion pollsters) in the "frontstage" of their lives while still harboring deep racist imagery, stereotyping, and proclivities in their minds and everyday orientations to the world, especially as they interact with other whites in the "backstage" of their lives. Interesting too in McKinney's accounts is the fact that much of the repertoire of racist thought and action is not seen by young whites as racist.

Living lives apart from people of color is common for whites outside big central city areas. Most of these white students had very limited contacts with people of color before they came to college. Most grew up in overwhelmingly white communities and went to mostly white schools, even in this era of supposed school desegregation. They often see their childhoods as times of innocence when they did not know about "race" or other racial matters. Thus, they often record their first contacts with people of color as dramatic if not painful. They have lived lives of great isolation, which tends to breed the white arrogance to which Du Bois refers.

If they did not have much contact with African Americans and other Americans of color, where then did they get their notions and stereotypes about racial "others" and about their own racial privileges? For the most part, as McKinney shows well, they did not learn their sincere fictions on racial matters from verbal lessons taught by their parents. Few recount such verbal instructions. Instead, their lessons have come from observing what parents, other relatives, and older friends do and say about people of color and white privilege. It is adult behavior from which children quietly and regularly learn the broad repertoire of words, thoughts, phrases, metaphors, and practices that constitute the hard reality of everyday racism.

At the heart of many of McKinney's student accounts lie what Hernan Vera and I have called the "sincere fictions of the white self." Sincere fictions are images, notions, and ideas that whites hold that reproduce aspects of a broad racist ideology at the level of their everyday lives. Thus, whites often describe themselves, or their friends and relatives, as "not racist" or as "good people," while simultaneously these whites often express negative notions about African Americans or other Americans of color. Like older whites, young whites periodically assert their innocence with assertions of not being racist or of their family's innocence in regard to slavery or segregation. Evidently, guiltlessness is professed in all white generations, not just among older whites. Repeatedly, these students privilege whiteness and white perspectives while not being conscious—or not being fully conscious—of what they are doing. Not only is whiteness the national normative structure of the United States, it is the implicit standard for many everyday racial understandings of young white Americans.

Since they but rarely analyze the sources and meaning of racial inequality in the society, these young whites, like older whites, are mostly unaware of how their racial identities are rooted strongly in an ancient and underlying racial order. Rarely do they link continuing racial inequality to this age-old system of white racism. Indeed, one price systemic racism exacts from whites is a studied ignorance and lack of awareness. Most whites exhibit an uncritical cast of mind that not only asserts the existing racial order as normal but also resists questioning other types of oppression in society. Cultivated un-thinking on matters of "race" is often associated with thoughtlessness about sexism, classism, and heterosexism. This is a huge price for continuing racism paid by a society faced by many serious societal problems that demand much new critical thinking.

One of the most intriguing and significant findings here is what I have found in my own research on white men and women of all ages. Most simply do not see how centuries of slavery, legal segregation, and contemporary discrimination have brought them major social, economic, and political privileges and benefits. Clearly, most of these students do not feel that whites as a group, and they themselves as individuals, have benefited greatly from discrimination targeting African Americans and other Americans of color. Clearly, too, they do not see a need for significant new antidiscrimination action, much less reparations, to remedy the impact of past and present discrimination.

Conspicuous too in McKinney's autobiographical accounts is the way in which young whites feel that *they* now are the *victims* of discrimination and inattention. In several chapters of this book we see unmistakably how many white students deny the realities of the racism facing Americans of color by seeing themselves as victims today. Thus, some see themselves and other whites as left out of racial-ethnic events and activities, or out of governmental concern. Some portray themselves, or whites generally, as victims of reverse discrimination and affirmative action, or as now having a socioeconomic disadvantage in the United States. Some feel that whiteness is now an empty category or meaningless.

The challenge signaled by these data is clear. Today as in the past, much white effort, both conscious and unconscious, has been put into mythologizing U.S. history and society so that most young white Americans do not "see" the institutional racism that is the foundation of the society and that continues to privilege most of them greatly. In this manner, they make themselves and the larger society appear blameless for the racial brutality and oppression that they, and their ancestors, have perpetrated on Americans of color.

It is perhaps not surprising that, as McKinney shows, many white media commentators and white academics have difficulty with the idea of "whiteness studies." The main reason for these objections seems to be that most whites of all ages and stations simply do not see anything about whiteness that needs much study. Following the sage advice of scholars like Du Bois and Toni Morrison, instead of these white critics, McKinney here gets us deeply into how young whites relate, implicitly and explicitly, to being white and to whiteness in a still white-racist society.

Preface
"A White Woman from the South"

Oh very young, what will you leave us this time? You're only dancing on this earth for a short while . . ..Oh very young, what will you leave us this time? There'll never be a better chance to change your mind.

Yusuf Islam (formerly known as Cat Stevens), "Oh Very Young"

A white male student once told me that he did not think he could learn about race from a "white woman from the South." I wrote back to him and, trying to remain impersonal, encouraged him to reconsider his views of a North–South difference in race relations today. I added that urban–rural distinctions might influence one's racial attitudes more than broad geographical differences between Northerners and Southerners. Still, his question about my identity reminded me that I am not racially "unmarked" in the classroom; being a "Southern woman" impacts how my message is received. I am now more vigilant about how the dimensions of my identity mediate the course content and my interactions with students—in ways perhaps not completely visible to me.

While writing this book, I also found that being a white woman has an impact on my research in three major ways. First, my role as a researcher has been more difficult to negotiate when studying whites than when researching people of color. Although I do not believe "objectivity" is possible in research, I attempt to be balanced by assuming the perspective of my respondents. Unlike people of color, whites are likely to enjoy certain privileges in U.S. society based on their race. Although all whites do not equally benefit from white privilege, to some degree each has advantages that people of color cannot take for granted. In studying the more privileged group, I found it harder to negotiate my stance as a researcher toward the respondents. I have had to struggle to relate to their perspectives in order to represent their views in the proper context.

Often whites are unaware of their privileges. As this research will show, they may quite conversely believe they are disadvantaged by whiteness. Some harbor negative views of people of color. Repeatedly, I was challenged by my disagreement with some of the beliefs of my respondents. As social science researchers, we are taught an ethic that suggests that "the respondent is always right"—that we are to take the position of our respondent. With this comes the sense that the researcher should not offer disconfirming evidence or arguments against what the respondent states. Charles Gallagher addressed this dilemma of white researchers studying whites and suggested that the researcher should offer counterarguments in interviews with whites who hold factually inaccurate views.[1] In her participatory action research with white teachers, Alice McIntyre also struggles with her role as a white researcher of whites and decides to critique statements of her interviewees that reinforce racist notions.[2] In this book I too sometimes offer counterevidence to respondents' statements. I discuss how certain beliefs they espouse about being white are "fictions" that, left unchallenged, help to sustain societal racism. I believe that I as the researcher can take this position while still maintaining the respect for my respondents that my ethics require. I am able to do this because I am aware that these fictions are part of the collective experience of whiteness—none of these individuals needs to be maliciously racist for these fictions to survive and sustain racism. While my role always causes me to feel I should "treat my respondents as I would want to be treated," this was not always as straightforward as it might sound; as a white person who believes that whites have much to do to end racism, I had to find an analytically and ethically suitable position between the two extremes of being too easy on and too critical of white people. Most helpful was to recognize that it was not individual whites who were my unit of analysis, but stories and discourses representing whiteness.

Throughout the process of writing, I had to negotiate my role as a cultural "insider" studying an identity I shared with my respondents. Sometimes the reaction of other whites to my project highlighted my role as an insider. When I told some whites that I was studying whiteness, they reacted with a congratulatory stance, as if to say "Good for you! We've given enough attention to *them*, it's time someone academic gave some attention to us." Needless to say, my research is likely to disappoint these individuals. Others went somewhat blank. Whiteness is so widely taken for granted that for many whites it does not require attention or explanation. As many of my respondents put it, "We are just white." If I further elaborated that I had chosen to analyze written autobiographies focusing on what it means to be white, some seemed to understand, but then became dismissive: "Oh, none of them know, I bet." To many, this inability to express whiteness seemed to be the end of the story. Subtly or not, many whites tried to remind me that matters of race need not be questioned. In this sense, I was treated as an "outsider." Because I was questioning something that most whites believed did not need explanation, I placed myself in a position alien to most whites, and to my respondents.

As a white person familiar with white culture, I understood how respondents have come to the views that they have. On the other hand, as a white person reading the writing of white respondents, I was frustrated and sometimes even outraged by their statements. As Richard Delgado suggests, one of the ways that whites can help the cause of antiracism is through "subversion from within."[3] Whites who wish to be allies to people of color should work to change the ideas of other whites that perpetuate a culture of racism. For example, as Delgado mentions, whites can help other whites to see that elite whites, not people of color, are responsible for the economic pressures on middle-class and working-class whites. I hope that this book can serve as "subversion from within."

I also keep in mind my own life story while utilizing the life stories of other whites. As in the case of most of my respondents, my parents did not give my sister and me many explicit verbal messages addressing whiteness as we grew up. They did, however, speak to us about racial differences as we encountered them. I recall my father telling others that he did not like them to use racial epithets, and I remember that my mother would not let my sister and me watch certain television shows, such as *All in the Family,* because of the prejudiced attitudes expressed by characters on the show. However ironic those opinions might have been intended to be, I believe she was right in assuming that our young minds would fail to distinguish between parody and realism. These are only two of the many messages about how to "do race" I received from my parents during my childhood and adolescence. I believe that my parents' strong spirituality had a great deal to do with what I learned about race from them. In church we sang "Jesus loves the little children, all the children of the world . . . red and yellow, black and white, they are precious in his sight," and learned that "God loves everyone the same." Whatever the values of anyone else we came into contact with, my parents took "the golden rule" very seriously, and I believe they still do. It was in large part through growing up in their home that I learned a version of "whiteness" that includes a desire for racial equality. For me, this is the part of my life that is about a woman who grew up in the South.

An indigenous, "insider" perspective can be used to gain different insights into data than would come from an outsider's perspective. Especially in whiteness studies, this indigenous perspective can be a useful resource. Some have specifically undertaken whiteness studies with such an approach, in the attempt to better understand complexities of white identity, but also in the hopes of ending racism.[4] It is important to note, however, that whites are separated by many lines of difference, and the role of an "insider" is a relative one. Not every white person would view me as "one of them."[5]

A final challenge in this project lay in my role as a teacher studying and analyzing her own students. Most autobiographies included here are from my students. As a teacher, I feel an inherent sense of protectiveness and desire to be a helpful and knowledgeable ally to my students. But many of the perspectives offered by the students demonstrated conceptions of whiteness that uphold structural racism. White students usually conceptualize racism only in individual terms and have difficulty envisioning structural racism. They seem to believe that when I discuss racism, I am in effect calling each of them a "racist." Many white students react with hostility and resentment to race and ethnicity course discussions and readings, often indicating that they are "tired of being made to feel guilty for being white."[6] Also, having grown up in a time when "not noticing" race (being "colorblind") is equated with being antiracist,[7] I find that most white students are committed to the myth that we live in a complete meritocracy—that all who work hard enough will receive the economic returns they deserve, whatever their racial or ethnic classification. The racism my white students seem most comfortable discussing is so-called "reverse" racism. Many feel that they as whites are facing racial victimization.

Many of the same ideas and attitudes with which I had become familiar in the classroom were reflected in the students' writing. Although often I found some of their opinions perplexing or even distressing, I was gratified that they felt free to share them with me. After several years of interacting with students of all ethnic backgrounds, I am not as often annoyed at an individual student because of the opinions he or she expresses in an autobiography, though I may be worried or puzzled by them. I am instead dismayed by the culture that produces the ideologies reflected there. I do not locate the ideas primarily in the individual student. First, there is too much complexity revealed in their autobiographies to label any student a "racist" in simple terms. Second, countless times, even after they have left my classroom, students surprise me by coming by or emailing to tell me how they have begun to see things differently, and that something they read in my class, or that I or a fellow student said influenced that. We are *all* always "works in progress," and I have rarely met a student with whom I cannot find some common ground, especially after reading about their lives. Striving to present a nonjudgmental attitude to them might have some impact on the forthrightness of their writing. Third, these ideas are so widely shared among the respondents that it is impossible to believe that they reflect individual pathologies or prejudices, revealing instead cultural constructions of race and whiteness. Finally, there is complexity and contradiction in the students' writing—many express antiprejudiced or antiracist sentiments along with visceral expressions of victimization. What is important is not to determine which whites are "racist" or "nonracist" but to try to uncover what whites think about being white, how they have come to think these things, and what impact this may have on the racial system.

Based on the comments of several respondents, the process of writing the autobiography may have benefited them, by serving as a catalyst for a first deep consideration of race. For instance, although she could expect thanks for her contribution, Karen thanks me not only for giving her the opportunity to write her autobiography, but also for reading it:

In closing I would like to thank you for the opportunity to write this autobiography as well as for your time in reading it. It has allowed me to examine my own beliefs and thoughts on racism and learn more about myself. I hope this will be useful to you in your research. Once again, thank you.

Karen implies that it is not the finished product of the paper that is most important, but the dual *processes* of her writing it and my reading it. Interestingly, she includes *both* as valuable for her. Perhaps, in some sense, knowing that someone else has read her words fixes the process as a turning point for Karen. Many other students expressed similar sentiments of personal transformation.

I hope that this process provided such insights to each of the students involved, for without them this project could not have taken place. Autobiographical writing is a very personal process, and I am humbled by the generosity of these young people in allowing their autobiographies to be read by a wider audience. Particularly in writing about a sensitive and complex topic such as race, these authors have placed themselves in a potentially vulnerable position. I have learned an enormous amount from reading their writing. The autobiographies were often profound and were always deeply moving in their sincere approach to the topic of whiteness. Aside from the substantive themes I will discuss from the data, what comes through most is that young people struggle with ethical issues that they realize are of great importance to their own lives and the future of our society. I thank them for their honesty and for allowing me the opportunity to understand whiteness better as we begin the twenty-first century.

Chapter 1
"I Could Tell My Life Story Without Mentioning My Race": Exploring Everyday Whiteness

In my everyday normal life I don't even think about being white. It has no value or gives me no feeling of superiority. . . . Being white means fitting in, I will never be ashamed of the fact that I am white. I do find it hard to talk about whiteness without mentioning any other races. I do feel I could tell my life story without mentioning my race.

Amy[1], a respondent

I was nineteen before I ever thought about what it means to be white. When I was a sophomore in college, as we were studying one night, a close African American friend asked me, "Are you proud to be white?" My mind went blank, and then frantically spun, looking for an answer. I realized that not only did I not know if I was "proud" to be white, I didn't even know what it was to be white—how it felt, what it meant—anything. The question was unanswerable in that the term "white," for me, was empty of any meaning. If anything, "white" seemed to me boring and bland. I have relatives who have pursued our Scottish heritage. Is reclaiming ethnicity a way to fill in the emptiness of whiteness? Perhaps we as white people long to be "different," envying the quality dominant culture teaches us to abhor.

Author's reflection, written March 1998

When I wrote these words, like my respondents (who were asked to write about how race entered their life stories), I had rarely thought about my racial identity. My recognition that I had something in common with my respondents is

1

important. Accepting that white people do have things in common begins to break down the misconception that there is no "white culture," that white people never act as a group. At the same time, this understanding guides my approach as a researcher—I am not a passive, objective observer, but occupy a more complex insider/outsider position in this study.[2]

This book is based on autobiographies of young white people, collected in one Northern and three Southern universities between 1998 and 2003.[3] All of the authors were asked to write a "racial and/or ethnic autobiography" that would take the reader through their lives from their earliest memories of thinking about or noticing race to the present. These autobiographies were in a sense "accounts" of race. Accounts are usually asked for and given as explanations for unusual phenomena. As Lyman and Scott note,

> By an account, then, we mean a statement made by a social actor to explain unanticipated or untoward behavior. . . . An account is not called for when people engage in routine, common-sense behavior in a cultural environment that recognizes that behavior as such. . . . These questions are not asked because they have been settled in advance in our culture. . . . When such taken-for-granted phenomena are called into question, the inquirer (if a member of the same culture group) is regarded as 'just fooling around,' or perhaps as being 'sick.'[4]

Initially, my white respondents thought it inane to talk about something so obvious. They thought whiteness was self-evident and did not require an explanation. In this book, I show how most whites do not think about being white unless they are asked to do so. As such, whiteness could be said to be a *prompted* identity, one that becomes a topic of interest when respondents are directly asked to talk about it.

Recent public opinion research paints a rosy picture of the attitudes of young Americans toward racial and ethnic diversity. A recent Gallup Poll reports that 91% of the young people (aged 13–17) surveyed agree with interracial marriages between whites and blacks and more than eight out of ten teens say that they do not mind whether their college roommate is black, white, Hispanic or Asian.[5] The author of the report concludes that race is virtually a "non-issue" for young people. Of course, another more detailed report about the same poll reveals that eight percent of whites would not like a black roommate and twelve percent would not like a Hispanic roommate.[6] Thus, at least some young whites still reported discomfort with roommates of another racial background. In terms of religious tolerance, in all the racial groups combined, twenty-nine percent stated they would not like a Muslim roommate. Given the political climate in the post-September 11 United States, this finding likely reveals not only religious but also ethnic bias. Still, not only these two Gallup Polls but also others reach the conclusion that young people have moved beyond the issue of race, and racial prejudices are nonexistent in this generation. For example, in two other Gallup Polls the conclusion is reached that about two-thirds of U.S. young people have "at least a few friends" of other races and ethnic backgrounds.[7] These findings differed by geographical region, with teens in the Northeast reporting some of the lowest levels of integration. Still, most young people stated that there was a negligible amount of racial segregation in their lives and schools.

Although not based on a nationally representative sample, my qualitative research reveals a contrasting picture of young whites' perceptions and attitudes. The data was gathered in two regions of the country. Allowed to write about their own lives in detail, these respondents discuss many lingering discomforts, fears, and struggles with racial issues. Most still discuss a sense of distance from people of color not revealed in the public opinion surveys. Although roommate situations can lead to turning points in their racial identities, most of these young whites were at first quite apprehensive about sharing their domestic space with a person of a different racial or ethnic background. Most importantly, this research will show how the majority of young whites construct whiteness as a liability, while some recognize it as an undeserved privilege when prompted to discuss their racial identities. This research is an exploration of the white self as presented in written autobiographical accounts.[8] The next section describes the analytical framework of this book.

Exploring Everyday Whiteness

> My project is an effort to avert the critical gaze from the racial object to the racial subject; from the described and imagined to the describers and imaginers; from the serving to the served.

> Toni Morrison[9]

In describing her literary project in *Playing in the Dark: Whiteness and the Literary Imagination*, Toni Morrison mirrors my sociological interest. Before reading her words, I had not yet found anyone else using the metaphor I had envisioned for my research. I wanted my study to turn the critical gaze away from the racialized Other, onto racialized whites. In this sense, my research consists of "othering" whiteness—treating it as exotic. One of the privileges of whiteness is to be able to remain racially invisible, unnamed.[10] As in a child's "peek-a-boo" game, as white people we are able to cover *our* eyes to consciousness of "race"[11] and, in doing so, fool ourselves into thinking that, because we do not "see" race, we will not be *seen* as racialized beings. In this state of pseudo-invisibility, whites have more often consumed the stories of racialized others, while their own lives remain unexplored.[12]

My data reveals that many young whites are themselves convinced of this invisibility of white culture, and until we have first outlined the contours of whiteness in everyday experience, we will not be able to make whiteness visible. Just as there is no one "blackness" (i.e., blacks belong to diverse socioeconomic, religious, and political backgrounds), there is no essential whiteness—white people are divided by ethnic, regional, religious, class, and gender differences, among others. Not every white person experiences whiteness the same way. For example, as George Lipsitz points out, all whites do not benefit equally from their whiteness. However, the "possessive investment" in whiteness does affect every white person's life opportunities.[13] Because of this, a "white life" is more likely to include certain elements than the life of a person of color does in the United States.

Aside from the substantive content of group experiences (slavery vs. freedom, oppression vs. advantage), the major difference between whiteness and blackness is that whiteness has not been *held accountable* to the extent that blackness has. I use the word "accountable" here in two ways; both in the non-academic, ethical/moral sense, and in the academic/theoretical sense. Even after those in academia began to treat racism as a white and not a black problem, whites have very rarely been held equally accountable for helping to end racism.[14] Most whites, unless they are overtly racist, in the sense of involvement in white supremacist activity or the expression of old-style prejudice, feel absolved of implication in "racism."

Second, blackness, in popular and academic discourse, is considered more account-worthy in that it is the non-normative or "marked" position, while whiteness, being normative, or "unmarked," usually is not, literally, *accountable*. So as much as scholars of race and ethnicity may believe that racism is a white, and not a black problem, most empirical studies of racism still focus on people of color, as the victims of racism, and not on whites, its perpetrators. Thus in both the literary and the moral sense, African Americans and other people of color are held more "accountable" than whites, both in popular culture and in the academy. Rather than taking whiteness for granted as invisible and self-evident, this study holds it accountable. That is, using student racial autobiographies, this book questions the way whiteness is talked about in popular and academic discourse. At the same time, my research is intended to draw direct connections between how whites see themselves and the larger problem of modern racism.

Until relatively recently, research on whites has focused on "heroes" and "villains," that is, antiracist white activists and members of white supremacist groups. Only the two extremes of those who directly challenge white privilege and those who struggle to maintain it received attention from researchers. Presumably, most "average" whites would not align themselves with either group. Yet it is these average whites who are involved in everyday racism.[15] This is the type of racism that routinely affects the lives of people of color, and its root causes depend on average whites' support of the racist status quo, or lack of recognition of or resistance to structural discrimination.

Some have called for more research on what whites think about being white. For example, Feagin and Vera write:

> Most research on whites' racial attitudes is focused on how whites see the 'others.' The question of how whites see themselves as they participate in a

racist society has been neglected. . . . While we do not underestimate the value of learning about others, we believe that one way to begin to address white racism in this society is to reorient social science research to a thorough investigation of whites' own self-definitions and self-concepts.[16]

The primary goal of this research is to examine what average whites believe it means today to be white. In the next section I describe how I went about doing my research from this perspective.

Collecting and Making Sense of Autobiographical Data

> The personal is political.
>
> Traditional feminist adage

> We are always coming up with the emphatic facts of history in our private experience and verifying them here. All history becomes subjective; in other words, there is properly no history, only biography. Every mind must know the whole lesson for itself—must go over the whole ground. What it does not see, what is does not live, it will not know. . . . In like manner, all public facts are to be individualized, all private facts are to be generalized. Then at once History becomes fluid and true, and Biography deep and sublime.
>
> Ralph Waldo Emerson[17]

Examining life stories holds promise for deciphering whiteness and the way white people interact with people of color, as noted here by the authors of *Storied Lives*:

> To the sociologically oriented investigator, studying narratives is additionally useful for what they reveal about social life—culture 'speaks itself' through an individual's story. It is possible to examine gender inequality, racial oppression and other practices of power that may be taken for granted by individual speakers. Narrators speak in terms that seem natural, but we can analyze how culturally and historically contingent these terms are.[18]

In individual white people's life stories lies a rich source of information about white culture, even though that culture is often invisible to the storytellers themselves.

Some researchers assert that change is the operative metaphor in autobiographical discourse.[19] As such, autobiography is particularly suited for a study of whiteness at the millennium, because the racial and ethnic makeup of the population is shifting. Written autobiography has not often been used as sociological data, although it seems particularly able to make "the personal political" by exploring the relationship between the experiences of individuals and larger social patterns.[20] Robert Blauner, in his introduction to *Black Lives, White Lives*, reminds us that the great sociologist C. Wright Mills believed "investigating the relation between public issues and private troubles is sociology's special mandate."[21] Thus Blauner chose a life story approach to study how white and African American adults make sense of race in their lives.

While many sociologists have used *oral* life history narratives as research data, few have examined written autobiographies. When written autobiographies are used, it is usually popular autobiographies, or autobiographies of the famous that are examined.[22] Anthropological research, on the other hand, has produced multiple volumes using autobiography as data, with many focusing on the life story of the researcher, or "autoethnography."[23] As Rosenwald and Ochberg argue in *Storied Lives,* autobiography can be particularly useful in exploring the construction of identity:

> How individuals recount their histories—what they emphasize and omit, their stance as protagonists or victims, the relationship the story establishes between teller and audience—all shape what individuals can claim of their own lives. Personal stories are not merely a way of telling someone (or oneself) about one's life; they are the means by which identities may be fashioned.[24]

Some whites have written autobiographies chronicling how they came to know themselves as white. These autobiographies include stories of white individuals joining families of color or bringing people of color into their families,[25] stories of whites who have discovered they are *already* related to people of color,[26] memoirs of "race traitors" and race "pretenders,"[27] and chronicles of racial understandings reached in the life histories of various whites.[28] Additionally, some have published anthologies of multiple personal narratives about race (by whites, people of color, and biracial Americans) with varying degrees of accompanying analysis.[29] With the exception of Bob Blauner's and Studs Terkel's compilations of narratives, most autobiographies are written by racially aware whites, since they are more inclined to reflect on these issues. Where average whites (who usually do not notice their whiteness) are concerned, the story of "everyday whiteness" has not yet been fully explored.

I have found few studies in which authors have used students' writing as data in studies of race and racism. Two are Jerome Rabow's *Voices of Pain and Voices of Hope* and James Waller's *Prejudice Across America*, both of which use students' journal entries from a college course to discuss contemporary prejudice and racism.[30] A third is edited by Thomas Dublin, titled *Becoming American, Becoming Ethnic*.[31] In this book, Dublin, after a brief, but insightful introduction, simply reproduces students' ethnic life stories, written for his courses, in their entirety. Finally, Margery Mazie and her colleagues use writing from a course on race to show how the teacher and students "deconstructed whiteness" throughout the semester.[32]

My data was collected in college classes that I or my colleagues taught.[33] I developed the syllabus for my first race and ethnicity course (in which I first collected data for this book in 1998), after having recently done interviews with white women who had dated African American men.[34] In that study, my respondents told childhood stories about becoming aware of race in general and their own whiteness in particular. Through their encounters with "difference" in various settings, such as homes, neighborhoods, schools, or in the media, some of the women I interviewed "noticed" their whiteness in early childhood, as well as their attraction to people of color. Others spoke of specific watershed experiences, or epiphanies, with race that they believed to have awakened them and shaped their current views.[35]

Thus, I developed an interest in how white people's life stories may provide a "usable past" in regard to their race and ethnicity.[36] I was also intrigued by how whites "do race" in their present everyday lives.[37] I included in the syllabus for my race and ethnicity course a final journal assignment in which students were to write their "racial or ethnic autobiography." After many of the white students voiced concerns about completing the project, I handed out a guide listing questions they might address in their papers.[38] I asked them to take the reader through their lives from earliest childhood memories, emphasizing incidents, parental messages, educational encounters or media content, all of which, I theorized, may have influenced their understanding of their own and other's race and ethnicity.

When I first asked students to write autobiographies for my race and ethnicity class, I did not intend to use them as data. My experience was similar to that of Dublin (*Becoming American, Becoming Ethnic*), who gathered ethnic family stories from his college students. He too was impressed by the quality of student autobiographies. I do not remember specifically what made me think to ask students to write autobiographies as a course assignment; I only recall that I wanted to try to get students to consider how race had affected them personally. On a more selfish note, after reading much more traditional-style essays and research papers for the entire summer, I wanted at least one assignment to be a bit different, and perhaps more enjoyable to read.

I remember vividly my growing excitement as I began to read the students' papers. The depth of their thought, the passion with which many of them wrote, the insights they raised—all of these things were evident to me as I read and graded their papers. Further, I noticed certain patterns and themes in their writing, and this was when I began to believe that the papers I was reading were valuable sociological data. I discussed my ideas with my mentor, Joe Feagin, and colleagues, and the project began to take shape.

The Respondents

The data for this book were collected from 1998 to 2003 at four universities, three southern and one northern. Most of the authors range in age from eighteen to twenty-one. The entire sample, including both the southern and northern samples, included 193 respondents, made up of 54% autobiographies from women ($n = 105$) and 46% autobiographies from men ($n = 88$). The southern subsamples are summarized in table 1.1, and the northern subsamples in table 1.2.

There are many similarities in the lives of my respondents prior to coming to the university. Most had very limited contact with people of color until they began college, growing up in predominantly white communities and attending white schools, although this differs somewhat between the southern and northern samples.[39] They describe childhood as a time of racial innocence and sometimes of instinctively knowing racial "truth," which they wish they could retain throughout their lives. Many respondents remember first noticing race through contact with neighborhood children or school acquaintances. As others have found in their research, several of these respondents remember their first interactions with people of color as dramatic or even painful.[40] For example, when first confronted with people of color in school, they sometimes describe feeling fearful and outnumbered, even though most were in a significant majority. Many note the racial segregation on their high school campuses and believe it to have been equally the choice of whites and of people of color.

Perhaps the most notable similarity in the stories of almost all the respondents is that they received virtually *no* verbal parental messages about race,

TABLE 1.1 Summary of Southern Subsamples

Sample	Gathered	Female	Male	Nontraditional (age 30 years+)	Total
1	Summer 1998 (my class)	74% ($n = 17$)	26% ($n = 6$)	4.3% ($n = 1$)	37% ($n = 23$)
2–5*	Fall 1998 and spring 1999	60% ($n = 24$)	40% ($n = 16$)	—	63% ($n = 40$)
Total	All Semesters	65% ($n = 41$)	35% ($n = 22$)	1.5% ($n = 1$)	$n = 63$

*These Southern subsamples were collected in the classes of four colleagues, who offered their students extra credit for writing an autobiography for my research. Thus, in four of the subsamples, students knew *before* writing their papers that they could be used in research. Together, these data were collected over the period from June 1998 to December 1999. All of the students in this first sample lived in the Southeast, although many were born or had lived in other regions of the country. I did not separate the Southern subsamples that were collected in colleagues' courses from one another, since they were collected in the same ways, under the same conditions. All but one were collected at the same university. The main difference that I believe is important to recognize is in the number of autobiographies collected in my own classes versus the number that were collected in others' classes. I will discuss notable findings regarding differences between the Southern and Northern samples in appendix B.

TABLE 1.2 Summary of Northern Subsamples

Sample	Gathered	Female	Male	Nontraditional (age 30 years+)	Total
1	Fall 2000	50% ($n = 5$)	50% ($n = 5$)	20% ($n = 2$)	7.7% ($n = 10$)
2	Spring 2001	50% ($n = 22$)	50% ($n = 22$)	2.3% ($n = 1$)	33.8% ($n = 44$)
3	Fall 2001	64% ($n = 9$)	36% ($n = 5$)	—	10.8% ($n = 14$)
4	Spring 2003	45% ($n = 28$)	55% ($n = 34$)	9.7% ($n = 6$)	47.7% ($n = 62$)
Total	All semesters	49% ($n = 64$)	51% ($n = 66$)	7% ($n = 9$)	$n = 130$

All of these "Northern" subsamples were gathered in my own race and ethnicity courses between 2000 and 2003. In the first two subsamples, all students were required to write autobiographies, submitted in two chapters, as part of the course. At the end of the semester they were asked to allow me to use their autobiographies for my research, and if they agreed, they resubmitted them and were given extra credit for allowing me to do so. Students were, of course, offered other types of opportunities to receive extra credit, should they choose not to allow me to use their autobiographies in my research. My university's Institutional Review Board (IRB) approved this research technique, including the informed consent form that students were given and signed. In the third subsample the autobiographies were not part of the course requirements, but were offered *only* as an extra credit assignment and written for that purpose. The fourth subsample was similar to first two, except that students submitted the autobiography only as *one* paper, which counted for less of their overall course grade and was shorter. They were asked shortly *before* submission whether they would allow me to use their papers in my research, whereas the other students in the Northern sample were asked after submitting their papers. Thus, in only one of the Northern subsamples did the students know their papers could be used in research as they were writing them.

nor had any discussions with their parents regarding what it means to be white. Previous research is consistent with this finding and also suggests that white parents not only do not discuss race with their children, but silence them when their children try to bring up the topic.[41] This reaction is perhaps best explained by the growing tendency, since the end of the Civil Rights Movement, for whites to equate not noticing race (being "colorblind"), or at least not mentioning it, with nonracism.

These respondents did carefully watch their parents' *behavior* regarding race and drew many conclusions about racial etiquette based on their observations. When asked to discuss their own racial autobiography, most told their life story moving from the first person of color they remember to the most recent. As I will discuss in chapter 3, many whites seem to construct what it means to be white based on their sense of what they are *not*—a person of color. This is indeed evident in the structure of their autobiographical narratives.

The primary focus of this book is young white people's attitudes toward race and racial identity as reflected in their autobiographies. Youth is an important factor in this research. Although whiteness is a social position that is anchored in other statuses such as gender, class, and local setting,[42] it is also influenced by age and generational affiliation. White young people may be especially sensitive to current changes in white identity. Young people today are exposed to different societal events and discourses of race than their parents and grandparents were, and thus they have different resources for the construction of everyday whiteness, and a different understanding of race relations, than do older generations. White young people are also, because of social desirability bias, often less willing to express belief in stereotypes than previous generations were, and are more concerned with presenting themselves as "non-racist." Generational differences arise primarily because of the influences of contemporary events and differences in exposure to people of color.[43]

Thus, white students constitute perhaps the most appropriate population for a study of contemporary whiteness, for several reasons: (1) in their often more subtle, covert, or colorblind attitudes, they exhibit a different style of racism than their parents or grandparents, who may have engaged in more overt and blatant hostility and discrimination; (2) with acts of young white-male violence being commonplace and sometimes racialized, more research is needed to address the racial components of their hostility and alienation; (3) because of the nation's changing racial demography, most young whites will have more contact with people of color than their parents or grandparents; and (4) young whites will become policymakers and voters and, as they replace the older generation, they will have a greater impact on whether racism will be eradicated.

The Beginnings of Whiteness Research

This section provides the novice reader with a general overview of the background of social science research on whiteness. Specifically, after briefly describing the history of whiteness studies, I review the major scholarly works in this area and show how this book builds on the previous research by focusing on how young whites see themselves in relation to people of color.

Historical Overview: The African American Contribution

It was people of color, and not white academics, who pioneered the field of whiteness studies, without referring to it as such. An edited volume by David Roediger, entitled *Black on White: Black Writers on What It Means to Be White*, filled an important research gap by reminding race theorists that long before white studies became part of academia, people of color, and particularly African Americans, had been writing about whiteness.[44] Historically, people of color have had to take an interest in whites. Their status as members of a minority group, combined with their economic dependence has compelled people of color to be familiar with white culture. Even while they were enslaved, African Americans analyzed the behavior of their captors, as in the writing of Harriet Jacobs, a young slave who wrote the "plain truth" about living in a white Southern home in her 1861 memoir, *Incidents in the Life of a Slave Girl*.[45] Thus, much of the current whiteness research builds on or echoes the works of African American authors from decades or even centuries ago. It is a sad testimony to their privilege that only when white people began to write about themselves that a field called "white studies" was created to support their interest.

Many African American authors wrote works specifically about the challenges of dealing with "white folks." For example, before it became common (with the work of such theorists as Roediger, Theodore Allen, and Omi and Winant[46]) to write of the "social construction of whiteness," African American scholars had recognized race as a social rather than biological trait, and the fact that one "becomes," rather than is born, white.[47] Ralph Ellison and Malcolm X both highlighted the observation that the quickest way for an immigrant to "become" white, and thus feel "instantly American," was to learn to deride African Americans.[48] James Baldwin, in his essay "On Being 'White' . . . and Other Lies," notes that "[n]o one was white before he/she came to America."[49] According to Baldwin, whiteness entails a moral choice—a choice to justify black oppression and also to include certain positive aspects of human experience in one's life and to exclude other negative things, which are subsequently relegated to the racial Other. Baldwin concludes thus that there can really be no white "community," because no community can be based on "so genocidal a lie."[50] In *Notes of a Native Son*, Baldwin considers the role whiteness plays as a societal norm, as well as the fact that this is a shifting reality that is subject to change.

Another broad theme addressed first by African American writers was the role of class and capitalism in fostering racial division and tension. Before any white scholar gave the topic serious consideration, W. E. B. Du Bois, Oliver C. Cox, and other African American labor historians considered the economic aspects of white privilege. As will be discussed in later chapters, Du Bois formulated what is perhaps one of the most useful concepts in class analyses of racism: the "psychological wages of whiteness."[51]

Research on White Identity

More research has been done on minority group racial identity than on white racial identity, presumably because positive racial identity can be used as a coping mechanism against discrimination.[52] Fewer theorists have recognized the need to explore white racial identity in order to dismantle racism. One of the few models of white racial identity, and by far the most influential, is that of Janet Helms. Helms offers a developmental model of white racial identity, in which whites move through several stages on their way to an autonomous white identity. Operating on the assumption that racism is damaging to white identity, Helms attempts to suggest a way for whites to move out of denial of race to a positive white identity. Helms' model categorizes several stages of white racial identity. The first is the *contact* stage, in which whites encounter people of color, sometimes with fear or curiosity, but deny that their own whiteness causes them to benefit from racism. In the second stage, *disintegration*, a white person first encounters moral conflicts involved in the recognition of whiteness. It is not until the third stage, *reintegration*, that a white person consciously acknowledges a white identity, but the content of it is white supremacy. Helms asserts that it is usually a personally jarring event that serves to move a person out of this stage of racist white identity.

In the fourth, *pseudo-independent* stage, a white person begins to create a positive, nonracist white identity. In this stage, a white person begins to question the assumption of white superiority and African American inferiority. The fifth stage of white identity development is that of *immersion/ emersion*, in which a white person replaces stereotypical assumptions of race with accurate information about what it has historically meant to be white in the United States and in the world at large. The final stage of white identity development, according to Helms, is *autonomy*. The autonomous white person no longer must oppress, denigrate, *or* idealize people of color in order to have a positive white identity. Helms sees this stage as more of an ongoing process, in which whites learn to apply their new conceptions of whiteness, as well as continue their vigilant opposition to institutional and personal racism.[53]

Since introducing her identity theory, Helms has applied her work to create an activist guide for "being a white person or understanding the white person in your life."[54] This volume represents perhaps one of the first practically oriented attempts to problematize whiteness. Others have used Helms' work as a foundation in their attempts to further elaborate on white racial identity.[55]

White Racism Research

Another aspect of research on whiteness has focused on the link between white privilege and racism. Historically, whiteness has been about claiming certain rights by virtue of one's skin color. Whereas young whites may identify racially "by default," because they have lost touch with much of their ethnic traditions, earlier generations still had close ties to their ethnic heritage and thus had the choice of retaining an ethnic identity. Those who chose instead to identify as white, implicitly or explicitly, expressed the desire to set themselves apart as racially distinct and superior, and so to benefit from the privileges of that identification.[56] Indeed, in recent years, the only whites to claim a white identity explicitly have usually been white supremacists.[57]

Researchers have explored the psychological dimensions of racism for whites. Such work has typically treated racism as a "disease" of white Americans and has attempted to find its causes and cures.[58] Despite the significant contributions of these studies to understanding prejudice, their focus on racism as resulting from *individual* white personality disorders or developmental conflicts leaves unexamined the structural and cultural bases of white privilege. Ending prejudice is a noble goal, but it may not be necessary, or even effective, without simultaneously working to end discrimination. Robert Merton's typology of prejudiced and discriminatory personality types demonstrates, for example, how people can be prejudiced without practicing discrimination or can even practice discrimination without holding prejudiced attitudes.[59] If Merton's assertions are true, then it is more important to work to end discrimination, and the racist system that results from it, than to try to change the attitudes of every prejudiced white individual. Thus, studies of prejudiced attitudes alone cannot show us how discrimination persists in the routine workings of our institutions. We should also attend to the ideologies and practices of racism.

More recent research has studied "everyday racism," the institutionally-supported daily oppression of people of color by the white dominant system in U.S. society.[60] Such work highlights the fact that discrimination is neither infrequent nor the fault of individual sick white minds. Instead, it is pervasive and is supported not only by many prejudiced whites but also by a culture of racism.[61] Some of these studies demonstrate how racism harms people of color, whites, and the entire society.[62]

For example, in *White Racism: The Basics,* Feagin and Vera interviewed whites to explore how they construct whiteness in a way that allows them to retain certain "sincere fictions" of the white self.[63] Feagin and Vera demonstrate how whiteness itself serves as a foundation for racism. Further, they show how it is racist notions of *average* whites that form the basis for everyday racism.

Another body of research examines the various positions that white people adopt regarding race and whiteness. Some of these studies categorize whites in terms of their stance on racism. Perhaps the most influential of these is Ruth Frankenberg's typology, presented in *White Women, Race Matters: The Social Construction of Whiteness.*[64] In this volume, Frankenberg describes three distinct perspectives on race: the "essentialist," "colorblind" (power-evasive), and the "race/power conscious" views. According to Frankenberg, white individuals move through these three phases on their way to antiracism. Frankenberg's typology has been extremely valuable in describing racism and asserting that white people may be acting according to different perspectives on race. Her research has helped to show the complexity of racism and, like Feagin and Vera's, has also contributed to dispelling the notion that the only contributors to racism are extremists. Since publication of her book, other authors have begun to apply Frankenberg's typology to their research and have elaborated on the various perspectives she outlines.[65] Particularly, Frankenberg's discussion of colorblind racism has been useful for understanding how whites may see themselves as nonracist and yet still contribute to a societal system of racism and white privilege.

Indeed, numerous scholars have shown that a primary characteristic of modern racism is the denial that it still exists.[66] Correspondent with this denial is a stance of colorblindness toward racial identity.[67] This line of reasoning assumes that because whiteness is not important to whites, blackness is not, or *should not* be important to blacks, Latino-ness to Latinos, and so on. Further, according to this ideology, racism is all but demolished, so if we just remove the remaining vestiges of race recognition, such as affirmative action, racism will completely disappear. Colorblindness also denies white privilege.

This knowledge has added to existing work aimed at increasing white awareness and thus combating racism.[68] Yet although many studies have explored whiteness at the extremes of racism and antiracism, very little significant research has empirically demonstrated how average whites in the U.S. think and feel about *their own* race and ethnicity, as well as that of others.[69] This sociological attention to whiteness as a "thing" to be studied is relatively new, compared to the studies of white racial identity, white ethnic identity, and white racism that have preceded it.

Contemporary Research: Whiteness as a Social Construction

Whiteness research blossomed in the late 1990s, when theorists began to study whiteness as a social construct.[70] Early on, this research area was dominated by cultural studies practitioners, particularly those doing work in literary and film studies. Two seminal works in cultural studies have been frequently cited as the first examples of white studies. First, Toni Morrison, in *Playing in the Dark,* questions the taken-for-granted, normal status of whiteness.[71] Similarly, in his ground-breaking book, *White,* Richard Dyer examines images of whiteness in film, photography, and visual art in order to discover how whiteness takes the position of "ordinariness" in Western culture.[72] Indeed, Dyer is credited with some of the first statements describing the invisibility of whiteness. For example, in an article titled "White," published in 1988, he states that "Trying to think about the representation of whiteness as an ethnic category in mainstream film is difficult, partly because white power secures its dominance by seeming not to be anything in particular, but also because . . . it is often revealed as emptiness, absence, denial or even a kind of death."[73] Dyer goes on to describe how whiteness has come to seem "normal," or a "historical accident."[74] Dyer's theoretical discoveries were based on the observation that whiteness in a sense is never explicitly represented in film. Instead, it is always replaced with ethnicity, class, or regional identity. He concluded that one of the ways that whiteness retains power is by seeming cultureless, or nonexistent. This idea would become important in the work of others, across academic disciplines, and I found it to be an integral part of my respondents' experience.[75]

Since the publication of these two works, there has been a proliferation of research on whiteness, especially in the interdisciplinary field of cultural studies.[76] Whiteness has been examined in film,[77] media photography,[78] and in broader cultural and political discourse and theory.[79] Most of these studies look at how cultural representations of whiteness influence everyday discourse and behavior surrounding race. Cultural studies treats whiteness as a social construction, which, once created, further constructs other aspects of the social environment. After its beginnings as a subfield of cultural studies, whiteness theory and research later began to be evidenced in history, legal theory, autobiography, sociology, and several anthologies.

For example, there have been studies of how European immigrant groups came to be constructed as "white."[80] Others have provided in-depth analyses of the "whitening" of particular groups, such as the Irish,[81] the British working class,[82] and Jewish Americans.[83] Some of the most important work in the area of historical studies of whiteness has been that of Omi and Winant. In their seminal work, *Racial Formation in the United States: From the 1960s to the 1980s*, Omi and Winant trace how various groups were defined as white through historical, political, and economic circumstances.

Legal theorists have examined the role that law has played in the social construction and maintenance of whiteness. In an insightful article, Cheryl Harris discusses the construction of whiteness as "property," protected by law.[84] Similarly, in his 1996 work, *White by Law*, Ian Lopez shows through the analysis of court cases how the boundaries of whiteness are maintained in law.[85] Legal scholars have also questioned the colorblind standard for race neutrality in the workplace, asserting that what passes for "colorblind" is actually based on "transparent" white norms of behavior.[86] Claims about the neutrality of decision making in the workplace must be treated with skepticism, particularly when all decision makers are white.[87] Others have used criticism of color-blind ideology to explore its implications in public policy, politics, and culture. This research elucidates how white people are "invested" in whiteness both as a source of material rewards and as resource for their identity construction.[88] The overall goal of the this line of inquiry has been to expose the advantaged status of whites in Western societies, a status that comes at the expense of oppressing people of color.

Since the beginning of the field of whiteness studies in the area of literary and cultural studies, there has been debate over its impact and its purpose.[89] Some argue that it amounts to little more than returning white people to the center of the white intellectual research establishment or, even worse, a growing body of apologetics for white privilege that does little to work against racism. Others assert that whiteness studies can become part of the foundation for antiracism. As a whole, since its beginnings, the field of whiteness studies, or "white studies," often has baffled those outside academia and spurred debate amongst academics. For example, in a 1997 article in the popular online journal, *Salon*, Tim Duggan writes

[W]hiteness studies [is] the trendiest and most perplexing new field in academia. . . . A mix of liberal anti-racism, muddled postmodern theory and embarrassing white guilt, the study of "whiteness" has opened the floodgates of a new scholarly market. And with over 70 books, hundreds of journal articles and two recent conferences on the subject, it has all the trappings of a bona fide movement. But how far it'll be moving—and what it actually has to teach us about race—is less than clear. . . .

The author goes on to discuss the work of some of the most noted authors in whiteness studies. He then describes a whiteness studies conference he attended, which he found to be "chilling" in terms of its "heated oratory," but, perhaps even worse, incoherent in its message. Duggan adds:

[W]hile whiteness studies seems to have found its place on the scholarly radar, it's having a much tougher time finding some kind of cohesion. . . . In spite of all the conflict and confusion, one could argue that many people are now willing to see that white is indeed a color of its own. And as scholars of all stripes joust over the direction of the field, they might take solace in the fact that they are marching together under the banner of whiteness. Whatever that means.[91]

Although he is not a expert in the field, I cite this author because I am interested in his overall perception of the field of whiteness studies—described in a popular magazine—its incoherence, inaccessibility, and in the end, irrelevance to the lives of everyday white people.

Certainly some theorists in the area of whiteness studies are working very hard to ensure that their research has a practical impact in changing racial circumstances. Many strive to make the connection between whiteness and structural racism clear in their analysis. There is also evidence that whiteness studies may be beginning to have an impact outside academia. For example, in a recent issue of *Diversity Inc.*, a magazine whose primary audience is the business community, an article about whiteness studies explicitly asserts that academic whiteness studies can help whites in the business world to have a more accepting attitude toward a diverse workforce: "[M]any people are not aware of the impact of their behavior and biases, and . . . this lack of awareness isolates people of color and impedes the success of organizations. White managers may have certain blind spots generated by centuries of being the dominant culture, but without being made conscious of those blind spots, they may not perceive that they have a problem."[92]

Still, because most of the writing in whiteness studies has remained theoretical and historical, many people have a difficult time relating it to their everyday experiences. Additionally, the field of whiteness studies, and our critique of whiteness, can progress only so far until we begin to do more research that asks everyday white people what *they* believe it means to be white. A very fruitful line of inquiry is to understand what whiteness means to white people. As social activists, it is these people we must convince to relinquish their white privilege. Although we know, historically, politically and socially, what "whiteness" means, we must also know what it means as part of the identities, experiences, and ideologies of white people.

If the goal of whiteness studies is to abolish white privilege and ask whites to give up their status, then I would go a step further than Duggan. I would ask: How realistic can a movement based on eliminating white privilege and racism be if we do not first study the experiential dimensions of this "whiteness" that we are asking white people to renounce? How grounded is a movement built on very little empirical work with its main subjects of interest? In this study, I proceed from the belief that in order to better oppose everyday racism, it is crucial that we explore everyday *whiteness*.[93] No doubt whiteness, as historically and presently practiced, is destructive, to whites, but most devastatingly, to people of color. We must understand it completely to disarm it effectively. Studies aimed at this understanding are only just beginning to be done.[94]

Some have argued that it is whiteness that is the underpinning of the system of categorization that is race. Kalpana Sheshadri-Crooks writes:

By Whiteness, I do not mean a physical or ideological property. . . . By Whiteness, I refer to a master signifier (without a signified) that establishes a structure of relations, a signifying chain that through a process of inclusions and exclusions constitutes a pattern for organizing human difference. This chain provides subjects with certain symbolic positions such as 'black,' 'white,' 'Asian,' etc., in relation to the master signifier. 'Race,' in other words, is a system of categorization that once it has been organized shapes human difference in seemingly predetermined ways.[95]

It is essential that antiracist scholars understand how whiteness is grounded in everyday experience so that the categorization scheme that has long privileged whites at the cost of every other racial and ethnic group in the United States can be undermined.

Themes of Whiteness

Most respondents noted that had they not been asked to write about whiteness, they would not have mentioned it when discussing who they are. In this sense, whiteness is a prompted identity. Once asked to consider their whiteness, respondents tell stories that describe what it means to them to be white. This book is organized around themes from these stories of whiteness; it aims to show how whites see themselves in relation to other racial groups. For the most part, being white goes unnoticed by those in my study. Still, there are times in their lives when whiteness becomes visible and salient. In Chapter 2, I show how whites sometimes recognize whiteness through turning points, or moments when they become conscious of being white. After these experiences, the research participants became more aware of differences between whites and people of color.

Next, I explore the various ways being white, or white identity, is used by young people. Chapters 3, 4, and 5 all describe whiteness as a liability. Specifically, chapter 3 shows how my respondents write about whiteness as culturally empty and meaningless. I demonstrate in chapter 4 how, for my young respondents, whiteness makes them vulnerable to accusations of racism and denies them equal participation in ethnic events and practices. Thus, whiteness in the twenty-first century brings a sense of cultural victimization. Chapter 5 focuses on whites' perceptions of their economic status. Rather than understanding whiteness as a privileged status, my respondents state that being white causes economic disadvantage. In this chapter I juxtapose their accounts against available research on affirmative action and its effect on whites.

Chapter 6 describes how the group I studied sometimes recognizes whiteness as a privilege. Here I also discuss how my respondents struggled with their responsibilities as recipients of undeserved privilege. Throughout chapter 6 I point out how the students themselves found ways to question their whiteness. As a whole, the autobiographies analyzed in this book are about two contrasting themes: whiteness as a liability, and whiteness as a privilege. Collective white identity is constructed through individual white struggles with these two positions. Young whites struggle with their position in part because of global and national changes in the status of whites. In chapter 6 I also consider the political climate that has paved the way for a "collective white identity crisis" and its impact on how whites describe themselves. Finally, chapter 6 concludes the book with a discussion of how antiracist pedagogy can challenge whites' misperceptions of whiteness as a social liability.

Chapter 2
"I Began to See How Important Race Could Be": Turning Points in Whiteness

Despite my time studying race and ethnicity, I have been in the racial minority very seldom. It is even rarer that these situations are for any prolonged or regular period of time. One of the most memorable was when I tutored for a juvenile probation program. This was transformative, though not necessarily in the most obvious ways. Most would expect me to be surprised by the difficult lives led by many of the young men, and therefore made grateful for my comparatively carefree one. This was partly true, but I was also surprised to find that several of the young men were as intelligent and capable as I. I expected to "learn" from them, certainly, in "life lessons" or "street smarts," but I had not expected to realize that many could have taken my college classes and impressed my professors with their intellect and insight (even as high school students). I have been surprised and dismayed by reactions to my "work" with "troubled youth," and this has been a sort of epiphany of whiteness for me. I recently rediscovered a long-forgotten newspaper feature on my volunteer work. In it, I fear I appear a privileged young white woman donating some of her busy life to dubiously worthy black young men. In retrospect, I think I took from them much more than I gave, trying on various "white shoes" or racial positionings, and stumbling repeatedly. I never found the right way to "help" while remaining human and allowing them to do the same. My only consolation is that I was very young.

When visiting my husband's family in Miami, I find I am part of a racial and ethnic minority in the city, in 2004. My whiteness seems startling, garish, and out of place. I am conscious of my status as a white female, and more careful of the impression I make and the signals I send. Now, these temporary concerns are overshadowed by all the positive things the city brings me, in both familial association and cultural diversity. Still, being in the minority is not a common experience for those of us in the majority. The first time a white person finds her or himself in the minority can serve as a turning-point experience, although it may also be uncomfortable, in that it can bring one's whiteness into sudden visibility. Each time thereafter, being in the minority can be a reminder that there is social meaning to being white.

Prompted Whiteness

Perhaps one of the most important findings of this study is that whiteness is a *prompted identity*; that is, most of the respondents insist that they had not thought in any depth about whiteness until asked to do so by the writing guide. Other researchers have similarly found that the most common response that whites give when asked what it means to be white is that they have never before considered their white identity.[1] As previously mentioned, one legal scholar has labeled this unconsciousness the "transparency" characteristic of white identity.[2] For these respondents, their whiteness is indeed "transparent," and many indicated they would not think to discuss it were if they were not being asked to do so. For example, Neal writes:

> I think it is difficult to talk about whiteness because I'm really not sure what it means to me. I have pondered this for many days . . . Actually when I think of whiteness it has nothing to do with race but I think of purity. Since I couldn't figure out what whiteness exactly meant to me I began to ask others. Needless to say I received a lot of stupid stares. I did get one answer so I thought I'd tell you what this person told me. I asked, 'What does whiteness mean to you' and she said when she thinks of whiteness she thinks about the perfect family. She also said she thinks about the All-American Family. Sort of like the Walton's or The Brady Bunch. The idea of a nice house, the perfect family, a nice car, and a good income was what whiteness meant to her.

Whiteness was constructed in the autobiographies after having been prompted. Thus the particular autobiographical constructions of white identity arose specifically in the context of this research, and are undoubtedly shaped by its purposes. Whiteness is not self-evident. For many respondents, like Neal, the notion of whiteness evokes thoughts of being part of the "all-American" norm.

According to other studies, many white people, were they not asked to consider what being white means, would evidently never do so. In a study of young British whites, Ann Phoenix found that most of them had not thought about what it means to be white and did not consider themselves proud to be white, because individualist notions cause them to believe one should be proud only of individual achievement.[3] Many were also reluctant to voice pride in being white because they believed that only white supremacists would do so. Phoenix also found that having grown up relatively isolated from people of color allowed the young people to retain stereotypical views of them. Phoenix suggested the need for whiteness to become an "overt identity," and for further research into the racialized identities of young whites.[4] Most of these respondents state that they have never given race very much thought, and they go on to construct themselves as passive recipients of racial messages from their parents and the larger society. Many suggest that after being given these messages, their thoughts on race were "set," and they have given little thought to their own race since. Once prompted to consider their whiteness, they are faced with what, if any, their role should be in a world they recognize as highly racialized.

Before writing this autobiography, many of the respondents had very likely had to think about their race or ethnicity only when filling out forms, which, given their age, has probably not been a regular occurrence for them yet. As Deanna states,

> I really do not know how to discuss what it is like to be white. I just am. . . . I live in a place, one of the few places left, where everyone is the same when it comes to race. Race and ethnicity is not talked about, and it is not brought up. The only time that I ever really think about it, is when filling out some sort of paper work that requires it. For example, an application for a job asks for race. I still do not understand what race has to do with someone's ability to do a job. . . . The person best fit for the job should be hired, no matter what their race or ethnicity. . . . I would definitely have no problem at all telling my life story without mentioning race or ethnicity. Even when I describe myself, white does not pop into my head. I guess this is because I was brought up in a family where race did not matter. Everyone is equal. They definitely believe in equality, or at least that is what they let me believe so that I could make up my mind for myself from my own personal experiences.

Deanna brings up two reasons why race, to her, is not a necessary part of her life story. First, the area in which she grew up was predominantly white, as was the case for many of the respondents. For many whites, a sense of a racialized self is dependent on awareness of and contact with a racialized "Other." Many of these young people have had no such contact until coming to college, in the few years before writing their autobiography. Thus for most of their lives, they have not thought of themselves as "white." Second, many whites believe that the only way to a truly egalitarian society is through colorblindness. They believe that "race" is only invoked in the pursuit of inequality, as in the case of the so-called "reverse discrimination" that results from the utilization of affirmative action goals and policies. It seems important to their sense of equality and fairness to maintain a stance of "not noticing race." To overlook race includes not giving attention to one's own race, and this is discursively linked with being colorblind to others' race—and thus being nonracist.

In the following passage, Elysia, like Deanna, mentions that because she lives in a small town, her white identity has never been salient to her. She has had contacts only with other white people. Since whiteness is the norm in society, for most whites, without significant interpersonal contact with a person of color, whiteness might never become an overt identity. Unlike the reality for people of color, whiteness is not even mentioned in the media routinely; so for a white child growing up in an all-white environment, whiteness would likely remain invisible. Elysia also alludes to other reasons that whiteness is a "prompted" identity:

> If/when I am asked to identify myself, I seem to focus more on age and gender as the most important, relevant features. In my small town community "whiteness" is not often the topic of any conversation. For most of my life all of my friends, peers, and associates have been white. I don't recall ever having to define, defend, or even discuss my "whiteness."

Some respondents may have little sense of whiteness because other identity statuses take a greater priority for them. Elysia mentions that age and gender are more important parts of her identity than are race. This may be because the status positions she occupies in these categories—being young and female—are sometimes stigmatized statuses. Hence, she is more likely to be discriminated against based on these roles. Even if she has never faced discrimination based on being young or female, she is perhaps conscious of the possibility that this could happen. For whatever reason, other parts of her identity are more important to her than being white—whiteness must be invoked, whereas Elysia would introduce age and gender as relevant to her identity.

Elysia also mentions that she has never had to "defend" her whiteness. Molly also mentions not being reminded by others of her whiteness:

> I think my race is less important to me than it is to members of other groups. I feel that this is true because I take my race for granted. I don't have to be conscious of it all the time, so I forget the benefits it brings. I also think that African Americans and other minorities are more aware of their race because they are constantly reminded that they are different.

As other respondents in this study note, part of white privilege is not having to face discrimination. Although respondents may suggest that they face as much "reverse discrimination" today as other groups face in more traditional discrimination, some do recognize that whites have generally not faced discrimination on the same level as other groups have. This may, however, be another reason that whites have little sense of being "white." When one is constantly reminded of one's racial or ethnic identity through routine discrimination, that identity is likely to become more salient for the person.[5]

One student, Dylan, explicitly discusses his perception that whiteness in invoked based on the race of one's audience:

> I feel it would be easier to tell a white person my life story without mentioning race or ethnicity. The reasons being that white people could better understand a life where you don't think about your race every day. To me, telling a black person my life would involve me stressing that my classrooms were always made up of white children and my neighbors white. I feel I would have to describe racially my background more to the black whereas the white would already assume that is how it was.

Dylan's consciousness that *others'* racial identities may be more salient to them than his is to him is insightful. In realizing that his whiteness becomes salient in the context of his interactions with people of other racial backgrounds, he understands the normative position of whiteness in U.S. society, and that this is the reason he is not usually called upon to account for it.

Ophelia's writing evidences another facet of prompted whiteness:

> If I were to describe myself I wouldn't say that I was white, I would say that I was human, moral, respectful, etc., but I wouldn't think to identify myself as white until the question was asked. I don't really think that it matters what race I am. What race someone is a part of is very important in society today. I really hate to admit that this is so, but it is. It is a good thing that society has changed it's ways in the last 50 or 60 years, but we still have problems with race that still need to be sought out. . . . I could not possibly understand what it is like to not be white in America. . . . I do find it incomprehensible though to think of what it is like to be of another race.

It may seem at first as though Ophelia is simply contradicting herself. If she were asked to describe herself, she would not identify as white, and she does not believe it matters what race she is. However, she does understand that one's racial categorization is important in society—in other words, although her racial identity does not mean much to her, she realizes that it does mean something to others. She may even recognize the existence of a racial hierarchy. It is perhaps because of this that she cannot imagine being of a race other than white.

Racial Turning-Point Stories

Some have noted a literary genre called the "racial conversion narrative" in the autobiographical writings of authors such as Lillian Smith, James McBride Dabbs, Sarah Patton Boyle, and Will Campbell.[6] This style of writing, which first appeared in white autobiography in the 1940s, is similar in several ways to the Puritan religious conversion narrative. Like Puritan conversions, racial conversions include an announcement and confession of past racial "sins" and a need for redemption, a description of a dramatic transformation in one's racial attitudes or behaviors, and a subsequent impulse to "witness" to others, or "testify" about one's conversion. In fact, this testifying can serve as the ultimate proof of one's conversion.[7]

The racial conversion is different from a religious conversion in that instead of following a minister's leading, a person listens to her or his own conscience, first to be "convicted" of *social* sins and then to find the way to *secular* salvation.[8] The social sins for which the person must be redeemed are not only that person's, but also that of her or his racial group, and are committed not toward one person, but against an entire other group. Additionally, racial conversions, unlike religious conversions, usually do *not* lead a person "back to the fold" from which they came, but instead cause them to leave behind the white community, at least in some sense.[9]

Many autobiographies include stories of moments when the author became conscious of whiteness, or of race or racism, and came to some new understanding of what it means to be white. Most of these would probably not fit the criteria for a "racial conversion," in that they do not follow the narrative pattern of a person being "lost" in a racist quagmire, then "saved" by an extremely dramatic experience, to live a completely transformed life. Still, these are "turning points," in that they are moments when respondents came to new understandings of race.

As Norman Denzin points out, "the biographical method [is] the studied use and collection of life documents that describe turning-point moments in an individual's life."[10] This chapter focuses on turning points in whiteness. Denzin's typology of epiphanies includes "major events," "representative events," "minor epiphanies," and "reliving experience."[11] Although I characterize them differently, my analysis reveals some of the same types. Turning points in whiteness may be "major" or "minor," in terms of being more or less dramatic. They may be "representative," having become a recurring event. Finally, some respondents "relive experiences," reflecting on them after learning more about race relations.

Because whites generally receive few verbal messages from parents about what it means to be white, whiteness is an particularly *storied* identity; a part of one's self that is communicated most effectively through storytelling, or remembered experiences. For these respondents, whiteness is not grounded in verbal messages about who one is but in stories that reveal one as a racialized person. In this study, a *turning point* is a moment of *conscious whiteness*, when a respondent gained insight into the racialized nature of her or his life. An *epiphany* could be described as a more dramatic change of thinking and behavior in regards to race, usually built on a series of racial turning points.

For the purposes of this book, turning points are not about "correct" understandings of race or whiteness, but simply *different* or *new* understandings.

Respondents recognized their whiteness or understood something new about race or racism, and in this sense, these turning points are positive stories. Many of these new understandings are more antiracist than previously held beliefs. Some stories tell of beginning to recognize the fallacies supporting a fiction of whiteness. Other situations raise new questions and even some new confusions about race and whiteness. Most stories are not the "final word" on the person's ideas about race. They are as likely to be told in the middle of an essay as at the end, and the person may have had other experiences that either contradict or support the new understanding later. Although the turning point may lead a respondent closer to an antiracist consciousness, it does not necessarily transform the respondent into an antiracist.

Agents of Epiphany

Most turning points and epiphanies discussed in this chapter occur as a result of interactions with others whom I call *agents of epiphany*. In stories of whiteness, the usual agents of epiphany are African Americans.[12] An agent of epiphany is usually a friend, classmate, or, occasionally, a teacher. Less often, agents of epiphany are other whites, also sometimes a friend or teacher, but in some cases a family member.[13] Agents of epiphany are usually remembered in detail and almost always called by name. In the following discussions of types of turning-point events, agents of epiphany can be recognized as catalysts of thought-provoking incidents. Simply because the person telling the story was involved in the situation does not mean that the experience was "about" them. In some of the turning-point stories, the focus is still on the "other," not on the author as "white." In these scenarios, the racial Other is, in many ways, still more "object" than agent. Still, these autobiographers gain new understandings of race and racism through interactions with people of color, even limited or temporary.

"Crossings:" Interactions with People of Color

By far the most common turning point stories are interactions with people of color. One might describe these as "crossings" because they are times in the respondents' lives when they, usually for the first time, closely bond with a person of color. This bond could be a friendship, a close teacher-student relationship, or a romantic relationship. Traditionally, the racial divide keeping people of color and white people from close relationships has been described as a "color line." Thus, in these relationships, one has "crossed" this line.

Much scholarly debate has centered on interracial contact as a solution to racial prejudice. The "contact hypothesis" suggests that interactions between members of different racial and ethnic groups can diminish stereotyping and increase understanding and empathy.[14] Supporters suggest that interracial contact provides firsthand experience with and information about other groups that may translate into positive attitudes toward the group.[15] Presumably, interracial contact may convince a prejudiced person that other racial groups are not inherently inferior or superior to their own.[16] Some important social policies of the 1960s were based on the theory that bringing white and black children together in schools would improve race relations in society at large.[17]

Although one-to-one contact may help to end racism, some researchers, such as Gordon Allport, have asserted that the contact must be under certain conditions to reduce prejudice. Specifically, the actors should be of equal social status, working toward a common goal in a noncompetitive, non-threatening situation. Ideally, the contact should be more than superficial, as well—it should involve a level of intimacy that allows mutual understanding. Finally, those in authority should endorse the contact.[18] Numerous studies have supported these ideas. For example, urban studies have shown that for interracial neighborhood contact to foster improved racial attitudes for whites, it must be with equal or higher-status blacks.[19]

Some have criticized contact theory for its micro-level approach: forming friendships, or "knowing" people of color alone may help to end prejudice, but will fall short of combating structural racism. Whites who form such friendships may be convinced that because they have "black friends," the problems of racism must be solved.[20] Others contend that contact theory focuses too much on attitudes, assuming that changed attitudes would lead to changed behavior.[21] In response to this criticism, some researchers have studied to what degree prior interracial contact affects present-day interracial ties. One of these studies found that those with interracial contact experiences in their schools and neighborhoods were more likely as adults to have interracial friendships, attend multiracial churches, and even to be interracially married.[22] Another found that various factors in controlling prejudiced attitudes as adults were related to childhood interracial experiences.[23] Some evidence indicates that interracial contact in childhood may affect adult behaviors.[24]

Others question the causal direction of interracial contact as a solution to racial prejudice and stereotyping. They have suggested that those who are already more racially tolerant or accepting are likely to engage in interracial contact and friendship. Thus the contact is not the cause, but evidence of positive feelings toward other racial groups. At least one study, of black attitudes toward whites, has found that this is not the case—interracial contact itself does seem to cause more positive feelings toward racial others.[25]

Some studies suggest that interracial contact is still relatively rare for most whites. When it does occur, it is likely to be superficial and brief. For example, many whites' primary interracial contact occurs when shopping or in the workplace. Nearly half of all whites report that they have no black friends or social acquaintances.[26] Nonetheless, perhaps in part *because* close personal relationships with people of color are rare for most whites, if they occur they have dramatic impact on the white person's racial consciousness. The other person in the relationship may become the "reality check" for the stereotypical racial notions heard or held throughout their lives. The close person of color may influence a skeptical white person to accept that racism still damages the lives of people of color. A white person who previously thought people of color were paranoid, exaggerating their claims of discrimination, may come to belief after hearing the same claims from a trusted friend.

Recently, in a meta-analysis of 515 studies of the contact hypothesis, Pettigrew and Tropp found that these studies overwhelmingly support the assertion that interracial contact is likely to reduce prejudice.[27] Specifically, 93% of the studies and 95% of the samples in the analysis showed an inverse relationship between contact and prejudice. Studies that use more rigorous, reliable, and multi-item scales find larger effects than less reliable studies. Their study also showed that the effects of intergroup contact can extend beyond the initial encounter to generalized attitudes toward the entire outgroup. Pettigrew and Tropp also explored the causal direction of the effects of intergroup contact. They found that although prejudiced people tend to avoid intergroup contact, contact does reduce prejudice in all types of people.

Pettigrew and Tropp also examined previous findings regarding situations in which intergroup contact yields most positive results. They discovered that educational and recreational settings are the most likely ones in which positive results occur, while contact during travel has the weakest effects, perhaps because it tends to be brief and superficial. Intergroup friendships, particularly, can lead to a change of attitudes because they usually involve most of Allport's optimal conditions for intergroup contact. However, Pettigrew and Tropp's meta-analysis found that the optimal conditions suggested for intergroup contact to yield positive effects are not mandatory but are instead important facilitating conditions. Positive outcomes can occur in the absence of some of these conditions.[28] As a whole, the contact hypothesis generally focuses on how "whites" can reduce their prejudice through more associations with people of color. My data suggests that by encouraging whites to consider their own racial status, contact with people of color does seem to improve whites' racial attitudes.

From this discussion, one might assume that interracial contact, or "crossings" are about what a person of color "does" for a white person.[29] Indeed, in the early stages of these relationships, this may be the case. People of color, given their historical status as minorities and as oppressed people, have known white people in a way that most whites have not known them. The famed African American sociologist W. E. B. DuBois referred to this as the "double consciousness" of people of color.[30] Audre Lorde summarized it well:

> Traditionally, in American [sic] society, it is the members of oppressed, objectified groups who are expected to stretch out and bridge the gap between the actualities of our lives and the consciousness of the oppressor. For in order to survive, those of us for whom oppression is as American as apple pie have always had to be watchers, to become familiar with the language and manners of the oppressor, even sometimes adopting them

for some illusion of protection. Whenever the need for some pretense of communication arises, those who profit from our oppression call upon us to share our knowledge with them. In other words, it is the responsibility of the oppressed to teach the oppressor their mistakes. . . . The oppressors maintain their position and evade responsibility for their own actions. There is a constant drain of energy which might be better used in redefining ourselves and devising realistic scenarios for altering the present and constructing the future.[31]

In the same vein, Roediger acknowledges this point in *Black on White*, quoting James Weldon Johnson: "[C]olored people of this country know and understand the white people better than the white people know and understand them."[32]

The unbalanced dynamics of these relationships notwithstanding, for the purpose of this analysis, I am most interested in the early stages of these "crossings," when a white person was confronted with what it means to be white through a relationship with someone who is not. This chapter will focus on turning-point stories that involve interactions with people of color. These include college relationships, other friendships, romantic partnerships, interactions begun because of geographical displacement (travel or relocation); interactions in which a white person is in the minority; vicarious victimization, relationship conflict, new family members and education.

Certainly many of these turning-point stories also involve other whites. Particularly in stories of relationship conflict and the addition of new family members, seeing other whites' reactions to people of color can sometimes be epiphanic. Additionally, stories of insights gained through education may have whites involved as actors, and of course the white author herself or himself is in some sense the center of the action in stories of gaining education in a classroom setting. Still, even in stories where whites play an important part, people of color serve as the catalyst for the racial turning points described by the respondents.

College Roommates and Friends

In college, white students encounter not only new ways of thinking, but also more diversity than they have experienced, and often experience a new sense of racial and ethnic identity.[33] Although whites are becoming more of a minority in the U.S., schools are resegregating dramatically.[34] Most respondents come from predominantly white high schools, and even if they attend primarily white colleges and universities, they come into closer contact with people of color than in high school and may be required to consider equality, fairness, and diversity both in and outside the classroom. Students in this study report significant racial segregation on college campuses. However, many cross racial lines, at limited times, such as in particular classes or study groups or in specific settings, such as in dorms. Justin notes, in his autobiography titled "The Rural" [Justin here used the name of his home state to describe himself]:

> There were not a lot of racial differences in my hometown. . . . Sure, I had classes in school that explained racial differences, but it all seemed so fake and unclear to me since I was not exposed to it. It was not until I came to college that I was exposed to the "real-world". . . . I admit, at first I was prejudiced towards people of different races, but in time I have realized that every one is equal and to treat them with nothing but respect. . . . If I had not gone to college, I do not think I would feel the way I do about people of difference races and ethnicities. It has been a life changing experience. . . . I was never aware of how oppressive we can be as human beings. . . . [C]ollege has been the main reason for my change of views and heart as a person . . . Still today, I am faced with the backlash and prejudice that comes with rural life and small town living.

Many students, particularly northerners, mention being frightened of people of color before meeting them in college. White students and students of color come into contact in an especially intimate way in dorms as neighbors or roommates—situations that may at first cause tensions, which sometimes are unresolved, and the white person may end up feeling victimized and pessimistic about race relations generally. On the other hand, sometimes roommate or dorm neighbor relationships become friendships that help a white person to a new understanding of whiteness, involving realization that one might be seen as a member of an outside group. Here, Valerie describes the value of living with her Asian American roommate:

> I grew up in an extremely small, old-fashioned town. . . . exposed to racist views from my family and older friends. None of these people expressed their racism in any physical way, it just seemed that there was a general conception that being white was better. Growing up in an almost purely white environment . . . really left me in the dark. . . . The first time that I remember realizing that there are other races closer than I imagined was when I got a letter from [the university] telling me who my roommate was going to be. . . . I instantly recognized [it] to be a non-white name. . . . I talked to her on the phone and found out that she was Asian American. I also found out that she was quite similar to me, and after just one conversation I realized that no matter what race she was, we were going to hit it off great as roommates. That is exactly what happened too.
>   . . . . [W]hen I do not understand something about a minority or their ways, she is there to provide an answer, since she . . . grew up with many different races; and when she cannot make sense of a white person's ways, I provide her with the best definition. . . . Another way this

relationship has proved to be educational is that I am meeting a lot of different types of people through her. [She] generally hangs out with African Americans, so . . . I get introduced to a variety of people. . . . I have never been subject to any discrimination based on my color, however, when [her] friends ask about me they refer to me as her white roommate. I do not find this as being racist because I know to them, I am just as different as they are to me.

Although one could read her description of "minority ways" and "white ways" as essentialist, it could be seen as more progressive than the typical colorblind stance. Valerie conceptualizes the relationship as an *equal exchange* of culture. She does not approach the relationship as a cultural tourist, but believes that she too has culture to share—she acknowledges that whites, too, have "culture." In recognizing that whites have a culture for which to account, Valerie differs from many other respondents, who place whiteness as the norm that needs be no explanation. Further, Valerie is not offended when she is referred to as the "white roommate," because she understands her positioning as a member of a racialized group. Whites generally are used to and insist on being treated as "individuals," meaning their race should not be brought up—this is a privilege of being in the majority. Additionally, that may be the way they treat each other, since some research suggests that we tend to treat members of our in-group as individuals and tend to see those in the outgroup as a generalized mass, undifferentiated and stereotypical.[35] Valerie is willing to be seen as part of a group, relinquishing, in the dorm microsociety and circle of friends, her position of privilege; and, importantly, understanding how nonwhites might see her.

Others, like Valerie, link their dorm situations to forming relationships that were significant in changing their outlook on race. For example, Linshyan writes:

While in the process of getting a hold of my first roommate I did not even think about the possibility of her being of another background until a friend had pointed out to me the fact that she was probably wondering the same about me because of how my name is of an Asian-Chinese origin. This made me think about how I would feel if I were set up with a roommate with a different background: would we not get along because of our heritage, would we not like the same music, would we hate each other's friends?. . . . I had never really known anyone nor had I been friends with anyone who was of another race. I knew I was not and am not a racist, but I had heard so many stereotypes and really did not know what to expect. I remember the first time I talked to her on the phone the first words out of my mouth were that I wasn't Chinese, just that my mom likes interesting names. It was a harmless funny joke at the time that helped to break the ice, but now I look back and wonder why it was that I felt the need to declare that to her. Was I afraid that she would not want to live with someone who was Chinese? Was it the fact that I would not want to? Why did I worry about an issue that could not be changed? Anyway we proved to hit it off, although we have many differences and live together again this year . . .

Linshyan expresses anxiety about the possibility of living with a roommate of a different racial background. Assuming others may have the same fears, she attempts to reassure her prospective roommate that despite her name, she is "not Chinese." That she felt it necessary to do so is the first episode leading her to question her notions of race. Linshyan continues:

The first few months at college I mostly made friends with people who were like me: white. I think this was a subconscious decision . . . that it was easier to talk and meet people who share similarities with you [*Linshyan, like some other students, discusses here that she believes the university segregates students by race in the dorms, contributing to campus separation.*]. . . . I did meet my future roommate during my first year of college. She is Philippine and Asian. . . . I had never thought about 'heritage' before . . . I had to do a project . . . surveying people who have a different background than I. That is how I got to know her. After the survey was done though, I found I was still interested and began talking to her more and more about her life, and she was equally curious to mine. . . . From her, I gained a new respect for those who chose to give up all familiarity and their home, to make a better life for their children. . . . This year I have made many new dear friends of all different background and from all over the world. My best friend here is from Africa, and next year she will be my roommate. . . . The thing I find most interesting about the things she has taught me is that she has taught me more about white people than about blacks. For instance, she made me think about the fact that the United States is one of the few places that even care about race: one of the few places that has racism. I had never thought about it like that before, but it is true.

After overcoming initial fears regarding diversity at the university, Linshyan begins to meet people of color—and two have been roommates. Further, she credits her best friend from Africa not just with teaching her about *Africans*, but about *whites*. Like Valerie, her cross-racial friendships grant her an outsider's perspective on whiteness.

Gabriel experiences an entirely new environment after leaving his small northeastern town for an early summer program in a southern college:

Living in the towers my freshman year made it easy and interesting meeting people. Black, White Latino, Chinese, there were tons of kids who stayed in this place. . . . And the crazy thing was, I got along with everyone and everyone liked me. I met one of my best friends my first semester at school that year. . . . He wished me Merry Christmas, I wished him a Happy Hanukah. I was a rock n' roller from the country, he was a rapper from the city. . . . We always joked around with each other about our different backgrounds, but we made such a good team. . . . By the second semester our click was pretty defined. . . . [Another friend,] Karno was half black and half white, but he identified himself as black. And he was my first black best friend. Karno kind of knew I hadn't had too much contact with 'black folks', as he referred to black people. And Karno always was joking around, and we would always talk black-white to each other on a very comedic [level] but never crossing the bounds of decency. Except for one time I accidentally put an 'er' instead of an 'a' after the word 'nigg' and Karno had to correct me. But we were best friends.

So if we look back to high school graduation I knew a couple of black kids, had a cousin who was black, and had no Jewish friends. I went away to [college] . . . , made friends, and changed my whole perspective on other races and ethnicity. I had to leave [that school and] come home to what I lived with for the first 18 years of my life. And the sad part is nothing has changed. I could come home and tell people that my best friends were a NIGGER and a JEW [*his emphasis*], but I don't. They wouldn't understand, I looked past everything that I grew up thinking, that all my friends thought. I tell them my best friends were Ivan and Karno, my boys. . . . My group of friends was what was so different from [my hometown]. . . . You have to surround yourself with diversity to truly find the person that lies within you. . . .

Gabriel describes his move to a college in the South as a "change in [his] whole perspective on other races." Earlier, he described his high school experience; in which he was isolated from any racial diversity. He and his friends laughed at racist humor and mocked white kids who "acted black." When he has to return home after changing his perspective, he realizes that his old friends would only consider his new friends in the same terms in which they had before—as a "nigger and a Jew." They certainly would not understand the new lens through which Gabriel saw once he removed ideas that previously inhibited his personal growth and limited his friendships.

Others mentioned crossing racial boundaries at colleges away from their predominantly white hometowns. Todd writes:

Most of my experiences that have made my race/ethnicity noticeable to me occurred while I was attending [college away from home]. My entire life was football . . . and since seventy-five percent of the team was African American, it was inevitable that race would come up. I can truthfully say that the racial interactions among the teammates were always that of a humorous nature. In society, African American males use the term 'nigga' to relate to each other. In our locker room, however, even the white players would be called that by the black players. A few of these players have left an indelible impression on me and I will never forget their names or the stories they have shared with me. . . . They liked my openness and were surprised that a 'back-woods country bumpkin' (their words) like myself could talk with them about things that other 'new guys' wouldn't. I told them how I enjoyed the outdoor sports like hunting and fishing and they told me about life in the inner city projects. This was a totally new experience for me. . . . It was then that I realized that most white people, like myself, had no perception of life outside of their own little world. At the same time I felt connected to these young men and yet still real-ized that I was a totally different person with completely different experiences. I know that they saw me as a teammate and a person but somehow I just felt like the 'white kid' who didn't really know what a hard life exists for some people.

Todd's cross-racial experiences begin with a shared interest in football and working toward a common goal as a team. Indeed, some researchers suggest that one of the ways interracial contact may reduce prejudice is if it involves cooperation toward a common goal. Todd's exprience also allows him to see that his whiteness has given him a narrow perspective. He continues:

While at [that college] I taught some of my African American teammates how to fish in a stream. . . . I visited [a player's] home with him. . . . where I was introduced to his parents. They were wonderful people. . . . Imagine that, a white guy from the mountains of [my northeastern state] sitting down to a meal with a black family in a run-down [city] neigh-borhood. Three generations ago it would have been unthinkable for someone like me to be doing this; I do believe that change is a wonderful thing. . . . I am very proud of [my friend]. Two years ago he was drafted by [an NFL team]. He overcame his tough childhood and is now living the life of luxury, with a college degree to boot.

When I transferred to [this college in my hometown], I left all my African American friends at [the other school]. I returned to the life that I had known since childhood. The town I lived in was white again and all the people I talked to as friends were now white again as well. The only thing different about me now was that I had a newfound apprecia-tion for people from all walks of life and I no longer judged people by the way they looked. . . . The reason that I only have a white circle of friends is the fact that everywhere I like to hang out, white people are the only ones there.

Today, Todd's friendship circle is limited not by choice, but environment. His fiancée, with whom he has a son, is an Asian American Buddhist. He attributes these changes to friendship with African Americans in college.

In one form or another, most respondents placed their college experience as transformative. For some, that experience remained more like "cultural tourism." For others, it was a catalyst for rethinking whiteness on a deeper level (for a more in-depth discussion of cultural tourism, see chapter 3).

Other Friendships

Other crossings involved adolescent or adult friendships that changed a white person's thoughts about race. These stories differ from those about friendships in early life, because childhood friendships help form what the person thinks of whiteness, whereas adult friendships often *change* this perception. A woman from the South writes of a transforming friendship:

> Because I grew up in a mostly white town most of my friends were white. If you only see white people, they're the only people you can be friends with. Once I moved to [a large northeastern city], my friendships became more diverse and have continued to be so. I think this is because I tend to look past exteriors. Even in my hometown I tended to be friends with the 'outcasts'. My more popular friends would ask how I could do that but to me it wasn't an issue, and it still isn't. . . .
>
> When I moved to [a Northern city] after high school, I began to see how important race could be. I was the only white woman in the bank I worked at but I was never made to feel uncomfortable. I was teased because they thought I was a country girl and because I was young, but never because of my race. I became best friends with a thirty-six year old black woman with two children. She and I would go to Chucky Cheese's when the kids were at school and just have fun. We would also go to a barbecue shack in the inner city that I loved. She warned me not to go there without her because there could be trouble because of my race.

This friendship crosses both racial and generational lines. Lisa is entrusted with "insider" knowledge about where to get good barbecue, as well as warnings not to go there alone. Because of this move to the city and new relationships Lisa "began to see how important race could be."

Some discussed friendships before college that changed their thinking about race or whiteness. For example, Jeff writes of a friendship forged during high school:

> I had a best friend in high school named Jerrell. He was a black guy. He decided to start dating this girl named Julie. They . . . both clearly had feelings for each other, but the problem was that Julie was white and

Jerrell was black. Mixed couples aren't exactly accepted in a hick town like the one I lived in.

. . . . People would say things like 'White girl, gets hurt by white [guys] so she goes black' and 'dumb nigger thinks he's going to be treated like a white guy if he dates a white girl.' A lot of people both black and white criticized the relationship, and but no matter how much people would complain, the two stayed together.

Then Jerrell was 16, I was 15 and so was Julie. Now Jerrell is going on [20] and his steady girlfriend Julie is now 19. The two are still together and it's amazing how much they care for each other. The verbal abuse they endured only helped to strengthen their relationship.

Until the time of their relationship I felt extremely peace-oriented. I hated fights and conflicts and would do anything I could to avoid them. I used to tell Jerrell that maybe he should reconsider dating Julie to avoid all the verbal abuse. He would tell me, 'love is a conflict, man, and when it comes down to your heart, black and white just aren't that important.' I'll remember that for as long I live.

From watching his friends' interracial relationship outlast the harassment of those in the town, Jeff learns that crossing racial lines to form connections can be worth confrontation. Elsewhere, Jeff expresses the belief that he has created a friendship with Jerrell that truly transcends racial distinctions.

Kendall writes in depth about the impression his lifelong friendship with two African Americans has made on his attitudes toward race and his own whiteness:

Other times my race is most visible to me but at the same time not noticeable at all is when I am with my three best friends: two African American guys and another white guy. I notice it because two of us are black and the other two of us are white. However, it is not noticeable to us because the four of us are friends for who we are. That may sound slightly corny but it is the truth. While I notice that I am white when we are around each other, I also notice that our race does not matter because of how good of friends we are, especially since I recognize myself more as Irish than white when I am around them because I do not notice the skin color. However when I am not hanging around them, I notice myself thinking more that I am white than Irish or Italian even. . . . In short, race and ethnic relations were very prominent in my life, are very prominent in my life and will be very prominent for the rest of my life.

When with his friends, Kendall's race is "visible" but "at the same time not noticeable at all." This could be partly because Kendall feels more "ethnic" when with his black friends and more "white" when he is not. In contrast, many respondents' identities become more racialized when they are around people of color. Perhaps, unlike many other whites, Kendall understands the *ethnic* basis of African American identity, and this brings his own ethnicity to the fore. Kendall also states that his friendship in some ways makes him not notice race. He adds: "[I]t was and will be, John, myself, Lavel and Will hanging out and having a blast; two black guys and two white guys having fun and seeing past racial lines, not even thinking about racial lines and being friends because we like each other. . . ."

Kendall's statements are not entirely "colorblind." A more careful reading suggests that rather than refusing to "see" difference at all, he has "seen" the differences between him and his friends and accepted and valued those differences. He does not deny the role that race and ethnicity have played and will play in his life, and he expresses an appreciation for diversity that he has learned through his friendships, rather than an insistence that everyone is "the same."

After moving to an affluent part of a midwestern city, Stefan only learns about people of color "from watching T.V." As he states, "Ignorance was bliss to me; I never once experienced anything controversial or even close to disturbing my perfect little world." However, Stefan forms an interracial friendship that changes him:

> I met one of the most influential people in my life and boy did it shock me that he was black. . . . he had taught my father when my father was in high school. Over the years the two of them had become good friends and had kept in touch. . . . and often worked together on projects for the school. I remember very vividly the first time I met Mr. Howard. . . . My father and I were going to drive to [another city] for a [high school] football game. . . . I was horrified to find out that we were going to be giving this guy a ride to the game too. I wanted to spend time with my father alone. . . . When I first saw him I was very intimidated, he was about 6'6" and was 240 lbs. of mostly muscle. . . . That first night I didn't really say much I just kind of sat in awe of the man. . . . the most odd thing was that he was black.
>
> After that first night . . . I just kind of put it out of my mind. . . . As I grew up a little bit more . . . color became a very large barrier. I wasn't really sure what to do about black people. I never really interacted with them but when I did it was very uncomfortable for me. I started to make generalizations about them and stopped looking at them as people and started looking at them as inferior. I was very young yet and I was really sure about what I felt and I never thought about it being wrong, to me it wasn't. I was looking at myself as superior and I *knew* that my beliefs were right. I knew that I was better than black people, I lived in a bigger house, I had money, I wasn't a thief, and most importantly I wasn't black. I had become very prejudiced in a very short period of time and nothing could convince me otherwise, or so I thought. I had this idea in my head about black

people, that they were inferior, stupid, weak and all mean. Mr. Howard turned my beliefs about black people and about people in general upside down.

As my father [and I] became more involved with [the school], Mr. Howard was a more frequent presence in my life. I learned to respect him and his beliefs. I also learned to not make generalizations about people because that they may fit some but not others, and the generalizations I had made certainly did not fit this man. I soon became his friend and because of this friendship I learned a lot about people and myself. Mr. Howard would eventually take the position of principal at my high school, and this would lead to many pushes forward in my own life and my view of others.

As Stefan matures, he is confronted with what to "do about black people." In a racist society, this is a question every white person will face. Because he has few interactions with African Americans, he begins to accept stereotypical ideas about them. It is through his relationship with Mr. Howard, an African-American man who becomes a role model for him, that these generalizations begin to break down.

Romantic Partnerships

Researchers have observed that whites have varying levels of comfort with people of color. Many who would not object to working with people of color might reject having them as neighbors. Some who are comfortable with a neighbor of color would not want a person of color for a close friend. Many would object to a friend or daughter dating a person of color. Most race theorists agree that the final racial boundary for many white people is to date a person of color themselves.[36] This is one of the last racial taboos, even for white liberals. When respondents date or even flirt interracially, it is usually a notable experience. Doing so shows willingness to rebel against one of society's strongest racial norms. Helen's mother reacted strongly to her date with an African American boy:

> I never felt any restrictions because of my race until high school. While my ideas of racial differences remained the same, I began to question the reasons why I had these ideas. For example in tenth grade a boy who was half-Indian and half African American asked me to a dance. I accepted, and when he came to pick me up my family welcomed him. After the dance we continued to keep in touch through nightly phone conversations, and that's when my mom asked me 'You're not going to date him are you?' The question sounded like she already had an answer, and coming from such an accepting, loving woman I was confused. She continued to say that her concern was not stemmed from the boy, but rather society's reaction to us as a biracial couple. Another

experience that made me more aware of my restrictions, was when I went to junior prom with an African American. We began to discuss our family's views of racial differences, and I confessed that my family discouraged biracial relationships, but did not forbid them. He went on to tell me that his mother would not allow it, no matter who the girl was. I realized once again, at a point when I thought I knew everything, that racial differences played a much bigger role than I had thought.

Helen's mother insists she has no problem with her dating interracially, but that "society" would, and on these grounds she disapproves. Many white parents claim that their opposition to interracial dating is based on fears of how society will treat their children or potential grandchildren.[37] Whether this is the real concern or the parents themselves object, situations like Helen's are often "training grounds" for whiteness. These attempts to cross the racial dating line are the first times Helen "felt any restrictions because of [my] race." This is true for many white people, who are not routinely restricted by discrimination in movement and behavior as are African Americans and other people of color. It is epiphanal for white people to feel any racially based restrictions, especially from their parents. It can also be a turning point for whites to see the prejudices of other whites expressed.

Respondents who progress romantically with people of color frequently experience the beginnings of those relationships as epiphanies. In her autobiography, "Boundaries," Gail describes an experience dating outside her ethnic group:

> It was my first year of college that was a turning point in my life, in that it brought diversity into my life. The first few months . . . , I felt overwhelmed with the vast array of race and ethnicities. It was an awkward situation at first, as I didn't know how to interact with people of various . . . groups. I didn't want to accidentally say something inappropriate. . . . My lack of interaction with other races became prevalent in a conversation with an African-American. I hesitated when it came to racial classification: Should I say black or African-American? He took one look at me and said: 'You've never interacted with different races before, have you?' He then informed me that using 'black' to refer to African-Americans is acceptable. This experience made me realize just how 'white' I was in that I had no clue how to interact with someone who was black. . . .
>
> I became close friends with this person, who taught me a lot about racial and ethnic diversity and about various forms of discrimination that he has experienced as an African-American—discrimination that I never noticed. I guess I grew up naïve of the inequalities present in the world. One day I realized I was discriminating against a race and not living by my belief in equality for all. I wouldn't date this person, simply because I kept seeing the racial issues that were bound to arise through a black and

white relationship. . . . Eventually, I began dating this man, and now I don't even notice the difference in our skin tone until others point it out.

Living in a predominantly white environment, it seems, to Gail as she writes earlier, that "racial issues are non-existent." Whites in these environments do not see themselves as part of a racialized group. She first considers "racial issues," such as discrimination, through her contact with an African American man. The real turning point comes when Gail questions her own resistance to probably the closest form of interracial "crossing" experience—dating someone of another racial group. It is in crossing this boundary that Gail believes she has overcome a crucial aspect of her naïve whiteness, and her own failure to live up to ideals of equality.

Perhaps the ultimate crossing experience is an interracial marriage like Sandra's with Frank, a Latino man:

One month before I graduated from High School my girlfriends and I decided to throw a party. . . . Around thirty people showed up to my friend's house and one guy with dark features kept staring at me. I had no idea what ethnicity he was. . . . He continued to stare and smile at me for the rest of the evening until I started to leave. He then approached me, tried to start a conversation, and introduced himself as Frank Morez. . . . We talked for a few hours that night and he asked me for a date the following night. . . . When we were at dinner I had this overwhelming urge to ask him 'So what is your background?' I tried as long as I could to hold off asking that question because he was obviously American. After I asked him the million-dollar question a look on his face told me he knew I was going to ask eventually. He told me he was 'Spanish, Cuban, and Malaysian.' I was cool with his heritage and now my parents would be put to the test the following night. When dinner was halfway over at my parent's house, my mother just had to ask 'So what are you?' After he told everyone, they just said 'Oh.' We have been together every day since May 10, 1991 and got married on November 6, 1992. Every time Frank met one of my friends, no matter what ethnicity they belonged to the popular question for him was 'So what are you?' He was very conditioned to being asked that question and even explaining that his grandfather was from Cuba, his grandmother from Spain, and his dad was from the Philippines.

Sandra notices Frank immediately, and is curious about his ethnic background. She remembers waiting anxiously through their first date to ask about his heritage, and after she does, declares that she is "cool with" it. This is a typical pattern in the data: White people judge the uses of race and various racial "positionings" and decide whether to accept them. Sandra has some realization of this, since she notes that her parents and friends asked Frank "So, what are you?," and Frank himself is "conditioned" to this.

Often white people are insensitive in phrasing questions of background to people of color, so many end up asking, instead of "Where are you from?" questions like "What are you?" Questions of heritage asked too early or without reciprocal discussions of the white person's background may be offensive, but may be doubly so when put in such terms as *What* are you?"

Sandra continues her story:

> Meeting Frank's family was very scary for me. I did not know how they would feel about Frank dating a 'white' girl. I did not know if they were going to speak in Spanish and talk about me or if they would just accept me for who I am. I once dated a Greek boy named Chris, and his parents were of the Greek Orthodox religion. Even though I went to every Greek festivity, Chris's parents hated me just because I was not Greek, could not speak the language, and therefore would not give me the time of day. I was afraid that I would get the same reception by Frank's parents and family. To my surprise they were very accepting of me, and did not speak in Spanish to talk about me. The whole family had completely assimilated . . . and tried to tell everyone they were 'white' Spanish. I also noticed throughout the time we dated that Frank always checked the 'white' box on an application form when asked what ethnicity he was because there is no such thing as a 'white Spanish' box on the application form. I remember taking Frank on a modeling assignment with me once where there were many people of color present. The photographer requested one shot to contain only 'white' people in it. I was curious as to where they would place Frank, with the colored people or me. I was surprised that they put him in the 'white' group with me. I was neither happy nor disagreeable about it; I was just surprised at how other people saw him.

Sandra is pleasantly surprised when Frank's family does not reject her based on race. She attributes this to their being "assimilated." Indeed, for those of obvious "ethnicity" who want to be considered "white," adding a white family member might be perceived positively. Knowing Frank's family, and witnessing Frank being considered "white" are turning points for Sandra, who begins to see that race is socially constructed in everyday life. Having a biracial child causes her to think further about this:

> After Frank and I were married, the next big step in my relationship with Frank was starting a family. When I learned I was pregnant I was so curious as to what my child would look like. I had a feeling that he or she would look mostly like my husband because dark features are usually dominant traits. Throughout the time I was pregnant, I could not even imagine what our child would look like because Frank and I have no similar features. Some people say that when two people have been together for a long time, they start to look like brother and sister. I knew

that would never be possible for me and my husband. No one we know could imagine what our child was going to look like. When our son, Dillon, was born we finally got to see what the mixture of our genes would produce. Of course he had a dark complexion, with dark hair and charcoal black eyes. I make a joke sometimes and say, 'We're still wondering if I'm the real mother' because my son looks nothing like me. The bite of reality came when I had to fill out paperwork in the hospital and check a box for Dillon's racial identity. Frank and I both talked about it and decided to check the 'white' box. The nurse who took the paperwork looked at me and said, 'He's white?' I really was not sure what the politically correct answer was.

Sandra's pregnancy and the birth of her child are a reminder of what she will *not* experience that white people who marry other whites may: her child will not look like her, and she and her husband will never "start to look like brother and sister." This comes as a personal "bite of reality" for Sandra. This "reality" is symbolized in boxes to be selected on forms. When Sandra and Frank's choice of "white" for their son is questioned, Sandra is left wondering what is "politically correct." She understands that her choice is subject to judgment.

Geographical Displacement

A third type of experience that sometimes helps one to view whiteness or race in a new way is geographical displacement. Sometimes this displacement comes through relocating and sometimes it is temporary travel to another state or country. Both can place a person in an unfamiliar context and thus lead to a questioning of identity.

Parents' jobs require many respondents to live in a variety of areas. Moving can highlight contrasts in the ways people in various areas view race, and may call into question the stability of the racial constructs with which whites grow up. Karen discovers an unfamiliar dichotomy when she moves from a state in the South to one in the "Deep South":

Sixth grade my mother remarried and we moved to [another state]. I have not seen a more racist area since then. The first day I go to school on the bus, which is almost a three hour ordeal since everyone lives so far apart, I am approached with the question: 'Are you a prep or a redneck?' Since I had no clue as to which either of the two really meant I just sat there somewhat stumped for a little while and then asked for an explanation. . . . .I was told that a prep dressed in nice designer clothing while a redneck generally dressed in jeans, boots, a flannel shirt, and was possibly a member of the KKK. This shocked me because I had somewhat heard of the KKK, but was not really familiar with what it was all about. Come to find out throughout the following days riding to and

from school that many of the kids' parents and themselves were involved or knew someone involved in the KKK. This frightened me, but I
was too scared being the new kid at the school to say anything about it
to anyone. I usually would just sit in my seat with a friend and listen to
what they would have to say. At least there were no black kids on our
bus so it did not offend anyone as far as I could see. The more I listened
to them talk the more I wanted to know why they thought so differently
of the black race and especially why they thought that they had a right to
harm them and 'take back what was theirs.' I asked my parents what they
thought of all of this and they said that racism and the KKK were terrible
things and said that many of these kids were not very educated. They
continued on to say that we should treat everyone the same. I told
them of a few interracial couples at school and how they were so ridi-
culed that they would be made fun of almost every day and occasionally be beaten up for it. They said that they thought it very sad that the
students resorted to violence, but that they also didn't agree with
interracial relationships and definitely not interracial marriage. They
said the reasoning behind it was not that they were inferior in any way,
but simply that they had an entirely different culture and value system
than we did.

Karen learns quickly that in her new environment there are two acceptable
forms of whiteness: being a "prep" or a "redneck." Not sure where she fits in,
Karen is forced to think about ways of being white. These experiences also lead
to conversations with her parents about interracial dating. In a sense, Karen is
resocialized into the role of whiteness.

Will writes that a move from the northern U.S. to the South profoundly
influenced his ideas about race:

When my teen years rolled around I moved from [a northern city], to [a
southern city]. I saw a big change in people's thoughts of one another.
Most of the schools in [the northern state] had certain boundaries that
each school pertained to. This kept most white neighborhoods white and
black neighborhoods black. When I came to [the southern city], the
schools bussed students from poor areas to the schools in the wealthy
areas. This, in my eyes, caused some serious problems. The poor students
didn't have what the wealthy students had, it mixed different racial
groups together which brought about fights, and demanded more from
the poor students. I had never been scared to go to school until I moved
to [the southern city]. Where I came from in [the northern state], there
wasn't much talk about how people hated blacks or Hispanics. When we
met a person from a different race, we treated him/her with respect just
like anyone else. In [the southern city], it was an entire different story.
Whites called blacks 'stupid Niggers' and the blacks called whites 'little
white boys.' Along with these comments came fights and disputes. I think

the main reason was the idea of the poor mixed with the wealthy. I
learned not to fear people of other races, but to be friends with them. I
think my fear of blacks was something that I just grew out of, like my fear
of clowns. I think by this time I was eleven or twelve years old, and was
ready to deal with the world. . I saw many problems arise from jealousy
from the poor students and mocking from the wealthy students. This I
think led to the name-calling and racism. What race one is was definitely
more important in [the southern city] than it was [in the northern city].

Racial problems sometimes seem absent in settings that are predominantly
white. While it may be the case that overt racial tensions were not visible in the
northern school Will attended, subtle racial biases may have existed that were
simply not evoked by the presence of students of color. When people of color
are not present, often whites believe that "race" itself is absent. Whites, feeling
that they have no "race," recognize the relevance of race when they interact
with people of color.

While recognizing that some tensions in the southern school were based on
race, Will adds a class dimension to his discussion, suggesting that mixing
poor and wealthy students caused many disputes. Note also that Will uses a
common line of argument to suggest that everyone is equally "racist," mentioning that whites called African Americans names and vice versa.[38] The
important consideration here is not the logic of Will's argument, but the way
he contrasts the two places he has lived and links this to his new view of how
the world works, racially.

Although he does not directly connect it with the relocation, Will adds that
he has overcome his fear of people of other races. Will's metaphor is striking:
he "grew out of" his fear of people of color, just as he outgrew his "fear of
clowns." It is not uncommon in our culture to hear of children being afraid of
clowns. Clowns are often included as symbols of evil packaged as innocence in
horror movies that include children. By referencing clowns, Will may imply
that as he matured, he realized African Americans were not menacing threats,
but innocent and nonthreatening. Although he may not realize the implica-
tion, comparing African Americans to clowns constructs them as harmless,
entertaining and "fun," but not to be taken seriously.

Another respondent grew up in an isolated, all-white northeastern town
that she considered "racist." For Denise, leaving this town enables her to think
differently about matters of race:

Of course I'm describing all of this to you with the power of hindsight.
Had I not moved to [a larger southeastern city] my freshman year in
high school I may not have been able to see how wrong the feelings and
beliefs of my hometown were. Even worse I may have fallen to the racist
views of my parents and begun to pass them on to my own family.
Instead I attended a high school which may have only been 6% black but
it was enough to make this white girl petrified on the first day and give

her the biggest and best lessons in life from then on out. I may still have some major prejudices and fall to racist opinions at times but I try my best not think in terms of race and to be as open minded as someone who grew up where I did can be. I am proud to say also that my parents are a lot more open minded since being transferred to [this city] and that they fully accept that my best friend is Korean and my last boy-friend was Asian American. It may sound cheesy to most but for a girl who told a Puerto Rican friend that she could no longer talk to him because he wasn't white, it is a huge step in a positive direction. To be able to bring home and have accepted friends and boyfriends of differ-ent races and ethnic backgrounds is more from my parents than I ever would have expected.

Moving becomes a transforming experience for both Denise and her parents. She characterizes her racial perspective as a "near miss" situation: Denise came very close to being what she considers a racist, but was saved by her move to a larger city. Had she never moved, even writing this type of autobiography probably would have been impossible.

Another occasion serving as a catalyst for stories of conscious whiteness is traveling. Traveling is similar to moving in placing a person in new sur-roundings. This may allow the person to question if previous ways of thought are really "how things are" or a product of having seen them in only one context. Gary writes about traveling on a new job:

As a white male raised in a rural community in [the northeast], I never was put into a position to defend my ethnic identity. . . . When entering my second year of college, I took a job with a company who primarily deal with extreme/action sports. . . . [N]ever could I have imagined the different kinds of people that I would meet. . . . Being 19 years old, and traveling to countless cities throughout the year . . . . The people you meet and the stories they tell are simply amazing!. . . . I feel classes teaching about culture and ethnic differences are beneficial, but a hands on approach is far superior, if available. . . . I always think of what would happen if you put some of these people from around here in a diverse place like Miami or Los Angeles. Nonetheless, you cannot change these types of people. The important part is to keep what you know as *right* in the back of your mind, and not fall victim to following the easy path of those who are narrow-minded and scared of change. . . . I have been blessed not having to explain myself, like so many people do. However, I try not to rely and take advantage of this, because I have talked to so many who struggle with this. I can honestly say that I would like to think that my racial/ethnic identity will not affect my future, but I feel it will do so in a positive manner. While being a certain skin color should not produce any specific preferential treatment, I feel that it does.

Gary is able to see white privilege because he has talked to those who do not benefit from it. While recognizing the value of diversity courses, he asserts that they are less able to show a different perspective than everyday contact with people of color. This is the experience that many in his predominantly white community lack.

In this data, most of the transformative stories involving travel are of joining the military. Regardless of one's stance on current military conflicts or other armed forces issues, in diversity and affirmative action it has been one of the most progressive organizations in the United States. In speaking with people familiar with the history of racial issues in the military, I have gained some insights into why this is so. First, even when the military was segregated, in the all-black units, men were gaining the experience to advance in rank. Thus, when the various branches desegregated, they were positioned to move into higher ranks in the newly diverse military, simply by the status of their earned rank. Second, the military has a strict system honoring rank, that engrains in soldiers that they are not to question authority, regardless of the color, race, or ethnicity of the person in authority.[39] Obviously, this does not always work; but the chain of command in the military supports the standing of people of color. Third, the military has always used affirmative action, and still strongly supports it. During the recent Supreme Court arguments over affirmative action in academia, members of the military wrote an amicus brief in support of affirmative action, stating that it is crucial to military morale to have people of all races and ethnicities in positions of various ranking, particularly serving as officers, as leaders and role models.[40] The military is firmly committed to affirmative action in admissions to higher education, to produce this diverse officer corps.[41]

Thus it is not surprising that students, after military service, seem to gain a new understanding of other racial and ethnic groups, and sometimes of themselves as whites. As one student was told, "In the Marines, there's no black and white—we're all green." Another, Luke, writes:

My senior T.I. [Training Instructor in the Air Force] was Latino American and two out of the three assistants were also of Latino descent, the other white American. All three T.I.s would speak both languages (Spanish and English) and they spoke both very well. . . . The members of my flight were from different cultures. . . . We were basically all paranoid of each other through the myths we had embedded in our brains from our upbringing. To our T.I.s we were all Airman Basic skinheads. . . . We were taught, that, while in the Military Service we were all equal and we would have discussions about our cultures and most importantly we were taught how to coexist because it may be someone that we had prejudiced opinions about that may someday save our life. . . . An odd thing happened, the entire flight conformed to the Military way of thinking as a family should do and we all wanted to stay together [after graduation]. . . .

Luke's supervisors were people of color, who set a diverse example by being bilingual. He worked and lived with people of various backgrounds. Informal or perhaps formal discussions took place regarding diversity and prejudice. All of these factors helped the men to overcome their initial fear and distrust eventually to feel like a "family."

Dylan writes about his introduction to the military:

> I lived a very secluded life from what most people have probably experienced. My family didn't have the money to travel or buy most things that a lot of people experienced. I was 14 before I traveled out of the state and even then it was only to Maryland. It was this lack of experience that made my later trip to Army Basic Training and then to college, such dramatic experiences racially and ethnically. . . . The most influential experience that reshaped my way of thinking was the four months I spent in Alabama in Army Basic Training. Any previous opinion of how blacks acted or the amount of respect they deserved was shredded within seconds of arriving. . . . My 'holier than thou' attitude was stomped on by a 5'9" black female drill sergeant named Drill Sergeant White. I remember staring at her and wondering how the heck she became a drill sergeant. I had no sooner completed that thought when she caught me staring at her. For those who don't know, staring at a drill sergeant is a big no-no. Never in my life have I been screamed at and so degraded. . . . as I was by her. As soon as she saw me she ran over and got right in my face. With her nose half an inch from mine she yelled, 'What are you looking at private? Do you like what you see? Do you want me to be your girlfriend? You'd like that wouldn't you?' She then proceeded to call me every name in the book and in doing so attracted the attention of the other seven drill sergeants in my company who all took their turn reaming me out. It might be hard to believe but that one incidence brought me to treat black women with a lot more respect.

Dylan's most transformative experiences in the Army are at first the most traumatic, even frightening to him. In this interaction with the drill sergeant, Dylan's turning point occurs at the cross-section of race and gender. This woman disrupts his preconceived notions not only of African Americans, but also of women. Dylan's story continues in this same vein, as he also writes about his first awkward encounters with his African American bunkmate, and how he develops from his friendship with him an empathy for the discrimination that African Americans face.

The military brings some into contact not only with people of color who are fellow soldiers, but with those from diverse world cultures. Dale writes:

> Throughout my military career, I have been fortunate to visit many countries including Europe, Africa, Cuba, Haiti, and the Middle East. I

have experienced various different cultures and ethnicities that are much different than mine. I was once corrected after attempting to hug an Arab female in a restaurant located in Abu Dhabi. I learned that public affection was prohibited within that particular community. . . . While serving in Somalia, I have learned about the Muslim faith through many hours of public prayer, which was heard over loud speakers. I was amazed at the commitment towards religious faith after observing entire communities being shut down in order to pray. Upon returning to the civilian world, I chose to broaden my education by attending college. My experiences have allowed me to appreciate diversity and the various people of the world. I also began to gain interest in my own race and ethnicity and made significant advances towards learning about my family history.

Dale has learned things about the cultures of various countries in which he served. Admittedly, it is impossible to tell what judgments he has formed about these cultures, since he only expresses admiration for the Somalis' Muslim faith and does not comment positively or negatively on other cultural practices. However, he has gained some information, does not write in an overtly negative way, and it is likely that in future encounters with those different from him, they at least will not seem quite as "foreign." Further, learning about other cultures has encouraged him to explore his own, which some deem a positive step for white Americans.[42]

Traveling can remove people from the security of home and place a white person in the minority for the first time, in itself a turning point experience. Sylvie has "a pure epiphany" after returning from the Dominican Republic:

My most recent and perhaps most powerful race revelation came last year right before I turned 19. I went to the Dominican Republic, where they are mostly of very dark complexion. I returned home and began to develop my pictures. There were many occasions where group photos were taken with Dominicans and myself. As I was flipping through the pictures I landed on one that changed my life, one that made me sick to my stomach, a pure epiphany. It was a picture of me surrounded by ten Dominicans, I stuck out like a sore thumb, a white ghost in the blackness. For that instant and every time I look at that picture I am reminded of what it must feel like for a minority amongst sameness. What it was like for those two black students at my high school that ruptured the array of white in the class photos. The ones that when they are older cannot hold their class picture in front of their grandchildren and ask them—'Try to find me.'

I am a white girl who lives in an all white town. I know what it's like to insult another race with no excuse other than pure ignorance. I know what it's like to watch a child suffer for no other reason than her parents falling in love. I've seen people lose friends, get into fights, and support hate. But the most important thing I know is what it is like to experience the other side of the spectrum.

The "minority" experience is immortalized in photos triggering Sylvie's "racial revelation." She now understands what it is like to experience race from a different perspective. Like Sylvie, Lona returns with important lessons from a trip to Japan as an exchange student:

> In my hometown, my race has never really stood out. I live in an all white community. I do know however, what it is like to be in the minority. When I was in high school I went to Japan via an exchange program. . . . Another exchange student and myself were the only people with blond hair in my school. We also were the only people who spoke fluent English. . . . My year spent abroad really opened my eyes to what many new immigrants to the U.S. face. I was in a country that did not speak my language and I did not speak theirs. . . . That experience. . . . helped me get over my prejudices against other races and cultures. I can actually sympathize with many of the Spanish-speaking people in the U.S. I know what people say to them. I used to be one of those people who said, 'If you don't speak English, get out of the country.' I don't say that anymore.
>
> I found that when in the minority you have to go along with the majority. I, being white, had never been in the minority; I had always been in the majority. It was a BIG shock to me. When I was in Japan, I was treated great. Everyone welcomed me. I was really surprised about that, considering the past issues that we have had with them. . . . I noticed that the Japanese people were more willing to forgive and forget about it then many people here in America. I formed many close relationships with classmates and members of my host families. . . . After I was. . . . able to communicate. . . . I had assimilated into Japanese culture. I consider myself bi-cultural, like some consider themselves as bi-racial. . . . It was not easy, but it was a great learning experience. It showed me what new immigrants to the U.S. face. It also taught me how to be patient with people who are different from me either racially or culturally.
>
> Because of my experience as a foreign exchange student, my views on other races and ethnicities have changed. . . . When I was younger I thought that the only way to be was white. I thought that white was right. I realize now that I was wrong to think that. . . . the color of one's skin is not what is important. It is the person that matters. My friends now encompass all walks of life. I have friends that are white, as well as African-American, Latino-Americans, Asian Americans and Arab-Americans.

Most white Americans never develop the bicultural orientation that those in racial minority groups must have for everyday survival in the United States.

Subordinate groups must understand the dominant culture as well as their own—they must have a "double consciousness."[43] Living in Japan has given Lona a sense of what it is like to be part of a minority group. Specifically, Lona has learned a new acceptance of linguistic difference.

Being in the Minority

As discussed above, an unfamiliar experience that often elicits stories of whiteness is being in the minority. Many white people who do not travel abroad live their entire lives never being in a situation where they are racially the minority. Some who do experience this unusual circumstance find it changes their perspective enough to perceive how it might feel to be a minority throughout life. Fiona stays with a Latino and African-American family for much of a summer and experiences feelings of inferiority based on her whiteness:

> Last summer was an eye-opening experience for me. I agreed to live with my friend for about a month on and off. . . . The way that he and his family acted towards me made me realize that for the first time in my life, I was a minority. Trey and his family were born in Puerto Rico. . . . His sister . . . is married to an African American. They have a five-year-old son. At first I was surprised at how differently his household was run compared to mine. They sat down for dinner almost every night and didn't talk; they just ate. My family chats about their day. The kids also do a lot more for their parents, or at least the parents expect them to. Maybe this seemed different to me because I'm the baby and in my family and we all work together to accomplish tasks, we don't divvy out duties. They also spoke a lot of Spanish. This was hard for me to get used to. Sometimes his mother would ask me to do something in Spanish and I would have to remind her that I couldn't speak Spanish. This made me feel inferior to the rest of the family. I have never been in a situation where I felt like I couldn't communicate with a person. The first time I met Trey's nephew, it was quite an experience. He looked me square in the face and said, 'What's the matter with your eyes?' I told him that nothing was wrong. They're just blue. He responded by saying, 'Well, everyone in my family has brown eyes and you don't so you shouldn't be here!' I was mortified and a bit upset because this was only day three, and no one had ever talked like that to me, especially a five-year-old. It made me wonder if maybe he had heard things in his home that had made him believe that people with blue eyes were inferior to those with brown eyes. Even though his parents were perfectly nice to me, children always reflect what their parents are truly thinking. . . . There I was, a blue-eyed Irish girl who felt like I was inferior to everyone in that house. I don't think that they meant it to be this way, I just think that they didn't realize what they were saying made me uncomfortable.

Her unfamiliarity with Spanish, and physical and cultural differences, make Fiona feel like an outsider. She experiences the complex nature of race relations in having to guess what the other side "really" means. Stefan experiences a situation in which he is the minority in the workplace. Like Fiona, it is in part lack of familiarity with another language that highlights his status as an outsider:

> I was working in a Chinese restaurant and I was the only white male working there. I found out rather quickly that I was being made fun of, and talked about behind my back. I don't know why this happened, maybe because I didn't speak Chinese or maybe it was because I was white, but I do know that I felt unwanted and I didn't care for that feeling. This one experience changed my whole perspective about racism. I didn't work in that restaurant for long.
>
> In this single case I was the minority and I was discriminated against. I was not treated as an equal because I was white and I didn't conform to their ideals. Because of this fact I believe that racism and discrimination are relative to the situation. If whites were the minority in this country and we lived in a black-dominated culture the situation would probably be reversed.
>
> I'm not trying to justify what is going on in terms of racism but I am trying to explain what it is to be white. If I lived a "typical" white man's life this experience would never have happened. I believe that being white is being isolated and believing in the ideal case for oneself. What I have experienced is rare for white people, if it wasn't then I don't believe racism would be such a problem.

Although Stefan believes he faced discrimination in this situation, he also understands that it would take a "black-dominated culture" for whites to experience a "reversed" situation of racism. As Stefan notes, if more whites were to experience a situation in which they were in the minority, it could begin to change the attitudes that are a foundation for white racism.

For some, the experience of being in the minority is briefer, but still has enough of an impact for them to note it in their autobiographies. Like many other college students, Molly's first experience of being in the minority is at a party:

> During my life I have had experiences that have made my race very visible to me. One of these experiences was earlier this year at a party. My friend Devon and I were dancing and having a good time when we realized that the other white students had left. We noticed that we were the only ones in the party who were not black. We started to feel uncomfortable because we did not know anyone there and we were unsure if we were welcome. We eventually just decided to leave the party. This was a unique experience for me because it was the first time I felt like a

minority. Looking back on this experience, I wish I had stayed at the party and met some of the people there. I think that I would have had a good time and met some great people if I had decided to stay.

Molly realizes that this experience of being in the minority was incomplete, since she and her friend did not stay at the party. However, remaining there as long as she did, and feeling discomfort, was a turning point for her. Initially uncomfortable experiences with negative feelings may become ones that change perceptions.

Lewis experiences being in the minority in an athletic competition:

In 1999 I was selected to play basketball in the USA Junior Nationals Basketball Game. . . . There were 200 boys selected for this tournament. If you could just imagine for a moment; a 5'10" white country hick, in a group of 6' 10" black city boys. It was quite an experience. I had to keep an open mind and do what I went there to accomplish. During the first round of games, I didn't get the ball more than twice during the game. . . . After they found out I could play ball, things got a little better. By the time the games were over and we had to leave, we were all getting along fine. I learned a lot from this experience. Being from a predominately white area, I can only imagine what it would be like to be a minority in a hostile environment. Even if the majority has no intention of being prejudiced, it would make you want to be on the offensive all the time.

Institutional discrimination is usually a difficult concept for whites to comprehend and empathize with. As one of the few white participants in a basketball tournament, Lewis learns how institutional discrimination works. He also can imagine how "a minority in a hostile environment" would constantly need to be looking out for such treatment.

Greg attends a summer course at a community college, and writes:

My first day as a student opened my eyes to a new universe. I walked into my art class that I was taking and was the first one to his seat. Slowly, as people began taking their seats it came to my attention that I was the only white person in the entire class of 33. I was for once in my life now the minority, to say the least and would experience emotions that I have never felt before in my life. At first I was very apprehentious [*sic*] of what this class would bring me, not academically, but culturally and regarding maturity. As it turns out, the class was great, I received the highest mark and so did ninety percent of the rest of the class. I saw this experience as one that let me acknowledge that I did not receive the highest marks because I was white; everyone is smart in their own way, regardless of race or ethnicity. What still bothered me was the fact how this school, which was only a county college, seemed to house only African American students and various other races and ethnicities. Why is it that all the minorities are funneled into this county college when the status of the work they produce is indicative of a [state college] student? This is a trouble that society has faced in regards to education. The segregation of races during this free and civil time frustrates me in that although we are passed [*sic*] the civil rights era in our history and every man is equal, they are not in essence. This is what society tells me today, that we are not equal, we are segregated still, though not by law, by physical mindset, we are still segregated.

Here, segregation becomes experientially realized. Because the minority students at the community college are able to achieve the same academic standards as Greg, he sees them in a new light. Only by being in the minority does Greg realize how segregated education is, and that this segregation is not based on ability, but on race and class.

Similarly to Greg, Lauren's first experience of being in the minority comes when she attends college:

I think the first time my race was really visible to me was when I went to my first semester at [college]. That was the first time I noticed some of the different styles and customs of other races. I really felt 'white' in instances like when I was in the bathroom and I was the only 'white' person in there or when I was walking to class when there was not many people around and I would pass a group of some people of other races other than white. It is not that I was scared but it was just the first time that I felt the feeling of being the minority. I was always nice and smiled at people (all people no matter their race) but I have always been more reluctant to talk to people of other races especially African Americans. . . . I am afraid of that because I sometimes feel that other races' (especially African Americans) race and ethnicity are more important to them than mine is. Their ancestors have probably had a much harder life than mine have had. In comparing how much I think of my race as to how much someone of another race might think of their race, I am guessing that they think of theirs a lot more than I think of mine. Everyday society forces them to think of it.

Lauren becomes self-conscious of her whiteness, almost overwhelmed by her concerns, when she is in the minority. Again we note that being in this unusual situation allows whites to experience life in ways that they otherwise do not. It also may lead them to realizations that they had not previously considered. For example, Lauren states that the reason she has previously not been as concerned about race as have others is likely because of the discrimination African Americans have faced.

After writing about attending school in the midst of a community of color, Marcy tells of her experience being a minority; by choice:

> In the eighth grade, when I was fourteen, the Navy Reserve Officer Training Commission (NJROTC) Drill Team came to the middle school for a demonstration intended to recruit members. I still remember some of the preppie girls saying things like 'only niggers are on that drill team' and, 'anybody that was somebody would not join.' Even my older brother said similar things. At this point in my life, I had already decided to go into the military when I graduated high school. I thought 'Why not get some experience in NJROTC before joining the real deal.' Consequently, when I became a freshman in high school, I joined NJROTC and my brother disowned me for the next three years. It seemed that the general assumption was that only the lower class, uneducated, or African Americans were in this program. Ironically, that same year and the year that followed more and more atypical white people joined. We changed the stereotype that NJROTC was only for African Americans. Looking back to that time, I was a minority. But, I truly did not think about that until now. The reason I did not think about it is most likely because I was never taught that I was a minority.

Placing a future goal as a higher priority than peer approval for fulfilling the obligations of whiteness, Marcy singlehandedly integrates the drill team. By being in the minority, Marcy learns more about white people's views of whiteness than those of people of color. In fact, she did not think of being a minority "most likely because [she] was never taught that [she] was a minority," meaning by the African-American girls on the team. Marcy does proceed to enlist in the military, and is again in situations where she is the racial minority.

Robert has had school situations where he has been one of few white students:

> [My middle school] had a large population of Blacks, and I believe that they were more than fifty percent of the school's population. Being part of the minority was something I had never experienced before, and it was a little strange. During this time, my attitudes towards other races began to change. I began to see that African Americans were no different than whites. I had a few Black friends, and they seemed to prove to me that there was nothing wrong with Blacks, and that it is wrong of whites to discriminate against them. I also had a few friends who did not share the same viewpoints that I did. One of friends grew up in a traditional Southern household, and it was his belief that Blacks were inferior to whites, and often used the term 'nigger' to describe them. I often used to tell him that it was wrong to discriminate people like that, but he did not listen, and kept using those words.

Being at a school where people of color make up half the population may make it less likely that a white student will only associate with other whites, although this can still happen. In Robert's case, being in the minority, or at least in a situation where whites were not the clear majority, possibly encouraged him to have "a few Black friends." These friendships convinced Robert that "there was nothing wrong with Blacks," and that they "were no different than whites." While this could be perceived as a "color-blind" statement, these data suggest that some dimensions of a color-blind perspective may lead to more positive whiteness. For whites to believe that people of color are "the same" in terms of having equal potential for certain abilities, personal characteristics, talents, or proclivities seems to be an important step toward destroying stereotypes. However, when "color-blindness" is extended to a belief that every group's *experiences* are the same, in terms of opportunities and power, it is not constructive of positive whiteness or antiracism.

Vicarious Victimization

One of the most profound epiphanal stories of whiteness I call "vicarious victimization." In this type of epiphany, a white person has probably also had a crossing experience—becoming close to a person of color. Vicarious victimization happens when a white person, through association with a person of color, witnesses differential treatment firsthand. A common example is a white person going to a restaurant with a person of color and finding that they receive poorer service than when in white company. Another situation regularly mentioned is that when shopping with a person of color, a white person may encounter a much different attention than usually experienced. For example, Annette notes:

> As I teenager, I rebelled against my parents. . . . I began having a racially mixed group of friends. . . . They began to accept this as long as I was just friends with them. When I was nineteen, I became very good friends with an African American girl I worked with, we hung out and did everything together. I can remember going to the mall one afternoon and people just stared at us. I said to her 'do I have something on my face?' She responded, 'No they are staring at you because you are walking with me.' I think that this was my first experience [with] the outside world of racism.

Annette, like many whites, is accustomed to stares only when something is wrong or out of place. In this case, nothing is wrong with her, but she herself is seen as out of place in walking with a person of color—unusual in her small town. Even whites in urban settings, when out with friends of color, may receive unusual attention in public. For instance, they may be asked immediately upon entering a store "May I help you?" or both may be followed while browsing. Linshyan wrote of this experience:

It is almost like I had an awakening this year when it comes to racism and discrimination. For instance, I went to Wal-Mart with a friend of mine, who happened to be Puerto Rican. We were followed as soon as we entered the store. I was furious, never had I been treated like that before anywhere . . . I was in such a state of rage, yet she posed no real concern other than the words we exchanged between each other about the people following us. I could not believe that she was not upset, I expected her to be more upset than I, but she explained to me how this was not the first time that this had happened to her, and it would not be the last. She told me, 'You get used to it' and my heart . . . dropped out of my chest. . . . I can understand why white Americans, in particular, may truly believe that racism does not exist in the world today, or at least not enough to complain about. However, they most definitely are only around white people because in my experience, after a few times of hanging around with a minority, you will encounter a racist event.

Linshyan further explains that she felt "ignorant" before realizing that racism still exists. For many whites, denial of the "everyday life" reality of racism is not caused by malicious intent, but by ignorance of the experience of being a person of color in the United States. African Americans and other people of color make allowances for the fact that many whites do not deny racism out of ill intent, but simply from living a different everyday experience.[44] The closest many whites will come to an understanding of the experiences of people of color is, as Linshyan points out, by "a few times of hanging around with a minority." For whites who never cross racial boundaries in their friendships, such an understanding may never come about.

Several respondents experienced vicarious victimization with close friends of color. Most often women experienced these turning points. Vanessa tells this story:

I have observed and experienced many racial conflicts. My best friend, who is white, has a son who has a black father, which makes him half black. There have been many occasions in which we would be out with her son and other white and black people have given us dirty looks. I'm assuming this comes from people not agreeing with interracial relationships etc. Her little boy is only 5 years old and doesn't yet understand why some of the other kids say mean things to him and refuse to play with him because of his skin color, or because he's different than them in some ways. It really hurts my feelings to hear him say that the kids at school make fun of him, and even call him names such as "nigger."

Here racial understanding comes from observing the plight of intimate others. Because Vanessa is close to this family, she has been with them when they receive hateful stares of disapproval in public. Consequently, when the young biracial child is referred to by racial epithets, Vanessa says that it "hurts [her] feelings." Vicarious victimization is often noted by women who date interracially, as a sense of being "on stage."[45] However, in this sample most women describe vicarious victimization as experienced through nonromantic friendships.

Tricia and a white friend were threatened at gunpoint by African-American men a few years before she wrote her autobiography. Throughout her essay, she describes her attempts to overcome her lasting fear and anger toward African-American men. Here she speaks of her friendship with a Jamaican woman:

> Since this incident, I have tried to come to grips with my prejudiced attitude but I know some of the feelings I still possess toward black males are negative. The incident did not affect my feelings about black females. I have always had black acquaintances but have never been friends with blacks on a personal level. During my freshman year of college at [another university] in [another city], I lived with a Jamaican girl named Marlie.
>
> My true feelings were immediately tested. The first thought I had, although I had always been friends with black girls, was extremely negative. I could not fathom the idea of having to share a room with someone who was 'different' than me. This experience turned out to be worthwhile. I learned that people of color do have to work harder than whites at some things.
>
> Marlie had African-American friends who frequently visited us. I had more fun with these girls than I did with some of the white girls who lived around me. One night Marlie, two of her friends, and I went out to eat and to the movies. I felt the stares they have to experience everyday of their lives. Marlie and her friends were comfortable enough with their race that they were able to make jokes about the white girl being with these black girls. They were comfortable, but I felt awkward, not being used to these foreign stares.

Tricia's friendship with Marlie and the vicarious sense of the white gaze that she experiences have helped her begin to overcome negative feelings from personal violence. Being out in public with Marlie and her friends shows Tricia that although the women of color are comfortable with their race, she feels "awkward" perhaps with their race or perhaps with her own. Not only have Tricia's attitudes changed; but she goes on to explain that so have concrete circumstances of her life, such as the neighborhood where she lives. She attributes these changes to knowing Marlie.

Another female respondent also had a violent encounter with an African-American man and an interracial friendship with a black woman. While many respondents express racialized fear for their physical safety, these are the *only* two who actually *experienced* personal attacks by strangers. Other acts of violence described are either altercations involving both the white person and the person of color or violence about which the respondents heard in the media.

Rhonda, who faced a personal attack, is an older student and mother. She spends nearly a third of her autobiography describing the impact of her friend Christy on her conceptions of race:

Through my friendship with Christy I have learned much about myself and about racism. . . . There has never been another person in my life who I have been closer to. . . . Christy understands me like no one else ever could. She is my soul mate. . . . We used to joke about race. Whenever we went out we would always get a lot of double take looks from people. . . . and we would laugh about the looks people would give us. When I moved to [the Midwest] Christy came to visit me. I never realized how 'white' my life in [that state] was. I lived in a predominantly white neighborhood, all of my friends were white, and all of the places I went were filled with white people. We went on a skiing trip to [a northern state], and Christy was the only black person on the slopes. When we returned to [her home city], we went to a bar, and an African American friend of my sister's from high school was in the bar. Christy was staring at him so much that he asked her 'What's the matter haven't you ever seen a black man before?' Her response was classic—she said 'Not in [this state].'

. . . . Christy came to visit me right after I moved to [the southern state she lives in now]. We ran into some discriminatory situations, and this ruined our time together. We talked and talked and talked about racism, and we made a pact that we would never let racism affect our friendship, but it has. She hates coming to [this state] because of the racist experiences she has had here, but she still comes. The second time she came to [the state] to visit it was like walking on egg shells. I was like—oh God I hope nobody does or says anything racist. . . . The last time Christy came to visit it was much better. She has found a way to deal with racism, which is basically—screw them. . . . I have tried to explain to her that a lot of white people are unaware of what constitutes prejudice to a black person. The only reason I know as much as I do is because of my friendship with her. These are sorry statements for our society—that white people are not aware of what constitutes prejudice and that she should have to find a way to deal with racism just to be able to live her life. What's up with that?

Christy's presence in Rhonda's life brings its whiteness into visibility. How "white" Rhonda's life is becomes clear, and racism becomes more evident to her. Rhonda feels that she shares in discriminatory incidents when Christy visits. It is clear that she only encounters discrimination when she is with Christy. Rhonda wants to shield Christy from racism. Rather than "I hope Christy doesn't *think* anyone is being racist today," Rhonda hopes "nobody does or says anything racist." She recognizes her friend's ability to distinguish racist behaviors. Further, Rhonda validates Christy's experience in her final statements. She faults whites for not knowing "what constitutes prejudice" and regrets that her friend must cope with racism "just to be able to live her life."

Marcy, in the racial minority in the Navy, is now a police officer, writing:

> When I was twenty three, I was assigned to the Navy Absentee Collection Unit. My best friend in the unit was an African American women named Cindy. Cindy had a one year old son named Stefan. Sometimes, I would baby-sit Stefan so that Cindy could have a break. Plus I liked Stefan. One day, I was babysitting Stefan at my house and had just got him down for a nap when a friend of mine came in. She asked me 'What are you doing with that niglet baby?' I was furious. I managed to tell her to shut up and to never say that again in my presence. This incident helped me see a side of my friend that I did not know existed. It also hurt my feelings that an adult, who should have known better, could be so stupid.

Here an understanding of the pain of racial epithets is reached through vicarious victimization. Marcy is accustomed to spending time with people of various racial and ethnic groups. It therefore shocks her when her friend uses a racial epithet to suggest she should not have an African-American baby in her home. Evidently, Marcy feels vicariously victimized, since the comment "hurt [her] feelings." What "hurts" Marcy, most likely, is not only that a child she treats as quasi-family has been insulted; but the realization that for many whites, part of whiteness is hostility toward people of color, which may disrupt her friendships with them. This experience is an epiphany because it makes clarifies for Marcy how her sense of whiteness differs from that of others who formerly were close to her.

One young man had an experience that, early in life, was a turning point in his racial identity. In his autobiography, "Half a Year as Somebody Else," Jack writes:

> One of my very first memories of actual racial discrimination has to have been in my third-grade year at school. My school was and still mostly is predominately white, but that year we had an African American girl join our school. . . . but she only stayed in school for half of the year. She was constantly teased, and I actually made friends with her. I used to walk her home from school because she lived close to me. I couldn't understand the stares, and shouts that ensued when we walked down the street. I carried her books for her, because my mother taught me how to be a gentleman to all girls, no matter what color they were. My parents always taught me to treat everybody as equals and that racism was wrong. So after several weeks of walking her home and talking she became my first girlfriend, I know I was young, but he I didn't think it could hurt anything; I was sadly mistaken.

One day on the way home I noticed a large group of boys, a little older than us, following us and yelling things at her like: 'Careful you don't trip over her lips,' and, 'Go back to your country Nigger.' This was not a one-sided racial bashing, they had their turn on me as well calling me a 'Nigger Lover,' then they started to chase us. We ran towards her house and I had time to get her inside and continue down the street to draw the attention to myself; needless to say it worked. They did a good number on me and I had bruised ribs and a black eye for awhile, but my pride was hurt and I didn't understand why they hurt me over having a friend. After that [she] wouldn't be my friend any more, wouldn't talk to me, and wouldn't let me walk her home anymore because she didn't want to see me get hurt.

I don't feel that I could, in all good conscience, write about my life without including that half a year of my life when I was no longer just Jack but known as 'Nigger Lover,' I was no longer white, I was magically a different color because of the company I chose to keep; kids can be cruel.

For Jack, the physical and psychological toll of racism is felt through this tragic incident. This early experience changes his outlook. When he and his friend are verbally and physically attacked, he retrospectively perceives it as aimed at both of them, no matter who is targeted by the actual epithet. Most dramatically, Jack learns that he could lose his whiteness—he can become "magically a different color" by associating across the color line. Whiteness is no longer a fixed, stable essence one possesses, but a flexible, transferable quality negotiated in everyday interactions. It can shelter one from the treatment a person of color may receive—but losing or relinquishing it means one may be subjected to the same treatment as they.

Relationship Conflict

Intergenerational conflict is a common theme in American culture. Teenagers are almost expected at some point to have disagreements with their parents' values, attitudes, or lifestyles. As the United States becomes more diverse, younger white generations are offered the opportunity to associate with people of color or, seen another way, are required to come into contact with them. Conversely, many in their parents' and grandparents' generations could live out most of their lives with only brief and superficial encounters with people of color. As evidenced in the respondents' discussions of parental messages about race, some parents still harbor attitudes about people of color that are ambivalent if not negative. As one respondent, Racina, said, "Racism was my father's middle name and he imposed his ideas upon me as I grew up." Other parents may not have particularly hostile attitudes, but still believe it is best for whites and people of color to remain segregated from one another. Respondents who forge friendships across racial barriers may come into conflict with their parents because of this choice. When they pursue the friendships in opposition to their parents' wishes, the experience may serve as a landmark in their conception of their own whiteness. Not only have they crossed a racial line; they have rebelled against their parents.

Nina is surprised by her parents' reaction to her friendship with an African American young man:

My first experience with prejudice came when I was in about ninth grade. I was hanging around a group of friends that included a Black boy. On Monday nights a group of us would go out to . . . have dinner and we went to movies together and did lots of things together. I don't remember how it all got started but this Black boy, Daniel, would call me and we would talk for a long time and we were beginning to be good friends. One night, my parents told me that they thought Daniel might start to like me. They did not approve of that and they told me I could not hang around my friends if Daniel was around and basically, I couldn't be friends with Daniel anymore. This made me very angry. I did not like my parents judging Daniel based on his skin color. Not once did my parents ever have a conversation with him but made this ignorant judgment based on his skin color. If my parents had ever gotten to know Daniel, they would have found out that he was a smart, sweet, kind, and wonderful person. I decided that my parents were wrong and I began writing notes to Daniel at school and calling him on the phone late at night when my parents were sleeping.

As in Nina's story, dating relationships often begin when a group of teenagers spends time together, and then two in the group begin to pair off alone. Nina's parents attempt to put things back as they were when they were younger and groups of friends were usually racially homogenous, by cutting Daniel out of Nina's friendship circle. Nina responds by continuing the relationship through subterfuge. What is perhaps most poignant in this passage is Nina's assertion that this was her "first experience with prejudice." Given the importance respondents place on the influence of their parents in racial matters, realizing her parents had prejudiced attitudes was most likely profound. Another female respondent, Denise, tells a similar story involving her parents:

As I mentioned, earlier in the seventh grade I was assigned a family roots project. Upon completion of this project our class was to take a field trip to Ellis Island to visit where many of our ancestors had passed through. There was however a little more to it than that. We were not the only school that was going to be attending this trip. We were to be joined by an inner city school from [a nearby town]. Probably because of something our parents had said we anticipated the worst; however, after a few large interactive group activities we realized that these kids were for the most part just like us. They were just glad to be out of the classroom for the day. In fact as seventh grade girls often are, we were a little on the boy-crazy side and decided to exchange phone numbers with some of the boys from [the other school]. I honestly never thought that they would call nor did I have any intentions of calling them because, to put it mildly, I knew my parents would strongly disapprove. When my dad picked up the phone several days later and heard the voice of a young boy with a Puerto Rican accent asking for me I knew I was in trouble. More importantly I realized I had let my parents down and I couldn't even understand why. It was the first time I really questioned the values they had raised me to believe in. They assured me that it was for my own good and left it at that. I never brought it up again and told the boy not to call me at home anymore. Instead I would talk to him at my best friend's house who had also been talking to one of the boys from [the other school], that is until her parents got the phone bill. We decided that it wasn't worth disappointing our parents to continue the relationship but it was difficult to explain to the boys and to ourselves why that had to be. I knew deep down that just because these guys weren't rich and from my all white school that it was no reason to not associate with them. If, at the age of thirteen, I knew this then why couldn't my parents who were supposed to be older and wiser see that what they were saying was so unfair and wrong. I know now that it came from years of their parent's racist attitudes that had simply just been ignorantly passed on through the generations.

As with Nina, this interaction with her parents over race is a "first" for Denise—it is the first time she has questioned her parents' standards. Denise realizes her parents will object to her relationship with a Puerto Rican boy, but she does not understand why. When, as she expected, her parents tell her she cannot talk to the boy, "for [her] own good," Denise resorts to deceit to continue the budding friendship. Later, she and a friend who is engaging in similar behavior decide that continuing the friendships is not important enough to them to disappoint their parents. Still, for Denise the experience has been a turning point—"the first time [she] really questioned the values they had raised [her] to believe in." Thinking about racial matters for herself for the first time, Denise finds areas in which she disagrees with her parents.

Jackie had similar conflicts with her parents first in high school and then even as a college student:

My second job was in a mostly African American neighborhood. I was always polite and courteous to the customers . . . My feeling was that I owed it to them to be extra nice because of the discrimination they had to put up with. As time went on I began to notice that black men were polite and flirtatious with me. Several times I was asked to go out but I declined out of the fear of my father finding out. One gentleman in particular . . . was very attractive, and I had thought . . . that I would really like it if he were to ask me out. Then the day came that he did . . . The one thing that I remember most is that my father's best friend came and stood right behind us as he asked me out. He was there to make sure I was not being harassed by this black man and that I would turn his offer down. Which I regrettably did. To this day I wonder what kind of fun I had missed out . . .

My next experience was when I came to college. I became very attracted to a guy named Will, who happened to be African American. . . . I would tell my family about the time and activities that I had done with Will. They were happy that I had found a person to have fun with at college, until the day that they met him in person. After that day they wanted to make sure that we were just friends. Many times . . . they would say 'that's nice but you're just friends right? You know that's all it can be right?' This was one of the most hurtful times in my life so far. I was unable to be with the person that made me the happiest. I was not allowed to even see if he could have been the one for me. . . . Now that I have gotten together with my high school love I am happy that I did not get with Will. [My boyfriend] also takes his parent's attitude that African Americans and whites should not 'mix.' This is why I think him and my parents get along. He is everything they always wanted for me. My boyfriend is sweet, polite, mannerly, and of course white.

Jackie's experience is interesting in that not only her own family, but the extended quasi-family, in the form of her father's best friend, is engaged to ensure her behavior falls well within the standards of racial separation with which she has been raised. This story hearkens back to a time when any white woman was assumed to need protection by all white men from African-American men. Another young woman, Annette, actually begins dating an African-American young man, and faces familial conflict consequently:

Since I have come [to college], I have met many African American guys and girls, and have become very good friends with many of them. In this time, I have met an African American guy that I have begun dating. I figured that this would cause some controversy with my parents, so I decided to hide it from them for awhile. I went home for Spring Break, and my dad asked me if I had met any guys at school. I said 'Yes . . .' Then my dad proceeded to ask me if he was black or white. I hesitated and he said 'He's black isn't he?' I said yes, and he was very angry and disappointed in me.

For the rest of the week, I battled with my parents to make them understand why I am dating him and why I like him. They did not seem to care. I guess I did not know exactly how racist my parents are until this very moment. My dad told me that he thought that they had brought me up better than this. I told them that I was not doing this to get some sort of revenge on them, but I was doing this because I liked him.

After about a week of fighting about my choices, I was told that I was to stop seeing him, or they would pull me out of school. My choice was evident. I stopped dating him. Although, I still continue to be friends with him today. . . . I told my parents that my morals and beliefs may be different than theirs, and they are going to have to deal with that fact. I will not raise my children to only associate with people of their own race.

When Annette can be controlled no other way, her parents choose to use the threat of the withdrawal of financial support for her education to maintain their way of life in her behavior. For Annette and the other respondents, relationship conflict can be an experience serving to remind them of the boundaries of whiteness. These respondents are placed in a situation where they must do a "cost/benefit" analysis of the consequences of crossing racial lines in their intimate relationships. In effect, they are then cast into a complex relationship conflict. First, they experience a conflict with their parents, as they realize they do not share the same values in regards to racial acceptance. Growing up in all-white communities, many are not confronted with these differences in attitude until they reach college and begin to make friendships with people of color. Prior to this time, "race" may have rarely been an issue in their homes, except when a media event brought it to attention—as respondents sometimes noted. Fundamentally, theirs is a conflict in choosing between two relationships that are important to them—one with a significant other, and one with the parents. Other researchers likewise have found that young whites in this position often feel white families require a "racial loyalty" that comes into conflict with their relationships with people of color who are significant to them.[46]

New Family Members

For some, relationship conflict had arisen when siblings brought "race" into the family through the introduction of a family member who is racially "marked." Until that time, in a white family, it is as if "race" does not exist. For example, Keith writes of his sister's relationship with an Asian man:

I was sitting at the computer one evening in eleventh grade when the phone rang. My mother picked up the phone; it was my sister, who was attending [college]. I could hear some crying at the bottom of the stairs. After the phone call was complete, my father came up the stairs to where I was sitting. He told me in his words, 'Your sister is pregnant to some chink.' Hearing these words from my father sent chills through me. He stood there like he expected some outrageous response from me as well; I just sat there with a blank stare, trying not to lash out at my father. . . . My sister's pregnancy did not shock me nearly the same as it did my parents; I knew that she was seeing this guy. She was not scared to tell me about her relationship, but she wouldn't dare tell my father. . . . I couldn't fathom my father's anger when considering that his grandchild would also be half-[Asian].

In the second chapter of his autobiography, he continues:

As things progressed in my sister's relationship . . . , there was still much skepticism on my father's part. But Matthew has brought a magnificent change in my father's beliefs as well. At first sight none of us could help to show anything but unconditional love for this child. Matthew's birth has been an earth-shattering blow to my father's racial hang-ups. My sister and John were married about a year ago; and to be honest with you I don't think my father would have given his blessing on such a marriage without Matthew's birth. . . . Although my sister's pregnancy might not have been at the most convenient time, the results couldn't have been any better; I have a beautiful nephew and my father is expanding his racial horizons everyday.

Interracial marriages and their offspring can transform racial attitudes. Although, admittedly, Keith's sister's unplanned pregnancy at first caused trauma in her immediate family, its end result, according to Keith, was to help change her father's prejudiced attitudes toward Asians. Of course, one could question whether Keith's father has simply created an "exception" in his mind for his son-in-law and grandson. Still, perhaps even imperfect contact or incomplete transformation is cause for optimism and a starting place for ending prejudices.

Similarly to Keith, Courtney and her family change their racial understandings when a new child is born into the family. Courtney writes:

Up until this point in my life, I was extremely sheltered. I wasn't able to see or understand any racial problems that society faced. But it all came into focus when my sister hit her rebelling stage. Before I knew it, she was pregnant to a black man. . . . My dad was the first and the loudest to speak up. You see, my dad is an interesting person. It's okay that he is prejudiced because he once had a best friend who was black. It's as if he has already paid his dues, like it is a charity he can ignore by saying he donated last year. . . . The idea of his daughter having a 'nigger baby' outraged him. . . . It seemed that his mind was made up and he would never change, but a lot has happened since then. . . .

The real turning point came in my life. . . . [when] Mariah Courtney Carn was born. At this point I decided that people would accept her or I would not accept them. This included my father. She has dramatically changed his thinking more than I expected. . . . I cannot describe how much having her in my life has changed me. I was sleeping and she woke me up to a whole new world. All of a sudden, I heard the racist jokes and remarks that were casually made. I could see what had really been going on all around me my entire life. Why couldn't I see it before? Simply because it wasn't personal. I think I hear a lot more racial remarks than Mari might because people let their guard down when there are only whites around. I often noticed someone glaring at me in disgust when I took Mari somewhere. They thought I was the young mother of a black baby. People make comments not knowing I will take offense to it. I like this in a way because it is a good time to challenge peoples' thinking. It catches them off guard and they are not prepared to defend their negative remarks. I sometimes make the mistake of taking something personal when it really wasn't personal at all. Another bad aspect of being an invisible target is that I see the stupidity that the ignorance feeds off of. This is the same ignorance that will one day send this little girl home in tears. . . . I want her to know it is wrong, but it does exist, and if you let it get to you, they win.

Courtney describes the birth of her niece as the event that woke her from a state of sleep. She reasons that it was because "it wasn't personal" that she had not seen racism before. She even understands the dilemma of having to judge what ostensibly racially motivated behaviors and comments from whites are and are not "personal;" something few whites ever experience.

Later, Courtney writes:

I also have some experiences involving race at my job. I work at a small country club a couple days a week. There are no black members, and most likely never will be. The place is like a den for insecure white males to hide. My sister works there also. The fact that she had a black man's baby disgusted some of the members. They sit there in the dimmed bar area like it is their territory and get extremely threatened if a black person comes in the club, which happens about twice a year. You can hear everyone whispering, 'They're not here to get a membership are they?'

. . . . [I]f it were not for Mari, I would still be blind to many things in our society. She helped me and everyone around her, whether it was directly or indirectly, to open their eyes and take another look. . . . She has made more progress with individuals than any legislation ever could have. I think in order to change, people need things to be on a person level. Think of how different it would be if there were more biracial people uniting black and whites.

Having a family member of a different racial background has made Courtney more conscious of racial prejudice in other settings, such as in her workplace. It has also perhaps made her more likely than some other respondents to be aware of the low proportion of people of color on her college campus, which she also mentions in her discussion (while other respondents feel "overwhelmed" by diversity at the same school). Similarly to Gary, quoted previously, Courtney believes that it is through interracial contact that whites can begin to significantly change their understanding of race and racism, rather than through formal mechanisms.

Another respondent, Sue, first describes her father as a man with prejudiced attitudes openly expressed toward African Americans and then discusses a transformation in the family:

> [T]he next incident that occurred . . . solidified my opinion on race and ethnicity. It was an incident that shook the core foundational beliefs of our family and helped resettle them into what they are today. This incident was the adoption of my biracial nieces. . . . Even my father being as racist as he was benefited from the adoption of Jessica. I have not heard him nor anyone in my family crack a racist joke about anything since. . . .
>
> That is not to say that the years have gone by without trials and tribulations. . . . [the parents adopted another biracial child] When [the girls] were two years old, my sister . . . was babysitting them in a small town. . . . The town was in an uproar that evening because the Ku Klux Klan was planning a rally and was planning to burn a 50-foot cross in the middle of town. Several of [my sister's] neighbors aggressively confronted her about 'getting those black kids out of their town.' This event really made my family band together to confront racism. . . . I will continue to learn from [the girls] and be more aware of the effects of racism. . . . I only wish that everyone could have the opportunity to learn the way I did.

Sometimes one family member's interracial interactions initially cause tensions within the family. However, from the autobiographies it seems that, if a family can find a way not only to tolerate the new family member but to appreciate and learn from that person and that person's interactions with other whites, there is much to be gained from these initially tense situations.

Education and Insights

Many of my respondents wrote about turning points that come from learning about race relations in an educational environment. Very few respondents write of notable racial learning experiences in high school. Most discuss only learning about African Americans during Black History Month or when discussing slavery; and discussing "other cultures" only at similar token moments. Roger writes about one teacher who stands out in his memory because his history class was unusual:

> [This history teacher] was going over the American history and the problems with our perception. It was the first time that I had heard of the wrongs committed by the Europeans towards the Native Americans. Until this time I was always taught that the Europeans and the Native Americans got along fine with one another, when the Europeans first came to this country. As we went over the lesson, my mind flashed back

when I was in first grade. We were going over the first Thanksgiving, and the way that the teacher was presenting it, did not mirror what [this history teacher] was saying. My First grade teacher left out that Europeans butchered Native Americans. Brought diseases and famine upon many of the Native American tribes in the new Americas. Destroyed many of the villages and then enslaved the Native Americans for profit. As he spoke a painful realization was taking place. My mind focused on old cowboy movies. 'That's why they fought with cowboys,' I remember thinking to myself. Then [this history teacher] began to speak about Christopher Columbus. He began, 'Well who here thinks that Christopher Columbus was a great individual?' Of course the entire room raised their hands. We had always been taught that Columbus was a great man. He stood up to the world and proved to everyone that the world was not flat. [This history teacher] smiled with his confident crooked smile and said, 'Now what would you think if I told you that Columbus also did these things to Native Americans?' The room was in total shock. No, Columbus couldn't have done this. He was their friend. Then [this history teacher] explained to us something that no other teacher had ever attempted to explain. He described how our perception of the world was influenced by American history. We did understand that there were two sides to every story.

Education is an important tool in fighting racism. Here, in recognizing colonialism's impact on Native Americans, Roger begins to see that when history is told only from a white perspective, it may leave out the viewpoint of other groups. Additionally, the racial implications of interactions may also be unexplored.

Two women, Karen and Daphne, learned some about race prior to college. Karen's teacher introduces her to the Harlem Renaissance:

In tenth grade things were about the same way. My only new experience was that my English teacher taught us about the Harlem Renaissance. [My English teacher] was a young, white, male teacher. He had a very passionate and innovative teaching style. . . . He introduced me to black writers like Langston Hughes, Richard Wright, Alain Locke, James Johnson, Countee Cullen, and Marcus Garvey. I learned some of their history and came to understand their hurt and their pain from discrimination. One of my favorite poems is Hughes's *Theme for English B;* it describes how although he lives in a different neighborhood and may be discriminated against he is a part of the same America that his white instructor is a part of. This made me realize how useless racism and discrimination are—we are all living in the same world and can learn so much from each other and be more productive if we could put aside our differences and selfish thoughts. I also began to foster a sense of pride for my black friends realizing what they go through on a day to day basis and also what their ancestors went through. [My English teacher] gave me such a respect and different hue on the racial issue that I had never thought of before.

Apparently Karen's class covered the Harlem Renaissance in some degree of detail. The class and this teacher certainly opened her eyes to the literary talent of African Americans so often overlooked in high school. Karen's use of metaphor here is interesting also, that her teacher gave her a "different hue" on racial matters.

Daphne also has a high school teacher who believes it is important to spend time covering issues of African-American history year-round, instead of only during African-American History Month:

My American History teacher found the civil rights movement an extremely important topic to discuss. We spent at least a third of the year learning about the civil rights movement. It is so strange to think that I did not learn about the civil rights movement until I was seventeen years old. In previous years of school we had learned about Harriet Tubman and Martin Luther King Jr., but I never really understood who these people were until my junior year of high school. My teacher . . . was the first person to explain to me the hardships that other ethnic groups had to encounter in our country in the past. I learned everything there is to know about the civil rights movement and the struggle blacks had to endure in our country, but I never learned about the struggle blacks have to endure in today's times. It was not until my sophomore year in college that I learned about the struggle blacks still have to endure.

Later, she adds

College has not just taught me what it feels like to be a minority; it has also taught me about the discrimination minorities have had to encounter their entire life. I have heard black students explain how hard it is to go places without worrying about if you're going to be treated different because of your race.

Daphne commends her high school history teacher for covering the Civil Rights Movement so thoroughly. Still, she criticizes the school system for her not having heard about this earlier and then complains she did not learn about *present*-day discrimination until college. Although the college experience has taught her much about discrimination, she believes that, in general, predominantly white school systems lag behind in teaching students about racism.

Like Daphne, most respondents learned very little in high school about present-day race relations. As noted previously, most also have had little interaction with people of color in their racially isolated environments. Hence, the college experience itself serves as a turning point for many. Mary Waters notes for many young whites, leaving home to attend college is a significant experience. It allows them their first chance to test their families' beliefs against experience by bringing them into contact with people who are "different."[47] She also explains how inexperience on the part of white students can lead to low levels of racial tension on college campuses.[47] Students' college experiences frequently conflict with what they have learned from their families.

Some respondents describe how their thoughts about race changed over the course of a semester as a result of the classes they were taking. Kim writes:

> My dad would never comment about a person's race to their face, but he has done it many times behind their backs. I can tell now that their views have rubbed off on me. I never saw myself as being a racist person, but after having taken this class, [in race and ethnicity], I have changed some of my points of view. I had always been given the impression by my family that Blacks were, for the most part, just lazy and took advantage of the welfare system because they did not want to get jobs. I also agreed with my dad that blacks just accused white people of being racist because it was a good excuse for them being unsuccessful. Now I realize that there is still racism and still people who are discriminated against. I thought it was a thing of the past, but that is because I was fortunate enough never to have been someone who has had to face any of it. The first few times our [race and ethnicity] class met, all I could do was sit there and think how stupid everyone was and wonder why they didn't realize that everything they were saying about racism and discrimination was just a facade. As the class continued to meet, and as I had to read more and more, I began to think that maybe I was the one with the wrong idea about all of this. I used to have such a strong opinion about it all, but now I am more confused. I now think that in a way it is unfair for me to even speak my opinion to anyone else because I couldn't possibly know what it is like to be someone of a different race. It is because I am white that I do not see racism as a problem in our country.

Here we see how education can have an impact on students by presenting a more complex picture of the world. Kim, who grew up in a family where prejudiced opinions were freely expressed, has had a transformation of her consciousness because of her experiences in a course she is taking. One can see white students' first reaction to evidence of existing racism is often denial and defensiveness, which may be replaced with a more accepting attitude. The most important way the class has changed her views is she has been able to see the notion that we live in a meritocratic system as a myth. Kim now "realize[s] that there is still racism and still people who are discriminated against."

Before, she thought that claims of discrimination were only a "good excuse for them being unsuccessful."

This passage also conveys something instructors who teach courses in diversity, social problems, or race and ethnicity must consider. Kim says while her former "strong opinion" about it has been dismantled, "now [she is] more confused." College courses may do an adequate or even superb job of breaking down the ideas students bring to college, but sometimes are unable to replace those ideas with ones suggesting what to "do next" about racism. White identities based on superiority over others are displaced, but students are not assisted in replacing them with positive antiracist white identities. Of course, this may be a difficult task to undertake in the time allotted for a typical college course, but instructors should be mindful of the need to suggest solutions to racism.

Kim illustrates another potential problem for white students when discussing topics of race and racism. She comments that she "now think[s] that in a way it is unfair for me to even speak my opinion to anyone else because I couldn't possibly know what it is like to be someone of a different race." It is challenging for instructors to ensure that their classroom is a safe environment for people of color to speak out about racism in their lives and to hear those topics discussed. However, instructors must also create a place in the classroom for *white* students to feel comfortable speaking out about race and racism, even when what they have to say may not seem to hold merit. It is only through doing so that white students can learn where their arguments are faulty, and new ways to consider race and racism. This is perhaps the greatest challenge of teaching courses in race and diversity—to be sure that *all* students feel it is "fair" for them to speak, but to protect students from the possible pain that can be caused by another's comments.

Finally, Rita's experience in a college race and ethnicity course, combined with the influence of her boyfriend, Mick, together have a dramatic impact on her:

The diversity at the university level was phenomenal. I remember filling out a form that was used for the purpose of assigning you to a roommate. You can probably guess the remarks made by my family: 'How funny it would be if you got a black roommate.' Honestly, at the time I was petrified of this. . . . In retrospect, I realize this was only because I knew nothing about the 'other' races. . . . It was definitely a dichotomized campus. Socially, there were little interracial activities. But, one thing was different compared to high school, I was actually exposed to the 'other' races. This allowed me the opportunity to test out what I had been taught all my life. At this point I had only heard of other racial groups other than passing by them on the street. I would try to instigate conversations with other minority groups, but would inevitably fail. Could this mean my father had been right? At the time I concluded just this. However, now I realize that I was practicing the benefits of being white. I was talking to other groups as if they were like me. In other words, I did not understand why they could not be like me. So, it ends up my dad was right about one thing, other races are different from us. However, they are not negatively different from us, they are merely comparably different from us. It is left up to the individual to decide if this difference is negative or positive. This gave me a way out from my family's teachings.

Rita's analysis here is insightful. As Waters suggests about going away to college, Rita perceives the experience as a chance to "test out what [she] had been taught all [her] life." Although her college is segregated by race, like most, it is different from high school because she is "exposed" to people of other races. When she at first feels socially rejected by people of color, she wonders if her father's views of them were correct. Because of the course she has taken and conversations with her boyfriend, Rita realizes she was speaking to people of color as if they were white, and that this is one of the privileges of whiteness. This is a relatively sophisticated analysis of white privilege.

Rita also has been able to construct a new perception of difference. Instead of believing people of color to be "different" in terms of inferiority, she now conceives of them as "different" "comparably"—in terms of experiences. The "negative" or "positive" aspect of difference is based on individuals, not racial groups. College has given her "a way out from [her] family's teachings," in that she can understand how they came to believe what they do but has constructed a new belief system. Rita later writes:

> The most recent learning experience I have had is being in your class. Never before in my educational career have I taken a course about other races. . . . The most important information that I think I have learned from this class is the notion of the benefits associated with being white. Mick would tell me this, . . . he illustrated his point by saying this, 'these people have been suppressed for so long that it is not a fair race. It is like the white race has a head start towards the finish line.'

Learning about white privilege in class in conjunction with conversing with another white person about issues of race changed Rita's perception, again allowing her to see white privilege and, as she states elsewhere, to see that opportunity is not yet "equal." Rita ends her paper by writing:

> I cannot make up for my attitudes and behaviors in the past. My only option is changing them now. I am truly grateful to be who I am today and now realize I took the benefits of being white for granted. I hope this revelation will lead me down the right path in the future. This class has given me the base knowledge about other races and ethnic groups to

better understand what is going on around me, rather than scapegoat the 'other' groups. . . . In our world today, not understanding people's differences gives us an automatic disadvantage.

Rita says the class gave her a "base knowledge" for a better understanding of issues of race. Coupled with her discussions with her boyfriend, she has had what can be referred to as an epiphanal experience. Some might wonder whether Rita will continue to think as she does if her relationship with Mick ends. Janet Helms asserts that white people who have reached the next-to-last level of racial identity need the support of other conscious whites in order not to "backslide" into lower levels of racial identity.[49] While I do not conceptualize whiteness as a "staged" process, I do agree that for whites who have not been conscious of whiteness for very long to keep considering ways to be positively white, the support of other similarly race-conscious whites is beneficial.

Conclusion

This chapter highlighted experiences in respondents' life stories that served as "turning points" in their understandings of themselves as white or of the social meanings of race. Sometimes these turning points were epiphanal—they radically transformed their beliefs or attitudes. Other turning points were more subtle, yet still led the respondent to a new understanding of herself or himself as a white person or of the life circumstances of those in other groups. Respondents began to better understand racial inequality, white privilege, and that being white may make one's perspective different than others. Most of the turning-point experiences involved a white person first coming into sustained contact with a person of color. This happened through being college roommates, through creating other friendships, in romantic relationships, because of geographical displacement, by being in the minority, through vicarious victimization, through adding family members of color, or from education about the experiences of people of color.

"Turning points" for whites are very different than for people of color, and this difference highlights white privilege. Many people of color have been given verbal messages from their parents about race and their racial identity. They are also reminded of race through the discrimination they face regularly. For people in racial minority groups, their first racial "turning-point" experience might be traumatic, in that it reminds them of being outsiders in U.S. communities or workplaces. The transformative racial experience comes about through this realization of an "outsider" status, and through finding a way to create a positive identity within the framework imposed by it. In this sense, for people of color, being aware of race is an everyday necessity.

Whites, however, seldom have their race brought to their attention through discrimination. Most received no parental messages about what it means to be white. Race only becomes meaningful, and their racial identities significant, under unusual circumstances. For the whites in this research, racial turning points were primarily about becoming aware of the plight of others and then understanding their place in a system that has created unjust circumstances for people of color. Some turning points were more "colorblind" in nature—whites simply conclude after contact with others they have things in common and are not as "different" as they previously assumed. Whatever the outcome of the experience, for whites, unlike for people of color, these racial turning points are situations from which they could turn away. This in itself is a luxury, a privilege of whiteness—the option to confront race or avoid it. In contrast to the experiences of people of color, whose very survival may depend on learning how to deal with a "turning-point" experience, the only consequence for a white person's failure to engage the situation is a moral one—"if I don't learn how to get along with people in other groups, I am not a good person." This is a self-imposed moral principle, not a requirement imposed by society to learn how to deal with discrimination. Thus a racial "turning point" for a white person is always very different from what it is for people of color, in that it is voluntary—representing another privilege of whiteness.

In this chapter, turning-point experiences were positive encounters in that they led to new understandings of whiteness. Certainly, not every encounter between a white person and a person of color becomes a "turning-point" in this sense. Sometimes interracial contact can further ensconce the white person in stereotypical or hostile attitudes toward a person of color. Interracial contact can also create awkwardness and further misunderstanding. Although interracial contact can lead to negative attitudes, my data suggests that it for the most part leads to positive outcomes. For example, it was those who reported little to no interracial contact that were also more likely to express negative attitudes toward those of other racial groups. Of course, one must acknowledge that in turning-point experiences, the white person's response to the encounter was integral to the experience being a positive one and it may be relatively open-minded whites who are willing to engage in interracial contact.

For these respondents, dealing with race is a matter of voluntary engagement. For example, students who find themselves with roommates of a different race or ethnicity may generally avoid that person, or request a different roommate, rather than being open to a cross-racial friendship. In choosing to pursue a relationship with a significant other who is a person of color, respondents go against family and community norms. This generates a complex turning-point experience, encompassing not only the cross-racial relationship but also a break with family attitudes. Similarly, deciding to accept and even protect a person of color as a family member lays a foundation for many new experiences with race and even racism.

What is noteworthy here is that racial awareness for whites continues to be voluntary. White privilege allows respondents to engage people of color when they desire. People of color learn about white culture as a prerequisite for education and employment, but for whites, knowing about cultural others is an act of goodwill. We must consider the inequity of this situation. The voluntary nature of whites engaging others implicitly reinforces their dominant status. On the other hand, demographic changes (such as the growth of populations of people of color in the United States) may eventually bring balance to this situation. Gradually, understanding people of color and their experiences may become a practical necessity for whites. Their job opportunities and economic survival might depend on it.

Chapter 3
"Being Born in the U.S. to White Parents is Almost Boring": Whiteness as a Meaningless Identity

I became interested in our Scottish heritage and culture only in later life; and I believe that this is true with many people. I suppose advancing age makes us more conscious of those who have gone before, the void they leave, and all that we are losing of their collective memory and experience . . . it is sad that we don't seem to get very interested in our ancestry until those who can tell us about it are already gone. . . . Moreover, I guess that the changes in American society over my lifetime may have provided some impetus toward the past and my "identity."

I am sure that in Ireland, Scotland, Spain, France, Germany, and so forth the youth are taught in school what it means to be Irish or Scottish or whatever. The particularities of their cultures are seen, with regional variations, throughout their countries and are bound up with their national histories. But America is the great melting pot. When I was young, ethnic distinctions were ignored or minimized in the schools' teaching and programs. History and culture began with the Mayflower and were "American," not an amalgam of older traditions. It is not that the system was trying to deceive, or to pursue some sinister agenda; the country was, relatively speaking, young and sensitive about its lack of home-grown traditions and about the condescension it got from older nations. Despite the lingering white ethnic consciousness of the big centers of immigration like New York, where being Irish-American or Italian-American or Polish-American may even today serve to pigeonhole one, my experience in a mid-size-metropolitan South was that ethnicity among whites was nonexistent, or at least unrecognized. Sure, there were Polack jokes occasionally heard, but we really didn't know why they should be funny. They were funny only in their absurdity, not in their ethnicity.

Today, minorities such as African-Americans and Hispanics have programs in school to teach them what is distinctive and worthwhile in their heritage, and the Jewish heritage is taught in religious venues. The white European "Christian" majority, on the other hand, adheres for the most part to the melting-pot philosophy and sublimates the subgroups' cultural differences to the concept of the whole. There is strength here, of course— political and economic (though eroding)—and much more harmony than is evident between Scots and English, or Poles and Russians, for example, in their native lands. But what have we lost? We grow up knowing nothing about where we came from and lose the richness of our (white) diversity while trumpeting the virtues of a white/nonwhite diversity. (Digression— The challenge for your generation: achieving the benefits of diversity while subduing divisiveness.)

My father, Roy McKinney, Jr., April 1999

As you can tell, I am not big on ethnic identity or heritage. I would have to say that my own ethnicity is not very important in my opinion. . . . I believe this is true for most white people living in the United States. White people of the United States are very multicultural and most cannot identify with just one ethnicity. I, for instance, am Irish, English, Scottish, Italian, and German. . . . there are so many ethnic heritages to learn. I tend not to think about my own race or ethnicity. I believe I am a person from the United States living in [this state], in [this city].

Josh, a respondent

Recently, a mailed solicitation suggested that I "celebrate [my] Irish heritage" while "enjoy[ing] the convenience and financial freedom" of a particular credit card. Pictured in the full-color insert were three credit cards I could select, each with Celtic symbols, Irish flags, or Irish castle ruins, presumably so that with each purchase, I can identify with my "Irish roots." Several years back, my choices were more varied—I received a Visa application purporting to be "The Card That Celebrates Your Unique Heritage." It stated: "You take great pride in your ancestry and the distinctive customs and culture that define its unique way of life." I opened the pamphlet fully to reveal the *fourteen* cards from which the company said I could choose, each with an image meant to reflect a "heritage:" China, Cuba, England, France, Germany, India, Ireland, Italy, Japan, Korea, Poland, Scotland, Sweden, and Vietnam. Excepting China, Japan, Vietnam, India, and Cuba, each country is made up of "white" people. Aside from India and Cuba, each country's population is relatively light-skinned, and to many Americans, Asians are a "model minority," or "honorary whites" in the United States. Many Cubans, also, have been accepted into the mainstream, particularly arrivals in the first wave of migration: politically conservative, upper-class, and lighter-skinned. African-American heritage was completely absent, as were Middle Eastern and non-Cuban Latino national identities. As a white person, I was offered a neatly packaged opportunity to "feel ethnic"— but only certain types of ethnicity.

As my father's and Josh's comments demonstrate, many whites today feel a lack of connection to their ethnic pasts. Consumer culture exploits the notion that whites long to identify beyond racial terms, as more than "just white." If I wanted to advertise my heritage on credit cards, or in other symbolism, because I am white, I can choose to adopt any of several ethnic backgrounds, more than one or none at all. This may vary throughout life—as a teen, I found an "Irish" heritage appealing; no doubt because I liked musicians Enya and U2, but as an adult, perhaps because my father traced our Scottish heritage, I have identified primarily with a Scottish ethnicity, if at all.

Marilyn Halter, in *Shopping for Identity,* says the "ethnic revival" of the 1970s provided marketers with a new "hook" for increasing consumerism. This movement initially began as whites' response to the ethnic pride movements of minority groups in the 1960s. Whites felt a need to express their own ethnic pride and to defend their ethnic neighborhoods. That this revival had permeated the culture of the United States is evidenced in the Ethnic Heritage Act of 1974, a bill intended to support funding for ethnicity programs. Corporations began to respond to the cultural ethos, as they must do to remain solvent. Rather than mass-marketing their products, companies began to use segmentation, to target specific ethnic populations.[1] This strategy continues to be successful in the U.S. mainstream because of a positive regard for ethnic identity.

Early immigrants found it necessary to assimilate quickly, yielding ethnic traditions, accents, and distinctive traits to "become American."[2] For these early immigrants, "becoming American" was "becoming white." As George Lipsitz asserts, "[f]rom the start, European settlers in North America established structures encouraging a possessive investment in whiteness."[3] Citizenship was limited to "whites," and slavery was relegated to Africans. Land was taken from Native Americans, who did not have the rights that were granted to whites. Later, laws were passed to restrict immigration and naturalization of Asians. Whiteness in this racialized system has brought social and concrete material, economic benefits from the beginnings of our society.[4]

When groups first arrived and were not yet considered "white," there was every reason to begin to relinquish ethnic traditions, if necessary to take on a racialized identity.

Yet, as Halter points out,

Third- and fourth-generation upwardly mobile ethnics are now secure enough to proclaim their distinctiveness without risk of it becoming a hindrance to achieving middle-class respectability. In fact, it can be a plus in the workplace as a way of not only establishing connections among coethnics but also of relating to those of cultural backgrounds different from one's own.[5]

Halter's study suggests that for most Americans, ethnicity remains important, but in a largely symbolic way, as Richard Alba predicted, and that "Ethnicity is increasingly manifest through self-conscious consumption of goods and services and, at the same time, these commodities assist in negotiating and enforcing identity differences."[6] Some ethnicities are probably more accessible simply because they are more widely marketed and shared. For example, respondent Lacey wrote:

[O]ddly, we really don't have many Irish 'traditions.' On St. Patrick's Day my mother always dressed the family in green, had us wear pins that read, 'Kiss me, I'm Irish,' and made us eat corn beef hash. However during the rest of the year, our Irish heritage was never really recognized. It seems as if my family's Irish heritage is more of a symbolic ethnicity; it has faded with marital assimilation and is only acknowledged once a year. Moreover, I wonder if we would even celebrate St. Patrick's Day if the American society didn't advertise it so much within industries and the media. I think that my parent's two heritages have melted together so much that certain aspects of ethnic traditions have disappeared, leaving a more Americanized family.[7]

Lacey's family, as she reveals elsewhere in her autobiography, celebrates their Italian ethnicity more routinely. She recognizes that they perhaps would not celebrate their Irish heritage at all, were it not for media attention and the marketing of St. Patrick's Day merchandise. Further, she feels that both of her ethnic backgrounds have faded into more of a national identity.

Although Halter notes that ethnicity is important in the United States generally and that it is to some degree commodified for all groups, we should distinguish between voluntary ethnic identity for whites and the involuntary ethnicity of nonwhites. This is crucial, because it means that ethnicity is important for the two groups for very different reasons. In the early 1990s, Mary Waters noted the voluntary character of contemporary white ethnicity. Unlike people of color, whites can choose among multiple ethnic backgrounds or opt to be simply "American" or "white."[8] People of color are deemed "ethnic" whether or not they choose to be, and their ethnicity is neither symbolic nor without cost. This "ethnic option" is a privilege of whiteness and has been treated as such in the research literature. Whites can choose whether or not to be "ethnic," and it is important to them only to the extent they *wish* for it to be. Cultural visibility or invisibility differs according to a group's institutional power.[9]

Very little research has explored young whites' *perceptions* of their ethnic identity. Charles Gallagher, using data based on interviews with white students, found that paradoxically, while most of them see themselves as "colorblind," they also see their whiteness as a liability.[10] Believing themselves to live in a meritocracy, these white young people view affirmative action as "reverse discrimination" and hold African American entertainers and sports figures up as evidence of "equal opportunity." Additionally, most of his white students, feeling no sense of ethnicity, have undergone a process of "racialization," in which a racial identity takes precedence over an ethnic identification.[11] Many of these same themes arise in the autobiographies of the young whites in my research.

Another study of two high schools, one predominantly white and the other mixed, found that young whites perceive themselves as "cultureless" and construct this identity through two processes: normalization and rationalization.[12] In normalization, used in the predominantly white setting, whiteness is the "norm," the standard against which other groups should be judged. Rationalization is used where whites are the minority, and nonwhite groups are characterized as unsophisticated, and whites as advanced. This conception of whiteness is created by invoking the Western hegemonic ideal of superior, white, rational, future-oriented societies, with ethnic "Others" denigrated as arcane, irrational, and clinging to the past in traditions and cultural practices.[13] In this study, the researcher, Pamela Perry, disputes the lack of a "white American culture," which she argues dominates not only the area in which she conducted her research but most of the United States. She describes this culture, which most whites fail to see:

> By 'white American culture,' I refer to two features of American culture, broadly. First, . . . several of its core characteristics are of European origin. These include, as I have already suggested, the values and practices derived from the European Enlightenment, Anglican Protestantism, and Western colonialism, such as rationalism, individualism, personal responsibility, a strong worth ethnic [*sic*], self-effacement, and mastery over nature. I include, also, carryover or "melted" material cultures of Western, Eastern and Southern European peoples, such as hamburgers, spaghetti, cupcakes, parades, and line dancing. Second, by virtue of being numerically and politically dominant, whites tend to share certain dispositions, world views, and identities constituted by that, especially in predominantly white communities. Currently, a race-neutral or 'colorblind' worldview and sense of oneself as normal are examples of that.[14]

Perry goes on to describe features of white culture in the settings she studied. Most features probably would not be recognized as "white culture" by whites, but thought of as just "normal"; indeed, they have been described thus in these data. Most often, it is people of color who describe "white culture" as a "culture," because they have the outsider's perspective to be able to see that it exists.[15]

As groups immigrated, they had to assimilate to European culture to escape prejudice and discrimination, find work, and ultimately "become" white.[16] It surprises many students when told, for example, that the second wave of Irish and Italian immigrants, ancestors to many of them, were actually considered a different *race*, not just a different ethnic group, when they first arrived in the United States, based on differences from the dominant population, especially their Catholicism. Fiona, for instance, learned this from family stories:

> I'm not really troubled by my ethnicity in anyway, because it doesn't cause me to face any sort of discrimination. It was much different 100 years ago. My dad tells me stories about the Irish immigrants that were settling in America around the turn of the 20th century. Much like other ethnic groups, Italians, Eastern Europeans, the Irish were discriminated against and relegated to the most menial jobs. On the other hand, being Irish is rewarding at certain times of the year, especially during St. Patrick's Day. On this day, everyone wants to be Irish, and those that even have a little bit of Irish running through their blood, take part in the festivities. Every person that is walking down the street is wearing green to show his or her support for St. Patty's Day.[17]

Many white students see the transformation white ethnics underwent not as a reason to question the social construction of race; they use it instead as a means to claim equal oppression with African Americans and other ethnic minority groups, and to question their "lack of progress" in society.[18] Also, because assimilation earned European Americans social progress, many believe that it is still the solution to racial problems:

> In today's society, racial and ethnic problems are slowly disappearing. I do not think that they will ever disappear completely, but as long as people are willing to assimilate, then society will change. Of course change is always occurring, it is just a matter of time before major changes happen. Look back even a hundred years ago and one can see how society has changed.
>
> Deanna

"American" culture[19] *is* a melding of many cultures, but only to the extent that the dominant Anglo majority permits inserting elements of other ethnic cultures while allowing the group to assimilate and progress. The process of "becoming white" has been much easier for some groups. For early European immigrant groups, whose ethnic identifiability was based solely on markers such as language, holidays, and religion, the desire to become American and the necessity of feeding their families made it a given that they would adopt a more privatized or symbolic ethnicity. However, for groups identified by physical markers such as skin color, "becoming white" was not an option. Even if their ethnic traditions and language are privatized, physical appearance marks them as the "Other." Assimilation can only go so far for groups who stand out as physically distinguishable. In the United States, ethnicity and success often become a tradeoff: to become middle- or upper-class, one must be part of a family that long ago lost a close identification with an ethnic heritage. Kendall wrote about this point:

> What is whiteness? I suppose one could associate whiteness with assimilation. . . . . [S]ince assimilation meant acting like the majority (white people), the immigrants were to be as white as possible. . . . My ancestors that came from Italy were probably of those same immigrants that were forced to assimilate; to become white. . . . I suppose that it can be assumed that being white is just like being "lucky". . . . Being white is being part of the majority and being part of the majority is getting all of the breaks. . . .
>
> [M]y ancestors have been in America for so long that many traditions and cultures of my family that came from Ireland have been lost throughout the years. If I were to describe myself, . . . being white would be one of the last things I mention. However, there are a few Irish traditions still celebrated in my family that are related, mostly, to my religion which include celebrating Christmas strongly like many others, but also celebrating St. Patrick's Day. . . .
>
> I would say that being white is not as important to me as being black is to African Americans or being Latino is to Latinos. . . . [E]thnicity is more real to these minorities and other minorities because their ancestors held on to their traditions much stronger than many Europeans, like my ancestors, that felt it was [more] important to assimilate than to keep their ethnicity. . . . [Their assimilation] has made life easier for all of my ancestors' descendants.

Some suggest that a "cost" of racism is that because of it, many whites do not know about their ethnic heritage.[20] Conversely, if one retains a close connection to an ethnic heritage, that person may not assimilate fully into the mainstream and has a difficult time reaching success. Whether or not this lack of an ethnic heritage is a "cost" that is significant when placed against those faced by members of other ethnic groups; it is recognized by young whites, as found in Perry's study. Whiteness, for her respondents, meant "not having to say you're ethnic." In this study, however, although whiteness was sometimes defined through normalization and rationalization, often it was defined through comparison, resulting in a sort of cultural envy. Young whites defined the "culturelessness" of whiteness through *comparison* to the other culture, incorporating a sense of *envy* or *desire* for ethnic identity. Instead of "whiteness [meaning] never *having* to say you're ethnic," as with Perry's respondents,[21] whiteness for many of my respondents meant never *getting* to say you're ethnic. Whiteness provides no "culture" to draw on in identity formation, whereas respondents describe others as possessing an abundance of cultural resources merely by having been born a person of color. Carol writes about her sense of whiteness:

> Being white to me is to be someone who is without a working knowledge of their ancestry and cultural traditions. I am a member of the fifth generation of my family who has come to the United States and my parents as well as their parents were fully assimilated and consider themselves to be only American. When I ask my parents about my ethnicity they can only say that we are part English, Dutch and German but they do not know any more than just that. So since I know very little about my ethnic background I am left with only my racial identity, which is white.
>
> I guess being white also means that I have a hard time trying to identify with others who hold strong to their ethnic backgrounds since I have no recollection of my own culture and traditions. . . . As I look at other cultures celebrating their different traditions, I almost feel that I have missed out on something. I don't even know what my cultural traditions are. . . . Other cultures seem to me to be wise in teaching their children about their culture in order to keep their culture alive. . . . As Europeans we gave up all our traditions and became [the] "norm" and the American backdrop. Since many European Americans feel that they are normal, they think that anyone who is not the same as them are abnormal.

Carol's statement is exemplary of the ideas expressed in many of the autobiographies. Because she is many generations removed from the immigrant experience, she has lost touch with a "usable" ethnic heritage. Thus, as Charles Gallagher and others have found in studies of young whites, her identity has become racialized.[22] When she is asked to account for whiteness, Carol constructs her white identity in opposition to that of others. Finally, instead of an ethnic or racial identity, like other respondents, Carol may think of herself more as simply "American."

Given respondents' perception of cultural emptiness, the autobiographies include accounts of constructing white identity in four ways: (1) through usable (symbolic) ethnicity; (2) through tourist ethnicity; (3) through mirrored whiteness; and (4) through supplanted whiteness. In this struggle to fill the emptiness of whiteness, these autobiographies show the identity work of being white.

Usable Ethnicity

Sometimes a student describes ethnicity as having little personal significance but then discusses its use for various practical, seemingly trivial, purposes. This "usable" sense of ethnicity is not a stable feature of either everyday encounters or major life decisions; but it is utilized sparingly in identity work. Usable ethnicity most closely resembles what Alba and Gans termed "symbolic ethnicity,"[23] and Alba the "privatization" of ethnicity.[24] According to these theorists, the "ethnic revival" requires no commitment to ethnicity in concrete decision making about institutional involvement, living in ethnic enclaves, or marrying within one's own ethnicity.[25] Instead, for most white Americans, any lingering ethnicity involves a vague sense of "feeling" ethnic, and is displayed infrequently on recognized ethnic occasions or holidays. One of my respondents, Rick, writes of such ethnic symbolism in his family:

> A few years back . . . my mother went on a genealogical spree. She contacted every known relative. . . . I found out that I have a third cousin who currently pitches for the New York Yankees. We found out that my grandfather's grandfather died as a prisoner of war at the Andersonville Prison in Georgia during the Civil War. . . . One of my great-great aunts had records of the family clear back until the late 1600's. . . . Ivan Clavenhach emigrated from Germany in the early to middle 1700's, and descendents eventually took the name Cleavenhook. . . . This aunt also had a picture of the family coat-of-arms and a description of the colors. . . . Colors and emblems . . . represent the characteristics of the original bearer and were granted only if he be worthy of their symbolisms. . . . [*Rick describes the colors and emblems on the family crest at length*]. . . . She also found that one of our ancestors married a Native American. But that was a lot of generations before mine. My mother taught my brother and I a lot of our heritage during this time because she wanted us to know where we came from and what our family was about.

Rick's sense of ethnicity centers on family, ancestry, and, quite literally, symbols. Respondents usually wrote about European ethnicity in terms of this "usable," but fairly transient, form, which they used in various ways to construct a sense of identity. In the following pages, I offer a typology of usable ethnicity.

Inborn Traits

Some writers used their sense of European ethnicity primarily to account for what they believe are inborn traits. Some of these are physical traits, while others are characteristics of temperament, talents, or even food preferences. Rachel uses her Scandinavian heritage for an innovative purpose:

> Although I have a wide range of ethnic backgrounds, the one I identify most with is Scandinavian. . . . [T]hinking about myself as Scandinavian often helps my self-esteem. I often fall into the desire to want what the society sees as attractive, which are women who are quite thin. Yet, knowing my ethnicity, I understand that my body frame and structure, as a Scandinavian is built much more strong than other ethnicity's. It's physically impossible for me to be what society defines as "attractive."

> My sister has always been embarrassed by her "thunder-thighs," as most
> Scandinavians are accustomed to having, but I take pride in mine. My
> thighs are the one aspect of me that I really feel exemplifies my ethnicity.

Rachel proceeds to write that her family "never needed to discuss topics [such]
as race or ethnicity." Instead they have a "good time together"—presumably
discussing race and ethnicity would inhibit having a good time. She has, however, found a purpose for her distant Scandinavian heritage. Using it, she insu-
lates herself from the personal damage caused by failure to meet this culture's
physical ideal for women. My analysis shows that young women in particular
are likely to link physical characteristics to an ethnic heritage. Some, like
Rachel, apparently do so to combat negative self-conceptions (for example,
linking a large nose to Italian ethnicity), while others may simply enjoy possessing features or traits they believe signal group membership. For example,
many female respondents mention dark hair and skin as their sole connection
to a distant Italian heritage. For others, ethnicity explains their physical
appearance as well as some food preferences. Marilyn discusses her German
and Italian ethnicity:

> My mother is half Italian. . . . My Father is pretty much split half German
> and half Italian. This has a stereotype back home as being mean, a good
> cook and a wide back end. My grandmother. . . . is a very Italian individ-
> ual who fits the description of a typical Italian woman. She . . . believes
> that we should try to preserve our ethnic heritage. . . . If I had to pick 60
> words to explain myself the word white would not even be on the list.
> I have always seen myself as being Italian or German but never white.
> I don't think that white is a descriptive word to explain one's self. I think
> that describing my self as white is too broad it doesn't tell you anything.
> I believe that my ethnicity is a better way to describe myself. I think that
> it gives people a better understanding of some of your likes and dislikes.
> For instance I fit the Italian stereotype of liking pasta and if I told some-
> one that I was Italian when I first met them over the phone or by letter,
> I think that they can get a better description of what I look like and what
> kind of foods I enjoy. I believe that every one stereotypes people in one-
> way or another, however if I am going to be stereotyped then at least
> I am in a smaller group with my ethnicity.

Here, ethnicity is linked with many different inborn characteristics, such as
culinary talents, a "mean" personality, food preferences, and certain physical
characteristics. This sense of being Italian might be termed "symbolic," but it
is meaningful enough for Marilyn to construct her identity using ethnicity
rather than race. In other words, even a seemingly superficial ethnicity gives
her a resource on which to ground her identity, while whiteness is "too broad
[to] tell you anything." Several other students, like Fiona, similarly ground
their identity in Irish ethnicity:

I don't really consider myself a significant part of any ethnic group, but if I had to pick one, I suppose that it would be Irish. There are several reasons for this. The first one is . . . I guess that it makes me feel better to [be] more Irish rather than saying I'm mixed. I suppose with a name like Fiona Erin O'Brien, you might say it has a bit of an Irish ring to it . . . Another reason is that ever since I was a little girl, people have told me that I look Irish. The reason for this is because I have bright, blue eyes, light hair, light skin, and a ton of freckles. It's hard to describe what it means to me to be Irish. I guess that it means that a person has the same physical characteristics as me, likes to eat corned beef and cabbage, and loves St. Patrick's Day. I like to call myself Irish. When I tell people that I'm Irish, I think that it makes good conversation. . . . Every time I have to tell someone about myself or my family and our heritage, it is hard to leave out the Irish aspect. It is equally as hard to leave out the English part, but to me, Irish is more interesting.

Fiona relies on physical characteristics, name, and food preferences to explain her Irish identity. These traits seem to have served as a "self-fulfilling prophecy," a sort of catalyst that invoked her ethnic option, after which she chose an Irish heritage over other possibilities. Still she could have chosen an English identification—being Irish is just "more interesting," or as she later says, makes her feel "more important." She continues:

It is much easier for me to identify myself on ethnic terms instead of racial terms. This is because I don't have any characteristics that make it possible for me to identify with any other racial group but white American. The classification of "White American" is such a broad term that it makes me feel more important to identify with the ethnic group that it most dominant in my heritage.

Fiona knows enough about her "interesting" Irish heritage to use it, and chooses to do so instead of identifying as white; which seems to lack substance. She continues to discuss the implications of "Irishness:" "I don't think that I have missed any opportunities or been discriminated against because I'm Irish. . . . I don't really consider my heritage when I make important decisions, such as where to attend school or who I'll vote for in the next election." Fiona mentioned in her writing that Irish people face stereotyping related to alcohol consumption, but she understands they face little discrimination. As Waters, Alba, and Gans suggest, being Irish will not likely influence any major life decisions.[26] She can choose when to consider it and when to ignore it altogether.

Excusing Deviant Behavior

Some respondents reported using their heritage, usually Irish or Scottish/Irish or German, as a way to account for "leisure activities." Seth writes: "I am proud to be Scottish but it is more for fun and heritage than any serious set of beliefs." Many young men, especially, who claim Irishness as part of their ethnic heritage use it to explain their ability to drink large amounts of alcohol. For example, Allan explains:

> My ethnic background consists of French, German, Irish, and Lithuanian. I am especially proud of being German and Irish. I always have to cele-brate St. Patrick's Day. My brother and I get together with our friends and drink lots of green beer. All day long I talk with an Irish accent and usually piss everyone off after about the first hour. But I don't care because if my ancestors had stayed over there, I would be talking that way anyhow. Being German I also feel obligated that I have to drink beer, so I do. The only difference is that in Germany they like to drink it warm and I like mine ice cold. That is about all that I do to celebrate my ethnic heritage. However, when it comes to religion, my family and I cel-ebrate all of the Catholic holidays.[27]

Usable ethnicity can be invoked selectively to explain behaviors that respondents would probably engage in anyway. For several young men, eth-nicity is an excuse to "cut loose." Using Irish and German ethnicity as explanation, one can drink heavily, attribute it to one's ethnic "genes." Sev-eral other male respondents, like Allan, make this attribution. The implica-tion of this use of ethnicity is that "ethnic" people are more likely to engage in morally ambiguous behavior than "nonethnic" whites. They may choose these practices and blame the behavior on the parts of themselves that are still "ethnic." In this sense, white ethnicity is used as an "excuse" for deviant behavior.[28]

Family Names

Others know little about their ethnicity, but combine ethnicity with ancestry, frequently symbolized in their family name, to form a usable heritage. Michael's story characterizes this type of ethnic identity:

> My great grandfather came from Rome and my great grandmother came from Monesson. The Supericini name came from Italy. . . . I think it is neat that I am the last person right now to carry the Supericini name. I will probably use the middle name . . . for my children. I think it is important to name my children after Christians. . . . The funny thing about the name Supericini is automatically people assume I am Italian, but by the looks of me I am far from it. I have red hair, and white skin with freckles and very light complexion. . . . My dad on the other hand is very dark skinned and looks like an Italian man. During my younger years in travel baseball no one could ever pronounce my last name so they always made up a name which was "Michael the Superman." I always

found this to be very funny and enjoyed hearing my name called. Every-one always joked with my baseball team because ten out of our sixteen players were Italian and the announcers had a great amount of trouble pronouncing our names.[29]

Michael does not look Italian, but he is marked as ethnic by his obviously Italian name, so difficult to pronounce that teammates give him a nickname. For immigrants and others, usually nonwhites, who are treated as outsiders, having a name difficult to pronounce can reinforce difference and require them to provide an account for themselves.[30] European ethnics, no longer hav-ing to worry that their names can exclude them from white privilege, can enjoy the uniqueness of an "ethnic" name and laugh when others stumble over the pronunciation, rather than bracing themselves to see whether the other's discomfort will be turned against them.

Roger discussed his name with a teacher, but with a different conclusion:

What is in a name? Well, if you had my last name, confusion. I remem-ber asking my father, 'Dad what are we? I mean originally.' He replied to me that we were Scotch-Irish. I asked him how does he know that? He replied that's what his father told him that we were. I became curious however. Druschson is such a funny spelled name, how could it possibly be Scotch-Irish? I have always been interested in Celtic culture and could not see how my name sprang from there. So I did research on the name. I asked my teachers in high school where my name came from. The teachers I asked all told me the exact same thing. "Oh, Druschson that sounds like a German name." So instead of questioning my teachers, I questioned my father and then began to equate myself with the German people. I however, always kept what my father said in my mind. Besides, listen to how similar my last name sounds to the German name Drochssin, or Drauchssen. I thought that my ancestors were probably illiterate and through years of American assimilation corrupted the spelling and that is why my name was spelled that way. I believed that I had finally found where my ancestors were from. Then I went off to college and two years later took the German language. One day in my class the professor asked if anybody had a last name that was German. I raised my hand and said that I did. Then she looked at me and stated that my last name sounded and looked Celtic in nature to her. From that point on I was determined to find out where my last name came from. I went unto the Internet and looked it up. As it turns out, my father was right. Our last name is Celtic in origin. The first part of the name "Drusch" is a Scottish word that means, "resident of the hillside or valley." The last part of the name "son" denotes someone who came from the lowlands of Scotland, or who has relatives in Ireland. "Son" was a title left on the Celtic peo-ple, by the Viking culture. Either way I am Scotch-Irish as my father tried to tell me.[31]

There is, of course, more to the story of Roger's name than discovery of a usable ethnicity—there is his father's triumph over others who said his name was German. As revealed elsewhere in Roger's autobiography, his father was an orphan, in foster care, and of lower social status. He was less educated than Roger's teachers, who thought that his name was German. Roger and his father, and thus his family, are vindicated when he finds that his father is correct and the family is of Scotch-Irish ethnicity. Family and heritage are solidified for Roger in his name. Also significant is the amount of time and energy Roger expended researching his heritage. Ethnicity is an important source of identity for some white Americans.

Finally, the issue of family name is also poignant for Ted, a 44 year-old student who begins his paper this way:

> I will begin this paper with a diverse group of words that I have been required to place at the very beginning of almost every paper I've written since kindergarten class, my name . . . Ted. E. Presbylinski. I have always experienced anxious moments on the first day of school when everyone's name was called out, because I knew that mine would be the one that the teacher could not pronounce. Over the years I developed pride in that name that seemed so foreign to everyone, that pride developed as a result of the many wonderful and strong characters in the family stories I heard both my parents tell at various times in my childhood. . . . So in my case it wasn't a racial experience that I would refer to, after all I was the same "normal" color as 99.9% of the population. It was that feeling of being 'different' due to what the kids called a 'funny last name.' That last name came from a man who died when I was an infant, a Polish immigrant who came over on a ship with his parents to Ellis Island at the beginning of the century.

Ted's ethnicity is crystallized in his unusual name, which has at times caused him to stand out as "different." He goes on to discuss how ethnicity caused his family to face discrimination. As a whole, family names may become an inescapable connection with ethnicity.

Understanding Others' Ethnicity

For some respondents who discuss their ethnic past, part of the story they tell is one of discrimination and hardship experienced by their ancestors. These stories are more distant but still have resonance in their lives. For example, Riley writes:

> When [my family] got to the U.S. they were the typical Irish, working for almost nothing but surviving on what they got, working mostly as coal miners, and police. So, I feel that my ancestors were repressed almost as much, just because of their ethnicity. As time went on though the Irish became part of the 'white' population and not described by where they came from. . . .

To me I adhere, and will teach my children that their race and ethnicity is that of an American. A single grouping of people that came together, no matter how their ancestors got here. This country was founded on the premise of equality for all citizens, and although we disagree now the future generations will be the ones to bear the weight of fixing it. . . .

. . . I believe that no one should forget where they came from, but don't cling to it as a crutch when life does not go the way they think it should. Nor should any one race or ethnicity have precedence over another; this causes the inequality that we should all be fighting against, not creating.

The ideas expressed in this statement are reflected in many of the autobiographies. White ethnics are first established as people that have faced hardships and overcome them to succeed and assimilate as "Americans." With this story as the pattern, a colorblind standard is then suggested—that today any immigrant should be able to achieve a smooth transition into U.S. society through similar hard work.

In a recent study, Charles Gallagher showed how whites may play the "white ethnic card," constructing stories of ethnocentrism against whites to suggest that whites have suffered the same type of discrimination as have people of color.[32] Further, this "white ethnic card" is used to allow whites a foundation for race-based grievances—such as those that will be discussed in the next chapter—which allow them to maintain white privilege by denying that it still exists.[33] The "white ethnic card" is yet another way to assert the colorblind ideology that is currently common among whites.

Although many respondents used the "white ethnic card" to claim equal oppression with people of color, some others instead told stories of white ethnicity as a way of establishing a degree of empathy for the experience of people of color. As will be discussed later, some researchers assert that any empathy whites have for racism experienced by others is false empathy. However, some respondents note that although they can never understand the discrimination people of color face, knowing about their own ethnicity helps them be more accepting of the idea of difference and aware that ethnic discrimination has a history in the U.S. For example, Jill writes about her Jewish heritage:

My first experience of recognizing racial and ethnic differences was with my parents. My dad, who is Jewish, married my mom, who is Christian. . . . My dad's mother had a problem with my mom because she was not Jewish and she was not raising her grandchildren Jewish. This experienced has helped me become more aware of people's differences and to respect them. Having grown up on learning both religions has helped me become more open minded, open to new ideas and wanting to learn about my ethnicity and others. Since I learned to accept differences, I decided to take a friend of another race to a dance. My mom and dad were fine with the idea. . . .

> Being 'half' Jewish will not affect my future in any way and is not an important key factor in my life. It is not a recognizable difference. The only way it can be recognized is by my last name, which I will change when I marry anyways. . . . I have never been subject to discrimination. . . . [but] It gave me a chance to be more open minded and accepting of people's differences.

Because Jill's ethno-religious heritage does not create, for her, a visible difference from others, it has not brought her significant personal discrimination that she has noted. She does not use her white ethnicity to claim equal oppression with people of color. Rather she states that "being ethnic" allows her to be more comfortable with ethnic differences and more accepting of people of diverse groups. A few other respondents do have a more salient ethnic identity, more firmly grounded in everyday practices and decision making. These respondents note ethnic traditions celebrated by their families. Many are oriented toward food and holidays. Some are connected to their religious practices. Respondents with more of a salient ethnic identity use it either to claim equal victimization with people of color, or, in other instances, to develop a sense of empathy for them.

Also in contrast to the desire expressed for ethnicity pervading many autobiographies, a few are skeptical of the longing for ethnic identity. In the following passage, Ned questions what ethnic knowledge is "good for:"

> Up until I was about sixteen years old the only thing I really knew about "who" my family is was that I am part German because of my last name which is German, and Scottish because my mom said something about it one time. Around the time I was sixteen or so something sparked a little fire into my family as to finding out our lineage. My . . . dad's mother was given a Bible by someone in our family. . . . My dad began trying to recompose the family tree for personal reasons as well as just wanting to know "who" we are. Around about the same time all this was going on my Grandma and Grandaddy, who are my mother's parents, had come up with a family tree for their side of the family. This record revealed that my mom's side of the family are direct descendants of Robert Bruce who was crowned as the first kin[g] of Scotland in 1314. (Note: Robert Bruce was crowned as the king of Scotland in the end of the movie "Braveheart"). I'm sure my dad's interest in the Bible his mom had received had something to do with all of this on my mom's side of the family too. Anyway, my Grandaddy's sister spent several years and a lot of money to come up with all of this information. She had been through tons of family Bibles, state birth records, and other things. So for about two months there was all this hype about where we came from and then it all went away. Now I know that I'm of Scottish and German descent, but that does not help me a bit. First of all because no one ever asks what or who or where I am from ethnically, and second of all because it still does not help me explain what it is to be white.

Ned questions the practical purposes of European ethnicity, once it has been discovered. He also seems to suggest that *whiteness* is more in need of explanation in the United States today than is European ethnicity. Perhaps he understands that it is whiteness that is more operative in his everyday life. His is a rare perspective in the autobiographies, however. Most respondents that discuss ethnicity do so with a distinct desire to include more ethnic heritage in their lives.

Tourist Ethnicity

Some respondents create a sense of identity through "tourist ethnicity," by appropriating elements of other cultures, or by finding ethnic Others to teach them about "culture." Cultural critic bell hooks discusses "cultural tourism," describing it as the tendency of some whites, lacking a sense of their own culture, to appropriate the Others' cultures.[34] People of color have long recognized the contradiction of their inspiring both white hostility and fascination. In his 1927 essay, "The Caucasian Storms Harlem," Rudolph Fisher, a scientist and writer of the Harlem Renaissance, considered "this sudden, contagious interest in everything Negro" then prevalent.[35] Similarly, Langston Hughes, in his 1934 short story "Slaves on the Block," depicted "people who went in for Negroes."[36] In the 1990s, hooks and Karla Holloway pick up this analysis of white appropriation of other cultures. In her 1995 work, *Codes of Conduct*, cultural critic Holloway argues,

> An 'exchange' market in this era of superficially exchanged identities means white youth can harness the veneer of a popular black imagery . . . and assume a vicarious cultural difference without ever having to face the consequences and the real-life dangers of being culturally different from the endorsed (i.e. economically empowered) white identity.[37]

David Roediger analyzed the combination of fear and fascination in 1800s blackface minstrelsy and the role it played in the social construction of whiteness. Perhaps because of their long history in the United States and some of the particulars of their relationship with whites, African Americans frequently are the focus of whites' cultural appropriation.[38]

Cultural appropriation, more benignly called "cultural crossover," seems to have gained momentum recently, particularly with young whites' consumption, and more rarely, performance of the music and "street culture" of African Americans. A writer in the pop culture *Spin* magazine observes that "millions of white kids are defining themselves through nonwhite culture."[39] Some see this crossover as positive or at least harmless.[40] Others worry that cultural appropriation has more negative consequences in allowing whites a sense of "knowing" Others' cultures without necessarily knowing any *people* from those cultures or understanding their circumstances. Echoing Holloway, Charles Aaron recognizes that

[t]here are real social problems that hip-hop will never touch. In 1996, the typical black household had a net worth of $4,500, one-tenth that of the average white household; poverty among black children is at 40 percent; young black males are murdered at a still startling rate—111 per 100,000, according to 1995 figures. All of which puts impassioned white hip-hop-heads in an odd position.[41]

By borrowing the experiences of people of color embedded in their art, young whites can have a sense of culture without questioning their whiteness. Whites' using the cultures of people of color is not necessarily indicative of personal antiracism or even nonracism. When that use accompanies disregard of the structural conditions of race that privilege whiteness and disadvantage people of color, cultural borrowing may convince whites further that the problems of inequality are all but solved.

In class discussions, some argue that formerly, musical genres "belonged" to one group, and when whites delved into, for example, hip-hop music, "cultural tourism" might have described that behavior. Today, they contend, all music belongs equally to all groups, so it is no longer "appropriation" when whites enjoy rap or hip-hop yet have no African-American friends. Students regularly cite white rap stars like Eminem as evidence that rap now truly is everyone's music, equally. Eminem's experience does seem to differ from that of many white rap artists—he grew up among people of color, his career has been fostered by famous black artists, whom he credits, and he is well respected by African-American musicians and critics. Still, Eminem stands out as a white artist *because* he differs from other white artists—he is an exception to the rule in the credibility he has gained and in his understanding of black culture.[42] Students also argue that music now "belongs to everyone," using cultural borrowing itself as evidence; they state that "even farm kids who have never met a black person listen to rap" in order to prove that music that began as an African-American art form now belongs equally to rural white kids. Whatever their argument, when told they might be engaging in cultural tourism, most young whites disagree vehemently. Very few address this in their autobiographies, but it frequently becomes a topic of discussion in class. Bridget is one exception; and her argument is similar to that frequently heard in the classroom:

Why do you think that the "white" teenagers of America are so "into" the African American "hip-hop" culture of today more than any other type of music? Could it be because they are assimilating to the "black" culture? I think it is a combination of both assimilation of the host group to the minority group and the fact that a lot of the music is just down right good music. Do we really need an explanation for this? Can we not just say that we enjoy aspects of a different "race" without having to explain ourselves?

Bridget reasons that young whites "enjoy" African-American culture in part because of *white* assimilation to black culture. Many respondents place their use of another culture in the context of shifting demographics and growing diversity: new "culture" is out there to sample and enjoy, "without having to explain ourselves."

Bridget's explanation, and others', of the consumption of hip-hop by white youth rewrites the racial hierarchy so that all groups have equal cultural and economic power. From the colorblind perspective of many young whites, cultural exchange is on an equal footing; and group power is not a factor—thus two-way assimilation, or even majority assimilation to minority culture, is realistic. However, most whites have hardly "assimilated" to black culture; in fact, they maintain and carefully guard the parts of white culture that work to their benefit, economically, politically, and socially, and use bits and pieces of the experiences of people of color to add cultural flavor to their lives. A majority group's voluntary borrowing of pieces of a minority culture is not equivalent to the pervasive, usually involuntary, assimilation minority groups must do to survive in a hegemonic host culture.

While young whites may resent people of color for "having" culture, they are able to enjoy their cultural work, whether this be musical, athletic, theatrical, or just their everyday "lifestyle." Seth mentions: "I can always remember my father telling me how much he loved the mentality of inner city blacks (the way they talked, acted, etc). My dad and I would always go and play basketball with people and the majority of the people we played with were black, I always enjoyed those times." Seth and his father enjoy their games not only for the athletic competition, but also because they can partake of what they see as a distinct, essentialized "mentality," attractive because it differs from theirs. In the following passage, Rachel's reference to people of color as "landmarks" in her life is suggestive of the cultural tourism that bell hooks describes:

> I can recall three "landmark" incidents or relationships that helped progress my racial and ethnic awareness. . . . My first "landmark" was when I was young and in middle school, my best friend was from Puerto Rico. . . . My second "landmark" was when I was in high school and I had a part time job at a local McDonald's. . . . My fondest memories of my time at McDonald's were of the experiences and conversations I had with many of the African American girls. They loved to talk and were also very quick to defend themselves or fight for what they felt was right. I think that aggressiveness is part of their race because of the trials and tribulations African Americans have had to go through in the past. I give them credit for talking to me and being honest about their race and beliefs. They used to dance and sing to some of the music at work and I would "get into it" every now and then, which they just loved. I almost felt that I was trying to be like them and putting off a false impression of myself. . . . Right now, in college, my closest tie to someone of a different

race or ethnicity and my third "landmark," is a real good friend of mine, whose name is Raquel. She is from Puerto Rico and loves to talk about her racial and ethnic background. I learn something new from her everyday. . . . She is actually going to live with me in the fall and I have no apprehensions over that. . . . The cool thing about having relationships with people of different race and ethnicity other than your own is that you can learn so much from them. . . . Although I have had a few special friends of different race and ethnicity, the majority of my friends and of my relationships, have been the same race and ethnicity as mine.

Rachel attempts to learn about other cultures, and apparently believes that people of color have valuable knowledge to share, though perhaps restricted to a narrow set of topics. Openness to learning from other cultures is a commendable feature of many in this generation. However, constructing herself as "learner," and racial others as "teachers," Rachel is a passive recipient of "culture," except when she sings and dances to entertain her coworkers. But her singing and dancing is done in imitation of African Americans, almost reminiscent of a minstrel show. In this autobiography, there is no mention of how Rachel shares her own racial or ethnic identity with her black coworkers. An underlying assumption in cultural tourism is that whiteness is self-evidently normative and cannot be shared in the way that "otherness" can. People of color may serve as "landmarks," while primary friendships are with other whites.

Many respondents discuss how upon entering college, they welcome conversations with people of various races and ethnicities, questioning them about their traditions and backgrounds. This interest marks progress from the more disinterested approach of many older white Americans. Yet, sometimes whites approach people of color as a curiosity, which suggests exoticization rather than a genuine attempt at friendship.[43] Educating white people about one's traditions and culture is not the same as sharing experiences and developing a mutually satisfying relationship. Whites' questions to people of color may be asked before a solid friendship is formed. Further, questions sometimes are posed as if the person's ethnic experience is the only point of interest about him or her, and the only ethnicity of interest in the interaction. Hence, the white person becomes the cultural interrogator, and the ethnic Other a person on display, an object of curiosity. Yet from the position of these white students, one can understand how this type of relationship evolves. They are convinced they have nothing of interest to add to a conversation about "culture." The discourses surrounding young whites may encourage this view. Some suggest that a possible pitfall of multicultural education as frequently taught is that it may give young whites the perception that everyone *else* has a "culture" they can study (often for one day or week each year), while whites remain centered as the norm.[44] David remembers learning about Latino culture from John, a friend from Puerto Rico:

John and I hit it off and we became good friends. I can recall thinking that it was cool to have a friend who could speak Spanish. I recall the girls all flocked to him because he was 'different.' On occasion, I would visit John at his home. His family spoke Spanish amongst themselves at times, and I found this quite interesting. I was always welcomed into their home and treated like one of the family. I also found it interesting that they celebrated all of the Puerto Rican and Mexican holidays, and they were proud of their heritage. The exposure to John and his family gave me insight into a different culture. For me, there was no real sense of ethnic or racial pride—I was a white, blue-eyed, blonde-haired male. Being 'white' seemed boring to me. Being white did not seem like a race at all, it seemed more the absence of one. In addition, it appeared to me that the only people that declared pride in being 'white' were racist.

While enjoying learning from his friend, David realizes from observing his peers' reactions that part of John's appeal lay in his "difference." In other words, David is able to see that his friend was treated as exotic. Whether David believes he treated John this way is unclear; but he remarks that by comparing himself to John and his family he began to see whiteness as "boring." David also notes the linkage between claimed racial identity for whites and white supremacy. This data shows that whites searching for an answer to the question "what does it mean to be white?" find little information within their own experiences. Moving beyond personal experience in seeking an answer, most encounter only the lives and words of racists as examples of people who speak spontaneously of whiteness.

Tourist ethnicity may give white people the sense of "culture" they lack, and an identity based not on their own culture but on artifacts collected from the cultures of Others. Indeed, many student autobiographies are stories that move through encounters from one person of color to the next.

Mirrored Whiteness

I am white. Being white means my skin color is white. If you think about it, my skin really isn't white. It is peach colored. I think it is impossible to write about being white without the mention of other groups because there has to be something to compare it to. My skin is not brown or black. I am not Asian. I am not Latino. I am white.

Lona

Since most lack the sense of ethnic identity of past generations, some build whiteness through reference to racial others. Whiteness is a "mirrored" identity, constructed as a reflection of everything it is "not," as described by Ralph Ellison, in his 1970 essay "What America Would be Like Without Blacks:"

> Since the beginning of the nation, white Americans have suffered from a deep inner uncertainty as to who they really are. One of the ways that has been used to simplify the answer has been to seize upon the presence of black Americans and use them as a marker, a symbol of limits, a metaphor for the 'outsider.'[45]

To many respondents, whiteness lacks substantive content easily accessible as cultural resources. In the past, discourses of white supremacy compensated for this deficiency. One could always describe whiteness by its superiority to "blackness," "Asian-ness," "Latino-ness," or any type of "foreign-ness." Also in the past, white ethnicity could be accessed to compensate for white racial identity's lacking substance. Today, young whites who reject white supremacist discourse and know little of their ethnic heritage may create a mirrored whiteness. In this construction of whiteness, autobiographers do not "borrow" from others' cultures, they only contrast them with whiteness. For some, a trace of white supremacist discourse lingers on in their descriptions of what they were taught about whiteness in comparison to other groups. For example, Courtney writes:

> I am a 22-year old white woman. My heritage is mostly German with a splash of Irish mixed in as well. That is all I can say about my ethnic and racial make-up. I don't know which ancestors were from where or the problems they faced when they came to America. I was born and raised here. . . . I don't know exactly what percentage of minorities live in [this town], but I do know that it is *very* small. Small enough that I rarely remember ever seeing a minority around when I was growing up. It is still uncommon today to see two minorities at the same place. . . . There is a particular street that is usually considered a 'colored street'. . . . Then there is the housing developments or 'nigger hill.' 'Nigger hill' got its name because there are groups of black people who often go to the bars on the hill. I have never had a reason other than St. Patrick's Day to think about my ethnicity. I've never thought about my white heritage and what I did know was all bad. It was all about the harm the white race has done and the crazy white supremacy groups terrorizing people. The only race I knew anything about was African Americans. I had my own stereotypes about black people. They are positive ones, and I don't know where they came from, I just remember having them. I thought that black people were funny, athletic, and good singers. I was not exposed to other groups so I had nothing to compare myself to. There was an overall sense that whites were superior as I was growing up. It was like people were products, and 'white' was the name brand. The other products, 'black,' 'Asian,' 'Latino' or whatever are good brands for a cheaper price, but not quite as good as the name brand.

From the environment in which Courtney lives, she gleans information that leads her to see whiteness as normative, and in this sense superior to other racial groups. Further, she knows very little about her ethnic heritage, and thus is left to form an identity based primarily on her racial identity. Her white racial identity is constructed only at the extremes—as either "all bad" or "superior."

Theo explicitly chooses to discuss interactions with others rather than his own ethnicity: "The traditions of my family's racial and ethnic background really haven't been passed on to me. . . . Since I don't have any specific memories of racial and/or ethnic experiences in my family, I am choosing to write about my first experience with people of another race, the African American race to be specific." He continues, discussing when he was in third grade and an African American family moved into his neighborhood. Stories of his interactions with this family make up Theo's entire paper, which is, ironically, titled "The Story of Me." In Theo's case, these interactions were positive, and his mother left a lasting impression on him by being the first in the community to welcome this family.

Students were asked in the autobiography guide to consider whether they could discuss either their racial or ethnic identity without mentioning other groups. Very few could do so. Most white respondents wrote that it is impossible to talk about being white without referring to other groups, although some just attributed this to whiteness being "not important" to them. Others were more contemplative. For example, Ned writes:

'What am I?' This is a question I have never been asked before. It is probably a good thing because the only way I would have known to answer that question before would have been 'white.' And now I have been asked what is white and I do not know. I can not begin to describe to you what it means to be white. The only way I can think of describing my whiteness is to say that I am not Black or Indian or whatever else. I can not give you a definition of white. Now I ask myself: who can I be if I don't know what I'm being?

Here, Ned wrestles with the dearth of descriptors of whiteness. Setting aside whiteness as taken for granted, he cannot "begin to describe to you what it means to be white." If the answer to "what am I?" must go beyond the one word, "white," he has no cultural resources to utilize. Ned must construct whiteness based on what it is *not*: African American, Indian, or any other person of color.

While all racial and ethnic identity might in some sense be described as referential, theorists have noted that people of minority ethnic groups must know the cultures of dominant groups in order to survive in them, while majority groups typically do not understand minority cultures as well.[46]

Moreover, studies show that parents of children of color give them some verbal messages about traditions and culture, so they probably have more of a sense of what that culture means without reference to other ethnic groups.[47] Therefore, the oppositional identity of people of color is founded on a "double consciousness" of the content of one's own culture and that of whites. Mirrored *white* identity, in contrast, is built around less tangible knowledge of one's own or others' cultures. Accordingly, Seth writes,

> I could describe what it is like to be *white* [*his emphasis*] without referring to any other group but I think that would be irrelevant. . . . Being "white" is to have a lack of pigment in the skin, flowing hair. . . . without the reference to other groups there would be very few defining features among a specific group. This type of identification only exists because we have something to compare ourselves to.
>
> I think that other races in this country have a much stronger attachment to their race and ethnicity. This is probably because they live in the opposite world of what I do.

Seth asserts that race or ethnicity are only "relevant" in comparison to other groups. Trying to define whiteness without reference to others, he is left with physical descriptions. However, even these assertions of independent white identity are referential. Unstated, but implied in Seth's writing are the words "unlike *them*." "[Unlike them], I have a lack of pigment . . . and flowing hair." Whiteness is devoid of cultural content except referentially. Not only identity, but social environment is a mirrored reality—other groups inhabit an "opposite world."

Nathan finds it hard to describe whiteness without reference to others for several reasons:

> Whiteness to me seems normal because I have never been treated unfairly because I am white. I think of whiteness as intelligent, and law abiding. Whites are the prominent political figures that I have encountered throughout my life. I am not white trash, which is what people think of many Southern whites. I was born and raised in a southern city and I think of myself as a cracker. This term is used to describe native[s of this state] like myself. It seems somewhat difficult to speak about being white without referring to other groups.

Nathan hints at a point some theorists have observed; racial identity is usually more salient for groups facing discrimination.[48] If reminded of race by the unfair treatment from others, race will constitute a larger portion of one's overall identity. To some extent, minus this experiential dynamic, Nathan relies on regional identity to add dimension to whiteness.

Some explicitly state that the reason they describe whiteness using reference to others is because it is meaningless without considering the place whiteness holds in an unequal racial hierarchy. Molly writes:

Being white is being 'normal.' It is living a better life and having better experiences. Being white is also having the ability to enjoy life and not feel constantly bad about your identity. It is difficult to speak of whiteness without making reference to other groups. Whiteness wouldn't be what it is if there weren't other racial groups. Whiteness wouldn't matter if there were not other skin colors to compare it with. I feel that the difference in skin colors between whites and blacks would not matter if slavery had never existed. Skin can be many colors, but it is unfortunate that we value some colors more than others and that we let colors keep us separated. I don't believe that I could tell my life story without mentioning race or ethnicity because I have encountered individuals of various races over my lifetime.

Molly begins by describing whiteness as the norm, and a privileged existence. She continues by outlining what it is not—throughout this passage, Molly discusses what whiteness "would not" be without comparing other groups. She suggests that slavery made whiteness and blackness significant. Indeed, modern conceptions of whiteness and blackness were constructed around and in justification of that economic relationship.[49] Kendall reflects on this theme:

Being white is being part of the majority and being part of the majority is getting all of the breaks. Minorities have so many obstacles to face in their life that, we, members of the majority, do not have to face. I suppose that it is not difficult to speak of being white without mentioning other races because the whites are not being oppressed or have not been oppressed in any way by a majority race because whites are the majority. . . . I could describe my life story without mentioning the fact that I was white or anything else about race. However, by not mentioning race, one would notice that I am white because I never mentioned discrimination or any kind of past oppression because of the fact that most minorities have been discriminated against in even the littlest way.

Although saying it is "not difficult" to express whiteness without mentioning other groups, Kendall fails to do so. Each attempt to explain what it means to be white relies on reference to whiteness in relation to "otherness," specifically to *blackness*. Kendall especially relies on a majority-minority contrast, which is changing as whites become less of a majority. Still, he recognizes that whites have been more regularly in the position of oppressors than the oppressed.

Mike echoes a theme of Kendall's: that because he can omit his race in telling his life story, people would assume he was white:

> I am a white man. I have no comprehension of what it is like to be of any other race. Being white has been convenient for me since I have not experienced any racism against my group. Whiteness is not an easy topic to discuss without discussing other races. We represent the broader culture; therefore I usually consider my race in comparison to other races. White people are not reminded every day that they are white. Occasionally in conversation I may make a brief remark about my race. That statement is usually joking or in regards to a current event. For instance 'white men can't jump or dance.' I do not consider the color of my skin to be an important aspect of my personality. . . . I feel that my lifestyle, career choices, and hobbies play a more important role in my character than does my race. My beliefs would not be manipulated by my skin color. I like to think that if I were a different color I would have the same ideals. I could tell my life story without mentioning my race, but because I can do that everybody would know that I am white.

Mike understands that he makes reference to his race only when whiteness is brought up, sometimes humorously, in contrast to supposed characteristics of other groups. Like many others, Mike attributes his "mirrored" identity to whites being the majority racial group, and to the fact that white people usually are not the victims of racism. Even after recognizing these differences in experience, however, Mike adds a statement endorsing individualism as the basis of indentity for all groups.

The Black/White Paradigm

> I know this paper was concentrated on blacks, but it is all I know. I have not had much interaction with other groups.

Courtney

When whites define whiteness in terms of who they are "not," the contrasted are usually African American. Few respondents mentioned other racial groups. Even the Southern respondents, who live in a region where they could be expected to encounter Latinos, rarely mentioned them. Although one might expect variation according to where respondents grew up, all referred to African Americans more than any other group. Respondents not only mention African Americans more than others, but also are able to give full descriptions of stereotypes applied to them.

Respondents use the terms "African Americans" or "black people" almost interchangeably with the terms "people of color," "nonwhites," or "minority group members." Thus, the mirrored white identity is virtually dichotomous, constructed according to a black/white paradigm.[50] Although other groups are growing, with racism directed against them as well, one can argue that a black/white paradigm still holds for U.S. racism, for several reasons. The modern idea of "race" was constructed in response to the relationship between whites and African Americans. Other groups who have entered the United States have had to contend with this system and be judged by its standards. In this sense, it follows that we live in a "colorist" society more than a "racist" one. Further, African Americans were the only group ever held in long-term legal servitude in this country, and the only group whose enslavement was legitimized by the Constitution. For these reasons and others, the black experience in the United States has been so unique that racism to some extent persists and operates according to a black/white paradigm. Thus, it is unsurprising that many comments demonstrate that the mirrored white identity is usually built on a black/white paradigm. Helen writes about her reactions to African Americans:

> As a child there were no specific messages given to me about race, and especially not about ethnicity. . . . However, differences were addressed by telling me things such as, "never say nigger." African American people are the only people I can remember being aware of as different from my race as a child.

Later, Helen writes,

> The barrier that only existed with African Americans is still confusing for me, and I never really realized it was true until I wrote the autobiography. Maybe it has to do with African Americans being the largest group of minorities that surrounded me, or was I just not aware? Maybe I picked up on the stronger stereotypes related to African Americans, because of my southern nature and surroundings. Maybe I thought they looked the most different. I am still sorting through these possibilities.

Though other groups are increasing in the United States, and Latinos and Asians are the fastest growing ethnic groups, African Americans had until recently been the largest minority group in the United States—one reason that the black/white paradigm still holds. Helen acknowledges that the African-American stereotypes are often "stronger" than those applied to others. Nearly always, negative attitudes expressed in the autobiographies about other races were directed toward African Americans. Edward, the son of a police officer, who told of violence perpetrated by African-American men, writes: "I don't really have a problem with any other ethnic group, but only with blacks. I don't hate blacks I just don't accept them as quickly. I do have black friends. It just takes me longer to accept him as a friend because of my experiences." The phrase "because of my experiences" is a rhetorical device repeatedly appearing in the autobiographies, employed to validate the authenticity of the respondents' viewpoint. Just as the phrase "I have black friends" is sometimes used by whites as evidence that they are not racist, "because of my experiences" is utilized to transform what might be viewed as prejudiced thinking into reasonable judgment based on empirical data.

Like Edward, Stacey writes,

> But now as a 19-year old, I still know that racism is wrong, but I already have my opinions about people of other races, and unfortunately the views are slightly racist. . . . The main group of people I'm racist towards is blacks. Don't get me wrong, I do have black friends, as well as I have Asian and Mexican and friends of all ethnic backgrounds.

This is consistent with other studies of white Americans, which reveal they have the strongest feelings about African Americans.[51] Few in this study mention any other groups, even in discussions of affirmative action and economic concerns.

Political Events and Mirrored Whiteness

Global and national political events may bring certain groups into the social landscape of white Americans. After the terrorist attacks of September 11, 2001, references to Middle Eastern Americans, particularly Arab Americans, appeared more in the autobiographies; however, "more" means going from no mention at all to ten percent or less of each class mentioning this group (of course, in the fall of 2001 this figure was a bit higher). For example, in the fall of 2001, Jennifer writes:

> The biggest problem in the US today would have to be the September 11 attacks in New York. After the attacks, Muslims have been discriminated against. US citizens have turned against many thinking they are all terrorists. I have even heard stories of the Muslim frat at Penn State being stoned. Many of them even support our fight back and do not support the actions of the terrorists.

By the spring of 2003, out of 62 autobiographies, fewer than ten referred to Middle Eastern Americans explicitly. Although other groups occasionally register with white people based on national and global political events, overall, African Americans remain the most common stable referents, with Asian and Latino Americans coming in, together, a very distant second. Further, though other groups sometimes appeared in autobiographies, they were not used the same way as African Americans, as a mirror for white identity. Rarely did respondents specifically describe whiteness as "not" being another group except African American. Thus, when whiteness is constructed as a mirrored identity, it is almost invariably blackness with which it is contrasted.

Cultural Envy

> I think that minorities have a greater knowledge of global and international activities of their group. My mom is of Irish descent and my dad is

Irish and a bit of German and Swedish. Besides my mom's huge St. Patrick's Day celebration, very little of our heritage is discussed. I know that my mom wants to go to Ireland and see where her grandparents lived, my uncle has already been. I am disappointed in myself for not knowing about my relatives or never even asking. Many minority ethnic and racial groups are very educated on their personal and family histories—something I know very little about.

Beth

On an episode of the popular sitcom *Seinfeld*, Elaine, Seinfeld's (white) friend, dates a man of ambiguous ethnicity. Throughout the show, she tries to determine his "race." Elaine becomes increasingly pleased by the idea that she is in an interracial relationship, and when it is finally revealed that he is not black, Elaine asks why her boyfriend had stated that they were an interracial couple earlier. The boyfriend responds that he said they were interracial because "*You're* Hispanic." Elaine, who obviously does not identify as Hispanic, quickly declares "I don't think we should be talking about this." The boyfriend asks woefully, "So, we're just a couple of white people?" To which Elaine replies, also with disappointment, "I guess." After sitting dejectedly for a few seconds, Elaine asks, sounding a bit more hopeful, "So, you wanna go to the Gap?"

This vignette exemplifies the attitudes expressed by many young whites in these data. Part of the attraction between Elaine and her boyfriend is that they believe the other is of a more exotic race than "just" white. Elaine even believes that with a "black" boyfriend, she has gained entrance into "black culture," enough to call a black woman "sister." When both discover they are "just a couple of white people," they are disappointed, but then comforted by realizing that they can find solace in "the Gap." Whiteness is still dominant in consumer culture.

Many young whites do not see the hegemonic hold of whiteness on U.S. culture, and thus believe they have no "culture" at all. Perhaps because whiteness is ubiquitous, it is difficult to identify traditions, artistry, music, and other "culture" that young whites feel they can call their own.[52] Most of the youth in this study reported they grew up in predominantly white communities, with some variation by region.[53] Some connect the low salience of their ethnicity with this early environment. Gail writes: "Growing up white, in a predominantly white neighborhood, racial and ethnic issues were virtually non-existent. . . . As a child, I knew I was white, as was everyone else, and from an early age I learned about my multi-ethnic heritage, but it was more like a history lesson than anything that really defined who I was. . . . .it has never really shaped my life and I don't really feel it defines me in any way—it's just my heritage." Ethnicity is relegated to stale "history lessons," without real-life impact.

In addition to a sense of whiteness built around what it is "not," some respondents constructed a more specific referential identity, centered on envy for people perceived as "having culture." Two women, Lori and Stephanie, write eloquently of the emptiness of whiteness and their accompanying envy for the cultures of people of color. Lori discusses her family background:

> My Grandfather's ancestors were Irish. That just means he got toasted for St. Patrick's Day and developed an affinity for green. My grandmother on my real father's side . . . once told me that I was related to Charlemagne. That might have meant something except that at that point I had no idea who he was. Is my world influenced internally because of ethnicity? Nope. I don't celebrate anything that isn't inherently "American" or have customs that I have to explain. Is my world influenced externally? I think so. I have no idea when my ancestors came over on the boat or whether they owned slaves or what. But I have slowly begun to see privileges that I have because I am part of a dominant culture. I don't have to wonder if glances or phrases are due to my ethnicity. I don't have to worry about how my skin will speak for me before I open my mouth. . . . In a country whose latest fad is rediscovering their roots, I am grasping at straws. There are people who could not shed their ethnicity no matter how hard they might try. I have nothing to take on in this category. I have no new facet to add to my identity. . . . I never had any "specialty dishes" to bring on cultural awareness day. I feel neutral, plain about my ethnicity. It is only recently that I have realized that others may not see my race that way. I took it for granted that I fit into the apple pie, girl next door, American backdrop. My last name is "Smith." It's like "being everybody else."

Unlike some respondents, Lori recognizes that whiteness imparts privilege. She also acknowledges that while she has no sense of ethnicity, others lack the option of "shed[ding]" theirs. Further, although her *ethnicity* may seem "plain," Lori realizes members of other groups may see content in her *whiteness* that is invisible to her. Lori's story demonstrates that even when whites perceive whiteness as privilege, they can still experience it as a cultural liability. Identifying her frustration as a product of a new societal appreciation for "culture," she laments she has no "roots" to discover. With humor, she adds that even her last name[54] is generically American. Whiteness is described as the "norm," but to Lori this means being "neutral [and] plain."

Stephanie also writes extensively of her cultural envy:

> I have never seen [friends of other races] as different in a derogatory way, only more interesting than myself. When I think of my life, I am almost disappointed that I do not have more culture in my heritage. Being born in the United States to white parents also born here is almost boring to me. I have friends from Nicaragua and France and when they speak of their country and cultural heritage I find it extremely fascinating. They have different holidays, different customs and religions and different meals that their family prepares.

Stephanie is "disappointed" that she was born white in the United States, a status she finds "boring." One can "have" culture or not, and she in some ways romanticizes the culture her friends possess. Stephanie does not construct "difference" itself negatively but she has a negative response to it in that it highlights her "sameness," which she finds unappealing.

Some might argue that cultural envy is the pinnacle of white privilege: white people may overlook social and economic privileges, and even bemoan their status as part of the dominant group. Measured by any standard, whites have benefited from whiteness. For example, not only have whites benefited politically and economically from their status as part of the dominant group, they also have a longer life expectancy than people of color.[55] Being white brings concrete, valuable advantage. Despite their misconceptions of the status of whites, the respondents' views represent a significant shift from those of the immediately preceding generations, from a time when the popular phrase "free, white, and twenty-one" described a person with a comfortable and carefree life. Although some of their parents' and grandparents' generations may now view whiteness as an economic disadvantage because of affirmative action, and some respondents share this view, these young whites also find it less culturally rewarding than to be a person of color. The social construction of whiteness has shifted so that this generation sees culture as something others have and may bring into their lives. Although most comment generally, some note particular aspects of other cultures they admire or wish were emulated in white experience:

> I feel other groups take more pride in their race than what the whites around me do. For instance Black people have churches filled with dancing, singing and lots of vocal praise. The black churches seem to have great enthusiasm and joy. The white churches seem so bland in comparison.

Here Wanda writes specifically about the greater intensity she believes is found in African-American spirituality—a point often made by whites who are religious and either have visited a black congregation or seen one portrayed in the media. Other respondents note the same spirituality they believe can be found in black culture, along with other supposed cultural traits and symbols.

Lacey found that many of her close friendships were with people of color, and this has perhaps made her conscious of a lack of culture in her own heritage:

> *My* daily life was made up of people of all cultures. My best friend is Indian; my first kiss was with a Filipino boy, one of my good friends is Jamaican American, and my other good friend is Italian with an African American boyfriend. I think the reason for my friendships with many ethnic backgrounds is because as a child, I was never told that people are different based on the color of their skin; . . . I was taught to treat everyone equally. . . .

Lacey goes on to discuss friendships with others of Italian ethnicity that she feels are based on a shared understanding of Italian culture. Although she has a sense of being "Italian," still, she immediately writes:

> This glimpse of interaction with Italians is the only way I feel that I inter-act with a group about ethnicity. I think that I am almost jealous that I am not able to have more ethnic conversations, or ethnic celebrations. I think that because I am white, I have picked out the ethnicity that is more interesting to me in order to have that taste of culture. . . . This is pro-bably because my family had much more traditions for my father's Italian heritage than we did for my mother's Irish traditions. To me, the Italian culture is more interesting than the Irish culture, so that is why I would rather be associated with being Italian.

Lacey exercises an ethnic option, choosing to identify with her Italian heritage. This may be partly because she believes Irish culture is commodified more than Italian traditions. Neither ethnic identity, however, provides Lacey the sense of culture she desires. This is puzzling, since in her autobiography, she seems very "in touch" with her Italian roots. Still she desires more "ethnic conversations, or ethnic celebrations." Even when young white people are ethnically aware and use their ethnic option, that option is meaningless when the ethnicity it provides is superficial.

Most students, like Caitlin, simply do not believe they *have* an "ethnic option," although few refer to this as explicitly:

> It is hard being white, probably just as hard as it is to be anything else in life. . . . .Being white has disadvantages; you lose all sense of the culture that you come from. . . . I feel that whites are forced to give up [ethnicity] to fit in. Blacks and other groups claim that is what whites want them to do as well. I don't feel that this is the case. I would want to hold on to any traditions that I have of any of my ethnicities, if I knew what those were. Given that, I wouldn't expect anyone else to give that up. Blacks should be grateful that they at least know what their culture is like and are able to live it.
>
> Another thing that I have learned is that most whites do NOT have the so-called 'ethnic option.' I know that I definitely do not. I am so many different things and not one of them stands out in me, nor do I know anything about any of the cultures or traditions that make up my heritage. I would like to learn more about the traditions that go along with my heritage, but not even my parents really know what they are. That is why I feel that I fit into the national identification of "American". . . . I am like most whites, who think that they are the norm, or average. I never really thought that I got any special treatment for being white. . . .
>
> [M]y family has. . . . assimilated to the point where we can't get our culture or traditions back. We consider ourselves to be Americans, and

we celebrate the normal "American holidays." I wish that I knew how my great grandparents, who lived in other countries/cultures, celebrated holidays or the traditions that they held most important to them. If only I knew this, then I could pass these things on to my children when I have a family.

But instead of knowing these things, I have to deal with being just white, just an American, just normal, and just what society expects me to be. I feel that these are all responsibilities that society has placed upon whites. We have to fill these shoes, which can be quite stressful, and then we have to tip toe around races and ethnicities so that we don't step on their toes and discriminate against them . . .

I also feel that for some people, their race or ethnicity plays a big role as to where they live, what schools they go to and so forth. I however, do not feel that these things affect my decisions. . . . I do not see why people need to bring their race or ethnicity into decision making.

As noted in the last chapter, many whites describe whiteness as the norm, and identify primarily according to some other aspect of their personality. Caitlin clearly believes that being white has brought disadvantage, not privilege, by causing her to lose touch with her ethnic identity, and exposing her to claims of racial inequality. In fact, one hears a certain resentment, carrying throughout Caitlin's autobiography, toward others who still "know their culture" and consequently "should be grateful." She, conversely, must face "being *just* white, *just* American, *just* normal" (my emphasis). Like many of her peers, Caitlin experiences these characteristics not as a privilege, but a burden.

Supplanted Whiteness

In denying the importance of their whiteness, some respondents supplant their racial identity by discussing another identity that is more salient to them. They either do not mention whiteness at all, but instead only discuss the other identity, or they may use a nonracial identity as a modifier of whiteness. This coincides with Beverly Tatum's observation that young whites usually construct identities based on characteristics other than race, in part because society does not continuously remind them of their racial label.[56] When a respondent replaces the white identity altogether, writing that "whiteness is not important, but I can tell you about being an American," or "whiteness is not important, but I can tell you about being a woman," in effect she is implying that race does not matter: her experience would be the same were she an African-American person living in the United States or a Latina. Some respondents describe being in a particular group *within* the white racial group, such as "white male," "white middle-class," or "white trash." When linking the white identity to other identities, the effect is also to deny the importance of whiteness, in this case asserting that there are no areas of social life in which whiteness in and of itself is a privileged status.

While it is important to acknowledge that whiteness is not a monolithic experience, particularizing the white experience can imply that race does not matter. That is, this can translate into the assertion that being white does not affect the respondents' lives, that being a "white male," for example, or "white trash" impacts it more significantly. Along these lines, John Hartigan's ethnography of poor whites in Detroit alerts us to consider "differences within the body of the Same."[57] However, he acknowledges that "Given the national stage on which these [racial] dramas unfold, certain broad readings of racial groups across this country are warranted."[58] In the attempt to consider complexity of whiteness, one must not obscure the existence of a racial hierarchy in which it is still more beneficial, all else being equal, to be white than to be a person of color.

Nationality

Often when the word "American" is used alone, unless an ethnic identification is added, it is assumed that the person being referred to is white. Frank Wu writes:

> It isn't easy to call people on their unconscious errors. If I point out that they said 'American' when they meant 'white,' they will brush it off with 'Well, you know what I mean,' or 'Why are your bringing up race?' Yet it is worth pondering exactly what they do mean. What they have done through negligence, with barely any awareness, is equate race and citizenship. They may even become embarrassed once the effect is noticed. Asian Americans were upset when the MS-NBC website printed a headline announcing that 'American beats out Kwan' after Tara Lipinsky defeated Michelle Kwan in figure skating at the 1998 Winter Olympics. Like gold medallist Lipinsky, Kwan is an American. By implying that Kwan was a foreigner who had been defeated by an 'American,' the headline in effect announced that an Asian American had been defeated by a white American in a racialized contest. . . . If Kwan had won, it also would be unlikely for the victory to be described as "American beats out Lipinsky' or "Asian beats out white." Movie producer Christopher Lee recalls that when studio executives were considering making a film version of *Joy Luck Club*, they shied away from it because 'there were no Americans in it.' He told his colleagues 'There are Americans in it. They just don't look like you.'[59]

For many respondents, perhaps the most accessible identification to replace whiteness is "Americanness," since the white experience in America has come to be universalized as *the* American experience.

Will speaks of the "American" identity as accessible to all groups who assimilate:

> America does not accept anything that is not in the mainstream culture. I don't think that it is very important here to have strong ties with one's

past. It may interest some individuals . . . but most people don't seem to care about other people's backgrounds. . . . America offers an entire new form of ethnicity. People born and raised here in the past two decades know how America is becoming "one" culture. Many people here talk the same slang, dress similarly, and act similarly. It seems to me to be different from any other kind of ethnicity. It seems to be becoming its own. . . . I see most of my ethnicity right here in America and know little, compared to my American traditions, of those of my Czech ancestors.

This description is reminiscent of the melting-pot view of assimilation. Will presents a picture of a "new ethnicity" being formed in America, where everyone has equal opportunity to become part of "'one' culture." Further, because he is not interested in his ethnic background, Will assumes that generally "most people don't seem to care about other people's backgrounds." Yet most people of color would probably assert that they and others are still quite concerned with *their* "background." For people of color in the U.S., assimilation has typically been one-way. Instead of the "melting-pot" ideal, it has followed a model of Anglo-conformity.

Carol speaks of a female American identity that has become primary for her because she does not know about her ethnic heritage:

Until I took a sociology course on race and ethnicity I never really thought about what it means to me to be white. So if I were asked to tell my life history I would not have included my ethnic or racial backgrounds, at the most I may have included that I am an American. I would not have ever thought to include that I am white or that I am English, Dutch and German. I probably would identify more with my gender than anything else.

One of the first things I might say if I were asked to describe myself would probably [be] that I am a female. Although at times I have wished that I weren't, being female would be one of the first things I would say to identify myself. As a member of the female gender I am also part of the minority group, this is why I often wish that I was a male. There just seem to be so many more opportunities for males than for females especially in the occupations in which I have become interested. . . .

[My family does] not know anything about our cultural traditions or how in fact they have shaped our lives. My parents regard themselves as American and as practicing only American traditions. . . . I guess that my family along with myself have totally forgotten about the fact that our family didn't always live in the United States and identify just as white Americans. Claiming being American to me disregards the past and where we came from.

Carol acknowledges that without understanding her ethnicity, being female and "American" have become more important to her sense of identity. However, she is somewhat critical of the way whiteness has been replaced by "Americanness."

Gender

Although both male and female respondents mention gender in their autobiographies, women more than men explicitly discuss gender as being an important part of their identities. In much the same way that people of color must be more conscious of their racial identity than are whites, arguably women are required to be more conscious of their gender than are men. Many female respondents indicated that while they do not think of themselves as white, they do think of themselves as female. Anna begins her statement this way, however, her view is unique:

> The disadvantages I can think of are not because I am white, but because I am a female. Women have been more likely to present themselves as weak or dependent [while] men [have] been likely to project power and control. Women also have to deal with unsolicited comments of men in public situations like in bars or nightclubs. As to which racial group does it more I would have to say young black males. I've had personal experience with rude and crude gestures, which made me feel very uncomfortable. . . . By all means I'm not saying that white or Spanish young males don't do the same actions because they do, but I find it more often happening to me by black males.

Anna's statement is interesting in that while she does disassociate from her white identity, replacing it with a female identity, her mention of harassment by African-American males racializes her comment. Thus, although it seems her intention is to replace her racial identity with a gender identity, to some extent she discursively reassociates the two. In other words, in her experience it seems to matter not only that she is female but that she is a *white* female. Some other women, more than men, simply replace the white identity with a gender identity, without the implication of a racial linkage.

In the autobiographies, when men highlight gender, it is usually in the context of their perception of victimization as white men. Unlike women, few men discuss being male as an important part of their identity aside from their concerns over cultural and economic disadvantage as whites. This sense of economic disadvantage will be discussed more in chapter 5.

Class

Another status associated with whiteness in the autobiographies is class. A white racial identity alone may be indescribable, but when linked to class, whiteness takes on content. Some class positions, such as that of the middle class, can serve to make whiteness seem even *more* normative and empty. In contrast, other class positions may particularize the white experience—white upper-class status may enhance white privilege, while working-class whites may suffer from disadvantage.

One young woman describes shifts in her identity that come with changes in socioeconomic status. Claire began her life in the middle class, moved to the lower class, and now is part of the upper class. She writes:

> There are many separate ethnicities to the Caucasian race, but the two most prominent ones in today's society are the upper and lower class ones. Rich white people are viewed as complete opposites of poor white people, more commonly known to the world as "trailer trash" or just plain old "white trash." The stereotypes are very common, and all of the sociologists fail to see the difference or even acknowledge the poor white class as a different class or group.

In the introduction to their edited volume, entitled *White Trash*, Analee Newitz and Matt Wray paraphrase John Waters as stating that "'white trash' is not just a classist slur—it's also a racial epithet that marks out certain whites as a breed apart, a dysgenic race unto themselves."[60] Indeed, Claire constructs her class status *as* an "ethnicity," a "different group." She goes on to write about painful experiences of ridicule and poverty she undergoes as a member of the "white trash ethnicity." When she was older, Claire went to live with her wealthy father, escaping her "white trash" identity to become part of the white upper class:

> When I dress in expensive clothing and put on the good girl smile, I can do anything I set my mind to. I can get out of any speeding or accident ticket, which I have done four times. . . . I can get into any establishment I want to, whether it is the country club or the local nightclub. Fellow students and teachers automatically accept me. I am never asked to empty my bag in a shopping mall, even though many times I should be. Instead I am asked if I took anything, and when I say 'no' the sales ladies smile, apologize, and walk away. . . . Even though I was the white trash that I now so despise, I cannot seem to make myself break the barriers between them and me. . . . I am the one who ostracizes them in the classes I go to. I am one of the people I hated so much.

Claire's dramatic class shift allows her to take full advantage of white privilege. She goes on:

> The race gap between the poor white and the rich whites is very apparent to me and to other whites because there is such a dramatic one. . . . I personally think that more studies need to go into the "white trash" race, and how they are so different and segregated against in society. Even those that come from them segregate them. It is my race, it is my culture, and I would rather spit on it than tell people what I come from. It is the unmentioned race that no one confesses to. That is my race. That is who I am. That is what it is like to be white trash.

Elsewhere casting the "white trash race" as "the Hindu Untouchables of the American society," Claire writes that she now distances herself from her past identity. She unabashedly tells how she realizes that her upper-class status protects her from suspicion of various types of illegal activities, while lower-class whites would more likely be considered guilty. Claire constructs class as superseding race, by suggesting that class status would operate the same in other racial groups. Of course, studies have shown that middle-class black professionals still face regular discrimination, demonstrating that race matters aside from class.[61] Nonetheless, Claire insightfully suggests that sociologists should study the identities constructed at the cross sections of class and race. Indeed, some are realizing the importance of such inquiries. For example, Hartigan writes that "white trash designates ruptures of conventions that maintain whiteness as an unmarked, normative identity."[62]

Some respondents, although acknowledging that they experience some degree of racial privilege as whites, assert that it does not outweigh the disadvantages that they have experienced economically as members of the white working class. For example, Roger writes about his father:

> Before I was taught anything about race or ethnic lines, I was first taught about social and economical lines. My father would relate to me stories about his experiences growing up as a troubled youth, in placement homes. Now when my father was growing up, placement homes were not checked as they are now. It was basically a way for social services to pond [sic] children off to farms that needed the extra help. My father grew up in the 1940–1950's and this was an acceptable way to deal with kids whose families couldn't afford and/or didn't want them. My father would then tell me stories of how teachers and leaders of the community would look down upon my father and those like him. He was usually in trouble at school and would be embarrassed by teachers who thought themselves better than my father. He was discriminated against not because of skin color, not because of his ethnic identity; no he was discriminated against because of his social and economic class. Discrimination comes in many forms race and ethnicity are but a few.

Here Roger sets up "discrimination" as something that enters different people's lives in various forms; in his life, class discrimination played a more salient role than racial discrimination. This perspective was particularly common amongst the Northern respondents, perhaps because many of them are from working-class backgrounds, and the sample was gathered in a rural area that has suffered much from job layoffs and factory closings in recent years.

Thus national, gender, or class identities are sometimes used in respondents' autobiographies as a way of undermining the importance of race. By juxtaposing these identities against potential benefits of whiteness, a respondent seems to suggest that we are all minorities in one sense or another and that we all suffer from certain disadvantages. No doubt, citizenship, gender and class stratify U.S. society, but their existence does not diminish the enduring legacy of white privilege.

Conclusion

These data suggest that young whites have given little thought to what it means to be white and do not know how to describe it when asked. This chapter showed how respondents explain what it means to be white with reference to what whiteness is *not*. Primarily, in their perception, whiteness is not cultural. They assert that whiteness and European ethnicity, for the most part, give them no "culture" to draw on in creating identity. Further, far from claiming superiority to ethnic Others, at least in this dimension of life, they express longing for the "heritage," "tradition," and "culture" they believe them to have. The writers respond to this empty whiteness in different ways. Sometimes respondents assemble a usable ethnic identity in order to "have culture." Frequently, they engage in "cultural tourism." This data also reveals a mirrored aspect to contemporary whiteness. Whiteness is "not blackness," and respondents sometimes rely on this contrast for substance in an otherwise empty and indescribable identity. For some, mirrored whiteness is fundamentally a sense of cultural envy. Finally, some respondents create identity by linking whiteness to other statuses. In this way, they use identifications that have more meaning to them to give whiteness substance.

This is not to suggest that these students realize the implications of an involuntary "ethnic" label. In fact, I conclude that they are largely unaware of the "downside" to ethnicity, and that this is an integral part of their ethnic envy. Lack of awareness of differences in the experiences of whites and people of color contributes to the current colorblind perspective on race and underpins the system of white privilege maintaining the racial status quo. Nevertheless, while the ethnic option might have operated as a privilege for the parents and grandparents of this generation, they do not experience it as such. For the most part they see themselves as unable to exercise any option, in knowing nothing about their ethnicity. The respondents experience the lack of ethnicity not as a privilege, but one of many *liabilities* of whiteness.[63] Not only does claiming an ethnic identity seem impossible for most respondents, but whiteness itself is expressed as culturally empty.

Chapter 4
"I Feel 'Whiteness' When I Hear People Blaming Whites": Whiteness As Cultural Stigmatization

The word 'oppression' is. . . . much misused. . . . We hear that oppressing is oppressive to those who oppress as well as to those they oppress. . . . [T]he word 'oppression' is being stretched to meaninglessness; it is treated as though its scope includes any and all human experience of limitation or suffering, no matter the cause, degree or consequence. Once such usage has been put over on us, then if ever we deny that any person or group is oppressed, we seem to imply that we think they never suffer and have no feelings. We are accused of insensitivity; even of bigotry. . . . But this is nonsense. Human beings can be miserable without being oppressed, and it is perfectly consistent to deny that a person or group is oppressed without denying that they have feelings or that they suffer.

Marilyn Frye, "Oppression"

As shown in the last chapter, whites may express a sense of their racial identity as a *lack* of identity, overriding any real understanding of white privilege. Instead, they view whiteness as a cultural liability, responding to this sense of emptiness in a myriad of ways. Some autobiographies reflected a envy of other ethnic cultures. Sometimes, this envy was enacted in "borrowing" artifacts from these cultures—what bell hooks and others refer to as "cultural tourism." Still other whites find at least a symbolic sense of ethnicity in their own heritage. However, this may not provide the sense of identity most of them seek: what they see in people of color. In this chapter, I show the other side of the assessment that being white is a cultural disadvantage: not only is whiteness culturally empty, it exposes one to a barrage of external cultural assaults. This chapter will show that, for young whites, the new "white man's burden" is whiteness itself.[1] The perception of "cultural stigmatization" is exacerbated by the belief that whiteness offers no real sense of "culture." Not only does whiteness provide no "raw material" to serve as cultural resources usable to create an identity; but it is a cultural liability in a more actively negative sense—it leaves a white person vulnerable to cultural stigma.

To respondents, whiteness, far from enhancing a sense of self, or providing privilege, may spoil their identity and expose young whites to negative judgments.[2] This perception of whiteness as a stigma is constructed as a form of victimization. It was expressed in four specific complaints: that (1) people of color are oversensitive; (2) they are "living in the past" and unfairly accuse whites of racism; (3) they separate *themselves* voluntarily from whites, and that this separation is actually "special treatment;" and (4) white Americans are currently facing a situation in which they are required to accept other cultures, either through assimilating "Others" themselves, or accepting "foreign" languages and cultural traditions. Some respondents describe times when they believe they were personally victimized as whites.[3] In some passages, their writing reflects a broader conceptualization that whites as a group, or whiteness as a culture, is being treated unfairly.

People of Color are Oversensitive

Some whites resent people of color they encounter stemming from white beliefs that they are "oversensitive" about race. Many cite "political correctness," which is presumably making whites "have to be careful" of what they say, while others may speak their minds with impunity. For example, Hannah writes: "As a so-called 'white' person you have to specifically watch what you say or do because it could hurt someone of another race. I know when I was in high school I would have to be careful of what I said in history classes about slaves because I did not want to offend anyone." For many respondents, the chaos of racism is in the past, and it is now *whites* with a burden that people of color do not have: they must be careful not to "offend" people who still think about the past. Several other respondents also discuss their perception of having to "be careful." Mark writes:

> I am proud to be white because for the most part white people have nothing to be ashamed of (talking about how we act). If I were not asked to talk about race in this paper, yes I could even write more about my life story because race has not affected my life very much at all. . . . To me race has very little importance in my life. I define myself in more racial terms because I had never even heard of the word "ethnicity" until entering college. I am from a small town . . . where . . . No one had to soften the language of different races to keep from hurting somebody's feelings. If I were talking to someone over the phone or a computer and

they asked me to describe myself I would first say that I am a white man, so yes it must mean it ranks highly directing to my personality. . . . I do not believe that my race has as much importance to me as some others with different races. . . . Thinking about my race and how I feel about it, to say the least does not trouble me in any way. If anything it is rewarding to me that the race I classify myself as has been a dominant race throughout the country in which I live in.

Mark focuses here on whether or not he is proud of his racial or ethnic identity, and whether it is troubling or rewarding to him in any way. As throughout his essay, he shifts the focus from racial contrasts to draw a distinction between rural and city life, apparently more salient to him.[4] He asserts that back home, "[n]o one had to soften the language of different races to keep from hurting somebody's feelings." Mark points to oversensitivity not only of people of color, but all people who worry about "offense," ostensibly deracializing his criticism. He implies seemingly that all should be proud of their racial identity, but also should be able to hear "hard" or "real" language about race.

Although Mark says that being white is not important to him, and he could tell his life story more easily without a racial context, he does acknowledge that because he knows little about his ethnicity, his identity has become focused on race. Thus, Mark's experience supports the research finding that whites who have lost touch with their ethnicity will become racialized in their identification.[5] Still, it seems that Mark may have some sense of a white identity beyond this "default" whiteness; he says he is "proud to be white" because he feels there is no reason to be "ashamed" of it. Mark ends this segment with another reference to a group-based sense of pride in whiteness—it is rewarding because it has been dominant.

Many whites believe people of color are unforgiving about slavery, and "take things too seriously." Terri writes about the repercussions for whites:

Going to a mostly white school, we didn't encounter racism too much. There was about five or six black kids in our school, one in particular who everyone loved. . . . .He made everyone laugh and got along with everyone. It wasn't until my senior year of high school where we started to see racism as an issue. There was a kid who proudly displayed the rebel flag in the back of his truck, not meaning anything toward blacks, but just that he was a true redneck. This didn't fly well with one of the black girls in the school, and she caused all kinds of trouble for him.

After that incident, I started to change my views about racism. I was friends with both of them, and I felt that she was out of hand, and was taking the situation too seriously. I never had a problem with black people, but I get upset when they complain that they don't have any rights, and keep bringing up the past. It's over with, we need to forgive and forget.

Terri has positive feelings toward her black classmate who makes "everyone laugh" and gets "along with everyone." Respondents regularly describe African Americans considered as friends in these terms—as one who was the "class clown," and never had conflicts with anyone. Although cross-racial relationships show progress from past generations, perhaps young whites are less challenged by people of color placed in "safe," somewhat one-dimensional and perhaps stereotypical roles in their minds. The African American friend may be a fun-loving sidekick or talented athlete, but the white person is surprised or even threatened when the friend also proves to be a classroom competitor, a rival for the same girlfriend, or someone who challenges them ideologically.

It may be the case that these are not the only African American students that respondents knew, but simply the only people of color that they discuss— the only ones they took the time to get to know. Alternatively, they may be the only ones respondents remember, because they have tried to forget students of color who challenged their assumptions about race and whiteness. Finally, these may be the individuals they are most comfortable discussing, because they can tell the most pleasant stories about them.

Indeed, unlike Terri's African-American male classmate, the black female classmate who voices discomfort with the Confederate flag on a white classmate's truck quickly becomes unacceptable. Rather than seeing the young man's flag as causing problems for her black classmate, Terri views the young woman's *reaction* to the flag as making "all kinds of trouble" for the young man. This situation influences Terri to alter her views about racism and begin to see it as a problem caused by African Americans' complaints.

Terri's stance represents a struggle over who can claim victimization by manipulation of the Confederate flag imagery. Some whites have argued that the flag represents "heritage, not hate." Setting aside the difficulty of making a strong case for this in the *Northeast*, where Terri lives (and where the flag represents the "heritage" of very few), even if this is the message whites were trying to send, it cannot erase the symbolic meaning taken on by the flag over previous decades. The Confederate flag is the longest-standing symbol of white supremacy in the United States.[6] Consequently, several states have recently redesigned their state flags to remove Confederate imagery. It is unreasonable to suggest that the symbolic meaning of an object that has persisted for nearly 140 years can be rewritten within a decade simply because some whites, never the target of it, insist that it "does not mean hate" anymore. Associated with terrorism and violence toward African Americans, the flag will elicit negative images in members of that group's minds for decades to come. African Americans are in a unique position, as targets of the terrorism associated with it, to arbitrate the meaning of the symbol, to state whether the symbol is still harmful. Yet many whites feel that *they* and white culture are the ones being victimized when people of color protest the display of this symbol, and when they are asked to relinquish it. This is a prime example of struggles over claims-making that are an integral part of cultural victimization.

Like many respondents, Terri recommends that "we" need to "forgive and forget." From this perspective, whites and people of color have equal social footing, and *both groups* equally need apology and absolution. Terri continues: "All my life I was taught not to judge people and to love my enemies. Yet, sometimes I think some people can be out of hand and bring things upon themselves, such as racial discrimination. . . . I feel that racism is more of a problem, because black people make it a problem." Past racism has been erased; discussion of it in the present is defined as "racism," and people of color are primarily responsible for this.

Race-Based Humor

Whites often express confusion over what they perceive as double standards in using racial slurs and telling race-based jokes. The issue of oversenstivity specifically focuses on the perception that people of color, particularly African Americans, "take things too seriously," or "can't take a joke." Allan writes about having to censor himself:

> Throughout my life I have noticed that there are a lot of advantages of being white. People don't look at you as though you are different, you don't sense much discrimination against yourself from others, and you can find work easily. These are the advantages. However, it also has its drawbacks, especially if you are a white male. I have noticed that people other than white males think of us as being sexist and racist. . . . Just because our average income seems to be higher, we are automatically deemed to be unfair and overpowering. We always discriminate against female employees and are constantly making racial slurs. . . . This is what is thought about us all throughout the United States and even throughout the world. Could it not be as simple as maybe we are just better suited for the job? And about us making sexist and racist comments, 99.99% of the time they are jokes and they are meant to get a laugh. If they offend someone, then they shouldn't be listening to them. Everybody on this planet has said something racist or sexist even if it is just a joke, but it seems as if the white male takes all the heat for it.
>
> To me being white means watching your back and be careful what you say. I don't want this to sound racist in any way but if a white person were to call a black person a "nigger" there would be a major repercussion for it especially if it was in the workplace. That person would probably almost immediately be fired. Conversely, if a black person were to call a white person "white trash" probably next to nothing would happen. I can't say this would always happen, but this is what I've learned from television and other such sources. But even myself, I feel I have to watch every word I say because I don't want to say the wrong thing when the wrong person is around to hear it. . . . One wrong choice of words

could mean the end of a career. I guess this would be true for all people, but it just seems to happen more often to white males.

Allan's perception of victimization rests on his belief in a meritocratic society, in which all racial groups have equal power. In this worldview, although recognizing that white males have generally higher salaries, Allan believes they are higher because white men are "better suited for the job." Correspondingly, if society is meritocratic and fair, people can withdraw from situations causing them distress or hardship. If one chooses to remain in the situation, and then complains and causes another to be disciplined for using sexist or racist language, *that* person is at fault. Because Allan asserts that all obstacles have been removed for white women and people of color, he believes their claims of discrimination *constitute* discrimination against white males. Allan suggests that any remaining privileges of whiteness are offset by the risks to white men's careers from the oversensitivity of minorities and women to language that should be exempt from critique since it is "just as a joke." Interestingly, Allan's complaint about people of color (and white women) is that they base their claims of discrimination simply on identity. In actuality, the foundation for Allan's assertion of victimization rests in his identity as a white male. The argument seems to be that people make racially based claims that implicate white males unfairly—this argument, ironically, is a racially based claim itself.

Similarly to Allan, Will writes:

> I know that on TV many jokes are made about races and ethnic groups. I am not offended by these, nor have they influenced my thought about other's races and ethnic groups. . . . If the United States of America is too harsh of an environment, then they have the option of settling elsewhere or moving to a different part of the nation. I know that in the south people's attitudes towards race seem to be stronger. A minority with problems may be better off up north or out west.

Will suggests the people offended by racist humor are not strong enough—the normal environment is too "harsh" for them. Like Allan, he suggests that this is *their* problem; because Will is not offended by the jokes, no one should be. Notably, like many students, Will also suggests he is immune to the influence these media images might have on him. African-American poet and author Bruce Jacobs describes the different effects of jokes about people of color and about whites:

> I challenge you to tell me *one* 'white' joke. I don't mean a joke about a specific ethnic or cultural or physical subgroup of whites—WASPS, Poles, Germans, hillbillies, blonds. I mean a joke that makes fun of the broad, generally understood American idea of being white, in the same way that a black joke makes fun of the very idea of being black. . . . [W]hiteness is not in and of itself remarkable or funky or quaint. Whiteness is therefore not funny. It is featureless. It is invisible. It is the norm.

Tell a Polish joke, any Polish joke, even the most vulgar one imaginable. When you have finished, and the laughter has faded, the Polish farmer in the punch line strolls out of the joke and back onto the street, where he melds into the blanket identity of whiteness. In the sidewalk crowd he is no longer seen as the butt of a Polish joke. But what about the guy in the black joke? . . . He cannot merge with the throng of normalcy. He remains separate, noticed, 'a black guy.' And everybody knows what *that* means.[7]

The consequences for people of color of certain types of language, of being used *in* certain types of language, are different than for whites.

Racial Slurs, Epithets and Symbolism

Respondents believe linguistic double standards surround the use of particular words and phrases. Baffled regarding minority "oversensitivity" about racist jokes, many respondents are similarly perplexed about why people of color react more strongly to words like "nigger" than whites do to ethnic slurs referring to them. Tim Wise, a commentator on whiteness, writes:

As a white person I always saw terms like honky or cracker as evidence of how much more potent white racism was than any variation on the theme. . . . When a group of people has little or no power over you institutionally, they don't get to define the terms of your existence, they can't limit your opportunities, and you needn't worry much about the use of a slur to describe you and yours since, in all likelihood, the slur is as far as it's going to go. What are they going to do next: deny you a bank loan? Yeah, right. So whereas 'nigger' was and is a term used by whites to dehumanize blacks, to imply their inferiority, to 'put them in their place' if you will, the same cannot be said of honky: after all, you can't put white people in their place when they own the place to begin with.[8]

Wise's commentary applies to Bridget's statement; she, like Allan, writes about "double standards" in ethnic humor:

[My uncle] is from Lebanon and years ago he could not speak the English language very well. . . . The first time I met him, I cowered on the side of my mother's leg, I thought he was weird because he did not speak or look like me. He spoke with a very heavy accent, had dark eyes and olive-tinted skin. . . . Now, I know that when he did arrive here, he had to assimilate to the American culture. . . . [*She goes on to write about her Scottish aunt*] How much did she need to assimilate when she came to America? Obviously not much. My family just seemed to accept her like she had belonged to our family all along. Even to this day, they seem to like her much more than my uncle. . . . Never once in all of the years that she has been with my family have they ever made one racial slur about her. Even though they seem to do so about my uncle. . . . For example, "towel head" and "sand monkey" are a few of the more popular ones. He takes it all in fun because he makes fun of us Americans as well. But none of us seem to mind, because we all know how we really feel about each other.

This is a good point to discuss. Why do different racial groups take such offense to jokes told about their race or background? I know that when someone tells a stupid blonde joke, I never get offended. Also, when people tell dumb Pollock jokes, I never get uptight or angry with the person for telling it. Maybe we need to get to know each other a little better.

Bridget notes a difference in the assimilation experiences of her darker-skinned, Lebanese uncle and her white-skinned, Scottish aunt and discusses how her own family uses racial slurs to refer to her uncle. But this personal experience does not to her exemplify the difference skin color can make in the impact of racial language. Rather, her uncle's genial reaction to the family reinforces Bridget's perspective that everyone should respond as she does to ethnic slurs; or even to "blonde jokes." Bridget does not consider that while the racial slurs may not *seem* to bother her uncle, he could be putting on a brave front in order to get along with the family. Bridget continues:

As a white European American girl, I never really identified with my heritage too much in the past. I still do not to this day. . . . Except around holidays. . . . Also, I love eating Croatian and Polish foods. I surely am a true "hunkie" (slang for Polish-not "honkie") when it really comes down to it.

See? That is another thing that really bothers me. Why is it that white people are so much more passive about their racial backgrounds? I just said "hunkie" with no problem. I did not even think about it-it did not even bother me. If someone called me a "hunkie" or a "cracker" to may face I would just laugh it off. It would be humorous to me even if it was someone from a different racial or ethnic background. Think about this. What if I was hanging out with a bunch of people (who were racially mixed) and one of the white people called one of the black people a "nigger" or a "spook?" Holy cow, look out! There would be an outright racial war. I think that African Americans still like to hold on to the fact that the European Americans really screwed them in the past which is understandable. I might be a little perturbed as well. It just kind of makes me mad because I'm not the one who made their ancestors slaves. I know it is hard to say let bygones be bygones, but in reality, think about it, it could be worse—they could be Native Americans!

Race and ethnicity research establishes that whites, and young whites, particularly, tend to have a colorblind perspective regarding race.[9] From this outlook, many respondents fail to realize that they are assuming that white standards and practices are the norm for other groups. Like Will, Bridget expects her reactions to be the universal norm. Since "blonde jokes" and "hunkie" do not bother her, why should what *she* sees as parallels bother people of color? Bridget asks why 'whites are so passive' regarding their ethnicity, failing to realize the very different experience of of "ethnicity" between whites and people of color. Bridget has never identified with her ethnic heritage; for those who have, a slur linked to that heritage may have more meaning. Further, "hunkie" is probably meaningless to many Americans, and it also carries none of the cultural "baggage" of a term like "nigger." In their nationwide study of black professionals, Joe Feagin and Melvin Sikes found that "nigger" was lodged in the collective memory of African Americans. For example, a black professor stated:

> [M]ost white Americans. . . . feel that blacks tend to 'overreact'. . . . 'Nigger' to a white may simply be an epithet that should be ignored. To most blacks, the term brings into sharp and current focus all kinds of racism— murder, rape, torture, denial of constitutional rights, insults, limited opportunity structure, economic problems, unequal justice under the law and a myriad of. . . . other racist and discriminatory acts that occur daily.[10]

Still, Bridget's view is not only commonly expressed but is also logical in a sense. Holding everyone to identical standards, whites feel victimized when they believe people of color can be pardoned for racial slights that, if committed by whites, would be unforgivable. This view of language, however, does not consider speaker or context in interpreting the meaning of a word or phrase.

Bridget implies that Native Americans have faced more oppression than have African Americans. It is ironic that Bridget mentions Native Americans, who have also been the focus of debate surrounding racial symbolism. Native Americans have been caricatured in the United States as mascots for sports teams, supposedly "honoring" their history, despite activists' protestations that this is *not* the way their Nations wish to be honored. Recently, a group of American Indian activists at Northern Colorado University attempted to highlight the harm caused by transforming people into mascots by naming their intramural basketball team the "Fightin' Whites."[11] But in an ironic demonstration of the difference power makes in ethnic humor, not only did this fail to anger most whites, many actually enjoy being a mascot, and have purchased the team's gear, which pictures a smiling, conventional-looking white man. Wise speaks to this phenomenon:

> The difference is that it's tough to negatively objectify a group whose power and position allows them to define the meaning of another group's attempts at humor. . . . Perhaps if they had settled on 'slave-owning whiteys,' or 'murdering whiteys,' or 'land-stealing whiteys,' . . . or 'Native-people-butchering whiteys,' or 'mass raping whiteys,' the point would have been made. And instead of a smiling 'company man' logo, perhaps a Klansman, or skinhead as representative of the white race: now that

would have been a nice functional equivalent of the screaming Indian warrior . . . Simply put, what separates white racism from any other form, and what makes anti-black, anti-brown, anti-yellow or anti-red humor more biting and more dangerous than its anti-white equivalent is the ability of the former to become lodged in the minds and perceptions of the citizenry.[12]

Recently, the Fightin' Whites' merchandise has added as an option a new image for their mascot: a "hick" white man. Still, this image will also be less harmful to whites than are caricatures of people of color. There are two reasons that racial symbolism centered on whites is less harmful than that directed toward people of color. First, rarely are whites depicted as negatively as people of color are, and second, because of white cultural power, derogatory symbols of people of color have more potency, endurance and negative consequences.

Like Bridget, but focusing on the ownership of specific words, Stacy argues:

One thing that I don't really understand, but it bothers me is how black people can call each other the n-word, but when a person who is not black does it, they get upset. I remember seeing a fight happen in high school because of this. A white boy called a black kid the n-word, and the black boy was like, "What? What did you call me?," and then a fight broke up. Yet as soon as the fight was over I heard the black people saying things like "Yeah n*#@$, that's the way!" You hear it all the time on CD's and tapes too. To me it seems somewhat hypocritical to call someone that but then get mad if someone says it to you.

Stacey uses "equalizing" language in the last sentence in this passage. It is wrong to call "someone that" and become angry if "someone" calls you the "n-word." Using the word "someone" makes the race of these two "someones" irrelevant— it is a colorblind statement. In the "equal" society envisioned by most respondents, racial language should be acceptable for either everyone or no one. Again, white people cannot understand how the same behavior has different meanings when they as opposed to a person of color do it. Further, without friendships with people of color, and understanding the historical differences between themselves and other groups, white students may misunderstand the messages they receive from cultural artifacts like music, and the language used.

A solid argument has been made that it would serve society well, including African Americans, for everyone to discard ethnic slurs, particularly the word "nigger," given its historical significance, but the fact remains that these expressions have a very different meaning when used by whites versus people of color. Countless times, I have heard black people explain that they may use the word among themselves to strip it of some of its damaging power—to take it *out* of the hands of whites and in a way mock and devalue it. This makes some sense to me; but really it does not need to make sense to *me*. This is a point that is generally lost on my white students. Bruce Jacobs addresses this issue:

There is often a difference between how people refer to themselves and how they expect to be referred to by others. . . . Particularly within historically oppressed groups of Americans, such self-appellation can serve to strengthen a sense of unity, a feeling that some experience is 'just between us'. . . . It is hard to imagine any reasoned justification for blacks to use *nigger*—a word born of racism—in self-reference. . . . I believe that black children should be told of the epithet's wicked history and be taught not to use it. But those (such as I) who disapprove of the word must also beware of our own tendency to stereotype all blacks who use it. . . . To proclaim oneself a nigger is to declare to the disapproving mainstream, 'You can't fire me. I quit.' . . .

At the risk of stating the obvious, I will emphasize here that I have been talking strictly about the use of the word *by blacks*. If you are white, it is much simpler: use of *nigger* is completely off-limits, unless you happen to be one of the few whites so deeply assimilated into black life that it is not an issue. If you have to ask yourself whether using *nigger* is okay, it is not. An African American who cries nigger is playing with fire, but it is his own property—his identity—that he places at risk. A white American who cries nigger is lighting a blaze in someone else's house—and will likely be treated as an arsonist. There are as many ugly synonyms for whiteness as there are for blackness. . . . [but] through the sheer weight of white racism in our society, antiblack epithets carry much more destructive firepower than antiwhite ones.[13]

Part of the impact of white racism is that the meaning of certain language is determined not so much by the dictionary definition, but by history and the identity of the speaker.

People of Color are Living in the Past

I feel that although black people in the past had a hard life, let us just forgive one another and move forward with our lives. I honestly feel that black people can also discriminate against the white race, for instance if a minority and a white person apply for a job and the minority is not chosen, many times a discrimination suit will be filed.

Wanda

This type of statement, calling for people of all racial groups to "forgive one another and move forward," is oft-repeated in the writing of these young whites. While presumably seeking reconciliation, and thus well-intentioned, it is likely to raise the ire of many African Americans, who, because of past and present circumstances, may have a different perspective. Still, we must understand its place in the identity of young whites. Many respondents write that they are held responsible for the behavior of previous generations, and they are too easily accused of racism in the present— judged unfairly as members of a group, and not as individuals. For example, Mike states:

The truth is though that white society can only do so much. Other groups need to give in to the needs of our group too. . . . The best solution to the problem of racism is to think of the long term. Teach antiracist sentiment and encourage the groups to interact more. Social leaders always ask for the quick fix. Affirmative action is an example, while it has bolstered minority accomplishment it has recently caused job fear among whites and that inflames racism. It is important also to remember world history as well as American history. The Romans kept slaves from the Germanic tribes and Egypt, but the Germans and the Egyptians do not ask the Italians to apologize. That would not help the situation. I wish I could wave a magic wand and stop slavery from starting but I cannot. Likewise it is not my fault that it happened nor did I cause segregation. I do not have money to give minorities so that they can leave the inner cities and I cannot send business and industry back to them. I cannot even grant minorities equal justice. What I can do is treat everybody with equal respect personally and professionally. If most people do that, eventually the problem of racism will go away.

Mike's was one of the autobiographies that was particularly reflective. Still, many of these assertions are discursive strategies to release whites from the obligation to support concrete social policy measures to alleviate racial inequity. Specifically, stating that other societies have also had slavery is used in the data as an attempt to release the United States from responsibility for slavery here. The claim is that slavery was a common historical event for which no societies need to direct apologies or remedies in the present. Another discursive strategy used by whites is to deny individual responsibility for oppression, and in doing so to suggest that as individuals, they should not be required to help alleviate the effects of oppression today. Caitlin explains her view of unfair claims made by people of color:

[B]efore I thought that blacks were mistreated. Now I feel that they are not victims of discrimination anymore than you or I are victims of discrimination. . . . I think that some blacks seem to think that white people owe them something because they were enslaved by whites years ago. The thing I don't understand about this is that most of the blacks that are around today were not even around at the time of the slave trades. I am not saying that this is true of all blacks, but the ones that I have encountered . . . let me rephrase that, the ones that I see complaining about discrimination seem to be like that.

I can understand that there are groups out there that do not like blacks, so they would feel this way. But there are also groups out there that do not like whites, and we do not go around saying that we are discriminated against or that we deserve special privileges. For example, if whites went around saying things about black people and demanding organizations that were all white and for the advancement of whites, (i.e. NAACP for blacks) blacks would say that we are discriminating against them by doing so. Another example is the Miss Black USA pageant. Whites are not allowed to participate in this, but blacks must be included in the Miss USA pageant. It is fine for them to do this, but not for us to do so. Also, I feel the same way with affirmative action. Allotting a certain number of jobs for minorities, even if they are less qualified than whites, is discrimination to whites. Minorities seem to think that this is a very good idea and that we owe that much to them. . . . we have to tip toe around races and ethnicities so that we don't step on their toes and discriminate against them.

And it doesn't matter what kind of discrimination it is. We are held accountable for racial discrimination no matter what. If you do not hire a black woman for gender reasons, she will say it is because she is black, not because she is a female. It is discrimination either way, which is wrong, but some choose to play the race card.

As quoted in the last chapter, Caitlin expresses envy toward people of color for the ethnic identity she lacks. Thus, she places herself not as even on an equal footing, but culturally disadvantaged relative to people of color. Thus positioned, respondents perceive African American claims of discrimination as oppressive toward whites. Being accused of having privilege is itself victimization, particularly since people of color have access to culture whites desire. To many whites, African Americans can use the past for present gain in the form of "race cards" that they can "play" whenever they wish to make life easier. They, conversely, must deal with "being just white." To Caitlin and many young whites, racial identity has become a burden.

Other researchers have also found that whites are increasingly feeling victimized. For example, in her research on white teachers, Alice McIntyre found that because whites tend to see racism as existing only in the past, they believe that African Americans have better circumstances than whites in the United States today. Whites thus feel victimized in various ways, for example, by discussions of racism itself.[14]

Some theorists assert that white denial of the influence of the past on the present is part of a deliberate attempt to alleviate guilt or responsibility for the effects of slavery and racism. Others suggest that white people have bought so fully into the ideals of individualism, personal responsibility, and a "future" orientation that they are incapable of linking the present directly to the past.[15] Perhaps for some white people one of these conditions applies, while for others the alternative is more accurate. Perhaps both can be true in various contexts. But the result is the same—many white people, because of their ahistorical worldview, believe that other groups base too many present values and political assertions on the past. Many, like Lena, assert the need for a color-blind system of racial justice. Lena tells a story in which she is accused by a bar patron of racism when she refuses to serve him after hours:

That situation was totally uncalled for, and has made me very angry with the current situations today in this country. I didn't serve the man because it was against the law, not because he was an African-American.

I treat people how I would like to be treated. It is the golden rule. I do not treat people of different ethnic backgrounds, or of different racial identities, any differently. The particular situation in the bar has made me more aware of how I treat people, and I do not think that is fair. I was never cautious of talking with or being friends with people of different ethnic or racial backgrounds, in the past, and I do not want to have to feel like I am being cautious today. I respect every person the same. Since I do not feel that my being racially white has anything to do with who I am today, I do not want to be made to feel that others treat me a certain way because they see me as white.

An interesting point Lena brings up is that others' consciousness of their race, and claims of victimization based on race, have made her conscious of hers. The sudden visibility of her whiteness seems to make Lena uncomfortable. She links this visibility with people's reluctance to understand that "the past is the past." Although Lena states that she does not intend to compare whose ancestors had a more negative experience, in effect she does so. Lena states that

[i]n today's society, the most serious racial problem facing the U.S. is the simple fact that most people are still blaming each other for the problems and damaging past that our ancestors endured. Some people who are descendants of former slaves believe that reparations are owed to them . . . The idea that today's society owes people that have never even experienced these times of slavery, only their family, is ridiculous. Although my ancestors were never slaves, the struggles they were confronted with were probably as devastating. I do not intend to make this a competition of whose ancestors had it worse, but my point is the past is the past. I do not feel people of today's society owe people any kind of apology for something they did not partake in. The way I treat people today, should be the only determination of what kind of person I am. To treat people like human beings should be the civil thing to do, there should be no apologies, just respectful treatment towards everyone.

As discussed in the last chapter, many students discuss European ethnicity to compare white ethnic discrimination with the racism experienced by African Americans and other people of color. Lena brings up the hardships of her ancestors to support her point that African Americans have no more claim to reparations or verbal apology than any other group. Overlooked in this argument is that African Americans were *involuntary* immigrants, making their experience different from whites', particularly through limiting intergenerational transfer of wealth.[16]

Although there is a difference in wealth caused by different historical experience, many young whites, after learning of discrimination faced by European immigrants, use this as a basis to claim equal status as victims of discrimination with African Americans and other people of color and to set whites up as a type of "model minority." If ethnic Europeans could "make it" in the late 1800s and early 1900s, why cannot immigrants of color today?

Victor includes many different elements of white identity as a cultural liability:

> I am white and from a rural town in [a Northeastern state], but that doesn't make me racist or a redneck or a country bunkum, it just makes me a European American that knows a lot given the area that he is from. I feel the so-called 'whiteness' that I possess only when I hear something negative about white Americans. When you have other ethnic groups saying stereotypes of what they think that white people are then that is when I feel that the color of one's skin is more important than the person that is beneath the skin. It is my feeling today that most other racial groups, other than Caucasians, seem to be more racially biased today.

Victor's regional and class identity have been salient in his life, as he somewhat defensively states that he is not an uneducated "redneck" simply because he is from a small town. Victor establishes his whiteness as a victimized racial identity—he possesses it "only when [he hears] something negative about white Americans." Like Victor, Neal sees race, for whites, becoming more important because other groups bring race into issues when it should be irrelevant:

> I like being white. I wouldn't want to be any other color. Not because I don't like these people but because I'm proud to be white. . . . I also hate to be because we get blamed for everything from illiteracy to poverty of minorities.
>
> . . . . Although my racial identity wasn't an important aspect of my personality it is rapidly becoming important to me now. Now I'm older and it does mean more to me because of all things I read and see on TV. I'm interested in politics and race is always brought up. Also things I don't agree with like reparations and affirmative action are very hot topics right now.
>
> Many things over the past few years have really made my race more visible to me. When I hear people like Al Sharpton or Jesse Jackson blaming whites for everything wrong in America that makes me want to take a stand and argue why it isn't our fault. . . .
>
> . . . . I have not only thought about racist whites but also other minority groups who are also racist. Racism is not only practiced by whites but anyone can be racist. I think race and ethnicity is important in society today. It really isn't to me but I think it is to the overall society. It just

seems when something happens race is always brought into it. Just like the man the cops shot in Cincinnati recently. Everyone is saying he was shot because he was black. Why couldn't he have been shot because he is a criminal and the cops felt threatened? I just think the race card is used every chance blacks get.

Both of these young men view white identity as a defensive one, called forth in response to blame. Further, they feel connected to other whites through this sense of victimized whiteness. People of color use "race cards" that whites do not have access to, and in reaction to this, whites feel they must "take a stand" for themselves and other whites.

Separation and Special Treatment

Some passages focus on separation of people of color from whites and special treatment given to people of color. Directly after the passage just quoted, Victor describes what he sees as double standards:

It just seems that some of the things that other races get away with saying a white person would get in trouble. Also the issues of black colleges, making Spanish an official language, or ethnic scholarships are areas that I don't quite understand. Why are there such things as these, but if there were white colleges, just keeping English the one and only official language, or only white scholarships there would be extreme controversy and tension towards the white race. There shouldn't be any restrictions, either only black, only Spanish, or only white, on anything like this in my point of view because I think it causes more harm than good. . . . [Instead of "I am white" or "I am Mexican"] It should be more like 'I am a person' or 'I am American,' because to get along today that is how you have to view life. . . .

Here Victor elaborates on why he believes whites are culturally disadvantaged. They are not able to speak as freely as others, and he believes that other groups have exclusive holidays, colleges and universities, and argue for inclusion of their languages, whereas whites cannot do the same. From this perspective, people of color receive special treatment that whites do not. Victor does not perceive the dominant culture of the United States as a "white" culture, although most major institutions, especially in their leadership, are still predominantly white. Additionally, the culture of the United States is based on an Anglo-Saxon, Judeo-Christian foundation in its holidays, language, and major traditions. Because whiteness is invisible to most whites, they cannot see its ubiquitous presence in the culture. To Victor white culture is not an imposition on others, but quite the opposite. Although he states that all should be proud of their heritage, it seems Victor thinks that ideally, a national, "American" identity would help everyone "get along today." Often when people of color are asked to just be "American," they are being required to assimilate to white culture and relinquish their own.

The issue of separation and special treatment frequently arises in discussions of television stations that are specifically demarcated as "ethnic" in their programming. When white people are not used to seeing people of color on television, even one station focused on African American or Latino issues and programming, or a commercial featuring a family of color, stands out as a dramatic example of other cultures overwhelming white culture, particularly since nothing in the dominant culture is labeled "white"—it does not need to be. Whiteness is so invisible in popular culture that many respondents believe it is inadequately represented. Respondents directly link television stations like BET (Black Entertainment Television) to what they believe are unreasonable demands by African Americans for recompense for slavery. Ray focuses on television, but also on other issues he perceives to be cultural affronts against whites:

> I think racism in the world is becoming more equal. You always hear about white people being racist, but I think it goes both ways. Anytime a white person says something, the response is always that they're racist. More and more today though, I hear black people talking and believe their comments are racist. The other week, a friend of mine down the hall who is black, was talking to my roommate. They got into an argument about race and Jesse Jackson when my friend called him a "spoiled rich cracker." This may have been said jokingly, but I believe if my roommate would have used a racial slur towards my friend it would have been taken much more harshly. Another area which bothers me is music, all of the rappers using the word "nigger" in their music. If so many people are offended by that word including the rappers, then why are they using it to describe themselves. I would hate to see a white person use that word in his lyrics I don't think it would be taken lightly. I know that these are just a couple cases of racism and I know that white people are just as harsh towards black people, but I never hear about cases of black racism towards whites. I also believe that the television station, Black Entertainment Television (BET), is racist. I couldn't imagine having a white entertainment television, I think there would be protests galore. The same goes for colleges . . . , black schools in the south. There aren't such things as white colleges and now today Affirmative Action allows for minorities be accepted to a university while his/her white counterpart has the same or higher credentials. I think these are a few examples of what I believe to be racism towards whites.

Ray maintains that racism operates in the "reverse," both in everyday discourse and in institutions. Focusing on institutions, evidently Ray believes the segregation lingering in the United States is at least as much the fault of people of color as of whites. Specifically, this discussion paints a scenario where whites *who wish to be included* in predominantly minority activities and institutions are barred. There are problems with both of these assumptions. Certainly there are "historically black colleges and universities" (or "HBCUs"), but not only do they not *restrict* white students from admission, many give scholarships to whites to encourage diversity. Additionally, because whiteness is normative, young whites do not see the irony of complaining about the existence of predominantly black institutions. Most colleges and universities are still predominantly white, without even proportional representation of other groups. And historically black colleges were founded because white colleges excluded deserving African American students.[17] Aaron includes black colleges in his frustrations with voluntary separation of racial groups:

> Racism today is still apparent. There are rural areas that are notorious for harboring that animosity towards other races and they often earn the title of white trash, rednecks, or hicks. I guess it is not any better to call someone something as rebuttal for their being racist, but at least they had it coming. There is not one situation that calls for racism and it is never socially acceptable. . . . One of the major problems that I think are road blocking social equality's progress is the fact that the minority groups do not seem to want complete meshing of cultures. People do not have to let go of their traditions; however there will never be a tearing down of walls if we continue to have all black colleges or any other type of segregated groups. To me, this is an example of a lack of effort by a group that should put in their part. It is amazing to me how some things are acceptable for some ethnic groups and not for others. For example, the Black Entertainment Channel has a feature call Black Star Power. Imagine if there was a feature on television called White Star Power, let alone a White Entertainment Channel. I picture a Klan rally when I think of that. Another example of a lack effort to equalize social problems comes with societies, groups, and organizations that exclude all races or ethnicities but their own. There are universities that will only accept African Americans. In my opinion this creates an environment where it is impossible for people to be seen equally. There would never be an all white school today and since that has been abandoned, and rightly so, I believe that all these segregated organizations need to open their doors to all.

Aaron points to rural areas as "notorious" for racism. Although it is perhaps the case that those in rural areas have less contact with people of color, and if they have less education may also be less likely to censor themselves, they are not necessarily "more racist" than other whites. A common belief about white racism is that the working class is primarily responsible for it. However, without acquiescence and participation from those in the middle and upper classes, racism could not continue. It is these who have control over corporations, the media, and the political system that still systematically discriminates against people of color.

Aaron notes some difference in motivation behind using racial slurs—that although they are never appropriate, it is different when they are used "in rebuttal" than preemptively. But his understanding of the defensive use of racial survival strategies by people of color seems to end there. Aaron believes predominantly black universities are such because they "only accept African Americans." The fact is that relatively few white students seek admission there, and that some self-segregation of African Americans and other people of color is in response to years of *exclusion* by whites. Still, without this historical perspective, people only speak of the "racism" they believe they have experienced or can identify with, and many white students, having heard of "black colleges," believe that they are schools exclusively for African Americans. Failing to "see" white culture, they do not perceive that there are schools structured so that their admission is made easier and their attendance comfortable.

Campus Segregation

Some students focus on perceptions of special treatment of people of color in school. For example, Meg writes of a situation she encountered in high school:

> There was another black girl at school named Janine Scott. I don't think people viewed her as really black. . . . She was class President for three of those years, so I kind of looked up to her and tried to follow in her footsteps. It seemed that everyone in her class loved her. To me, it seemed like they loved her too much. I always wondered how she could be so well liked. It always seemed unfair, I was a year younger, but I thought that I was a better President than her for my class. Whenever I asked her a question, or tried to talk to her about something she had done my year, she always seemed disorganized. The icing on the cake however, was that she won both Prom Princess her junior year and then Prom Queen her senior year. I guess I was really jealous of her, being a class president also, I just didn't feel like my entire class loved me like her class loved her. So in the end, I always resolved the issue as, well, she is black, so I think her fellow classmates feel like they should be extra nice to her because of her race and because she is a 'good black person.'

Meg is apparently not in direct competition with Janine for president of her class, but she still feels threatened by Janine's success. She is able to resolve her jealousy by assuming that Janine has been successful only because she was given special treatment according to her race. Meg adds evidence that Janine does not deserve others' respect—"she always seemed disorganized."

Several are concerned specifically with campus segregation, seen primarily as the choice of African-American and other students of color. In his research on white students, Charles Gallagher also found the issue of separation on campus, particularly in race-based organizations, to elicit feelings of victimization in whites.[18] Molly writes: "While I found college to be a lesson and experience in diversity, others found it to intensify racial tensions. At college, individuals seemed to be more segregated along racial lines (by choice of course). . . . African Americans usually have their own sororities and fraternities and don't usually encourage other ethnicities to join. The sorority I joined consisted of no African Americans." Like most who write about separation on campus, Molly believes it equally the choice of whites and students of color. Another student, Julia, writes about segregation in the Greek system:

> Last fall I . . . came to discover how segregated this university was. Our rush was completely separated from the other rushes. . . . There are the African chapters, the Asian chapters, and there is the overwhelming number of white chapters. I never thought that people of other races would be hesitant to rush, but I guess they are the product of de facto segregation. By choice they choose to segregate themselves. I noticed many things about this university besides the segregated rush; white students run this school. The majority of the students in government are white. I know that no one tells people of different ethnicities and race that they are not allowed to run for positions; they choose [not] to on their own. It truly sickens me that people sit and complain, but yet they are not doing anything to change it. . . . It truly frustrates [me] that people cry wolf with discrimination, when the truth is they do it to themselves.

When reading this passage, one might initially expect that Julia will go on to discuss the role of white racism in keeping the Greek system and student government segregated. However, then she invokes, and misuses, the term "de facto segregation" to blame *people of color* for the separation of Greek systems. Julia goes on to note that "white students run this school." This circumstance, also, she blames on students of color. Since they are not overtly prohibited from participation, she cannot understand their lack of involvement. In the meritocratic campus situation she experiences, people of color are free to choose how and when to participate in campus activities. Within this view, enduring the "complaints" of people of color becomes one of the liabilities that whites are forced to tolerate based on their race. When Julia sees that students of color are not participating, she perceives them as troublemakers who "sit and complain" but take no action to change things. She also assumes that this segregation is what minorities are "complaining" about, when in fact their protest may be more focused on the lack of power that minority groups have on campus.

A young Northeastern woman, whose autobiography was titled "Small Town Girl," writes about college:

> The blacks here segregate themselves, as well as the Asians—the ones I have experienced at least. There's a "Black Student Union" and Black Entertainment Television—neither of which I have ever heard of until I came to college. Things like that really frustrate me because we don't have white groups like that, or Asian groups like that. It's like they automatically feel oppressed, and feel they need to segregate themselves, and especially make it known to everyone else. I haven't had too many

good experiences with African Americans in college so far. . . . But anyway, I've actually tried hard to understand blacks here and give them an over-equal chance than I would when meeting a white person for the first time, but they have all been the same so far. I'm hoping this will change when I move to [the nearby college town]—a bigger, more diverse environment [where a larger campus is located].

All in all, race used to not mean a lot to me, until, from my experiences, Blacks made it a "problem" or a "difference" in college. It never really had an impact on my life before college. And I could definitely tell my life story without including race because it means so little to me. . . . the other way it would, would be in my career with 'equal rights' and employment areas. But other than that, I don't see it affecting me. . . . And life, life is a challenge for me, and I want to conquer it.

Angie reports that she is going out of her way to accommodate the African American students she meets. Yet, in their assertions of ethnicity, she perceives that they "automatically feel oppressed" and further, seems to feel that their hostility regarding this oppression is aimed at all white people, including her. Her discomfort is centered around her perception that "they need to segregate themselves." The conclusion is that racism is a problem stemming from the actions not of whites, but people of color, in their insistence on bringing attention to lingering inequality, and taking steps to retain their culture. Maintenance of culture is itself constructed as an aggressive or threatening act. One woman in the South, Stacey, writes:

> Another thing that makes me frustrated with black people is how a lot of times they say they are being discriminated against. I know that there are many instances where they are victims of discrimination, but a lot of times I feel that they go overboard. One thing that really upsets me is Black History Month. I understand how it is important to learn about different cultures and all, but if there was ever a White History Month, I think that they would say it's discrimination. Many times I feel that black people bring on the way they are treated themselves. Take my schools for instance. . . . the black people all hung out together all of the time. In the cafeterias there was always a section for the black people. And at the sporting events and pep rallies, the black people always sat together. . . . I'm not trying to say that when black people are discriminated against it is their fault, but situations like these make me tend to feel that they are not as much a victim as they make it seem.

Stacey is not only angered by what African Americans *do*, but even more by what they *say*, the claims they make about discrimination. Further, although she espouses multiculturalism (it is "important to learn about different cultures") she does not understand why Black History Month is acceptable while White History Month would be considered racist. Some whites do not recognize that

"White History Month" is unnecessary because "American History" is usually taught as primarily "white history."[19]

Stacey presents a point repeated in the autobiographies: that separation according to race in school is done by everyone, and although not desirable, it is "natural" and no one's "fault." She suggests that since African Americans segregate *themselves*, they inspire racist treatment, only to complain of being "victims" later. Stacey's assumption is that they, in segregating themselves, are cutting off contact with white students who otherwise would not separate from African Americans. Studies show whites and people of color view and participate in campus segregation very differently. For example, a mid-1990s University of Michigan study reveals that students of color are much more likely than whites to dine and socialize across racial lines.[20]

Even were it true that students of color self-segregate more than whites, as Beverly Daniel Tatum argues in *Why are All the Black Kids Sitting Together in the Cafeteria?*, school cafeteria self-segregation is a good example of how past inequities can impart different meaning to behavior practiced by a minority group member compared to the same behavior on the part of a white person. Tatum states that high school students are just beginning to resolve their self-identity. For people of color, this includes coming to terms with their ethnic identity's meaning in society. White adolescents, not constantly reminded of their race, construct a self-identity based on other statuses. Thus, while young people of color may need to associate with others of their own ethnic group to learn what it means to be a member of that group, white students do not feel this need, unless raised in white supremacist families. Additionally, students of color may need support from those understanding their perspective when first learning to decide how to deal with potentially discriminatory treatment.[21]

A recent study explored the discourses college students use to explain campus racial segregation.[22] This study found that students of all racial groups sometimes explain that campus segregation is normative and due to cultural differences between whites and people of color. Additionally, some use accounts of campus segregation that show ambivalence and conflict. For example, they state that while this segregation is indeed problematic, and they would like more interracial contact, the separation is understandable, and they are unsure of how to achieve more significant interaction. Finally, the study found that African-American students were likely to explain campus racial segregation based on a need for a sense of social identity, even when this need led them to feel a dilemma, based on their conflicting desire for more meaningful contact with whites.

Other researchers have discussed the differences in students of color and whites' reasons for voluntary segregation. Paul Kivel explains:

[Y]ou might discover that most of the social groupings had to do with shared interests, experiences, and concerns. . . . We probably would not question the white students' sitting together in a similar manner.

Since so many public spaces in our society are white in tone, structure, and atmosphere, people of different ethnic groups need space to enjoy their own cultural uniqueness, strengths, and styles. They are not necessarily rejecting individual white people, or plotting revenge or revolution. . . . People of color are still routinely and persistently denied access to much public and most private space in this country. There is tremendous and undeniable segregation in housing, schools, jobs, and recreational facilities. . . . We segregate communities of color and rarely notice or challenge it. But when a group voluntarily congregates, we oppose its right to do so.[23]

Students of color may be focused on seeking unity and support in a predominantly white environment, while white students may feel awkward or fearful of interactions with people of color. Still a common complaint of the respondents is that if people of color want things to be "equal," why do they seem to set themselves apart by self-segregating, and asking for "special" treatment? Such an argument overlooks that equality of treatment does not require that groups are the *same*, or indistinguishable. Molly writes:

Growing up there were not many minority students at my school. Since there were few minorities, the minority students easily assimilated to the white society. I treated them as equals and felt that they were equals. After coming to college, I have seen that because there are more minorities they chose to not assimilate as fully as they did when I was growing up. They tend to have more friends of their own race and don't feel the need to become like the white students . . . In witnessing this I have realized that although I think people are equal, they are very different. . . . Here at college, African American students have certain organizations and functions that are solely for them. . . . Although these activities help to unite them, they also separate them from the rest of the students.

In Molly's school, students of color assimilated with white students because they were too few to form ethnic subcultures within the larger white majority. Thus, when Molly enters college, she is surprised to find clearly distinguishable subcultures. The existence of these separate groups has shown Molly there are ethnic differences, particularly between African Americans and whites; probably based on shared interests, as Kivel points out. However, Molly's final statement contains a degree of disapproval that these shared interests, although "unit[ing]" African Americans intraethnically, separate them interracially. Greg also writes about campus separation:

Does it really make a difference what race or color you are? Or what ethnicity you choose to be a part of and recognize?. . . . We are all the same people in the end. We have all the same vital organs and all the same tissue. We must begin to look past what race or color we are and look deeper into which we really are, within. . . . I recently attended a play on campus directed by one of the [theater] teachers. . . . , while watching this play it came to my attention that all of the actors and actresses were all African Americans, with only three White European Americans. This disturbs me because the. . . . teacher that was directing the play was African American. I see this as being discriminatory towards White European Americans.

. . . . I noticed that there is a Step dance team that is also on campus. The Step team also competes in competitions and they do talent shows and other events, but it is all African Americans on this dance team. I feel that no matter how you look at our [extra]curricular activities and clubs that are provided for the students on this campus it is always that the White European Americans and African Americans are always with their "own kind."

. . . [T]he B.S.U. (Black Student Union), this is a club that is provided on campus for the African Americans to get together and discuss situations that occur on campus and plan social activities and events for African Americans. I was disturbed to hear that they plan these events gearing them towards African Americans. . . . We as White European Americans have many different organizations that aren't just for us and groups that are on campus.

Greg begins with a colorblind assertion of equality and acceptance, which is then used as a foundation for his claim that whites are treated unfairly. He describes various scenarios that he perceives as exclusionary on the part of African Americans and threatening to interracial goodwill. I attended the same play to which Greg refers, three times. The theater instructor was actually a Brazilian woman. The cast was predominantly composed of students of color, African American and Latino, but at least one-fourth of the cast was white. This is exemplifies how, when whites see themselves as being in the minority, this perception may become exaggerated in memory.

Greg's perception of exclusion on campus may be magnified by an overlap and confusion of the concepts of "race" and "ethnicity."[24] Robert Blauner explains that when African Americans identify and organize ethnically, whites may see them as "'being racial,'" and for most whites, color consciousness is equated with racism. Thus, whites believe people of color are practicing "reverse racism" unless they are being "color-blind."[25] Whites then may believe they are justified in organizing racially as well—having a "white student union" in response to a black student union. Blauner argues that while such a group would be inappropriate and indeed racist, if whites organized *ethnically*, forming various groups such as an "Irish American" or "Italian American" club, given they were not simply covers for white supremacy, these could be legitimate, and even positive outlets for white identification.[26] Blauner argues the misunderstanding over ethnic and racial organizing on campuses contributes to whites and blacks "talking past each other" on issues of race.

Pamela Perry's empirical research in high schools suggests that it can be problematic to have "multicultural" programs and clubs focused on all groups except European or "white" cultures, because whiteness can become even more ensconced as the norm, and the "Other's" cultures even more "exotic" to white students.[27] Recognition of European ethnic groups as part of multiculturalism could help to dislodge whiteness as the cultural norm. However, other theorists have pointed out that sometimes ostensibly "ethnic" interest clubs for European students at high schools and colleges are actually a cover for racially based organizations.[28] Also, in some cases white students have used ethnic claims to go beyond establishing clubs to initiate academic units to study white European groups, such as at Queens College in New York City, where white students succeeded in establishing "Italian American studies."[29] Obviously, allocating funds to such subdisciplines diverts much-needed funding from the consideration of understudied people of color and flies in the face of the express purpose of establishing these types of academic units.

Invasion of "Our" Cultural and Physical Space

Finally, some respondents' identification as whites seemed based on a sense of whiteness imperiled by invasion by Others' "culture," in the growing numbers of nonwhite people themselves, or from insertion of the languages and traditions of those people into the mainstream. They assume that dominant white culture, usually substantively indescribable, is being overwhelmed by the cultures of people of color.

Recent studies show that whites tend to overestimate the proportion of people of color in the population. For example, a national study in the 1990s showed that white respondents estimated the African-American population at 24 percent, and the Asian and Latino proportion to be about 26 percent of the country. At the time these numbers were about double the actual percentages.[30] Researchers have found that one reason whites tend to overestimate the number of minorities in the population is that they believe people of color are "too vocal" about civil rights issues.[31] Other studies suggest that although immigrants have always been part of the United States, they are resented more today. This is because well-paying jobs are scarcer than they were at other times of peak immigration, such as during industrialization, and more importantly because the largest numbers of immigrants today are nonwhite (either Asian or Latino).[32] In the following sections, I will show how concerns about language and immigrants themselves overwhelming white culture are part of the view of whiteness as cultural victimization.

Language Concerns

Several students cited concerns about the imposition of "foreign" languages. Roger, in his autobiography, writes:

> I am not a racist by nature, but I found myself becoming upset with another minority in [a college] class. The professor was a . . . woman that had been teaching at the campus for quite a number of years. She was well respected by her peers and some students. However, I found myself starting to hate going to her class and listening to her speak. Her speech had a very thick accent and I could not decipher what she was actually saying. . . . This placed me in a position where prejudiced attitudes could develop. A small group of us in the class would laugh and make fun of her when she spoke. I do not believe that we were being prejudiced towards her, as much as we were rebelling against her way of teaching. If we were going to place this in terms of discrimination, one could draw parallels to the way slaves might have acted towards their owners. The owner being the professor was in a state of power over her slaves being we. We feared receiving a low grade therefore we submitted to her will. I understand that getting a bad grade in a class is small to losing your life, however, whites could draw parallels easier to this than they could to being a slave.

Because the professor is in a position of power, Roger imagines a metaphorical master-slave relationship. On some level, he is aware that this is a dubious comparison, "getting a bad grade in a class is small to losing your life," yet still draws the parallel. Roger is correct, however, in stating that whites find it hard to relate to the type of oppression African Americans have experienced, symbolized in slavery.

Often, primarily at the Northeastern university, students have complained to me about the accents of "foreign" professors. They appear frustrated by extra effort required to get used to the accent of some professors, despite exceptional abilities a professor may possess. Courtney, who writes in an otherwise nonracist tone through much of her autobiography, states: "I do have one confession about my college professors. I have always tried to pick a professor with an American name if possible. I did this simply because I was afraid of having trouble understanding a teacher if they had an accent." Often, I remind students of the irony of these complaints in the United States, where most are still monolingual, while most of the rest of the world is multilingual.[33] One student, Gilbert, wrote about his fellow students' lack of patience with professors' accents:

> When you attend college you are supposed to be more mature and open to new experiences. . . . One example of prejudice that I do remember was in a . . . class during my second semester of school. The professor was of [a non-European ethnic] background and she had a very strong accent. I remember students in the class mocking the way she spoke and making comments like, 'how can you teach us when you can't even speak English?' Some students even blamed their poor performance in

the class on the fact that the instructor did not speak clearly. They felt it was her responsibility to make sure that we understood what she said, not ours to ask questions if something was unclear.

Gilbert's perspective is a unique one in the autobiographies and in student comments I have heard on campuses.

Wanda's issue with language is a more general one:

I never thought of myself as a biased or prejudiced person until I went to California last year. . . . I felt like a minority, not because of skin color, it was because of all the different dialects spoken. . . . My family and I went on a tour of the Hearst Castle and there was several tour guides with different groups separated by the language that was spoken. This is the first time that I was really upset of other languages used other than English. For the first time in my life I found myself being prejudiced towards people in the United States that do not speak English. I now really hope that English will be the only official language ever to be used in the United States. I do feel that if an immigrant wants to work in the United States, they must speak English. I feel everyone has some degree of prejudicial beliefs, mine deals with the English language. . . . I must say at this time in my life I am not ashamed of my beliefs, maybe someday I will change my mind, but for now I only want English language used. I do enjoy hearing other languages being spoken and I do feel everyone should take a course in another language in high school, but in order for everyone to understand one another fully, I do feel anyone who wishes to work in the United States should be required to use the English language.

Wanda experiences culture shock on a trip to California, when clearly confronted with ethnic differences for the first time. She does discuss in more favorable terms certain commercialized aspects of Asian culture that she encounters, but expresses annoyance when she feels that the more authentic aspects of others' ethnicity, their languages, impose themselves into her everyday experiences. Ethnic culture is palatable to members of the dominant culture when they can decide when and how to incorporate it or consume it. When new cultures and peoples insert themselves into the dominant culture, sometimes they are not as welcome.

Wanda believes everyone has at least one area of prejudice, and she is willing to allow herself this one. When whites insist that people wanting to work in the United States should have to speak English, they demonstrate unfamiliarity with the dynamics of the labor market for new immigrants. Any new immigrant quickly learns that to succeed in the United States, she or he must learn English. Otherwise, that person will be forever relegated to the lowest-paying jobs and subject to exploitation by employers. Monolingual immigrants tend to be the newest entrants, young children, and the elderly. Echoing Wanda, Meg writes:

> Earlier this month, my parents drove down for my 21st birthday. . . . We spent an entire day in [an amusement park]. It was a lot of fun, but extremely annoying and frustrating. Besides for my parents, me and some of the employees there, I think everyone else was from another country. NO ONE spoke English. I have never been so annoyed. Where did these people come from? There must have been ten different ethnicities or languages, or whatever walking around that day. Makes you wonder what the face of America will look like in the next five to ten years. I think overall, I am definitely very ethnocentric in that I think that my culture and my ways are the best. But I think through the years I have become much more aware and have learned a lot. I think I started at just plain ignorance and now I'm much more accepting. . . . I think throughout my life I have surrounded myself with the same kind of people. College made a huge difference, because it forced me to be exposed to other ways of life and kinds of people. I think people in general surround themselves with people most like them. I don't think I'm by myself in that. It's a comfort thing and I think people will always do that.

A common theme emphasized in many universities is diversity and multiculturalism. However, clearly some students experience "diversity" not as a positive addition to their lives, but an "annoyance." The "ten different ethnicities" Meg encounters on her outing do not enhance that experience, but interfere with it. Further, she does not find it shameful to admit she is ethnocentric; but feels justified by the observation "people . . . surround themselves with people most like them." Again, white students observe others associating by common ethnicity and believe similar separation by whites is also legitimate and natural.

Concerns About Immigrants

Some white people are concerned not only about the languages immigrants bring with them, but about immigrants themselves. Keith writes:

> For many people the United States is still considered the land of opportunity. What makes us the land of opportunity is that we have the reputation to make somebody out of anybody. People flee to the United States everyday for a new start, a start in which they are free from persecution on behalf of racial identity, cultural beliefs, political beliefs, and religious beliefs. My personal beliefs are that we do not have the resources to accommodate everyone. As we are realizing, it is difficult to maintain a nation under such diverse humanity. I think that the United States' capabilities to inhabit such a racial and ethnic diversity have been

all but exhausted. Our racial barriers are pushed to their limits everyday. I cannot agree with the United States being [inhabited by] every racial and ethnic group of the world; that is a difficult assignment.

I honestly believe that the white male is becoming the minority figure in the United States if not in numbers, in treatment. I believe that affirmative action is the best example of what is happening in the United States. We are giving jobs to minority individuals that are less qualified than white workers. I do not consider equal rights to mean giving out freebees to minorities.

Keith communicates discomfort with the growing diversity in the United States. It is not just the growing *numbers* of people here that concern him, but that he believes the United States has exhausted its ability to absorb people of so many *different groups*. Keith presents something antiracists might find as positive, that immigration is pushing 'racial barriers,' as a negative process about which whites should be concerned. Clearly, Keith constructs the incorporation of these new Americans as signaling a loss in status for white males.

Several students contend that the immigrants need to change to accommodate whites, and not the reverse. Dane writes: "It is not fair to say that new immigrants should totally abandon their past, but on the other hand they need to realize that America needs to have a common thread." Josh's comment is even stronger:

I will need to become more aware of the different ethnicities that are migrating our way in order to get along in the new environment. I do not feel that I will be the one that will have to make significant changes, I do, however, believe the people that are coming to the United States will need to assimilate with the white-American people in order for them to get along in the future. Like it is said, whites control the United States and therefore you must try to act as white as you possibly can.

Josh engaged in antiracist action at work; a rare event in the autobiographies. He notes that racial change will come through demographic shifts, but he states bluntly that it will be unnecessary for him to change—people of color will have to assimilate and "act as white as they possibly can." Again, it is impossible to categorize individual white people as "racist" or "antiracist"; rather, twenty-first century whiteness is a collective and complex phenomenon. Elsewhere, Josh recognizes white privilege and even structural racist disadvantage, but here he seems to accept the racial status quo requiring one-way assimilation for nonwhites.

Randy writes the following, showing admiration of high school peers who assimilated:

It was difficult to become friend with the Latinos as they did not speak English, showed no real sign of American culture and for the most part wanted nothing to do with you. Asians in my school were split in half. Those who as we used to say were Americanized and spoke good English fit in well with the white students and generally had no problems. Though they often bonded together, there was still a large amount of white to Asian contact. I remember in seventh grade I had an art class with an Asian friend of mine named Ho Pak. He had been in the country four years and spoke good English. In that same class there was a new student who as we described him was Fresh Off the Boat or FOB. His name was Chan Soh. He would carry his English-Korean dictionary with him everywhere he went. I would help him as best as I could and so would Ho. I was amazed to see how well he progressed over the years. By the time he was a sophomore in high school you could hardly tell he had not grown up his whole life in the States. He basically changed his name to Vince and as we said became Americanized. He graduated from high school with me on time and was one of the seven valedictorians we had. . . .

'Vince' signed my senior yearbook and in it he wrote: 'Yo Randy, I've known you ever since I came over here when I was carrying my freaking English-Korean dictionary and had to look up every single . . . word there is in the world. Thanks for being there for me. . . . I only wish I could have spoken better English then so we could have had more fun. Good luck at [college] and my F.O.B ass is getting back on the boat . . . and going back to Korea. . . . I found this to be quite interesting and cherish it to this day.

For any immigrant, some assimilation must take place in order to succeed in a new society. Certainly Randy's friend's assimilation had some very positive outcomes for him—for example, he is a class valedictorian, which may open up opportunities for him. However, for Randy, "progress" for Chan Soh is assessed in that one "could hardly tell he had not grown up his whole life in the States." He had managed to put aside any trappings of his Asian culture in order to appear "Americanized," even to the point of taking an American name, "Vince." Chan Soh does return to Korea, so his "Americanization" may have been a mechanism for surviving the U.S. high school experience, arguably difficult for any adolescent.

Shawn believes that African Americans, particularly, are encroaching on the social space of whites. He is not primarily concerned with numbers but with values and culture:

Being white for me has primarily good benefits. . . . Some of the good things that I was able to think of was that the whites have a larger population and are able to have cultural power in relation to other races and that makes it nice for me. The reason I say this is because many white people having their own culture don't try to push anything white onto the black people or other minority communities. What I mean by this is that the whites have many different beliefs and customs and we really don't push the black community to learn about them or to even participate in them.

On the other hand, there are those in the black community who push a lot of their beliefs onto the whites. When some black guy dies with some importance we are to feel horrible and mourn for this person when we have no idea who he is or what he did. If we don't show remorse then we are looked as inconsiderate bastards who only care about our race and no other.

Unlike some others, Shawn acknowledges that white people have "cultural power in relation to other races," and that they "[have] their own culture" and share "many different beliefs and customs." He recognizes a shared white racial identity. However, as many other respondents, he does not see how as a person of color, living in a society where whites do have this cultural power, could feel as though "[something] white" was being "push[ed] onto the black people or other minority communities." Thus Shawn views the introduction of commemoration of black leaders and other African-American cultural markers as having the values of the "black community . . . push[ed] . . . onto the whites." Many whites view the historical and cultural contributions of people of color as an imposition.

Conclusion

A common element among white complaints of cultural victimization is what respondents construct as "double standards," but might more aptly be called "false parallels."[34] The sociologist Michael Schwalbe, who has studied men's movements, suggests that one draws a false parallel when equating the experiences of a less powerful group with those of a more powerful group to suggest that their reactions or behaviors in a given situation can be judged according to the same standards:[35]

Part of being sociologically mindful is taking history and context into account. . . . [I]n the United States blacks have never had the power to oppress or exploit whites; nor have whites had to suffer daily indignities at the hands of a black majority. . . . So if blacks, who are still a relatively powerless minority in the United States, disparage whites and try to maintain solidarity among themselves, this is not racism but *resistance* to racism. To say that blacks who are unfriendly to whites or who tell racist jokes about whites are 'just as racist' as whites who do the same things to blacks is a false parallel. It is false because it ignores the historical responsibility for racism; it ignores the huge differences in power between blacks and whites; and it ignores the different consequences that arise, depending on who is disparaging whom. Anyone can exhibit prejudice if they embrace stereotypes about members of another group. . . . But since blacks as a group do not have the power to discriminate against whites, any prejudice harbored by blacks is of little consequence. . . . Being sociologically mindful, we can see that doing racism requires not only prejudice but also the *power* to *discriminate* in ways that hurt others.[36]

Most claims that whites are victimized *as whites* rely on false parallels, as they ignore the power differences between whites and people of color at the group level. Schwalbe and others argue that while people of color can be prejudiced, just as whites can, they are not socially positioned as a group to be racist; in other words, to use power to put prejudiced attitudes to destructive use.

In these data, sometimes these false parallels rely on the old "golden rule" adage, as in the case of Lena, quoted previously in the chapter. Another example of the invocation of the golden rule to equalize the experiences of whites and people of color is this statement by Lauren:

> My parents have influenced the way I think about other people and other races. As I have mentioned before I was raised to treat all other people the way that I would treat myself. A lot of things have influenced the way I feel about other people. One thing that influenced the way that I feel about other people is thinking how I would feel if someone treated me that way. I do not really think about my race and ethnicity or anyone else's. I think the reason that I do not think about my race or ethnicity is because it was never something that was talked about when I was growing up. I guess probably because I have a wide background and not just one heritage. Since I do not think of my own background I do not think of anyone else's background either.

Similarly, Bridget asserts: "I just always try to keep in mind to treat people the way that I would want them to treat me. I think that is in the Bible somewhere. I will show someone as much respect as they show me." Numerous students repeat this "golden rule" ideology of "good" race relations. Although certainly the attempt to treat others as one would wish to be treated may improve interracial interactions, in understanding structural racial dynamics the "golden rule" approach can be problematic. The way that a white person wishes to be treated, or even *needs* to be treated, based on her or his experiences and membership in a racial group that is privileged, may be very different from the way a person of color wants to be or should be treated. To equate the two is almost inevitably to draw a false parallel. Indeed, Mary Waters points out the dangers in whites' lack of recognition of the asymmetries between their experiences and those of people of color. This oversight makes it harder for them to understand continuing inequality as caused by anything other than poor individual choices, and makes them unlikely to support policies that may alleviate this inequality, such as affirmative action.[37]

It is also difficult for white students to see that whites collectively hold more societal power than people of color, particularly when many, because of gender, class, or age, do not feel they individually are powerful. In my race and ethnicity courses, we discuss the terms "prejudice" and "racism" and why it is argued, as Schwalbe does, that people of color can be prejudiced, but not "racist," at least not in the same terms or scale that whites can. Beverly Daniel Tatum addresses this in her essay "Defining Racism: 'Can We Talk?'":

> [W]hen I am asked 'Can people of color be racist?' I reply, 'The answer depends on your definition of racism.' If one defines racism as racial prejudice, the answer is yes. People of color can and do have racial prejudices. However, if one defines racism as a system of advantage based on race, the answer is no. People of color are not racist because they do not systematically benefit from racism. And equally important, there is no systematic cultural and institutional support or sanction for the racial bigotry of people of color.[38]

This is the concept white students have perhaps the most difficulty grasping. I speculate this is in part because students struggle with thinking in sociological and structural rather than personal and individual terms, but I believe it is also because they often hear this statement as "*all* whites are racist" or "whites are morally worse people than people of color."

As I have learned to spend more time explaining these ideas, students understand better *why* theorists argue that only whites can be racist, but many still disagree. Some say that because now people of color are, in certain situations, in positions of power, they can in those contexts practice racism. Obviously, this does not negate the argument that on a group level people of color are not in a position to practice institutional racism. Others say that changing demographics ultimately will endow people of color with group power—but this does not contradict the fact that whites now dominate social, political, and economic institutions. Still others simply offer disagreement, without explanation. These are likely the most reluctant to recognize whites as in the position of having primary moral responsibility for solving racial inequities. Many of the arguments that arise in students' autobiographies include examples of "false parallels."

In her essay on white supremacy, Abby Ferber asserts that "Whiteness historically has equaled power, and when that equation is threatened, their own whiteness becomes visible to many white people for the first time."[39] One of the most salient elements of white identity for these young writers is the notion that whiteness today brings with it no cultural heritage, only cultural stigmatization. Respondents describe feeling culturally embattled, always having to "be careful" for fear that saying the wrong thing will damage them socially or economically. Worse yet, in their estimation, whites lack the sense of shared interests that other groups have, and thus, whites are not presenting a united front as a racial group. They describe a cultural landscape in which people of color misunderstand whites and accuse them of racism, when most are innocent of all but a tangential connection to "the past." Finally, many explain that they increasingly live in a world where they feel like cultural outsiders. Bobby sums up the feelings of many of the students regarding cultural stigmatization:

White people may not have the same amount or have the same degree of discrimination as other races, but that does not mean it does not exist. My race does not stick together or help each other out as much as other races do. There are no white scholarship funds, no white entertainment television stations, no national association for the advancement of white people, and there is no blaming problems or crimes on racism. I feel that if there were to be any of these things that the creator would then be sued for racism. It is something that white people are at a disadvantage in. . . . After learning that other races are discriminated against in getting jobs and are often paid less than whites, I was glad that I would not have to face that discrimination. However, I feel that whites often face discrimination as well.

. . . . At times I get angry about certain things about other groups. . . . It almost seems that if a mistake happens, then they can always blame it on racism and get what they want. . . . Presently, people are not listening to enough white people on their ideas of racism. If someone wants to find out problems dealing with racism, they will most likely go to a minority group. People do not listen to what white people have to say about racism today, and many white people are afraid to speak out about it because they feel that they will then be labeled a racist.

A racial scenario is constructed in these autobiographies in which Others have special access to "correct," socially approved discourses of race, to special privileges or "race cards," and to separate facilities. Most importantly, respondents believe that Others are afforded more cultural legitimacy to speak about race and be listened to.

Chapter 5
"I Was the Loser in this Rat Race":
Whiteness as Economic Disadvantage

Today society is based on superficial things, the way we look, what is our race, etc. Why do we run things this way? Why are all surveys, aptitude tests, and loan applications gender- and race-based? I mean why do they ask what "ethnic background" you are. Why do we get classified and categorized into groups based on the characteristics? What does it mean to the evaluator if "white Joe" scored 1290 on the SAT and "black Joe" scored 1300. What does that added-in statistical information tell him? Are we not both humans with brains?. . . . Should I give the unqualified black man the job to increase diversity, or should I hand it over to the more qualified white man. Should preferences be given to people because they are a certain color?

A male respondent

Black is beautiful, tan is grand, but white is the color of the big boss man.

From a slogan told to a respondent by her father

In February 2004, College Republicans at Roger Williams University in Rhode Island set up a scholarship for whites only. They took this action to protest scholarships for students of color. Like many white college students, they believed that such awards unfairly disadvantage whites.[1] Aside from the liability they believe whiteness represents culturally (discussed in the previous chapter), white students in my research most often discussed their white identity as an economic disadvantage. Most think this disadvantage is epitomized in affirmative action policies. Other research of young whites has shown that the issue of disadvantages of whiteness arises when affirmative action is the topic of discussion.[2] Some believe they have already been victims of reverse racism in college admissions. Others tell of family members who they believe lost their jobs to "less qualified" people of color. Many are convinced that their future success will likely be hindered by affirmative action. These concerns emerge in some of the strongest autobiographical passages. The forcefulness of these statements should be judged in light of the fact that fundamental ideologies of whiteness deny both the suggestion that whiteness brings economic privilege, and the policies used to remedy this inequality.

In this chapter, I will show how young whites construct whiteness as an economic disadvantage by (1) offering personal stories of disadvantages or fears of future victimization; (2) arguing that affirmative action is reverse discrimination and causes racial divisiveness; (3) casting affirmative action as fundamentally unreasonable, unfair, and illogical; and (4) asserting that the economic "playing field" is a level one in a colorblind and meritocratic society. I will present the respondents' arguments and place them in the context of counterarguments based on the available data surrounding the issue of affirmative action and the economics of race.

Stories and Fears of Victimization

Several participants include discussions of incidents in which whites already believe they have been treated unfairly according to their race, in ways that could affect their economic status in the present or the future. The message is indeed so widespread and so persistent that one respondent describes it this way:

> Due to being brought up in my community, a person tends to hear expressions that are reflective of the understandings of race of those who live in that community. It is always those few who have the wrong attitudes towards race, who falsely accuse people due to their skin color that you hear talking the loudest. I always felt as though it was natural to listen to the person who talks the most. For example: A mother bird feeds the chick that squawks the loudest, the rest just watch and wait, I fail to see how we are different when racial issues are discussed in my community. If a person is ranting and raving about how blacks are picked for employment due to affirmative action over a white guy, everybody in the community loves to listen. They assume the white guy was better qualified for the job. I try not to listen when I hear it, but sometimes when you walk by a running car and hear a song on the radio it gets stuck in your head. Just like the issue that is being discussed about race, you may not like the song at all but it still gets stuck in there.

Charles knows that in his blue-collar town the primary race-related topic is affirmative action and the prevailing theme is that unqualified black people are taking jobs from qualified whites. It is difficult for young white people to conceive of their whiteness as a privilege when it is consistently presented to them in everyday and political discourse as a liability. Almost daily, radio and television talk shows broadcast what purports to be intellectual analysis of the "economics" of race relations. Based on solid-sounding economics and color-blind ideology, many are convinced that white people, particularly white men, are now being discriminated against in the U.S. workplace. Politicians can capitalize on whites' sense of threat while still sounding "fair" and racially tolerant, because they can base the desire to end affirmative action on an ostensible desire for a colorblind society.

This mantra of economic victimization is seeping from the explicitly "political" realm into more accessible popular discourse. Politically slanted talk shows offer analyses of issues like affirmative action that often are very simplistic and go little beyond hyperbole and name-calling. In this context, it is no surprise, then, that these young people look for evidence of unfair treatment in their own lives and those of their family and friends. Especially when they are exposed to information in class discussions that could invoke guilt based on the discrimination that whites have brought to other groups, a very human reaction is to search for an equivalent personal experience that would counter the allegations of unfair advantage. This is the type of rhetorical move respondents employ in claiming that they have been economically victimized as whites. For example, several feel that whiteness has caused them or other whites to be disadvantaged when applying to college. Kim relates a friend's experience:

Clairecia [an African American friend] always got good grades and was very smart. When it came around time to apply to college, she applied for fall admission at the [state university]. My best friend also applied at [that university], but she applied summer because it is supposedly easier to get accepted. Clairecia had about a 3.7 GPA and something around a 1080 on her SAT's. She got accepted to the [university] and was even given a scholarship outside of her [State] Academic Scholarship based on her race. My best friend, with a 3.9 GPA and only a slightly lower SAT score, did not even get accepted to [the university] for summer. I saw this as being very unfair. I realize now that affirmative action involves integrating people of diverse races into different environments, including colleges and universities, but I still think it is unfair. It is discrimination against people who are perhaps better qualified. I think that asking someone what color or race they are on a college application is unnecessary. People should be admitted based solely on specific qualifications. As a white person, when I say something like this, people who are not white may argue that this is unfair because whites have had more privileges throughout this and past centuries. These privileges have supposedly given us an unfair advantage socially and economically. We are seen as having more educated families who make more money and are thus able to send us to better schools. Since we have received better educations for longer, if race is not an issue in college admissions, then blacks and other races will continue to lag behind whites in the world due to their lack of education.

I can understand this argument, but I still think that it is only slightly true. It is true that whites have had the privilege of many more benefits and have received better educations. But now, education is free and everyone has the same opportunities. Private schools aren't the only good schools out there. Public schools offer the same opportunities. Since education is free, everyone should be able to achieve success, provided they work for it.

Kim's objections to affirmative action are based on the assumption of a meritocratic society that offers equal opportunities for everyone. However, the facts point in a different direction. Repeated studies have shown that wide disparities in quality of secondary education still exist between suburban and urban schools, where students of color are disproportionately concentrated.[3] Far too often, race still makes a difference in the type of education a student will receive; and this in turn affects the student's chances for admission to universities. Affirmative action programs in admissions are in place in part to adjust for earlier educational inequality.

Regarding education at the university level, other issues arise. First, public university education is not "free." Even when a student pays less expensive in-state tuition, there are costs for books, fees, transportation, and living expenses. Kim has an understanding of the arguments for affirmative action that she has probably heard in her courses. Yet she discounts the serious disparity between the monetary and "cultural capital" she, as a white woman, has that helped her into college and the lack of capital of many people of color.[4] In his book *The Coming Race War?*, Richard Delgado describes cultural capital:

> [T]wo candidates, one white and one black . . . will often compete for the same job. Both are equally capable of doing a stellar job. But the interview, or job test, rewards the candidate who has the greatest store of cultural capital, the one who soaked it up so easily at his father's or mother's knee. The household had the right kind of music and books. The dinner table conversation taught precisely the mannerisms, conversational patterns, and small talk skills that the employer finds comforting, familiar, and reassuring. The more conventional candidate gets the job, even though the other one could have done just as well, maybe better.[5]

Kim extends her analysis to a discussion of racial bias in standardized tests:

> Another issue that we discussed in class was that the SAT is unfair because it is racially biased. I do not see how this could possibly be true. . . . I think that some people who complain about things like this are just

looking for excuses or ways to make things easier for themselves. If people want to be treated equally, they should have the same requirements.

For Kim, in order to be "equal," people must compete according to the same standards. She assumes that complaints from people of color are unjustified "excuses" or shortcuts. Again, what is omitted in Kim's remarks is that being white brings advantages preceding the college admissions process. These advantages could have provided her and other white students with skills difficult to quantify or measure, but which give them an advantage on standardized tests. The "same requirements" are usually "white" standards, so normative as to be invisible.[6] As such, these commonly used measures of qualifications for admission to colleges may not accurately predict the potential for nonwhite student achievement.[7] One author observes, for example, that to think philosophically does not necessarily require education or even traditionally measured "qualification."[8] College potential might be conceptualized in terms other than SAT scores and GPAs for individuals from groups more likely to have experienced particular societally embedded obstacles.

Some studies have negated the assertion that affirmative action policies allow unqualified students of color admission to universities. Even if a student is admitted to a university with the assistance of affirmative action policies, that student will not remain there because of them. Schools making the most use of affirmative action have the smallest racial gap in graduation rates.[9] Research conducted in 1998 at sixteen elite schools that utilize affirmative action extensively showed graduation rates for African Americans (the group whose qualifications are most questioned by whites) of 85 to 90 percent. Gaps in graduation rates, by contrast, were the highest, usually about 20 percentage points or more, at schools that admitted more applicants without using affirmative action.[10] Derek Bok, former President of Harvard University and Dean of Harvard Law School, explains: "By every measure of success . . . the more selective the school, the more blacks achieved (holding constant their initial test scores and grades)."[11] Affirmative action has been used most in college admissions beginning in the early 1990s, and since that time, graduation rates for African Americans have risen.[12]

Ironically, aside from the questions of validity of standardized tests as a predictor of academic and future success of minority students, some studies suggest that these tests may be relatively poor indicators of a member of *any* group's academic success. A student's high school GPA or class rank is slightly more reliable in predicting college performance than entrance exams such as the SAT. Yet somewhat lower SAT scores often exclude larger percentages of students in racial minority groups. According to the SAT firm (ETS)'s own research, high school grades, taken alone, can explain 29 percent of the variation in students' college GPAs, whereas the SAT alone can explain only 27 percent. Combining these to give a sort of "composite" grade-based view of a student's potential leaves two-thirds of the variation in college GPA still unexplained, leading one to believe that any number of other factors should be considered in college admissions, beyond a student's grades.[13]

The students in this sample are not unique in discussing abstract "diversity" in positive terms, while deriding the only methods that have been proven to be effective in achieving that goal. Recent research suggests that most support the *ideal* of diversity in higher education. A January 2003 survey of approximately 1,000 U.S. adults found that 85% of those polled believe college students are better prepared to live and work in society if they have gone to diverse universities.[14] However, they do not agree with using race as a factor in the application process. In this survey, approximately 80% of those surveyed disagreed with race-based affirmative action in college admissions. What is important to note, though, is that they also opposed the consideration of gender (83 percent), "legacy" status (75 percent), and athletic ability (56 percent)—"plus" factors usually not mentioned in affirmative action discussions.[15]

Wanda is another respondent who believes that being white has had economic costs that have affected her education:

> I get very upset with the whole state and federal college grant issues. I feel angry, maybe cheated, because I am employed full time and single. I receive approximately eight hundred dollars a year for student grants. Yes, I do appreciate the grants and I am thankful, but because I go to school part time I take out a lot of money in loans. I get very pissed off when I hear stories of single parents who receive so much assistance, they practically receive a free ride for their college education. I also hear stories of many adults who will quit work, go to college and the government practically pays for all of their education. I should do some research on this since I am only getting pissed off from stories that I hear. Maybe the government actually does distribute the grant money more equally than I realize.

Anecdotal arguments are frequently used by opponents of affirmative action, who rely on demonstrating how, in carefully chosen individual cases, seemingly unqualified or undeserving minority applicants benefited from affirmative action over more qualified or more needy whites. In doing so, commentators can make it seem as though affirmative action, while a good idea "in theory," never works in "real life." This data shows that these anecdotal arguments resonate with white students in that they play to one of their analytical weaknesses: the inability to envision a social structure that operates beyond their own experiences and environment.[16] When they hear political analysts making such arguments, it encourages them to pattern their arguments similarly. One can hear a competing social scientific paradigm in Wanda's comments— "I should do some research on this . . ." Still, personal experiences hold sway in shaping her ideologies: her autobiography has multiple passages that communicate her belief that, far from benefiting, she has been "cheated" as a white person.

Julia returns from a trip to Europe convinced understanding ethnicity is about appreciating "interesting foods," tolerating language differences, and realizing that "everyone is the same." Very quickly, her colorblind view conflicts with circumstances she encounters applying to college:

> I remember when I was applying to colleges, I wondered why on every application it asked your race and religion. I always thought to myself, 'does this really matter?' I went and asked my guidance counselor and she told me that schools have to fill quotas. I thought that was the most ridiculous thing I have ever heard. I never knew that schools based these important decisions on how many slots there are to fill. Affirmative Action began to take on a whole different meaning. I thought it was insane to let an unqualified person into a school because they are required to.

Julia's initial introduction to affirmative action policies comes through filling out college application forms. She describes this part of her life as something of an end to her colorblind innocence. Unfortunately, at a point when the guidance counselor could have shaped this young person's view of both the procedures and purposes of affirmative action in a positive way, she misinforms Julia that colleges "have to fill quotas." Julia then makes the cognitive leap that many whites make when they discuss affirmative action policies: she assumes they allow "unqualified" people to advance and are thus illogical or unfair. It is difficult for many whites to conceptualize affirmative action as opening opportunities to equally *qualified* persons of groups that have been traditionally excluded from advancement in society. Respondents envision "qualified" and "unqualified" in objective, clearly distinguishable terms. The assumption is made that persons of color (because it is hardly ever noted by respondents that white women also benefit from affirmative action) who are *unqualified* are assisted by affirmative action. One might argue that this amounts to a simple "slip of the tongue" on the part of respondents. Yet, I would argue that when the same verbal "slip" occurs repeatedly amongst a group of people, it amounts to more than a coincidence—it is a discursive construction that reveals something about the way whites see themselves and others. It seems hard for many whites, still, to conceptualize people of color as equally qualified to whites, both in educational and in work settings, as other data will show. Julia continues:

> I know that I worked very hard, and I thought that all that work would pay off with an acceptance letter. I was wrong. I know a girl named Erica that attends [another university]. She is Chinese and relatively smart. I know that my SATs and grades were a lot higher than hers, but I was rejected to [that school] and she was not. I felt like I had been the loser

in this rat race. I think that deep down she knows that she was the product of the quota system, but she enjoys the advantage. I began to have the feeling that being a white female, I was at a severe disadvantage. I did not seem to be getting any breaks. I put those feelings aside and attended [this university].

Similarly to Kim, Julia believes that her SAT scores should have "paid off;" instead, because of the "quota system" explained to her by a trusted guidance counselor, Julia believes that, as a white female, she is at a "severe disadvantage," "the loser in this rat race." Julia, like other respondents, believes affirmative action policies allow "unqualified" people to advance. As discussed in the last chapter, Julia further connects her perception of economic disadvantage with a sense of cultural victimization during the Greek rush process.

Ironically, many studies suggest that white women have benefited the most from affirmative action.[17] As women, they are considered a protected, underrepresented gender group, but as whites, they are socially located to best take advantage of the opportunities that are opened up to them by affirmative action. In other words, white women have the education, training and social networks that are necessary to make them 'equally qualified,' at least by commonly expected standards. Their gender may then act as a 'plus factor' to help them advance.

Because of family hardship, Will wants to take action to change policies used to allocate scholarships:

When I was a junior in high school, my father lost his job for several months due to an injury. We did not receive much compensation and my family went into debt. When it came time for a scholarship to finish my senior year of high school, I was only eligible for one scholarship because I was not a minority. Even though I was in greater need than the others receiving those scholarships, I was unable to apply for the scholarships. I think that this is a form of racism, and that all money for education should be awarded to the person who is most eligible. I had to struggle through school, making my family take grocery and medical money out of our budget so I could graduate with my friends. The students who received the scholarships had parents who made well over double mine. This experience has made me want to do something about the way financial aid is given out.

Will does not explain his certainty that those who received scholarships needed them less than he; however, he seems certain that there were many reserved for members of minority groups that were unavailable to him as a white male. It is a commonly believed fallacy that most scholarship money in the United States is earmarked for people of color. In fact, in the early 1990s, only about 4 percent of all scholarships in the United States were set aside for students of color.[18]

The conception of the college admissions procedure suggested by Will's statement is based on several mistaken assumptions. First, like many who question affirmative action in education, Will probably is unaware that a great deal of scholarship money and "quotas" historically have been inaccessible to people of color in the United States. For example, many Ivy League and even some public colleges and universities traditionally hold a certain number of seats in every entering class for children of alumni.[19] For example, at Harvard, "legacies" are three times as likely to be admitted; for more than forty years, one-fifth of the students admitted received this preference.[20] Among Ivy League schools, Harvard is no exception. At Yale the probability of admission is two and a half times greater for legacies, and Dartmouth and the University of Pennsylvania accepted well over half the applicants who were children of alumni in the year studied.[21] Obviously, these "set-asides" are disproportionately available to whites, whose parents and grandparents were more likely to attend college, especially Ivy League colleges. This practice is not limited to elite schools, however; and since white pupils are more likely to have had parents who attended any college, legacy preferences at public universities are more likely to benefit them also. At the University of Virginia and the University of California at Berkeley, children of alumni are automatically treated as in-state, regardless of residence—a distinct advantage.[22] When studied, Stanford's admission rate for legacies was twice that of nonlegacies, and Notre Dame actually set aside 25 percent of its incoming classes for children of alumni.[23]

Just as affirmative action is intended to do for minority students, legacy preferences are only supposed to benefit children of alumni *all else being equal*—in other words, if the student is "equally qualified," being a "legacy" can be a plus factor. However, some studies suggest that legacy students may actually be *less* qualified than their nonlegacy counterparts. In fact, they may lower the incoming class statistics.[24] So, although "affirmative action" in college admissions usually evokes images of nonwhite students gaining easier admission to universities based on race, white students, usually in the upper class, have also benefited from selectivity in admissions—something from which many media and political figures, who likely benefited from this type of whites-only "affirmative action" themselves, artfully direct white working- and middle-class students' attention.

Second, many white students believe that colleges and universities have racial "quotas" in place to increase minority enrollment. In fact, the 1978 *Bakke* case made racial quotas in higher education admissions illegal.[25] Colleges and universities use a variety of other systems to increase the enrollment of underrepresented groups. Some treat race as a "plus" factor, when other qualifications are equal between candidates. Alternatively, extra points on a scale may be added to a student's total if she or he is a member of a protected ethnic group. Some do not realize that in such a system, points are awarded for many other factors that universities believe worthy of protection, reward, or recruitment.

For example, the undergraduate affirmative action plan at the University of Michigan was scrutinized in one of two affirmative action cases argued before the Supreme Court in 2003. In that system, on a 150-point scale, minority undergraduate applicants received a twenty-point bonus. However, 110 of every student's total points were based on academic criteria, such as SAT scores and GPA. More importantly, many other criteria qualified for the possible 40-point nonacademic bonus. For example, ten points were awarded to Michigan residents, six to those from underrepresented Michigan counties, and two to applicants from underrepresented states. Four points were given to "legacies": applicants whose parent *or* step-parent went to the University of Michigan. Demonstrations of personal achievement, leadership, and service at the state, regional, and national levels were awarded points, up to five. Five points went to men entering the nursing profession. Finally, in addition to those from racial minority groups, scholarship athletes, the socioeconomically disadvantaged, and applicants in a category reserved for the "provost's discretion" were all eligible for twenty bonus points.[26]

The Michigan undergraduate point system was ruled unconstitutional by the Supreme Court on June 23, 2003, in *Gratz v. Bollinger*. However, this ruling was based on the program's specifics, not its spirit. In a six-to-three vote, the Court decided that the undergraduate program was unconstitutional because it used a numerical point system, which, in the words of Justice Sandra Day O'Connor, considered race in a "nonindividualized, mechanical" way.[27] The Court upheld the University of Michigan Law School's affirmative action plan, in *Grutter v. Bollinger*, by a vote of five to four, which they stated, in considering race a "plus factor," uses it in a "flexible, nonmechanical way."[28] This decision followed the precedent set in the *Bakke* case of 1978, which struck down strict quotas based on race, but allowed the use of race as a plus factor.[29] Some have argued that the point system used by the University of Michigan did represent the use of race as just one of many possible "plus factors" in a way that made it possible to manage the logistical nightmare of individualized evaluations for more than 25,000 applications annually received by that institution.[30] Yet the court did not believe this system represented an "individual" enough assessment, as they did the law school's nonnumerical, admissions-committee process.

Still, what was fundamentally important about these cases was that the Supreme Court affirmed the value of ensuring diversity in higher education and protected the opportunity provided by affirmative action programs to students from racial and ethnic minority groups.[31] One expert argued that if affirmative action ended at the law school alone, minority enrollment would decrease from 14.5 percent to 4 percent.[32] Considering such statistics, it is evident that white students are not yet losing places in large numbers to students of color, given their proportions in the United States; and were affirmative action plans to cease, students of color would lose many of their modest gains.

While confirming the Supreme Court's support of affirmative action, the Michigan cases prompted many other individuals, companies, and groups to demonstrate their avowal of those policies in amicus briefs. A group of Fortune 500 companies together filed an amicus brief in support of the University of Michigan, as did other individual companies, such as General Motors. After the Court's decision was announced, business leaders viewed it as an affirmation of their use of similar practices in hiring.[33] Business support centered around two themes. First, for success in the business world, students must learn how to interact across cultures and to approach issues from varied perspectives. Second, business leaders argued that ending affirmative action in colleges and universities would waste the human capital, the resources, represented by educated minority employees.[34]

Nevertheless, many white students in this study do not realize the benefits of being in a more diverse campus environment. Perhaps in part because "affirmative action" is equated with "racial minorities" in the media, when discussing their frustrations with it regarding college admissions, they do not complain about other groups benefiting from preferences based on group membership. As is often the case with young whites' constructions of whiteness, their sense of economic victimization is usually focused on African Americans, who they seem to perceive as particularly "unqualified," and thus undeserving.

A final fallacy embedded in many young white students' fears about economic disadvantage, especially in college admissions, is that "qualification" is clearly and objectively quantifiable. Will exemplifies this in stating that "all money for education should be awarded to the person who is most eligible." Class discussions reveal that students do not conceptualize of "qualified" or "most eligible" as subjective, and that they believe everyone can and should be equally accountable to objective standards. Consequently, after being held to identical standards, anyone meeting a certain level of achievement is *entitled* to admission to a university.

It is based on this reasoning that students like these believe that they have been "cheated" out of something rightfully theirs. In reality, though, college admission is not an entitlement. The admissions process is two-way; students choose universities, but universities also choose students and have an interest in acquiring students based on their own goals. In his expert opinion, written for *Grutter v. Bollinger* (the Michigan Law School case), Derek Bok asserts:

The university's obligation runs to the students whom it is to educate, and to the society at large that it is to serve. There is no escaping a university's obligation to try to serve the long-term interests of society. . . . Our society . . . is and will be multi-racial. . . . As a necessary predicate, it is important to recognize that a university should have the freedom to decide which students it will admit and which criteria it will use in its admissions decisions. . . . At bottom, admissions officers must decide which set of applicants, *considered individually and collectively,* will take fullest advantage of what the college has to offer, contribute most to the educational process in college, and be most successful in using what they have learned for the benefit of the larger society. . . . In my experience, in deciding among this group [of applicants with basic qualifications but who are not in the top category], a school does not start from the premise that any applicant has a 'right' to a place in a college or university. Instead, the starting premise is that a school has an obligation to make the best possible use of the limited number of places in each entering class so as to advance as effectively as possible the broad purposes the school seeks to serve. Within the very real limits imposed by the fallibility of any selection process of this kind, a school should try hard to be fair to every applicant; but the concept of fairness itself has to be understood within the context of the obligations of a university. Accordingly, in making these difficult choices among well-qualified candidates, considerations other than just test scores and grades come into play.[35]

Students are not guaranteed entrance to an institution merely because their test scores and GPA are at a certain level. Similarly, simply because a student who was denied entrance had the same test scores as those of another who gained entrance does not prove unfair treatment. Colleges and universities have a stated practice of choosing students to serve the university community. The student with slightly lower scores may be bringing something, in athletic or musical talent or in ethnic, racial, geographical, or socioeconomic diversity, that is at least as valuable to the university as is a certain test score or GPA. As Bowen and Bok write elsewhere:

Fairness should not be misinterpreted to mean that a particular criterion has to apply—that, for example, grades and test scores must always be considered more important than other qualities and characteristics so that no student with a B average can be accepted as long as some students with As are being turned down. . . . An individual's race may reveal something about how that person arrived at where he or she is today—what barriers were overcome, and what the individual's prospects are for further growth. Not every member of a minority group will have had to surmount obstacles. Moreover, other circumstances besides race can cause 'disadvantage.' Thus colleges and universities should and do give special consideration to the hard-working son of a family in Appalachia or the daughter of a recent immigrant from Russia. . . . But race is an important factor in its own right, given this nation's history and evidence presented in many studies of the continuing effects of discrimination and prejudice. Wishing it were otherwise does not make it otherwise.[36]

In these data alone, we see how isolated many white students are before entering college. Although demographically the country is changing, and whites are becoming more of a minority, U.S. schools are becoming more segregated, according to a recent Harvard Civil Rights Project Study.[37] Today, African-American students usually attend schools where fewer than 31 percent of their classmates are white.[38] Stated differently, a quarter of all black students in the Northeast and Midwest and one-sixth elsewhere attend schools that are almost 100 percent nonwhite.[39] Latino students go to schools where fewer than 29 percent of the students are white.[40] Asian American students are the most integrated of all groups, but they attend schools where 22 percent are Asian.[41] Of course, beyond the barriers posed to racial understanding caused by reseg-regation, it condemns disproportionate numbers of students of color to poorly funded schools in areas without the wealthy suburban tax base of those attended by white students.[42] Much of this resegregation occurs because of continued white flight to the suburbs and out of urban centers and because white parents have challenged desegregation plans, which courts have then done little to support.[43] White students are still the most segregated of all racial groups—making up approximately 61 percent of the total public school population, on average they attend schools that are 80 percent white.[44] Of particular interest is that white students interact with very few nonwhite students except in the South and Southwest.[45] Integration in Southern schools is more complete than in the North, although resegregation is beginning to become a problem there, also.[46]

Many participants do recognize that it was not until coming to college that they encountered "diversity," and some even perceive diversity as positive. However, rarely mentioned in the autobiographies is that affirmative action policies may have helped make this possible, and thus created a better campus environment for *all* students. As Bok states:

> A great deal of learning occurs informally. . . . The unplanned, casual encounters with roommates, fellow sufferers in class . . . student workers . . . teammates . . . can be subtle yet powerful sources of improved understanding and personal growth. Indeed, the data in our study prove what I have observed for years through experience—that . . . 'learning through diversity' actually occurs. Our study indicates that diversity is a benefit for all students, minorities and nonminorities alike.[47]

Indeed, studies have shown that the whites most supportive of affirmative action in universities are those who have attended schools that use affirmative action—in other words, those who have experienced how it benefits them.[48] Obviously not every African-American, Asian, Latino, or Middle Eastern person is alike, so one cannot say that simply bringing a white student into contact with any one Asian person, for example, will make the white student understand what "all" Asians are like. However, simply by having contact with people of various races and ethnic groups, stereotypes that white students who lack such contact hold might be challenged.

Aside from concerns about college admissions, some of the autobiographers tell of white people they know who they believe were victims of "reverse racism" in the workplace. Nadine, an older student, writes of her father's experiences in the 1960s:

> Affirmative action, which began in the later 1960's had a negative impact on my family, and many white working men of the time. . . . Many white men where my father worked . . . were laid off and told that the reason they were laid off was because a certain number of black people had to be hired. The men who were being laid off were asked to train the black men who were taking their places. This same thing happened to others around the country at the same time, you can imagine how what was basically a good concept, when implemented this way, would cause prejudice even where there was none before. I do not know what my father felt toward black people before this, but he is an extremely prejudiced person now. At around this same time there were maybe two black children in our elementary school but still, we were pulled out and put in a private Catholic school.

Like several of the autobiographers, Nadine argues that while she believes in affirmative action "in theory," in practice it "would cause prejudice . . . where there was none before." This argument is problematic. Affirmative action did not cause prejudice—prejudice, or more correctly racism, caused a *need* for affirmative action. However, her explanation of the impact on her family elucidates one of the most difficult aspects of affirmative action: in order for it to work, some individual white people, particularly men, who may not have *individually and intentionally* practiced racism, may pay a price.

This theme of job loss due to affirmative action is echoed in other autobiographies. Tim, a young man who writes about a dramatic racial "turning-point" experience, and now has black roommates, nevertheless ends his autobiography this way:

> I do have a problem with people who use race to get ahead in this world. I am tired of people saying that race should not be important and yet using it to get jobs or into college. Many of my uncles are firemen and this is what has happened to them. In order to get promoted you have to take a test and promotion is granted based on the results. Let's just say that it is supposed to be the top twenty percent that get the promotion, well if there are no black people in the top twenty percent they go and get enough blacks from the bottom of the list so that they are more equal in numbers of blacks and whites. That is one reason that one of my uncles has not made captain yet, he has always had a high score but once they get the blacks in there he is just short. This is disgusting because I don't care who saves my life just so long as they are the best person for the job. That is what really bothers me—color, not ability, is often too much of a factor in anything anymore. . . . These are the things that I hear about now. This is what racism is now. . . . We need to say this is it. Whether you are black, white, brown, or green this is what you have to do [meet certain

standards]. . . . I just think that we are a bunch of hypocrites. We stand and say that skin color doesn't matter but then we do things that go against that. We need to stop being two-faced and just be fair.

Believing that he and most whites have overcome being racist, Tim says race-conscious hiring policies are "what racism is now." He further asserts that supporters of affirmative action also usually hold colorblind ideals, and this makes them hypocritical. Tim feels compelled to highlight this hypocrisy: "we need to say this." Again, one sees the respondents' ahistorical and colorblind perspective in Tim's insistence that racism is, "now," about harm caused to whites. Also, as in the last chapter, some young whites are beginning to feel responsible for speaking up for their group interests, as they believe others are the only ones with a voice in racial issues.

The sense of whiteness as an economic liability is best captured in the next autobiography when a white respondent wishes he were black. Jerry writes,

> When graduating high school and going through the scholarship process, I thought for the first time that it would not be too bad to be black. Had I been black I would be a National Merit Scholar and had I been black I would not be taking a small loan to be here. . . . I am sure that when I do graduate college and attempt to trade bonds, on Wall Street, I will probably for the second time in my life wish that I were Black. . . . I was never confronted with blacks or other minorities until we were forced to compete, with unfair disadvantages I might add, against them for scholarships, college acceptance, and eventually jobs.

Throughout the data, one sees how white students construct the racial status quo as a "game" in which others hold more "cards"—and they play these "race cards" at every opportunity. Jerry perceives competition, perhaps previously considered in other terms, as now racialized—"us against them." The most striking thing about Jerry's comments may be his claim that because his whiteness is a liability, he has "wish[ed] that [he] were black," and probably will again. This statement characterizes the sentiments of many respondents, and contrasts with the racial beliefs and desires of their parents' and grandparents' generations. They see whiteness as both a cultural liability and an economic disadvantage, and many, blind to existing racism, find reasons to wish to be a person of color.

Affirmative Action Causes Harm

In this section I discuss how respondents see affirmative action as a social harm rather than a social good. Specifically, respondents perceive affirmative action as causing harm by inflicting reverse discrimination and causing racial tensions.

Reverse Discrimination

The subtext of respondents' complaints regarding their past experiences is that they believe being white has somehow caused them to be treated unfairly, or be "cheated." They believe they are essentially victims of economic "reverse discrimination." Dane discusses this more explicitly:

> I know that racism still exists in society today, but I wonder if it has been exaggerated. It is too easy for minorities to claim discrimination and gain compensation. My father works for a large financial company, and he is often in charge of the hiring and firing of employees. The company often has to go to trial to justify its firing of employees who claim that discrimination was the reason for their dismissal. While in reality the reasons for dismissal were purely work related. This holds true for not only minorities but women too. Just as I think racism is wrong I also think it is wrong for people to claim discrimination where there is none.

It has become part of the national discourse to assert that ours is a litigious society. For whites, this complaint may become centered on people of color "using" race to profit through litigation. Dane suggests that racism in society becomes exaggerated by false claims of workplace discrimination. Not only that, he believes such claims are easy to argue and win in court. This common assumption fails to hold up against actual evidence. For example, in comparing workplace sex discrimination cases to race discrimination cases, it appears that not only are more sex discrimination cases decided in favor of the plaintiff, at almost all judicial levels, but the standard of proof required for the two types of cases seems to be different.[49] In hostile sexual workplace environment cases, it has not been necessary for a victim to prove "severe psychological injury," or demonstrate that any one major discriminatory act occurred, to show that harassment occurs with enough frequency to "reasonably be termed pervasive."[50] Conversely, in cases at various levels, courts have placed a much more stringent burden of proof in racial workplace discrimination cases. The problem is that although both sexual harassment and racial discrimination cases require consideration of whether the treatment would affect "a reasonable employee in a similar situation," this standard is not applied in the same way in the two types of cases.[51] Feagin and McKinney suggest why it may be difficult for plaintiffs to win racial discrimination cases:

> To this point in time, the majority of U.S. courts have been more sympathetic to the arguments of women, mainly white women, that they face hostile, sexually harassing male workers in their workplaces—and thus hostile workplace climates—than they have been to the arguments of black workers that they face racially hostile white workers, and, thus, racially hostile workplace climates. Perhaps the reason for this is that in their own lives every white male judge and jury member has had close contacts with a woman, whether she be his grandmother, mother, daughter, wife, or friend. Thus, most will have some idea of what a 'reasonable woman' might find offensive, as well as have some sympathy

toward a white woman. However, white juries and judges often assess the evidence of racial hostility in white workplaces, and that evidence may be considered to be the 'perceptions' of some 'oversensitive' African Americans. Thus, the test presented by the courts, in which the standard of a 'reasonable person of the plaintiff's race' is invoked, is empty of meaning. Few white people have a real understanding of what African Americans' experience in white workplaces is like.[52]

Lacking a real knowledge of the outcome of such cases, like Dane, many whites believe that it is easy to play the "race card" in the workplace and either get out of difficulties or even make large amounts of money. Keith writes:

African Americans . . . are still the main focus of minority debate. I have to admit that I find myself stereotyping blacks on a regular basis. Throughout adolescence and high school I found myself shunning the attitude my father held. Although I do not always agree with [my father's] quiet racism, I have to admit that I understand his views. Before I came to college my interaction with blacks was limited. . . . My most significant eye opener came last summer when I worked as a security guard at [a] corporation. There is so much tension there between blacks and whites, especially between black workers and white management. The most basic problems turn into a heated racism issue. The misuse of the term racism was the most prevalent cause of disturbance. If a black person were to not show up for work five days in a row and was suspended for their actions it was most often blamed on the white manager for being racist. In a similar circumstance with a white person showing frequent tardiness, what was their excuse, they had none. A white person who is constantly late is immediately tested for alcohol or substance abuse problems. The problems with the black person are brushed under the carpet as quickly as possible to avoid any type of racially motivated lawsuits. Sure, this class is going to teach everyone that that is a misconception, but it is quickly found to be truthful once you step into the business world. All the education in the world cannot substitute for a hands-on experience. Everyone is trying to place the blame on someone other than himself or herself, and racism makes for an easy escape. I do not deny racism in the workforce by any means, I see that a lot also; I do, however believe that racially motivated excuses are used on a far too regular basis. I have seen these racially motivated accusations destroy the careers of many good people; they are just as much a victim as minorities whom are discriminated against.

Uninhibited about expressing opinions differing from information presented in class, Keith describes what he viewed as unfair practices in the workplace, as victimizing whites just as much as discrimination victimizes people of color. Note also that while Keith acknowledges the existence of racism, he offers no concrete way of addressing it.

A 1994 study of federal employees found that African-American employees are more than twice as likely to be fired as white employees. Particularly disheartening is that black workers face the most dismissal in occupations where they are most concentrated. For example, African-American janitorial and office workers are about four times more likely to be fired than their white counterparts.[53] Such studies suggest that large-scale discrimination still operates in the workplace experiences of people of color.

Some whites believe that people of color use claims of racism to lobby for continued affirmative action, as Dane writes:

> Affirmative action is an issue that is on the minds of both races. It seems that the public is ready to move past affirmative action and work for all races to be on equal footing. These laws only serve to reinforce that there is a difference between the races. It is reverse discrimination and it works against the princip[le] that the most qualified person gets the position. I think laws need to be made to stop discrimination, not encourage it.

Some recent studies reveal the majority of whites, especially men, believe they may be victimized by racial discrimination.[54] Further, they believe, like Tim, that "this is what racism is now": by a margin of two to one, respondents to these studies perceived whites at greater risk of facing discrimination at work than African Americans.[55] Despite the fact that many whites believe that affirmative action is causing whites, particularly males, significant harm, evidence does not bear this out. Two types of evidence are important to consider in this regard. First, very few complaints filed with the Equal Employment Opportunity Commission (EEOC) are for "reverse discrimination." Between 1987 and 1994, of the total 451,442 discrimination complaints filed, only 4 percent claimed reverse discrimination.[56] An even smaller percentage of the total cases that reached the court systems were so-called reverse discrimination cases. Lest one believe that this is because white men are less litigious than are others, apparently they do file complaints for discrimination they believe they have suffered—white men filed 80 percent of the EEOC age discrimination complaints in 1994.[57] Further, of the racial discrimination complaints filed by white men, very few are found credible by the EEOC (only 28 of the 7,000 filed in 1994); and between 1990 and 1994 U.S. district and appellate courts dismissed almost all as without merit.[58] Victor discusses the effects of affirmative action on white males:

> I think that it is over exaggerated to how great it is to be a white male in America today. We are seen as the elite group and that everything is given to us without a worry. Being a white male is seeing other groups get advantages over you that seem very unfair. You really can't describe

what it is to be racially without making any reference to any other racial group, because you must compare yourself to them and what they have that we don't have and what we have that they don't have. If you look at advantages, you look at things like Affirmative Action and you have to compare your chances to a woman's chances or a Mexican American's chances and an African American's chances of getting the same exact job and seeing that you are already at a disadvantage. . . . To be white is the same as it is to be African American or to be Mexican American or to be Asian American or to be Native American. Other groups see us as the advantaged, or as the ones with the free ride, but I say this is bullshit, pardon the language, because we have disadvantages too. . . . I am not saying that other groups are not disadvantaged because they are and definitely more so than the whites, but they shouldn't blame this on every single white person in America. I am from an area that has very little minorities and I haven't had to deal with the problem of people being put down and disadvantaged in looking for a job, buying a house or a car, or dealing with authority. The people around me could complain all they want about being disadvantaged, but it was just complaining because they didn't get what they wanted. I think that this is what is going on in America and I think that this should stop. I believe it should be the best man or woman for the job, whether they be white, black, Asian, Mexican, etc.

Candidly, Victor argues that being a white male means perceiving others as getting advantages he lacks, that "seem very unfair." As I will discuss later in the chapter, part of Victor's objection, as well as that of Keith and others, is that he believes people of color are misusing "race talk," complaining about racism when they should not be, and receiving privileges based on these complaints. Keeping in mind the importance of *understanding* these students' perspectives in order to reconstruct them, it is also crucial to see the weaknesses in them. In other words, so many students repeat these perceptions of how it feels to be white that it is impossible to ignore that there is some source of this feeling. Uncovering what this source is will be vital to effective antiracism.

Although Victor believes, like a majority of white Americans, that reverse discrimination is harming him, the evidence does not support this. It is true that individual whites, particularly men, may face job competition that they are not accustomed to from white women and people of color; and may indeed lose positions to some who are equally qualified because of affirmative action policies. However, white men as a group gained from decades of "affirmative action" as cronyism and "old boys' networks" that conferred advantage at the expense of people of color and white women.[59] They also had the basic advantage of the smaller labor pool afforded by the exclusion of white women and people of color. As Paul Kivel writes,

It is true that specific white people may not get specific job opportunities because of affirmative action policies and may suffer as a result. This lack of opportunity is unfortunate and we need to address the reasons that there are not enough jobs. We tend to forget that millions of specific people of color have also lost specific job opportunities as a result of racial discrimination. To be concerned only with the white applicants who don't get the job, while ignoring the people of color who don't get it, shows racial preference.[60]

Because of years of white dominance in business and social life, affirmative action policies, which are *not* strict numerical mandates but consist of "goals" and "good faith efforts," have done little to displace white men from their positions of power.[61] As of 1995, white men were 95 percent of U.S. senior management, but only 29 percent of the workforce.[62] Around the same time, U.S.-born white men constituted about 41 percent of the population, but held the majority of powerful positions in business and education, such as 97 percent of school superintendents, 80 percent of tenured professors, and 92 percent of Forbes 400 CEOs.[63] White men are still significantly overrepresented in every category of highly paid professional work, except professional athletics.[64]

On the other side of occupational segregation, in the mid-1990s, African Americans made up approximately 12.4 percent of the U.S. adult population, and Latinos, 9.5 percent. However, in the professions they fell far below proportional representation. For example, of the total physicians, African Americans composed approximately 4.2 percent, and Latinos 5.2 percent. About three percent of all lawyers were African American, and the same could be said of Latinos. African Americans were slightly more represented as engineers than were Latinos, at 3.7 percent and 3.3 percent, respectively, but both fell far below proportionality. Finally, only 5 percent of professors were African American, and 2.9 percent were Latino.[65] Until the percentages of people of color in the professions are at least proportional to their population numbers, affirmative action has not accomplished what was intended: to increase female and minority representation in workplaces where they are underrepresented. Claiming that it has begun to work in the opposite direction—actually to *overrepresent* minority workers, and disadvantage white men—is even more outrageous. One commentator writes regarding the suggestion that affirmative action in education is beginning to produce large numbers of unqualified professors of color:

My flaws are more easily forgiven because I am white. Some complain that affirmative action has meant the university is saddled with mediocre minority professors. I have no doubt that there are minority faculty who are mediocre, though I don't know very many. As Henry Louis Gates, Jr. once pointed out, if affirmative action policies were in place for the next hundred years, it's possible that . . . the university could have as many mediocre minority professors as it has mediocre white professors. That isn't meant as an insult to anyone, but it's a simple observation that white privilege has meant that scores of second-rate white professors have slid through the system because their flaws were overlooked out of solidarity based on race, as well as on gender, class and ideology.[66]

White men, and to some extent white women as well, have long benefited from informal, unstated affirmative action.

The lingering economic disparities between people of color and whites also indicate that "reverse discrimination" claims are unfounded. Other than Native Americans, African Americans are the least financially secure compared to whites, although they are the group respondents mention most as benefiting significantly from affirmative action. African American family income in 2000 was only about 66 percent of white family income. In 1998, African American male income was about 78 percent of white male income. With the same education, job experience, and credentials, the African American male, on average will still only make 85 percent of the income of his white counterpart.[67] Even more dramatic are the differences in white and black family wealth. Manning Marable writes, citing the work of sociologists Melvin Oliver and Thomas Shapiro:

> If affirmative action should be criticized, it might be on the grounds that it didn't go far enough in transforming the actual power relations between black and white within our society. More evidence for this is addressed by the sociologists Melvin Oliver and Thomas Shapiro in *Black Wealth/White Wealth* (1995). The authors point out that 'the typical black family has eleven cents of wealth for every dollar owned by the typical white family.' Even middle-class African-Americans . . . are significantly poorer than whites who earn identical incomes. If housing and vehicles owned are included in the definition of 'net wealth,' the median middle-class African-American family has only $8,300 in total assets, as against $56,000 for the comparable white family.[68]

Recently, in a *New York Times* editorial, sociologist Dalton Conley summarized the wealth gap in 2003:

> The typical white family enjoys a net worth that is more than eight times that of its black counterpart, according to the economist Edward Wolff. Even at equivalent income levels, gaps remain large. Among families earning less than $15,000 a year, the median African-American family has a net worth of zero, while the corresponding white family has $10,000 in equity. The typical white family earning $40,000 annually has a nest egg of around $80,000. Its black counterpart has about half that amount.
>
> This equity inequity is partly the result of the head start whites enjoy in accumulating and passing on assets. Some economists estimate that up to

80 percent of lifetime wealth accumulation results from gifts from earlier generations, ranging from the down payment on a home to a bequest from a parent.[69]

Most white families, because they did not face slavery, and because of government programs that benefited whites and not people of color, have more wealth for intergenerational transfer. Some of the most beneficial programs for whites were those set up for returning GIs after World War II. These in cluded educational benefits, which triggered the largest boom in middle-class college attendance ever; and job training programs.[70] Arguably the most advantageous programs for whites, and the most damaging for African Americans, were the mortgage loan programs. The Federal Housing Administration and the Veterans Administration guaranteed generous mortgage loans. These programs, which were in theory open to persons of any race or ethnicity, discriminated against African Americans because they would underwrite mortgages only in racially homogenous neighborhoods—restrictive covenants were openly stated FHA policy.[71] The FHA mortgage program allowed developers to refuse to sell to African Americans and created suburbanization for white Americans. Because whites moved to the suburbs first, only whites received the generous loans; to purchase what is generally the most important asset a person or family will ever own: their home.[72] In effect, the U.S. government subsidized "white flight" and urban decline.[73] Redlining, which was also systematically practiced by the FHA, exacerbated urban decline. Redlining, in which banks would not give loans for business development or home improvement in certain areas, ensured that African Americans trying to receive loans to improve their communities would not be able to do so.[74] The homes, education, and jobs that this generation of white Americans were able to secure with the help of the government, and without competition from people of color (or from single white women), helped them to acquire wealth and assets that were transferable to their children and grandchildren.

This evidence of income and wealth disparity suggests that there is a continuing need for policies encouraging equal treatment in the workplace. Despite respondents' insistence that "To be white is the same as it is to be African American or to be Mexican American or to be Asian American or to be Native American;" and protestations that they face race-based economic disadvantage as much as any other group, the data refute these claims.

Racial Divisiveness

Some respondents argue that affirmative action does more harm than good because it fosters resentment against people of color, and therefore it should be abandoned. Rhetorically, this is a creative argument, discrediting affirmative action while still maintaining the author's ideological innocence. It is reminiscent of white parents telling their children that they forbid them to date interracially, not because they personally have negative feelings about interracial dating or people of color, but because they know that *other* whites do and fear resentment directed from *them* towards their offspring. Such a stance supports the racial status quo by refusing to challenge whites who maintain racist ideologies.[75] Using such an argument, Neal writes:

> I think there are a few serious racial issues facing the United States today. I think Affirmative Action and Reparations are some of the more serious and damaging racial issues. I think both of these are racist. I feel Affirmative Action needs to be stopped in its tracks now before it gets any more ridiculous. I really think that if African Americans would receive reparations it would turn everyone against them. I think this would bother everyone in America. This I think would really destroy our country and separate people more than ever.
>
> . . . . I see whites playing a huge role in current race relations and current debates regarding race. I think the issues such as Affirmative Action and Reparations will make whites come to the forefront and fight against these issues. I have yet to talk to a white person who agrees with these issues. I have even talked to blacks that hate Affirmative Action because they feel it makes them look stupid and I tend to agree. They say it makes them feel stupid because they don't feel they should be given jobs or points on a test to excel. They feel they can do it themselves without help.

Neal's concerns include several aspects of the damage he believes affirmative action could cause. First, he asserts that such policies amount to racism, presumably against whites. Second, he perceives affirmative action, here linked to reparations, as racially divisive and suggests that both issues may mobilize whites against African Americans. In doing so, he implies that negative attitudes toward African Americans and other people of color are in some cases justified, or at least reasonable. Third, Neal argues that affirmative action stigmatizes its beneficiaries, using his African-American acquaintances as spokespersons to support this claim. Indeed, some black conservatives, such as Shelby Steele, Thomas Sowell, Walter Williams, and Clarence Thomas have attested that affirmative action stigmatizes not only those who benefit from it, but African Americans and others for whom it played no role in their hiring or college admission.[76] Such commentators argue that affirmative action may increase self-doubt among people of color; and cause whites to question the abilities of and resent the people of color they encounter in workplaces and universities.[77]

Despite these concerns, a 1995 Gallup poll found that very small percentages of African Americans or white women believed affirmative action had caused coworkers to question their skills or credentials.[78] Further, some people of color agree that there are white people who persistently question their abilities, and affirmative action may provide them additional ammunition to do so. However, they argue that without the policies, many African Americans and others may never have gained the opportunity to prove their abilities.[79] In proving stereotypes wrong, people of color may be able to work toward a day when affirmative action is no longer necessary. Thus, although affirmative action may fuel resentment among some whites, the alternative would be worse; many people of color would never get the chance to prove them wrong. Deanna writes about a college friend:

[M]y first lab partner was an African American. I would have to say that she is probably one of the nicest people that I have met in the past four years. I never really got to know her very well, but nothing ever came up in our conversations about race or racism. I do remember one talk though about her doing her internship. She was a very smart girl, but she felt as if the only reason she got the internship was because she was a minority student.

. . . . Which brings me to another point about affirmative action. In some ways it seems to be pulling society apart. Most jobs, employers have to fill quotas, and that is not fair to the person with better qualifications. A person should be hired for what that person can do not what they look like or where they came from. Everyone should be on an equal playing field. I know that in today's society that is not quite ready to happen. Especially when looking at the ratio of people who go to college and graduate, and even the people who graduate high school. Before going and hiring people to fill quotas something should be done with our education system so that every one gets a fair education.

Deanna's point is well taken, that better secondary education for all would make affirmative action less necessary, but ending those policies now would be unfair to people of color already in the workplace.

Mike's autobiography is especially insightful; he is self-critical and willing to consider how whiteness and privilege affect his life. He even questions to what degree he may harbor racism and prejudices. Still, he believes affirmative action is divisive: "White people are going to have to lead the way in furthering race relations. We need to voice our grievances with laws like affirmative action and not be afraid of offending minorities. . . . While it has bolstered minority accomplishment it has recently caused job fear among whites and that inflames racism." It is regarding affirmative action, and in the area of economics, that even many racially aware whites seem to feel that they are treated unfairly because of their whiteness. Many suggest that excluding this one arena of racial politics, they would have no lingering misgivings about those of other races.

Another respondent, Lauren, while opposing affirmative action, says "I can definitely see how this can cause bad feelings towards African Americans in a community. I think that if everyone wants to be treated as equals we all have to get the same treatment so that no one can sit and think that this person should not be here, they are just here because of affirmative action."

Despite many well-meaning whites' insistence that we all should be "treated as equals," people of color are still *not* receiving the same treatment in the workplace as are whites. For years, audit studies, with equally qualified black and white "applicants" applying in person for jobs, in order to see who is called back for interviews, have shown that whites are more likely to be given interviews or offered jobs in a variety of labor markets.[80] These findings have been supported recently by a disturbing study of the effect of one's name on the chance of being offered an interview.[81] In this study, researchers chose 1,300 help-wanted ads in Boston and Chicago newspapers and sent fictitious résumés to them. The applicants were the same, in education, skills, and experience, but their names differed. The researchers assigned first names on the résumés randomly, choosing from a set of common white and common black names.[82] The results were undeniable evidence of continuing racial discrimination in hiring. The "applicants" with white-sounding names were 50 percent more likely to be called for interviews than those with black-sounding names.[83] Particularly damaging to the aspirations of people of color could be the finding that whites' chances of being called for an interview rose with higher credentials, but higher credentials made much less difference for those with black-sounding names.[84] Despite whites' perceptions that race no longer matters in obtaining a job, research demonstrates consistently that it does.

Affirmative Action is Fundamentally Unreasonable

Another line of reasoning suggesting that whites are being victimized economically is that policies installed to help people of color progress economically are fundamentally unreasonable, because they compromise qualifications and impose inflexible quotas. Thus they are unfair to the qualified, whom respondents usually conceive of as white. Seth first discusses his mother's views:

> I think that my mother has drifted towards a more conservative view in recent years, she is very bitter about the incompetence she witnesses in minorities in the school system. I think that this has contributed to a level of racism in her life. I can sometimes see where she is coming from because it seems ridiculous that unqualified minorities get jobs and then keep them on the premise of being a minority. . . . Unfortunately, this is the way that Affirmative Action laws have been used in court. I am sure that in some cases it was justified and was necessary but now I see that things are being taken advantage of.

Again, many whites have the perception that affirmative action is a tool wielded frequently and effectively in courts to victimize whites. Like others, Seth admits affirmative action once may have been needed, but now it is "being taken advantage of." Later, he adds:

I am sure I have been discriminated based on my race or ethnicity but I don't remember them. Maybe I don't get as much scholarship money or something. Again, I am sure that my race has provided certain benefits, but I don't recall them because I don't think that they are important in life.... I think that my race gets blamed for the problems of other races in this country much more so than necessary. I understand what has happened to other races by mine, but these things happened many years ago and I am tired of being blamed for the mistakes of my ancestors. Also, I think that minorities (including females) blame white males for their problems in the workplace, etc. Again I know these things happen but to put the blame on all white males like they are some sort of disease is wrong. These extremist groups of people are the biggest hypocrites in the world. They want equality but mean to attain it through inequality. I don't understand this way of operating. Well, I guess I understand it, I just think it is wrong, and I don't understand how anyone could think it was right.

Characterizing minorities and women as "extremist groups" who "put the blame on all white males like they are some sort of disease," Seth struggles with the meaning of the word "equality." He believes equality of opportunity sought through affirmative action goals constitutes "inequality." Further, Seth cannot recall any privileges whiteness bestows because he believes they are unimportant; although he is able to think of ways he may have faced discrimination because he is white. Seth concludes by expressing his perplexity regarding those who promote race-consciousness in public life: he cannot "understand how anyone could think it was right." This is most likely because he writes from a white male perspective.

Compromised Qualifications?

At the Northern university, some respondents were students required to take my race and ethnicity course for their criminal justice program major. Several of these are convinced they are vulnerable to reverse discrimination in this field. Consider, for example, Keith's autobiography, which begins with expressing sympathetic views towards minorities (especially those who are victims of police brutality). However, his writing quickly moves to a criticism of affirmative action:

An issue that most disturbs me in the law enforcement field at this time is the way in which minorities are advancing without necessarily filling the same requirements as a white male. For instance, I know that you said earlier in the class that the argument about minorities having an advantage in the state police is false. I totally disagree, my [Asian] brother in law took the State Police exam and was given an extra five or ten points on his test due to the fact that he is a minority. The same is true for women taking the exam; a black woman taking the exam will be given ten extra points on her test which will boost her ahead of many white males whom are obviously much more qualified. I can tell you one thing, when I am in the field, I don't want my partner to be there just because they got extra points on their exam for being a minority; I want the most qualified to have my back.

Most whites are not angry about affirmative action because of belief that, when *equally qualified* white and nonwhite candidates are compared, the person of color will automatically be chosen. In nearly every instance, when discussing affirmative action specifically or white economic disadvantage more generally, respondents state that an "unqualified" or "under-qualified" person of color (usually African American) will probably get a job or university admission over them. Far from being an offhand remark, this common statement could be seen as a remnant of the old white superiority paradigm of previous generations. Instead of having minds open to the hypothetical applicant of color being equally qualified with the white person, the respondents typically make the assumption that the person of color (or white woman) would be *unqualified*, or at least less qualified than the white person for the position. As Keith states: "a black woman taking the exam will be given ten extra points . . . which will boost her ahead of many white males whom are obviously much more qualified." White men are "obviously . . . more qualified," and the "minority" person in the field is not conceptually linked as the "most qualified"—the two are set in logical contrast syntactically. It appears difficult for many whites to envision people of color as equal to them, both educationally and occupationally.

Allan discusses racism against whites:

> I wish everybody thought like I do, but people don't. There is still racism in the world today. One person that makes me aware that it is still around is Jesse Jackson. Almost every white person I know thinks that he is the most racist person on the planet. And I tend to agree with them. I honestly believe that he is doing more harm than good for the black community. He keeps on preaching and preaching and putting down the white man. This makes the white community angry and eventually leads to more hate group activity. You never see a white extremist complaining about racism or discrimination against whites, so why does he feel that he has to?

Here Allan expresses his frustration with the rhetoric of Jesse Jackson, which he believes is antiwhite. As discussed in the last chapter, the autobiographies reflect an impression held by most respondents that whiteness is under a cultural assault from many people of color. Allan believes Jackson is a leading voice in this attack. Further, the victims of hate crimes are in effect blamed for their own suffering. Allan provides a disclaimer for future racist attacks when he says "This makes the white community angry and eventually leads to more hate group activity." Finally, in contrast to evidence from the comments of numerous respondents, Allan asserts that whites do not complain about racism against them, to suggest that protests by people of color are illegitimate. Allan continues:

> If a black man and a white man were trying for the same position, for instance, in a fire station wouldn't you want the man who is better suited for the job? People's lives are at stake here. Say the white man does a better job in the physical aspect and in the interview, wouldn't you want him to show up when you're lying passed out under a burning bookcase? Most people would. However, if the fire company doesn't have enough black people on the force, then they have to hire him. I don't think this is right in any way especially when people's lives are on the line. . . . One thing that I feel treats the white community disproportionately is affirmative action. It really doesn't affect minorities at all, it helps them. It only affects the white community. It affects us because it may prevent us from getting a job simply because we are white and the company already has enough white people working for them, they need minorities so they do not have any room for us. I do not feel this is right at all. If someone is better suited for the job, then they should get the job. End of story. If someone is not suited for that particular line of work, then they should pursue a different line of work.

The recurring theme in Allan's writing is that unqualified people of color are unfairly displacing whites in the workforce and possibly endangering them. He views affirmative action not as "good faith efforts" intended to increase the presence of minorities and white women in businesses and universities, but as a mandate to hire and admit unqualified applicants. Barbara Reskin, probing the effects of affirmative action on whites, suggests that the reason so many white men, especially, believe they must be losing jobs to unqualified white women and people of color is because they are unaccustomed to competing unsuccessfully with them.[85] Thus, when this occurs, the only way they can explain it is to suggest that the person of color was not qualified, and only prevailed through racial preferences. This way of thinking carries old racist and sexist notions. Otherwise, why would it be a humiliation that *needed* justification to be "beaten" by a white woman or person of color? Why does this need more explanation than if another white man received the desired job?

Data shows that affirmative action has not resulted in the hiring of unqualified workers. Contradicting many respondents' particular career concerns, a study of Columbus, Ohio, female and minority police officers hired under an affirmative action policy showed they performed as well as the white males.[86]

More general studies of worker productivity reveal similar findings. A study of more than 3,000 entry-level employees in a variety of firms in Atlanta, Boston, Detroit, and Los Angeles demonstrated that performance evaluations of those hired using affirmative action did not differ from ratings of white men, or of white women and people of color hired without using affirmative action.[87] In other research, CEOs supported affirmative action, stating in one (72 percent) that it does not hurt productivity, and in another (41 percent) that it improves productivity.[88] Other studies have assessed whether profits differ between firms with higher or lower percentages of minority workers; in order to address the criticism sometimes lobbied that companies lower their standards when hiring people of color. No correlation was found, suggesting that companies with higher percentages of people of color have not compromised quality in meeting affirmative action goals.[89] In fact, some studies show quite the opposite: companies with better records of hiring and promoting people of color and white women average a higher return on investment than those with poorer records.[90]

Inflexible Quotas?

As previously alluded to, most whites hold serious misconceptions regarding what affirmative action requires of companies. Perhaps one of the most commonly held misconceptions about affirmative action is that it amounts to strict numerical quotas that companies must meet for hiring people of color. For example, Rick voices a common misconception regarding quotas:

> Being white in today's world is getting harder with every passing second. Sure, we still have the majority of the population in the United States but our percentage is going down everyday. Affirmative Action is starting to negatively affect white males like myself. At least in my future line of work, policing, the number of white males being hired is going down. I know that it may not be fair to complain considering how long African Americans lived with and still deal with job discrimination. But to me it doesn't make sense to have quotas on the number of each race in a police department, especially if affirmative action is forcing the hiring of under-qualified individuals because that person is a minority or a female.

Clearly, according to Rick, whiteness is under siege; circumstances in his own life and, very likely, in the political discourse around him have convinced him that being white is becoming steadily more cumbersome and oppressive. However, as is evident in several autobiographies, he does have a sense of an incongruity in what he is saying—Rick realizes that on some level, his troubles seem trivial compared to those of African Americans. Reading the students' words in context is a reminder of the complexity of their positions.

Meg writes of learning about affirmative action:

In my tenth grade history class we had to do a research paper. I didn't have any ideas on what to do, so I talked to my teacher, Mr. Mason and he suggested Affirmative Action. I had never even heard of it. He tried to briefly explain it, but I had to go to the library myself and research before I fully understood what it was all about. . . . After reading about it and going over Affirmative Action cases, I knew that I was completely against it. I couldn't even believe such practices went on. It seemed to me like reverse discrimination. Why would blacks want extra help in getting jobs or going to school? Haven't they heard of getting there on their own without little favors helping them along the way? What about pride in the fact that you got somewhere because you're qualified, not because someone had to meet a quota? I was baffled by the entire concept.

Meg presents affirmative action as logically flawed, implying that no reasonable person could think it fair. Like many whites, she also believes that affirmative action includes quotas, when in fact they are illegal except when a court prescribes them in extreme and unusual cases.[91] The experience of writing this high school report failed to correct her misconceptions.

David also brings up "quotas" in his discussion:

Soon, I will be applying for a position as a . . . State Trooper. I am told that as a twenty-two year old white male, I will have to meet stricter criteria than a minority applicant. Several years ago, my father applied for this same position. The Affirmative Action legislation had just passed. He passed the test, scoring in the 90th percentile. However, he was told that due to the change in legislation, he would have to be placed further down on the list. They would have to accept Blacks, Hispanics, and Women first. They had to meet a quota before they could accept White males. When my father heard this he was very disheartened. He could not understand why the State Police, of all people, would allow this to happen. He could not believe that the United States government would discriminate against a White male. This is a form of Reverse discrimination. I can only hope that the "quotas" are met for the minorities when I apply.

David views affirmative action as responsible for a legacy of reverse discrimination experienced in his family, because of the use of quotas. In fact, many affirmative action practices are neutral with respect to gender or race. They only work to eliminate as much subjectivity as possible from the hiring and promotion process.[92] Such strategies include geographically broadening recruiting, openly advertising available jobs, interviewing a wide variety of applicants, and standardizing practices to attempt to eliminate bias.[93] Other strategies do use characteristics such as race and gender as plus factors among comparably qualified candidates. Nonetheless, quotas are illegal and have been challenged and struck down in court when used by companies illegitimately. On rare occasions, when a court has found that a company has not made "good faith efforts" to increase diversity, a temporary quota may be imposed until progress is shown. However, sometimes there are good reasons that progress has not been made in hiring a more diverse workforce, despite an organization's best efforts. It is in part to allow for this possibility that strict numerical quotas are illegal, although goals for progress are encouraged.

Though opinion polls seem to suggest public opposition to affirmative action, people's opinions depend somewhat on how the question is asked. It is particularly important in surveys whether affirmative action is characterized as "quotas."[94] In most polls purporting to measure opinions about affirmative action, Americans are asked about illegal practices, like quotas. In a 1995 Gallup poll, fewer than one in eight supported hiring quotas.[95] Conversely, 70 percent *support* affirmative action when pollsters accurately describe it as *not* consisting of "quotas" or "preferences."[96] Most whites support the types of strategies actually used by companies. Three-quarters said they approve of employers recruiting qualified white women and people of color through increased outreach efforts, and most supported other race-neutral practices such as open advertising, job training, and tracking diversity.[97] As long as quotas and rigid preference systems are excluded, many whites understand the need for and fairness of affirmative action.

Level Playing Field: Colorblind Arguments of Meritocracy

In addition to making a case that whites are economically disadvantaged through the use of personal stories, by arguing that affirmative action causes harm and by suggesting that it is fundamentally unreasonable, some white respondents assert that affirmative action is no longer necessary because the U.S. marketplace is now a level playing field for people of all races and ethnicities. In such a system, where everyone is treated equally, for some to receive special consideration in hiring and admissions to universities seems fundamentally unfair.

To refer to race is first to acknowledge difference, whether one considers that difference to be a biological "truth" or a social construction. Recent research has asserted that for whites who do not want to appear racist, noticing difference at all has been taboo.[98] In other words, whites most often attempt to appear "colorblind." My data suggest that, at least for *young* whites, the question is *under what circumstances* one should notice or speak about race. Sometimes respondents avoid recognition of difference altogether. For example, they use coded language: words or phrases that are either neutral or ostensibly recognize and support sacred American ideals while covertly standing in for negative racial characterizations or implying that "others" are in opposition to these ideals. The substantive content of the autobiographical discourse is thus inundated with references to such supposedly race-neutral concepts as "bad neighborhoods," "certain people," and "crime," and other valued ideals such as "individualism," "equality," "respect," "merit," "hard work," and "responsibility."

Under many other circumstances, however, "difference" is acknowledged, at least to some degree. If there is one word that is used more than all others in these data, it is most likely the word "difference." The participants in this study apparently struggle more with how to cope with the increasing diversity in their environment than with almost any other issue of race. My research suggests that race is often equated with difference, or difference is used as code for race, which some respondents believe is wrong *ever* to invoke. A common assertion in the autobiographies is that one should try to ignore difference (thus ignore "race") to whatever degree is possible, a perspective close to the colorblind position described by race theorists.[99] However, even when this perspective is advanced in the autobiographies, it is often with mention of how it is nearly impossible to be colorblind. In other words, colorblindness is frequently discussed by these young whites as an ideal to be attained, not a reality. Another stance that some respondents take on race is that one should recognize people's "racial" differences, because what appear to be distinct biological differences between members of groups are fixed and stable and, further, can be predictors of their behavior, talents, and proclivities. Thus, racial differences can be used as a guide for future encounters with similar persons. This is an essentialist perspective, where differences are viewed as biological or cultural absolutes.[100]

Others are more "race-conscious," that is, they recognize that different experiences come from being labeled as part of a racial group, but there are no fixed and stable biological differences between members of racial groups, and thus there can be no conclusions drawn about behavior or personality of individuals based on their racial group membership. Finally, another way the respondents deal with difference in their writing is to laud it as something that adds "color" to our lives, and should be embraced. In the last two perspectives, "difference" may be cast as not only racial, though this might be the primary form, but also religious, ethnic, class, or ability/disability. By bringing in other forms of difference and diversity, the autobiographer effectively signals that she or he is not overly concerned with race. Each of these perspectives on difference represents a culturally sanctioned, "appropriate," use of race for whites, and more than one can be found in any one autobiography. Again, white individuals cannot be categorized in terms of the use of race they have chosen. Instead, each of these uses is part of collective whiteness.

Thus, in the autobiographies, "colorblindness" is evident and is constructed along a complex rubric of appropriate and inappropriate recognition of difference. However, respondents are not "colorblind" in all situations; in fact, they believe that one should note and respond to race in certain situations. In regards to several types of topical areas, respondents place themselves in a position of judges of the discourse of race, citing cases when race was invoked unjustifiably, in their mind. For the most part, throughout the autobiographies respondents are not angry about specific actions of people of color. They also do not, for the most part, advance traditional stereotypes of people of color (perhaps with the exception of their supposed proclivity to crime) and of white superiority. Instead, resentment and hostility toward people of color are expressed through skepticism about *their* complaints—that is, the evidence put forth by people of color regarding their own life experiences with discrimination is judged and found wanting.

Thus, the argument is not necessarily that people of color are "lazy," or "unmotivated," or whatever other traditional stereotypes are employed, but that *if they are not*, why do they, in today's meritocratic society, request or need "extra help" in the form of affirmative action, "quotas" or scholarships? This criticism is a double-edged sword: implied in the autobiographies is the assumption that either people of color *are* indeed lazy or unmotivated, or otherwise deficient—or that they are paranoid, and "using their race" to get ahead. This linguistic maneuver is characteristic of the new discourse of whiteness. It affords these white respondents and others in their generation a supposed neutral stance in the problem of race: they are the defenders of people of color against claims of innate inferiority, but are also in effect judge and jury of the legitimacy of their stories, able to silence or at least discount parts of them that violate today's racial discursive etiquette.

Near the middle of the last century, Gunnar Myrdal called race relations in this country "an American dilemma."[101] Specifically, the dilemma was between values that Americans professed to hold dear, such as equality, individualism and reward according to merit, and the reality of racism and discrimination. Since Myrdal, others have observed the hypocrisy of European American "values."[102] Today, the United States is still faced with the same dilemma, "talking American" still includes a great deal of "values" language that is not backed up with reality.[103] However, these autobiographies reveal a new twist: for many white people, it is not continuing inequality in current race relations, but the inappropriate invocation of race that threatens our democratic values. These respondents become the most adamant about race when they believe it is being improperly used to suggest that the racial status quo leaves people of color at a disadvantage. For example, Mark writes:

Personally, I feel that my race should never be brought up, whether it be for being seen with someone of a different race or be glorified for being the race that I am. I believe that it all goes back to my family's belief of work hard, believe in God, and you will get what you earn out of life.

Unequivocally, Mark insists that his race "should never be brought up," for any reason. Respondents do not always advance a colorblind perspective, but they are most likely to do so in order to protest what they believe to be unreasonable demands by people of color. Many passages in the autobiographies suggest that "difference" should be overlooked when to take note of it opposes individualism, if it challenges the ideal of meritocracy, or if racism is discussed as a feature of collective white power. Each of these represents an "inappropriate" use of race talk.

A foundational American fable is that anyone who works hard can "make it" in the United States. Part of the substantive discourse of whiteness is belief in this myth of meritocracy. Whites have a stake in believing this notion, for if it is false, they must question whether all their own accomplishments have come solely from personal abilities. In other words, they may question whether they deserved their achievements or to what extent being white helped them to attain success. Further, questioning the myth of meritocracy threatens a sense of entitlement—that they have "worked hard" and "deserve" to be rewarded. Thus, the premise that being white brings economic advantage seems preposterous to many; and conversely they cannot believe that nonwhites are disadvantaged as a counterpoint to their advantage. Fiona writes:

> The African-Americans however, didn't seem to be in the "upper class clique." I think that this was by choice, though. Right behind the high school, there is a neighborhood called Roxbury Estates. This was where the African-Americans lived, which was ironic because it was right across the street from Hunter Point, where the upper class lived. The African-Americans were a defined group in the school. They didn't really associate with any other ethnic or racial group. Needless to say, I always felt awkward when I walked past them in the hall. To this day, I don't feel as comfortable around African-Americans as I do around most other ethnic or racial groups. There is really no reason for it, except that they made me feel intimidated. I never let the way I feel keep me from trying to make friends. Some other people would have rather just kept to their own ethnic group, but I was raised to treat everyone the same, no matter what their skin color or ethnic background is. Besides the African-Americans sticking to their own ethnic group, the race or ethnicity of other people wasn't really a factor.

Richard Delgado notes that because of their different life experiences, whites and people of color have different myths. One of whites' myths is that of black progress and a level economic playing field. Delgado points out that without this myth, whites are in danger of being faced with guilt for the economic plight of African Americans.[104] As she grew up, Fiona was aware of the economic disparities between local racial groups. However, she believes the African

Americans have chosen to stay out of the upper class. Maintaining the myth of meritocracy, this young woman has convinced herself that people of color would choose to remain at a lower economic level. Also Fiona ties in what she sees as African Americans' voluntary *economic* segregation with cultural separation she believes is solely the choice of African American classmates. This conceptualization of the separation excuses her for still feeling "awkward" around black people—they made *her* "feel intimidated."

Because young whites believe racism is a problem of the distant past, in large part ended by their parents' and grandparents' generations, most embrace the idea that to think, talk, or act in a race-conscious way is itself racist.[105] They believe that the way to solve racial problems from this point on, is to act in a race-neutral manner. As touched on earlier, to admit that being white brings economic privilege would cause whites to question their success, and would also allow for the possibility that affirmative action is still needed, a notion fundamentally in opposition to colorblind ideology. Lisa writes:

> I think everyone should be treated exactly the same way, regardless of race. I understand the importance of quotas and affirmative action and agree that they are needed but when dealing with individuals in everyday life, I believe you should treat everyone the same.

Lisa does not realize the conflict between "treating individuals the same" and applying race-conscious remedies. Further, she somehow classifies affirmative action as "needed," but not used in "everyday life."

Caroline wrote her autobiography just after the September 11th attacks:

> There is too much going on in the world right now to have to worry about people in our own country that are at war with each other. I think that race and ethnicity is important in society today. It is a big issue when it comes to the workforce with affirmative action and everything. I do not really think that it should be as big an issue as society makes it. It really is not important what color a person is or what their ethnic background is. It makes no difference what race a person is, it is what they can do.

Caroline bases her colorblind ideology on a need for internal national unity in a time of crisis after the terrorist attacks. She understands that race has no real effect on job performance, but overlooks the fact that people often are still treated by employers as though their race *could* affect their job performance—and this is the reason for affirmative action. It is common for respondents to assume that because they try to act in a nonprejudiced way, others do the same, and remedies like affirmative action are unnecessary and even discriminatory against whites. Distinguishing the personal from the structural is a skill as yet unlearned by many college students.

Will purports to treat people fairly, without regard to race, but his discussion has an angrier tone:

> Because of many racist people out there, I think my status would change if I were of a different race. I would not let this stop me though. I think more minorities bitch and complain more than they do anything else about their problems. Most people are not out to get someone because of their race. I know this for a fact because the people that I hang out with view people of different races as the same as one another. I know that there are people out there who like to make life difficult for others. On a much lesser extent, this can be seen the other way around. I know what it is like to be treated poorly by a person because of my race and I don't like that. But everyone is not out to get minorities. There is a problem, but blaming people who are not racist is totally wrong. They like to say ' . . . it's [because of] people like you that I am the way I am . . . ' This really pisses me off mainly because I would not do anything to discriminate against anyone. If someone has it harder, they need to put forth a little more effort to reach their goals. I am sure I would have to do the same if I lived in somewhere like China or Japan. The point is that these minorities who constantly force into their minds that everyone is exploiting them are digging the hole they are in deeper and deeper. If other minorities can do it, then others should be able to as well. . . . I believe that racism is mostly based on a micro level. I believe that individuals who are racist ruin the reputations of the ones who are not racist, like me. Many minorities may look at me and think that I am a jerk because I am white and in the middle class. What they don't know is that I am a very friendly person and am nice and respectful to persons of all races.

For Will, the experiences of various groups do not differ; he assumes that in a meritocratic society, anyone who works hard enough can "reach their goals." In this perspective, all that is needed is the correct amount of effort, so if a group is not succeeding, it is that group's own fault. Although Will does not mention a specific group, he uses classic "model minority" rhetoric to suggest that if certain groups are lagging economically, they are not working hard enough, because other groups have "made it." This ignores that certain groups immigrated voluntarily, with monetary resources, and were allowed to involve themselves relatively freely in the economic system, whereas others were brought here involuntarily and legally kept out of the economic system for decades. Will also presents himself as a hypothetical "model minority," stating that if he moved to another country, he would have to work hard to succeed. This ties back to the point he makes in his opening sentence—that if he were a minority, he understands his status would change, but he "would not let this stop [him]." This, certainly, is the pinnacle of colorblindness. Many respondents seem to believe that living as white today is no different from living as any other race.

Conclusion

Few respondents recognize that being white brings them advantages. Such a recognition can threaten whites' worldview. Sometimes white students hear the phrase "white privilege" and assume that to suggest white people have benefited from being white means that they did not work hard. Robert Jensen, a white university professor, speaks to this issue:

> [W]hite folks have long cut other white folks a break. I know, because I am one of them. . . . I know I did not get where I am by merit alone, I benefited from, among other things, white privilege. That doesn't mean I don't deserve my job, or that if I weren't white I would never have gotten the job. It means simply that all through my life, I have soaked up benefits for being white. . . .
>
> There certainly is individual variation in experience. Some white people have had it easier than I. . . . Some white people have had it tougher than I. . . . But, in the end, white people have all drawn on white privilege somewhere in their lives.
>
> Like anyone, I have overcome certain hardships in my life. I have worked hard to get where I am, and I work hard to stay here. But to feel good about myself and my work, I do not have to believe that 'merit,' as defined by white people in a white country, alone got me here. I can acknowledge that in addition to all that hard work, I got a significant boost from white privilege, which continues to protect me every day of my life from certain hardships.
>
> At one time in my life, I would not have been able to say that, because I needed to believe that my success in life was due solely to my individual talent and effort. I saw myself as the heroic American, the rugged individualist. I was so deeply seduced by the culture's mythology that I couldn't see the fear that was binding me to those myths. Like all white Americans, I was living with the fear that maybe I didn't really deserve my success, that maybe luck and privilege had more to do with it than brains and hard work.

David Roediger, in *The Wages of Whiteness*, drawing on the work of W. E. B. Du Bois, traces how European ethnics began to identify racially as whites, rather than ethnically, or along class lines as working-class people. This was a great trick played on working-class whites by elite whites, because, rather than paying them the wages that they were worth, they instead paid them a "psychological wage of whiteness." In other words, workers got to think of themselves as white, superior to working men and women of other racial and ethnic groups, and identified with wealthy whites against their class interests. Being white carried some other nonwage benefits, such as unrestricted travel and escaping certain forms of discrimination. But in terms of monetary wages, whiteness carried no significant value for the working class. Had working-class whites instead identified along class lines, with other working people of various ethnic and racial groups, capitalist whites would not have been able to play working-class people against each other along racial lines, using working-class people of color as strikebreakers to keep whites' wages low.[106] Lillian Smith, writing about the white working class, highlighted how this "psychological wage" worked:

> To be 'superior,' to be the 'best people on the earth' with the 'best system' of making a living, because your sallow skin was white and you were 'Anglo-Saxon,' made you forget that you were eaten up with malaria and hookworm; made you forget that you lived in a shanty and ate potlikker and cornbread, and worked long hours for nothing. Nobody could take away from you this whiteness that made you and your way of life 'superior.' They could take your house, your job, your fun; they could steal your wages, keep you from acquiring knowledge; they could tax your vote or cheat you out of it; they could by arousing your anxieties make you impotent; but they could not strip your white skin off of you. It became the poor white's most precious possession, a 'charm' staving off utter dissolution. And in devious, perverse ways it helped maintain his sanity in an insane world, compensating him—as did his church's promise of h[e]aven—from so many spiritual bruises and material deprivations.[107]

For most whites, this misrecognition of their common interests with people of color still goes on today, and is one of the costs of racism for white people. Paul Kivel explains:

> [W]ealth is tremendously unequally distributed in our country. . . . The top . . . is almost exclusively white. There are also large numbers of white people in the middle and on the bottom. . . . With wealth so concentrated in the top 20 percent [the top 1 percent controls 47 percent of the total net financial wealth of the U.S., and the next 19 percent controls 44 percent of the net financial wealth], most white people have much to gain from working with people of color to redistribute wealth and opportunity. However racism often keeps poor, working- and middle-class white people from seeing common struggles with people of color. Feelings of racial solidarity keep many of us focused on our racial connections with people at the top rather than our economic connections with others lower down. The small amount of benefits we receive from being white can distract us from recognizing the amount of exploitation we receive at the hands of those at the top.[108]

The sense of class consciousness suggested here was reflected in the comments of a few respondents. For example, Marcy's working-class status, rather than causing her to resent people of color, apparently leads her to empathize with their plight:

When I was around twelve, I remember a couple of African American families bought land in the county near our farm. My dad had told me that you had to respect an African American with land because it was not given to him. About two years later, when I was fourteen my parents had to file bankruptcy. We lost all the land and equipment that my dad owned except for the five acres that our house was on. While we got to keep the house, my dad had to pay around six hundred dollars a month for a mortgage that had been paid off before the bankruptcy. Part of the reason my dad and other farmers were losing their land was because of big business monopolies. I know many people would look down on farmers who hired cheap labor. But, I understand why my father did it. He worked around the clock trying to make a living for his family and to keep what had been passed down to him. On August 26th 1986, my family's home burned while we were helping put out another person's barn fire. Unfortunately, my dad did not have home owner's insurance. So, we were forced to let the land go back to the bank. I have mentioned the above chapter of my life because I believe I can reasonably say that I know how it feels to have something taken away. This, in turn, makes me better able to sympathize with all racial groups that have lost property rights, or are unfairly dominated by rich white men.

Marcy believes that her family was treated unfairly by "rich white men," and thus feels a kinship with people of color, but she does not equate her experience with theirs. Marcy's father, commendably, taught her respect for people of color of similar occupational status, explaining to her that they were unlikely to have inherited the land that they were farming, as opposed to whites. Donna Langston suggests that the type of class consciousness Marcy shows could be the beginning of radical change:

> We need to overcome divisions among working people, not by ignoring the multiple oppressions many of us encounter, or by oppressing each other, but by becoming committed allies on all issues which affect working people: racism, sexism, classism, etc. An injury to one is an injury to all. Don't play by ruling class rules. . . . [109]

Another respondent, a "non-traditional" student, Bill, told of a time that he got into a fight in school with an African-American student. When he came home angry with the student, his father told him:

> 'The only difference between the Irish man and the colored man was that one was black on the outside and one was black on the inside.' . . . I had forgotten about it until I took this class and read about the minority labor forces and the immigrants competing for jobs by which group would work for the least money. This put that statement into perspective for me in that the Irish immigrants and the African Americans

were treated the same because we were perceived as having the same worth.

Some respondents recognize that whiteness can be an advantage to them, both materially and psychologically. Further, this psychological wage of whiteness can be used to drive a wedge between whites and people of color in the same economic position. However, despite some whites' recognition of privilege and of common economic interests with people of color, one of the most dominant views of whiteness in this research, along with the sense of whiteness as empty and as a cultural stigma, is that of economic disadvantage. Although this understanding of whites' status is based on many misunderstandings of the economic structure, one must understand it is a source of much frustration and resentment. The question is, Why are the economic benefits of whiteness and the consequences of the psychological wage not more often noticed by whites? Why is the prevailing view one of economic disadvantage or reverse discrimination against whites?

The answer seems to lie in a preoccupation with the issue of affirmative action. Studies show that whites who work in companies that utilize affirmative action are the most supportive of it; and whites who attend schools that use affirmative action the most have the most positive feelings about it.[110] It is whites who understand affirmative action the least who are the most resentful of it. Although this is cause for some optimism, respondents in this research were very sure of three things about affirmative action. First, they were hypersensitive to its adverse effects on whites. Second, they gave very little notice to its benefits in the lives of people of color. Finally, they did not acknowledge it as a practical solution to racial inequality.

This is more than a matter of intellectual curiosity. Unfortunately, sometimes whites' impressions of victimization can lead them to take actions to correct what they see as an imbalance against them. In 1998, about half of all of the 450 colleges and universities that reported to the FBI about hate crimes on campus had experienced at least one such incident. Of all of these bias-related crimes, 57% were motivated by race.[111] Whites' perceptions of economic and cultural victimization on college campuses may lead them to engage in violence on campus against people of color.[112] Researchers have pointed out that aside from overt attacks, on most campuses there exists a constant, underlying degree of racial tension and social awkwardness.[113]

Whites' perceptions that they are being taken advantage of economically in the workplace also have sometimes inspired them to take violent action against people of color. Several examples could be cited, but one that is perhaps most poignant is the murder of Vincent Chin, a twenty-seven-year-old Chinese man who was killed by white unemployed automobile workers in Detroit on the way to celebrate his upcoming wedding. These men mistook him for a Japanese person, and assaulted him due to their anger and resentment for losing their jobs in the auto industry.[114] Rather than understanding that it is other, more wealthy whites who cost working-class whites their jobs, middle- and working-class whites' anger is often directed toward people of color when they feel economically disadvantaged.

Further, even though most whites do not take violent action against people of color based on their construction of themselves as economic victims, they may lobby, speak, or vote against race-conscious hiring and admissions policies still needed to allow people of color to achieve full equality. Just as racist ideologies of superiority historically were used to justify existing systems of economic exploitation, now ideologies of victimization are used to legitimize dismissal of the need for corrective policies for economic inequality.

Chapter 6
"Being White is Like Being Free": Whiteness and the Potential for Antiracism[1]

This research has demonstrated that some characteristics of whiteness were common across the data. The young whites in my research, for the most part, view themselves as passive in regard to the many racialized aspects of their lives. They often describe themselves as recipients of parental messages and claim that certain attitudes are the result of what was put into their minds about "race" by others. Thus, writing about his middle school years, Stephen describes white, Black, and Latino gangs, and then adds "I was an observer, and what I was observing was very discouraging, not only as a white person, but also as a human being. It started to make me question my own heritage and upbringing." As young adults, these respondents tend to view themselves as passively involved in interracial interactions.

The major theme of whiteness expressed in the autobiographies is the belief that rather than bringing one advantage, whiteness is now a social liability. When whites are prompted to discuss the matter, they view whiteness as obscure, empty or boring. Many use racialized "others," particularly African Americans, to construct a white identity—in other words, they write of who they are by referring to who they are not. Many view whiteness as a socially and economically victimized identity. Even those who recognize personal white privilege and individual prejudice often lack an understanding of the systemic racism that has long been central to the United States.[2]

Systematic privilege and disadvantage is difficult for white students to understand, and challenging for teachers of college courses to communicate. Although in some of the autobiographical passages cited certain privileges of whiteness were noted or mentioned, rarely do the respondents suggest remedies for dismantling the unearned rewards of whiteness. In part, of course, this omission may be due to self-interest—why call for the reform of a system that has benefited your grandparents and parents, and from which you have been raised to believe you are entitled to benefit?

However, there may be another reason one reads few calls for fundamental change in the autobiographies. Most of the time, when respondents write about white privilege, they do not discuss it as an ongoing, systematic rewarding of whiteness. Most who admit white privilege exists write vaguely that there have "probably been times" they have benefited from being white. Few tell of specific instances when this was so. When they do mention specifics of white privilege, most noted are some more abstract items, or what might be considered matters of everyday, interactional convenience. For example, after reading a list of some forty items given by Peggy McIntosh that she as a white woman takes for granted and does not usually recognize as a privilege given her based on race,[3] many white students later identify with the more "microlevel" privileges McIntosh mentions, such as being able to find flesh-colored bandages that match one's skin. However, fewer mention in their writing privileges such as better job opportunities, or being able to live in the neighborhood of one's own choosing. For example, Stacey, who considers herself to be "somewhat racist," writes:

> I think that being white makes me have an advantage over people of other races. I don't necessarily feel superior to them, but society tends to sometimes discriminate against non white people. I've never really thought that much about being at an advantage until we studied race and racism in my social problems class. One of the articles we read had a whole list of advantages white people had. There are many of the same things that two people could do, yet if one person was of color, that would be noted. One of the main things in the list that stood out was the fact that I can get a band-aid in flesh color and it will basically match my skin. That is so true, because I have never seen a band-aid made to match a black person's skin color. I didn't really realize that I have so many privileges that come along with being white.

In the autobiographies, the matching Band-Aids were the most regularly mentioned privilege of whiteness. The other item most often discussed is that whites are never followed around in department stores, and how that would be very frustrating. While sometimes the most mundane, "everyday" indignities a person of color must suffer can be as damaging as the more structural inequities can be, it is crucial that white people understand that racism is much more than a list of "inconveniences."

For these respondents, whiteness usually includes an inability to envision any real disadvantages to being a person of color today, beyond the minor annoyances caused by individual, prejudiced white people. Almost entirely omitted in the autobiographies are references to *economic* white privilege and economic disadvantage for people of color. The collective whiteness constructed by this young generation is one where, economically and culturally, it "pays" to be a person of color, and conversely, whiteness is a liability. Thus, the most pronounced elements of white identity in these autobiographies are empty and victimized whiteness.

There are, however, passages in the autobiographies characterized by different perspectives on whiteness. When writing from these perspectives, the person is more likely to recognize the effects of white privilege on people of color beyond Band-Aids and shopping frustrations. In these instances, autobiographers are deeply reflexive about whiteness. In these passages, authors struggle with what whiteness means in their everyday lives and how to be "responsibly white." Writing reflexively, respondents recognize both sides of white privilege, how it advantages them and disadvantages others, and various levels of that privilege, such as the individual interactional level and also the structural level. In doing so, some search for ways to help to change the status quo.

In this chapter I turn to the various perspectives that were directed more toward antiracism in the autobiographies. Although certainly the autobiographies were characterized by a general belief that whiteness is a liability, there is also reason to believe that in this generation of young whites there is potential for antiracism. In this chapter I group the more antiracist responses into the following categories: fearful, directionless, antiprejudiced, and antiracist. I analyze each perspective and see how they are linked to the students' understandings of racism.

Again, mine is not an attempt to categorize each individual student into a specific category on a continuum of antiracism. Instead, it is important to note that my interest is in *collective* whiteness, and thus the unit of analysis is not the individual white person, but the individual story or unit of text. For many reasons, including current demographic changes, whiteness is in a state of flux, and the corresponding complexity of white identity is exemplified in this data. In the same autobiography, for example, respondents may write in one place in a "fearful" manner, only to write from an antiracist perspective later. Additionally, some of these are students who wrote of whiteness as a liability in other parts of their autobiographies.

Lingering Fears and Discomfort

Numerous respondents stated or implied that they have postponed their involvement in interracial interactions or even in antiracism because of fears regarding social tensions or awkwardness. Some students perceived that although they have been trying to act in opposition to racism, people of color are *the real problem* in that they are less open than whites, or resistant to whites' efforts. These students view actions opposing racism as fraught with the danger of their own victimization or rejection.

Because most of the respondents have an ahistorical view of race relations, and also believe strongly in the value of "treating everyone the same," they are likely to judge situations in which they believe a person of color is rude or unfriendly toward them as a blatantly personal affront. From a historical context, sometimes people of color have justifiable reasons to be suspicious of the overtures of white people, but this response can be seen as unfounded hostility and rejection by these respondents. The stories white respondents tell of social rejection focus on three main themes: (1) perceptions of having their attempts at friendship or other relationships rejected by people of color, (2) worries about having to "watch what [they] say" for fear of offending people of color in everyday conversations, and (3) resentment about having been accused of personal prejudice or racism. Helen, for example, writes about feeling rejected:

> My awareness finally started to broaden when I came to college. This may have been because the opportunity to get to know people was not given, and many judgments had to be made at first glance. This process made me realize what my first thoughts about people were, and I was disappointed in myself. For instance, I would clutch my purse when an African American would pass me at night on the campus. . . .
>
> My next big step towards unlearning my racism was when I registered for [race and ethnicity] class. . . . From the first night of class I felt an openness and readiness within myself to change and looked at it as a challenge to accept the things that were said about my race, rather than to become defensive. . . . After the first couple of classes I felt hopeful that I was making a change within myself and becoming more aware, but then I experienced a set back. One night, walking out of class, I saw a group of my African American classmates walking ahead of me, one of which I knew from a previous class. I debated whether or not to say hello because of the ratio of them to me, but convinced myself through my newfound hope to end my racist thoughts. As I said hello everyone was friendly, but looked somewhat suspicious of me. My friend and I began to talk about the class we had together previously, which was about the psychology of women. I joked with him that at least he was no longer the minority in this class like he was in the other and he replied, "yeah, now you are." The words were harsh and rebuilt my wall of defense.

Helen experiences this encounter as a "set back" that "rebuilt [her] wall of defense." Many respondents, like Helen, believing themselves to have made progress in becoming more racially "aware," expect their efforts to be taken at face value by people of color. When they are not, the respondent experiences this as a setback.

Blake, who plays pick-up basketball in his college gym, expresses the sense of alienation he feels when he finds it difficult to break into the African American player's friendship groups:

I started going to the gym in hopes of making some friends there that might be involved in some of the same sports I enjoy. I engaged in a pick-up basketball with a bunch of black kids the first time I went. We just threw a team together quick and started playing. I came back a few more times and played with the same kids. Never once did they introduce themselves to me or inquire to me about anything. I tried small talk and introducing but it never worked. All the black kids seemed like best friends, and I was just the outcast. I don't know if it was just because since there are so few black students on campus that it is automatic to assimilate with each other, or if it was a legitimate friendship that they had been working on in other places besides the gym. I felt left out. I was involved in the same activities they were and I was a regular, yet I couldn't be included in their clique because I wasn't black. Now that is just my assumption, but a credible assumption after what I had witnessed daily.

In *Why Are All the Black Kids Sitting Together in the Cafeteria?*, Beverly Daniel Tatum explains that African-American students group together on campus for the reasons that Blake mentions, particularly for support on campuses in which they are the minority and may not feel welcomed.[4] But it is important to notice the particular phrasing that Blake uses in his assessment of his treatment in the gym. He contrasts the black students bonding more easily with one another on campus because they are in the minority with "a *legitimate* friendship." In other words, although Blake understands that group solidarity could be an explanation for why the black basketball players more quickly and easily become friends, and for why he consequently feels "like an outcast," he does not consider this type of relationship "legitimate." It is hard for white students to understand that most people of color could report multiple experiences like the one Blake reports here, when they did not feel included in a clique simply because of the color of their skin. Still, Blake's obvious efforts to cross racial lines to form friendships are commendable, and his bafflement at what seems to him like personal rejection is palpable.

Other respondents' lingering fears about interracial interactions focus on worries about offending people of color. For example, Abigail explains:

I may be a coward but I am the type of person, who likes to avoid friction in my life, so when a heated racial incident is taking place near me, I do not perpetuate it nor do I become involved. A member of my class and I were talking one night about how he noticed that his co-workers, although they are his friends, try to avoid discussing things about race with him. I can identify with these people. When put into a situation like this I generally try to avoid the conversation more or less because I don't want to offend anyone or hurt anyone's feelings, especially if the people in the conversation are my friends. There is so much racial tension in the United States that as a white person I fear saying the wrong thing. I avoid these conversations not because I have nothing to say, but almost because I think I'm being nice. When I explained this to my classmate I think we learned from each other. I think he realized that when a white person had nothing to say, it was not necessarily because they are racist, but maybe they just care about his feeling and don't want to inadvertently say anything to hurt him. I learned from him that blacks perceive a white person avoiding these conversations as perpetuating the problems of racial inequality. They feel these things need to be talked about and discussed. He feels that talking may help in solving the problems. The night after I spoke with him, I felt really good. My eyes were opened a little bit more.

Fearing social rejection or awkwardness, Abigail usually avoids interracial discussions about racism. She explains this by saying that although it may seem like she is a "coward," she is just a person who avoids confrontation. This is a conception held by many well-meaning whites: that if racial problems in the past have been created by cruel things people have said to one another, such as expressions of prejudice, the best way to end racism is to avoid possibly controversial discussions of race. However, because racism is not just a matter of personal prejudice, but is also a system of inequality, simply not discussing it will not make it go away. Abigail has learned, from discussions with people of color in her classes, that avoiding conversations about race can "perpetuat[e] the problem."

In contemplating a friendship with an African American man, Mike also discusses whites' fears of offense that keep them from meaningful interaction across the color line:

I felt that I had to be more on guard in my conversations with Jim because I was afraid that I would say something offensive to him. Jim would laugh at me when he noticed me stumbling over my words so that I could find the most transparent, blanket statement with regards to my racial opinions. . . . Most white people feel this way; they stumble around issues when talking with minorities so that they do not offend anyone.

This fact points to a broader problem. I am not a racist but I still have difficulty dealing with blacks on a social level. This problem is limited to black people. I have a Hispanic friend . . . and I can talk frankly to him. With black people though I get uncomfortable. It is hard to explain my reasons for this. Even at work [*Mike is a security guard*] I find it more difficult to approach a black thief than a white one. I am not afraid that the black person is inherently more violent, that is a ludicrous idea. Rather I am afraid of being called a racist. White people in general have this fear. We tend to talk down to black people because we are afraid to be direct with them. This discomfort has been the source of personal, moral conflict. Why do I have a tendency to be shy around black people? I do not distrust them and I am not afraid of them. However I do not seek the same types of interaction with them as I do with whites or even other minorities. I cannot communicate my beliefs to black people because I am afraid they will disagree. . . .

These problems are especially bad problems for white people to have because we are the majority. As the majority we are in control. We should therefore be engaging minorities and downplaying racism. We have a responsibility to counteract the acid tongued racists in our group. We do not do that though. In fact the only whites who seem to be comfortable talking about race are the racists and the extremists. They in turn look like they represent white sentiment. . . . In order for me to avoid being labeled as a racist, I do not engage black people with issues that involve race relations. I wash my conversation of all that could possibly offend the most easily offended. Thus my conversation becomes jargon, the kind of blanket statements that third grade teachers tell their students. 'We are all the same on the inside.' It may or may not be true but either way it is a stupid comment to add to a serious conversation. The lack of communication between minorities and whites is the greatest problem in race relations. Racism cannot go away until we learn to communicate with each other.

Some have pointed out that racism in the United States was formed along a white-black continuum.[5] Thus it should come as no surprise that whites and African Americans experience particular racial tensions still today. As pointed out in chapter 3, whites still construct much of their sense of identity based on an understanding that they are *not* black. Mike theorizes that whites seem to feel particularly judged by African Americans, such that interracial conversations that could lead to increased understanding are inhibited. As this respondent notes, it is crucial for well-meaning whites to begin to communicate with African Americans, or else the interracial dialogue will be abandoned to racist whites.

One female respondent, Alexis, who writes in a particularly antiracist way in her autobiography, describes an experience of rejection based on her race, in which she was accused of being racist:

I went to school with two of [a nationally known African-American leader's] daughters. I didn't know anything about [him] before I got to Buchanan (my high school), but while there I learned quite a bit about him, his beliefs, and values—and where *I* fit into that system of thinking: typically at the bottom. By the time I was a junior, I had done a lot of reading of Black Lit. and discussed racial issues all the time with my friends, my family, in classes; however, I had not yet been accused of being 'White.' My junior year provided me with the opportunity of having one of [the man's] daughters in my P.E. class, I worked with the other one in the library.

One afternoon, as I was walking through a breezeway, I held the door open for one of the girls. She was behind me and I opened it to let her pass through (a habit that I have had for about as long as I can remember—it often drives men crazy). She started screaming all sorts of things at me. 'White bitch' this, 'oppressor' that, all sorts of stuff. I told her that I held the door for everyone, that it was just a habit. Nope. I was racist. Evil. Fortunately, a few of my friends happened to be coming up the stairs just outside the door and sort of stepped in. She said that I was lucky and then she told my friends that they were traitors. Gym class would never be the same again.

While Alexis writes of her contact with the man's daughters as an "opportunity," she is startled at the vehemence with which her seemingly polite gesture is met. She is accused of being a *racist*, however, tellingly, Alexis remembers this event as the first time she was ever accused of being *"White."* For her, being white is not an essential or fixed attribute, based on the color of her skin. Instead it is an attitude and set of behaviors towards people of color from which she has tried to distance herself. In fact, elsewhere in her autobiography, she discusses a time when she began to refer to herself as "green" to disassociate herself from feelings of guilt from being white. Alexis seems to gain an understanding that no matter how much she distances herself from it, some people of color will, because of their experiences, see her as white anyway. Indeed, even white antiracists benefit from certain privileges, although they can try to reject them. When Alexis approaches an interaction with a presumably racially conscious African-American young woman as if they are of equal social status, the gesture of holding the door open for her was perhaps seen as symbolically mocking or patronizing.

Another lingering source of discomfort for some respondents is guilt and shame they feel about being white, both in terms of past acts of racism (whether personal or collective) and/or about present white privilege. Helen reminisces about how she reacted to feeling guilt while in high school:

It was also in high school when I became more aware of the feelings and hostility felt by African Americans towards whites. Because I had avoided the topic, due to the risk of controversy, it took a teacher encouraging in class discussions to bring it up. I noticed African Americans seemed more confident and informed in their beliefs than in years before. This made conversations more informative for me than awkward. The class discussions often addressed simply the differences between African Americans and whites, and this was becoming a terribly familiar topic for me. Some of the class discussions throughout high school addressed anger towards the white race as a whole. While I knew that the anger was not towards me personally, I did feel attacked. I had been raised with no emphasis on my background, as far as religion or ethnicity, and therefore only identified myself as white. These conversations that blamed my race for the situation of the African Americans left me feeling as if the only characteristic that I had ever identified myself with wasn't one to be proud of. My race became the "bad race" to me, and because I couldn't change it I began to defend it with anger addressed towards the African Americans. I began to deny any notion of guilt and while I still had relationships with African Americans, I was forming prejudices against the race in general due to my anger.

Race theorists have noted that an emotion white people must often deal with who wish to be antiracist is guilt. Some place guilt as a part of a "stage" of white racial consciousness.[6] For example, Helms believes guilt may be one of the feelings that accompanies the second stage of the abandonment of racism for whites, "disintegration." Because this is only the second stage, Helms asserts that it is possible for a white person to return to the first state, "contact," because she or he is not able to resolve issues of guilt as well as other conflicts that accompany this stage of identity.

Others note that guilt can be counterproductive to antiracism. For example, Gloria Yamato discusses guilt:

> Then there's the guilt and the desire to end racism and how the two get all tangled up to the point that people, morbidly fascinated with their guilt, are immobilized. Rather than deal with ending racism, they sit and ponder their guilt and hope nobody notices how awful they are. Meanwhile, racism picks up momentum and keeps on keepin' on.[7]

Helen's sense of guilt comes from the association of whites with racism. Helen did not start her young life with a particular ethnic orientation. The only identity she knew to claim was as a white person, and because all she heard of whiteness was negative things, she began to feel guilt. Her response was to be angry and resentful. These feelings in turn caused her to defend whiteness against any criticism. She also notes that it was impossible for her to separate criticisms against white people as a *group* from personal attacks. Helen's insightful statement summarizes one important way that whiteness works to support racism—white guilt can lead to defensiveness. Later, she writes:

> The more classes progressed the more I learned about myself. I realized that compared to the other races and cultures in the class, I knew nothing about my own race and ethnicity. I considered myself white and couldn't describe it to someone or put a value on it. I never thought about it because I never had to. I was never discriminated against because of it, and if I received privileges because of it, I was so accustomed to it that I didn't even notice. I began to realize through the stories told by the African

American students, that I never had to worry about being accused of shoplifting, or fear police, or even be forbidden to live in a particular neighborhood. My race wasn't a factor in my life, but I began to realize the impact that my race had on others' lives.

Being in this high school class becomes a turning point for Helen. Instead of only reacting defensively to the statements of students of color, she begins to be able to look at herself and at whites generally as if from the perspective of a person of color. In doing so, she starts to understand that even if *she* does not think of her race, it does have an "impact . . . on others' lives." Helen begins to develop a sense of double consciousness, that is, being able to see whiteness through the eyes of the Other. Perhaps for some, guilt is a part of the process of becoming racially conscious.

Directionless Nonracism

Some respondents have relatively nonracist attitudes but lack direction in regard to putting those attitudes into action. Sometimes in these passages write about what they learned in courses but complain that these courses did not offer actions that a person can take to help dismantle racism. Put simply, the courses elucidated the "disease" in depth without offering any "cures."

These students' words can serve as a call to action. Instructors should try to offer students ways that they may act to help end racism. In their lack of direction, one can read in these respondents' words a sense of frustration about engaging in further discussions of racism. For example, Trent is unsure of his place in opposing racism. He comments:

So the question is whether being white gives any privileges or benefits, a question which is almost laughable. Of course it does. There are still a lot of people around who are . . . racist, and not being black or some other ethnicity can be a great benefit. So, if there are benefits, and if *responsibilities* always come with benefits, then what are my *responsibilities?* I haven't figured that out yet. I know I have a responsibility to try to end racism, within myself at the very least. Do I also have a responsibility to go on protests against racism? Do I have a *responsibility* to give away belongings that I obtained because of the privileges associated with my race? I haven't yet figured out just how far my responsibility goes, and whether I should be morally obligated to go even farther than just what I am responsible for. . . . As you can see, this hasn't been an important part of my life until recently.

Trent has a unique view among the respondents. He questions what "responsibility" means in terms of his future behavior. Trent reflects the uncertainty of whites about their responsibility to other ethnic and racial groups. It is the task of white antiracist scholars not only to expose white racism but also to suggest how whites might be accountable allies to people of color. These ideas must be taken beyond intellectual musings and made practically applicable in the lives of well-meaning whites.

One female student, Abigail, considers carefully both white privilege and several options that she as a white person has for responding to it:

> The Race/Ethnic Minorities class . . . is opening my eyes to the inequalities the different races possess. These inequalities affect me in all that I do, and I am only beginning to recognize them for what they entail. These inequalities are unspoken privileges that I have been given due to my race. From the moment I wake up in the morning and listen to a white newscaster report the white man's successes of the day, until the time I go to bed listening to a white radio broadcaster playing predominantly white music; I am unconsciously reminded of the status I own. Being born a white person in a country where white is considered normative has put me in a position where I can reliably expect to encounter people of my race wherever I choose to go. I will generally be welcome and feel comfortable in most situations when I leave my home, and if I don't, it probably won't have anything to do with my race. Realizations such as these weren't always in my conscious thought; it wasn't until recently that I came to recognize these privileges.

After discussing at length other specific privileges, such as in hiring and treatment in the criminal justice system, she goes on to discuss her options for handling these privileges:

> First, I can continue to naively accept these privileges as the way the United States works and continue to go through life without acknowledging the inequalities that exist in our society. Second, I can make an effort to be more appreciative of these privileges. In doing so, I would still be accepting, but I would consciously make an effort to recognize these things as they happen. This option, I believe is almost as bad as the first one, because it may lead a white person to feel superior or even grandiose. A third option would be to disregard these options and try to live in a way that promotes equality. I feel that this is the only acceptable option for me, but how to go about actively doing this isn't as clear. I do feel that it is my responsibility to point out racial discrimination when I see it. I feel I should inform people of their biased views, even if it offends them. I feel that I need to continue educating myself on the inequalities that exist in American society, because knowledge is truly the key to social change.

Understanding that to be just "more appreciative" of white privilege is not an effective strategy, Abigail wants to instead "promote equality." However, she is unsure of how to take action to do this. She has completed a course in race and ethnicity, has learned about white privilege and realized that she is responsible for trying to end it, but Abigail did not glean from the course concrete ways to actively oppose racism.

The Antiprejudiced View

Many theorists have discussed the current trend toward "colorblind" racism.[8] Instead of openly noting differences between whites and people of color and then asserting white superiority, many whites today state that they "don't notice color" and yet go on to support institutionalized racism actively or passively. The claim that one can be "colorblind" about race, and that this stance is even *desirable,* is one of the sincere fictions of whiteness.

Certainly colorblindness was a discernable element in many of the autobiographies. However, a distinct perspective expressed at least as often, and perhaps a relatively new sincere fiction of whiteness, I call the "antiprejudiced" view. Antiracist action involves an active resistance to discriminatory behavior, whether individual or institutionalized. The antiprejudiced perspective involves only stated resistance to negative *attitudes* about people of color, those held by the respondent or by other whites.

This perspective is not the same as colorblindness, in that these antiprejudiced whites usually do not claim to overlook the meaningful, although socially constructed, "racial" differences that elicit prejudices. However, theirs is not a strong antiracist response either but, at best, only a tentative move in an activist direction. Although ending prejudice can be a useful step in ending racism, it is not the only step. For most of those who are targets of racism, an end to *discrimination* is likely the primary concern, whether or not whites' attitudes become friendlier toward them. The antiprejudiced approach can waste precious energy fighting the battle of ending all prejudiced attitudes, while the larger war of dismantling racist practice is unfought.

When asked what they believe their future role will be in combating racism, numerous respondents write in their autobiographical statements about being sure that they themselves do not harbor negative attitudes about people of color, raising their children this way, and some mention helping other whites become less prejudiced or more "aware." Few realize that ending prejudice is *only a first step* toward ending racism. Briana puts it this way:

> I acknowledge that white people have the power and the privilege and I understand that discrimination does take place. It is the moral responsibility of whites to admit that racism and discrimination exist and to work toward combating them. I have taken several college courses that were geared toward cultural awareness and diversity. I have shared some of the knowledge I have gained with some of my family members. In the future, I plan to instill the same values in my children that my parents instilled in me.

Briana clearly states that it is *white people's* responsibility to combat racism. However, the only ways that she suggests they do so is through acknowledging and admitting there is a problem, becoming more aware of diversity individually and helping to educate other whites, primarily in their own families. Clearly these are commendable and important steps, but do not target structural racism.

Similarly, Lisa writes of working only on a "small scale," in part to keep from disrupting her life:

> I see myself trying to help race relations on a small scale. I try to correct people when they make ethnic jokes or slurs. I am not going to try and change the world because I want a quiet life. I feel that I can do good everyday just by treating people as equals. If I can get even one person to think before they say something racist, I believe I have done well. I also believe I will raise my children to look beyond race. I don't have kids yet but I have already decided to expose them to different lifestyles whenever I have the chance. I won't teach them they are good because they're white.

Like many respondents, Lisa combines various perspectives on racial matters. After asserting a colorblind position, she then switches to more diversity-conscious language. One reads here the complexity of whiteness and the impossibility of categorizing ordinary whites easily in terms of their perspectives on racial matters. These perspectives are discursive tools, used fluidly in telling stories of whiteness and constructing collective white identity, rather than static positions of individual identity.

An older student, Ted, has a teenage son whom he believes he is raising to be unprejudiced:

> I have taken it upon myself to raise an unbiased, objective thinking child on the subject of race and ethnicity. . . . hopefully what I have been teaching him in the form of non-prejudicial thinking will have an influence. . . . My role in the future of racial/ethnic relations is to take an individual stand against this social parasite in my home, school, workplace and community by not partaking in slur type language and jokes and by treating my fellow humans as I wish to be treated in all interactions. . . . I feel that a national solidarity must take place here in our nation if we are to overcome this destructive social disease that racial/ethnic discrimination brings to the table. When our founding fathers wrote the preface to the constitution they stated that all men were created equal—it is high time we as a nation practiced that belief. . . . I hold a race conscious view that is void of any overt discriminatory bias towards any other race or ethnic group. I am not perfect, I did not choose to be born white anymore than African or Native Americans chose to be born into oppression or poverty, but I am aware! . . . Perhaps, someday if we all do our share, America really can become the "land of the free!"

Again, Ted emphasizes overcoming prejudice, teaching one's children to do so, and, as do other antiprejudiced respondents, "being aware" as individuals in order to dismantle racism. Unlike some other respondents, Ted does mention the contradiction between the ideals of the United States and racial oppression. Yet, in his account he does not suggest specific ways that "we as a nation" might begin to practice the stated belief in equality.

Antiracism

Though much less frequently expressed than other positions, elements of a stronger antiracist position are conveyed in the autobiographical accounts of some students. The antiracist perspective suggests that the respondent opposes not just prejudiced attitudes but *racist behavior* or *institutionalized racism*. The antiracist perspective can be presented in contrast to how whiteness is most often conceptualized in the autobiographies. Again, it is crucial to remember that some of the respondents who are cited in this section are also cited in sections related to other types of whiteness. Because it is impossible to privilege one statement over another, and in doing so, to select which type of white identity individual whites "have," it is collective, not individual whiteness that is the focus of this study. The aim is *not* to characterize individual whites as having a certain type of identity, but to demonstrate the complexity of *collective* everyday whiteness. Perhaps in part because most whites have not given a great deal of thought to what whiteness means, white identity is, in a sense, a situational identity. That is, white people highlight various elements of whiteness depending on what reactions are called forth by circumstances in which they find themselves.

Reflexive, antiracist whiteness differs from other elements in several ways. When writing from a perspective of antiracist whiteness, respondents begin to use a double consciousness to discuss racism, acknowledge white privilege, theorize about whiteness, and take antiracist action.

Discussing Racism

Writing from a more antiracist perspective, respondents discuss racism in different terms than when writing from a more victimized perspective. For example, some student accounts reveal awareness of structural racism and of how traditional views are inadequate to address that reality. Stephanie explains the problem in her account:

> Despite efforts on the part of racial and ethnic groups to make society change, there has not been much progress in the big picture. People individually are more open and accepting now days than in the past and a greater effort towards equality is being made on a personal level than ever before. But, still there is not equality on a corporate and economic level.

Stephanie realizes that individuals being more "open and accepting" will not, alone, end racism—progress must also be made on an institutional level.

In addition to recognizing structural racism, contemplating whiteness more reflexively allows respondents to critique white racism almost as a cultural outsider. They are able to imagine, to some small degree, what it might be like to be a person of color, or at least are able to observe white behavior from "the outside in." In doing so, these whites may feel as if they have little in common with other white people. Some autobiographers described in detail instances of white racism they have witnessed. Sawyer writes:

> Education about racism has allowed me to see racism more clearly. Although being white only gives me an outside view upon black people, I still get to see instances of racism. I see white people hesitant to sit next to black men on the bus. Sometimes people will purposely go into a store to get out of the way of an oncoming group of blacks when they will not for a group of whites. I even see store workers come to assist me when both of us know that a black customer was there first. Knowing about such racist acts allows me to tell the worker that the other person was there first and not me.

Sawyer's learning makes him unable to ignore white racism. Here he discusses several recurrent behaviors he has observed, without trying to explain them away as somehow reasonable, based on white people's experiences. Sawyer also notes that in his case, understanding leads to action: because he notices racist acts, he takes action against them. Sawyer goes on to describe other white behavior:

> One thing that I see a lot being a white person is that other white people feel easy telling you their racist views when they ever feel this way. I think that for people, other white people being around are a comfort zone to express any racist views. It is funny how some people assume that no white person will care about what they say or that they will even support their beliefs. I don't doubt that acts of white people are discussed in groups of black people, but I can't help but understand. Blacks have only been free for thirty years and are still fighting for equal rights in certain circumstances. On the other hand, whites have always been free and hold more prestigious positions in society. Any issues that blacks discuss in groups are normal and understood.

Sawyer refuses to "cover" for racist white behavior. Here, he exposes the fact that white people often tell him "racist views," assuming that, because he is white, they have a "comfort zone" to do so. Insightfully, he also anticipates the false parallel many would use to argue against his point: that African Americans also talk about whites amongst themselves. Sawyer disposes of this argument by noting the recentness of the civil rights movement, and the continuing power differentials that make "[a]ny issues that blacks discuss in groups . . . normal and understood." Sawyer concludes his discussion:

Another thing that I get to see being white is that I see so many occur-
rences of blaming a group for the acts of a few members. I was once at a
baseball game and two black youths were walking down the parking lot
at the end of the night when the park was about to close. The remaining
ten or so of us saw them walking. As they walked past us, one began to
urinate on the road as he walked. When seeing this, the father of one of
my teammates began to yell and curse about how stupid and rude black
people are as a group. I'll admit that the act was very disgusting—but
what I heard in response was outrageous. The father did not care if one
of my family members or girlfriend was black. He felt comfortable giving his feelings no matter what kind of relations I may have had with a
black person. I can't say that I didn't expect what he said—I knew someone would express his feelings. I was just surprised that he expected no
one to take offense. What I did in response though was confirm his
belief and not say a word. I'm not sure that if I had said something
about his racist comments he would have stopped speaking that way in
public. Regardless, I do think I should have said something.

It is important for antiracist whites to be critical of the generalizations made
about minorities. What is perhaps most interesting about this passage is the
sense of possible vicarious victimization Sawyer expresses. He points out that
the father did not know whether Sawyer had a family member or girlfriend of
color, in which case his tirade would have offended Sawyer personally. Sawyer
is self-critical: he points out that in this instance he did not say anything to the
man and thinks now that he should have.

Lindsey, who grew up in a large city, comes to college in a small Northeastern town, and is surprised by the views of her classmates:

It wasn't until I got to [college] that I began to see things a lot differently. When I applied to colleges, I forgot to do one important piece of
research, find out the racial distribution on campus. Never in my life
have I been around this many white people. . . . I was so surprised at the
few minorities I saw on campus. . . . . Something that surprised me even
more than the racial ratio on campus, is other people's reaction to the
same thing. . . . I have heard enough racist comments and slurs to last
me my whole life within the time period of a few months. I have found
myself to be shocked and appalled by people's attitudes on race, and it
has made me more aware of the people around me. . . . Half of the time,
I don't think that they were aware of what they were saying, but sometimes, I think that it was intentional. There are times, especially in this
[race and ethnicity] class, that I feel like screaming at people for the

things that come out of their mouths. I can give one example . . . a boy described a school that he went to as 'all dark' because there were not many white students but mostly 'darkies.' When those words came out of his mouth, I almost felt sick to my stomach. . . . There was another time in . . . class when a different boy in the back of the room stated that there shouldn't be a problem with the difference in incomes between white and black people because there were plenty of black people in the NBA that made a lot of money. . . . To even try to use basketball players as an example of a minority group that makes a lot of money was so ignorant. Not only is that a miniscule part of the population, but I think that crediting black people with their ability in sports is condescending. . . . it implied that they were not as good at other things like school or intellectual based things.

Some researchers have noted that for white people who have recently come to a realization of discrimination against people of color, comments by whites who have not may seem intolerable.[9] Lindsey makes note of specific things about other whites' views that make her "sick to her stomach." Her comments express a sense of alienation from other white students based on their racial insensitivity.

Taking an antiracist perspective may also allow a white person to discuss her or his own prejudices or racism. For example, Mike questions himself:

Someone asked me once that if I were walking down a dark city street and I saw two groups of four individuals, one was young white males and the other young black males, which side of the street would I walk on? I said I would walk down the middle. That was a lie. The simple fact is that I would choose the white side ten out of ten times and I cannot give an honest reason why. I am not a racist. I do not discriminate against any person. I have a friend that is a black man. Despite all of this I still cannot answer that question. The fact is that prejudice is not always overt and blatant. Prejudice is a matter of choice. Why are almost all of my friends whites? Why did I not get to know more blacks in my youth? Why was I not exposed to more minorities?. . I do not understand my own prejudices. I do not feel any animosity towards minorities. I was raised to think that a racist was a social anomaly, a mistake that must be corrected. Racists were born and raised in my hometown. I would consider many of my childhood friends to be racists. Did I by some miracle grow up differently? I dated a minority. I would gladly hang out with people of all colors. Why then is it that I would and still always will walk down the white side of the street?

When whites write from an antiracist perspective, they are able to consider social structure in a way that even allows them to recognize that they are part of a racialized social context. Understanding this, Mike realizes that he may harbor unconscious biases that make him uncomfortable around African Americans.

Acknowledging Privilege

Even when writing about the liabilities of whiteness, respondents make passing reference to privilege throughout the autobiographies. However, sometimes respondents write about privilege from a more antiracist perspective. For example, they note not only that they have some occasional privileges but that whiteness is a systemic privilege because it is *normative*. Writing about whiteness as a liability, respondents regularly rationalize white privilege by claiming that whiteness brings more disadvantages than advantages. When looking at whiteness from an antiracist perspective, respondents view its privileges as vastly outweighing any liabilities it might bring. Finally, an antiracist perspective does not trivialize the plight of people of color by acknowledging only more insignificant white privileges (for example, that they have Band-Aids that match their skin tone). Here Beth highlights some very basic white privileges:

> Whiteness, to me, is not having to think about being white. I have nothing to prove to society, nobody will look at me and pass a judgment on my entire race on the basis of my individual actions, and I can make myself invisible in a majority of situations. As a white person, I will also be accepted in whatever choices I make, regardless of how radical they may be. If I choose to become romantically involved with someone of another religion, race, or ethnicity, I will not be shunned by that many people and I may even be celebrated for making a bold decision. I could definitely tell my life story without mentioning race, although it would be very easy to figure out my race due to my experiences, or more importantly, lack of experiences that come about because of how I look.

Beth understands that invisibility is a privilege in a world that still essentializes race while claiming to be colorblind. Further, she has thought about how she is allowed to make "radical" choices in a way that people of color are not. This point has been made by others in research on race and ethnicity; that is, white antiracists are more "acceptable," because they appear less self-interested, than are people of color with the same cause.[10] Beth's most profound statement, however, is that "Whiteness . . . is not having to think about being white." In other words, the very core of whiteness is that it does not need to *have* any describable essence, or any that one has to "think" about. Whiteness is constructed as the freedom not to think about identity.

Sawyer writes in depth about the privileges of whiteness:

> I think that what it means to be white in society is to have a bit of a head start. I never had to compete for much throughout school. Teachers

spent time with me as a learner and not a person in need of attention. I think that it has been a relatively easy life being a white member of society. No dirty looks in malls, no question of if I can afford items in stores, and pretty nice service in restaurants. Some terms that I could use to define what I feel about being white are comfortable, rewarding, educational, and appreciated.

Here whiteness is conceptualized as a "head start." As this respondent sees it, this has meant that he did not have to struggle to get a quality education, and that he has been able to go where he wants to go without being treated badly. It is especially insightful that Sawyer has noticed differential treatment by teachers toward whites and people of color. His teachers assumed that he would be able to learn, and their expectations were thus met. Sawyer admits that these privileges benefited him, even though doing so may call into question his own accomplishments and questions the myth of meritocracy. Later, Sawyer adds,

Although I do not think it is right or fair, there are definitely privileges and benefits associated with being white. So many white people often overlook these advantages and take them for granted but I have seen that they do exist. Even nonracist white people tend not to see the advantages over minorities in many aspects of their lives. Some people deny them, but I believe they are evident.

One example of a privilege that whites have that they may not realize is simply benefit of the doubt. Society is much less likely to doubt a white person's word than a black person's, especially if their words are conflicting. As whites, our honesty is often not questioned. Also, we are viewed as being generally less lazy, more intelligent, and more competent. I believe that in general, it would be easier for a white person to find a high-paying job than an equally qualified black person would. I find that in college, that black students tend to have to prove themselves and their eligibility to be there more than white students do. Most white people do not have to walk through their day feeling inferior to those that surround them. That confidence alone is a large enough benefit. White people also do not have to worry about the political leaders' agendas and if they will represent minorities' thoughts and views. White people know that those who govern their country share their same heritage and have similar backgrounds. Many minorities feel that government leaders do not relate to them and cannot possibly represent their needs accurately. This lack of trust is something that white people generally do not have to endure. I also believe that certain social problems affect my racial group disproportionately to other racial groups. I feel that it is more difficult for black people in general to get out of poverty, get off of welfare, or get a quality education than for white people who are in similar situations. I do not believe that this is because of individual qualities, but because of the way society views and treats each race.

A wide range of privileges is recognized in this quote: from having an easier time feeling confident and being able to trust politicians to being able to get out of poverty more easily, and being taken at one's word. In this passage being a person of color is seen as having to work a bit harder than whites at everything. People of color have to "prove themselves" in ways that whites do not, they must work harder in school, on the job, and even politically than whites do. Overall, Sawyer constructs whiteness not as a liability, but rather as having it "easier" than other groups do. Importantly, Sawyer understands these problems to be not the fault of the victims, but the result of institutional racism.

Dan also recognizes how whiteness has made life easier for him:

> Being of Bulgarian descent has made no major impact on my life, aside from having that mysterious pride one feels in knowing his or her roots. . . . However, I suppose the key factor in my life is not so much my ethnicity as it is my race. I am a White male, raised in the high end of an upper middle class household, living in a middle class society, with a stable family, and both parents. My race and class status has helped me through life. I am more fortunate than those around me. . . . In a world where I am a majority, my life can be as good as I strive for it to be. In a world where I am the majority, my race, not my culture, surrounds me. I am not saying that being White makes you the best, or even better. I am just saying that in a society where you are of the majority, the instruments for one to better themselves are more readily available, and more easily at one's disposal.

Dan understands that whiteness does not guarantee success, but being part of the majority gives whites access to opportunities for gaining success that others do not have. Similarly, Roger writes:

> Being Scotch-Irish is not the only identifier for me. I am also a white male. This term white male can hold many benefits if you were raised in a town such as where I was. The term meant that if you were not accepted as a hometown boy, you would always be considered white. That would always be in your favor. You didn't have to play sports; you didn't have to win any awards at the Four H Club. All you had to do was be white and you instantly became a member of the whole country town culture, a person that did fit in somewhere if nowhere else. However, this feeling was not really explained to each child as they grew up. It was an unwritten rule that each child just understood and accepted.

Being white means automatically "fitting in" in most places in the United States. There are subcultures within the white culture, and some whites are more acceptable than others, but as Roger makes clear, part of white privilege is that being white offers a certain base level of acceptance in almost any community. This acceptance serves as a foundation for success.

Finally, Dylan also understands that not only being white but being male brings him privilege in U.S. society:

> Using the word "whiteness" can sum up my identity. I can think of one word to describe what it is like to be a white male, awesome. Absolute freedom is another word that could describe whiteness. The only thing that is almost as good as being white is being a male. As a white male I do not have to worry about discrimination. If anything, white males have been the discriminators since this country was started. Living in an almost entirely white community, I don't feel like people are staring at me when I walk down the street because of the color of my skin. As a white male I can go just about anywhere I want and not feel threatened or inferior. . . . I am not saying the white race is better than others. I feel all races are equal. The color of your skin doesn't make you a better or more worthy person. The only trouble I have when thinking about my race is just how discriminatory it is. You name a race and white people have discriminated, persecuted, or in some way belittled, harassed or made them feel inferior to whites. . . . I can honestly say I have never been discriminated against. My racial background has only provided me with the privileges and benefits that are associated with whites. . . . I think the most serious racial issue facing the US today is the discrimination that occurs in the judicial system. . . . What people don't realize is that their discrimination is costing our society more money to keep blacks in jail for longer periods of time. This money could be used elsewhere to benefit society.

Dylan is able to compare his experience as a white male, able to travel freely in the United States, with the experiences of people of color, who are often harassed or restricted in their freedoms. The advantages of whiteness Dylan notes are not only of an everyday nature, but are also significant structural privileges in major institutions. He notes not only the costs to people of color brought by discrimination, but to society as a whole.

Theorizing About Whiteness

Antiracist whiteness also includes an ability to theorize about whiteness beyond what respondents have learned in classes, or in a way that applies theoretical concepts learned in classes to their own lives. For example, Susan discusses her understanding of whiteness:

> I think the greatest downfall of the 'white' race is that we do not celebrate being white in a positive manner. Sure, we have KKK rallies and white supremacy groups but those are all the white people who do not understand their race and are ignorant of understanding for other races. That is not celebrating being white that is celebrating our fear of being

black. African Americans celebrate their culture, Chinese, Japanese, Mexicans, Latinos, they all celebrate their cultures . . . how do whites celebrate our culture? Many do not because they are not sure of what their 'white' culture is. The idea of this paper was to answer the question, 'What does it mean to be white?' I am not so sure that I know what the answer to that is, but I have tried to at least scratch the surface.

One of the problems for antiracist whites is creating a positive white identity. Susan recognizes this difficulty, noting that those who celebrate whiteness are actually celebrating their fears of other groups. Yet it is these, white supremacists, who have monopolized the cultural dialogue on how to be white in a way that one can be proud of. Renee also discusses the problem of constructing white identity in terms that are meaningful to her:

> As I have written these last chapters I have really looked at my own identity and hope that some day I will be able to find something that satisfies me. Racial identity is not very important to me but I think that I need to find something that I can feel proud of. At this point in my life I am not proud of being "white" and I don't think I can fit into any other racial category very well. So now I guess the search begins for an identity, who knows what will happen from here.

When a white person realizes that whiteness as an identity includes little more than a history of domination and oppression of others, she or he may be left without a sense of who one can be as a white person. Antiracist educators are in a position to show white young people that a positive white identity may be constructed when whites position themselves as antiracist allies to people of color.[11]

This data suggests that some young whites make a distinction between racial identity and ethnic identity that allows them to see how ethnicity differs for whites and for people of color. For example, Stefan writes:

> I don't believe that racial identity is important in my life. I disregard race and therefore find myself with no need for a racial identity. On the other hand I do believe that ethnic identity is important. The difference between the two is very small but there is one. . . . .It gives me an opportunity to look back and see who my ancestors are, how they came to this country, and why. It doesn't tell me that I am white and that is it, rather this gives me a multi-cultural perspective on life.
>
> I don't think that it is important to think of oneself as black, or white. But I do pursue the belief that it is important to think of oneself as African, Asian, etc. I do intend on teaching my children their heritage. Without that we cannot grasp who and what we are. This may differ for black people. They may think racial identity is essential for survival especially in this country. I agree with this fact, the discrimination that they face,

that the only way to get by is for a common identity and to join together as one race. In my life I have experienced much that would lead me to believe that racism is the cancer that is choking this country.

Drawing a distinction between racial identity for whites and ethnic identity, Stefan asserts that white racial identity holds little meaning. Interestingly, he does not use white ethnicity to make a colorblind argument equating white and black experience. Rather, he states that in the United States racial identity actually might hold meaning for African Americans, since *discrimination* has given it meaning.

Respondents also consider whiteness in more abstract terms:

> I am not really sure what it means to be white. . . . In general terms to be white means to be free. There are exceptions that come along with any generalization, but for the most part white people experience a kind of total freedom. When that is taken away from [them] or an attempt to do so is made there is a great uproar. Whiteness is in essence total freedom.

> Stefan

One of the most important aspects of white privilege is being able to take full advantage of the freedoms promised in the United States. Whites, to this point in history, are the only group that has really ever been completely free to progress economically, educationally, and politically in our society. When whites perceive that others are beginning to take advantage of some of the same opportunities, they may believe their freedoms to be at risk, and they protest this vehemently, as Stefan insightfully points out.

Tim uses metaphor to communicate the "freedom" of whiteness:

> Being white is, in my personal point of view, like being free. It is like when you were a child and watched birds flying around—swooshing down and then soaring above the clouds—and you wish that for even a second you could touch the sky. Well the bird probably never even thinks about his freedom in flight, he just flies.

In this passage, Tim quite effectively describes how whiteness is an invisible privilege. Because it is all that white people have known, and because most do not make the type of contact with people of color that would awaken them to their experiences, it is taken for granted.

Taking Action

Few respondents write stories of having actually taken antiracist action. Those who do, interestingly, are mostly male. Jordan tells of an incident that occurred in his early teens:

We were hungry one morning so we walked over to a [doughnut shop]. While in the restaurant, a couple of black kids a little younger than ourselves walked in and ordered breakfast themselves. At the time [the doughnut chain] was running a promotion for free doughnuts and coffee. This contest consisted of scratch-off tickets that were given to you for each item that you bought. While eating I noticed that one of the black kids had apparently won a free doughnut. However, the Asian woman refused to give this boy his prize because she claimed that he scratched off a part that he was not supposed to. I went over to him and asked what was going on. After he explained what happened, he asked if I would try to redeem the ticket. I agreed but did not think she would accept it [from] me. To my dismay, they did not even question the ticket. I was totally shocked and outraged that this happened. After we confronted these women and I gave my new buddy his prize, I apologized on the employee's behalf. He told me it was not a big deal and that this kind of stuff happens to him and his friends all the time.

In his autobiography to this point, Jordan has not portrayed himself as a particularly antiracist person. However, in this instance we see that, taking the situation at face value, he believes he has witnessed a clear act of racism. The portion of this passage that makes Jordan's action antiracist is when he got involved by asking the young man what was going on. Most white people would not cross racial boundaries in order to involve themselves in a dispute involving a black stranger.

Simon writes about an ongoing workplace situation:

My first real contact with an actual racist was at my first job as a security officer at a local amusement park. It did not show itself right away, as the summer went on, I noticed things and behaviors of my co-workers when a person of any color other than white approached them. They were not treated the same as if a white person came in with the same problem. Soon after I heard the language used, directed at non-whites. Then I took notice and realized that no African American people worked with me or for the company either. Soon after, I quit the job; I was not going to be a part of what went on.

It is unusual to read in the autobiographies a white person noticing subtle discrimination in a workplace against people of color. It is even more rare for a respondent to have taken antiracist action, as Simon did, in that situation to the point of quitting a job. Larry also describes an instance of institutional racism:

Last summer when I was applying for a job at a sporting goods store . . . , as I was going into the manager's office to be interviewed, an African American man about my age was just leaving his interview with the same man who was about to interview me. After the very brief interview, he told me I had the job and that he trusts me more and told me I would be a better worker then the man he just interviewed. I was very stunned that he could and would hire me and make that statement even though he knew nothing about that other man and myself. And he made this decision based on the fact that the other man was African American and I was white. That was a summer job I wanted very much to work at but I definitely did not want to work for a person who was a bold face racist.

This is the only clear rejection of an offered advantage in the student autobiographies. Most respondents who recognize they receive privileges do not suggest dismantling the racist system by rejecting those privileges. Larry also ponders the future role of whites in challenging racism:

The role I see my racial/ethnic group playing in current racial/ethnic relations . . . is trying to get rid of racial stereotypes whether it's regarding Latinos, Asian Americans, African Americans, or Native Americans. Also, trying to get rid of racism in the workplace and in the schools.

Larry later suggests that getting rid of workplace racism entails getting the white decision makers to give up enough power to allow more people of color to be hired, and that this is a formidable challenge.

A Collective White Identity Crisis

In telling personal stories, people seek to establish coherence.[12] No doubt, these students are striving for coherence in their writing. However, seemingly inconsistent themes overlapped in students' autobiographies. In this study, I treat these contrasting themes not as contradictions but, instead, as characteristic of the complexity of twenty-first-century whiteness. As Stanford Lyman and Marvin Scott write:

Situations of account confusion are especially acute when a group is in transition from one status position to another and is undergoing a collective identity crisis. Racial groups provide numerous examples. . . . If a mutually agreed upon identity cannot be established, the giving and receiving of accounts may break up into conflict or show signs of anomie.[13]

I assert that presently there is a sort of collective crisis in white identity.[14] First, it exists on a global scale. It has, of course, always been the case that more people of dark complexion than of lighter skin tones have populated the world. One could argue, nonetheless, that today, with the formation of a world community, white people are less able to isolate themselves from the lives of racial Others than they—particularly white Westerners—used to be. The fact that they are a minority internationally may become more evident to whites. Further, the commodification of global culture has allowed whites to appropriate the artifacts and artistry of those of other ethnic groups increasingly while, of course, also sometimes exporting their own products. The last decade has seen the fall of the last formal system of racial separatism that kept a white minority in a state of legal supremacy over a black majority in a modern nation, with the dismantling of apartheid in South Africa. On a global level, this was the last bastion of "whiteness" in the world held in a position of *legal* superiority over others. Such a transition was certainly a symbolic if not literal blow to what had served for many both in South Africa and around the world as a firm grounding for a particular colonialist vision of "collective white identity."[15]

In her insightful empirical study of whites in South Africa after the fall of apartheid, *"Whiteness Just Isn't What it Used To Be": White Identity in a Changing South Africa*, Melissa Steyn asserts that

> In its extremity the South African situation has always been instructive, and the dramatic nature of the changes in the privileged position of 'whiteness' in recent years is no exception. Indeed, if it is true that some element of trauma or bafflement needs to be present to dislodge sedimented racial identity formations . . . , then the social and political unsettlement of contemporary South African society provides an interesting case study of a nation that has been provided with a prime (un)learning opportunity.[16]

Steyn's analysis demonstrates how white South Africans are motivated to renegotiate their racial identities because of structural shifts in the meaning of whiteness. In other words, because being white no longer holds the same place in South African society, white people are forced to rethink their whiteness. Although South Africa is the extreme case, one could argue that whites, globally, are presently being "repositioned" due to economic and political changes that are many and complex. Howard Winant argues that there are racial shifts occurring, in South Africa as well as in other global contexts. For example, in Europe the continued influx of immigrants from Africa, Turkey, and Asia is changing national ideas about racial and ethnic identity. In Asia, Southeast Asia, and the Middle East, conflicts continue that have what Winant calls "at least 'protoracial' features." He continues, "Arguably, the world today is a vast racial battlefield."[17] In sum, political and economic shifts and racial formations lead to transformations in racial identities.

Not only is this occurring globally; one could argue that today there is a similar U.S. collective confusion among whites regarding their identity, and thus the crisis in white identity is also a national one. Although there has not been a similar *single* dramatic event, as in the case of South Africa (the fall of apartheid), several factors suggest that white Americans may be headed for, if not already experiencing, a similar renegotiation of their racial identities. Michael Omi has asserted that the understanding that whites will soon be a minority in the United States has been a catalyst for an "emerging crisis of

white identity."[18] Since the Immigration Act of 1965 finally overturned preferential quotas that had maintained higher levels of European immigration, the
demographics of the United States have begun to change dramatically.[19] In
recent censuses, nearly one in every four Americans counted was of African,
Asian, Latino, or Native American ancestry.[20] Population projections suggest
that by the year 2050, white Americans will be at the lowest percentage ever in
the United States, about 53 per cent.[21] Others have suggested that whites will
be a minority in the United States. Already in the states of Hawaii, Florida,
Texas, and California, as well as the cities of New York, Los Angeles, Chicago,
and Houston, whites make up less than half of the population.[22] As the demographics of cities around the United States change, there is an increase in resi-
dential balkanization because of "white flight" from areas into which people of
color move, demonstrating the fearful reaction of many whites to increased
contact with people of color.[23] Because of the dramatic demographic changes
at work in the United States, Omi argues that there is a crisis of identity, which
has caused whites to become "racialized"—that is, to think of themselves as
members of a white racial group.

Young whites have more contact with people of color than did their parents
or grandparents, putting them in a situation where simply avoiding people of
color is increasingly impossible even if desired. In 1990, for people 70 years of
age or older, there were more than seven white people in the population for
every person of color. In contrast, for those younger than ten, there were only
about two white people for every person of color—making it much more
likely for a typical white young person to have contact with people of color.
Projections suggest that by 2050, the proportions will have just about evened
out; there will be about one white person for every person of color in the
United States.[24] Although more interracial contact is generally positive, simply
bringing people into more frequent contact does not necessarily ensure that
the contact will lead to lessening of prejudices and stereotyping.[25] Sometimes
such contact can actually increase prejudices, and sometimes, as is often the
case in colleges and universities, people of different racial and ethnic backgrounds simply keep their contact at a superficial level, reserving their meaningful relationships for those of the same racial group. Some research has
found that for white college students, contact with people of color can be experienced as traumatic. One study, for example, found that although students
entered college looking forward to the diversity they expected to encounter on
campus, and with generally positive feelings of acceptance toward people of
other racial groups, they left college with more prejudiced attitudes than when
they arrived.[26]

Omi asserts that before the Civil Rights movement, whiteness was "transparent" in meaning and "unproblematic."[27] It was after the Civil Rights movement
that whites began to reconsider what being white means. This reconsideration
continues in the present generation. Omi argues that after the Civil Rights
movement, when legal segregation was dismantled, no clear understanding of

race emerged to take the place of the old views. This has left a cultural vacuum into which neoconservative claims have emerged. Young whites have come of age during the years when talk of "reverse discrimination" has been at its peak. As men and women of color finally began to move into workplaces that were formerly all-white male environments, whites begin to see themselves as victims of affirmative action policies. The inclusion of people of color into white workplaces is often experienced as a loss of status and economic security and as unfair treatment by many whites, especially men.

Research has shown, and my study supports, that part of this racialization is based on the unprecedented perception that being white is now a cultural and economic handicap. Anti-immigrant rhetoric has become commonplace in popular discourse.[28] Certainly, worries about being "overrun" by immigrants and their economic impact, both of which are exaggerated and exploited by politicians, cause many white Americans (and some native-born people of color) to perceive their racial identities in ways that they never have before.[29] In doing so, respondents in this study regularly conflate "whiteness" with "Americanness." The tragic events of September 11, 2001 further exacerbated anxieties about immigration and, particularly, fears of immigrants from Middle Eastern countries. All of these factors have caused many white Americans to conceptualize whiteness as more of an economic and social disadvantage than a privilege.

In their autobiographies, as was discussed primarily in chapter 5, these young whites related stories of older fathers, uncles, grandfathers, and cousins (and sometimes themselves) "losing their jobs" to people of color. This generation of young whites is one of the first to be presented with the notion that whiteness will not bring them any special benefits. In his study of white young people, Charles Gallagher concluded that "whiteness is in the midst of a fundamental transformation."[30] According to his analysis, this transformation is fueled by (1) the perception that being white brings social and economic disadvantage, (2) their recognition of identity politics, (3) the influence of neoconservative political discourse, and (4) the decline in their sense of ethnicity.

Although economic disadvantage ("reverse discrimination") is a prevalent theme in the autobiographies and in the contemporary discourse about race, research shows that whites are still economically dominant in the United States. White income and wealth are still much higher than those of people of color.[31] In 1995 white men made up only 29 percent of the workforce but held 95 percent of all senior management positions.[32] As discussed in chapter 5, white men are still disproportionately represented in the most well-paying professions, and people of color are not present there in numbers proportional to the population.[33] Arguably, a dual labor market exists in the United States in which people of color remain positioned in lower-wage jobs as a result of past and present discrimination.[34] Despite these realities, it is true that white workers, as opposed to the white elite, are often less economically secure today.

The bottom fifth of the population has an income share that is one-tenth that of the top fifth today, compared to one-sixth that of the top fifth in the late 1960s.[35] However, white workers are manipulated into believing that the source of their economic insecurity is the influx of people of color into the workplace, rather than the decisions of elite whites that reduce job opportunities for everyone. Those in power in business are able to play on the racial fears of white working people to shift the focus from their own practices and keep the middle and working class divided along racial lines. Thus, the white elite reap more benefits from their whiteness than the white working class do. As George Lipsitz points out, all whites do not benefit equally from their whiteness.[36]

In addition to demographic changes and economic concerns, Omi also asserts that the "'twilight of white ethnicity'" means that racial identification will grow in significance for white people; in other words, the loss of ethnic identity is another factor in white racialization.[37] Ethnicity, for whites, has gradually developed into an optional identity.[38] This seemed to be the case for some of these respondents. The guidelines of the assignment allowed them to "fill in the blank" with whatever identification they most often use, whether it be a racial or ethnic one. In other words, they were to describe "what it means to be _____," and they could choose to fill the blank in with an ethnic identification, such as "Irish American," or "Italian American," rather than "white." Some did, but many more noted that they would prefer to identify with their ethnic roots if they could, but because they know very little about their ethnicity, they think of themselves instead as "just white." I found this sense of "culturelessness" to be an important aspect of whiteness for the respondents. Other studies show that many young whites are too far removed from their ethnic heritage to claim an ethnic identity. In his study of young whites, Gallagher found that most of his white students, feeling no sense of ethnicity, have undergone racialization.[39]

Finally, I believe that the "crisis in white identity" had a local relevance to this study. In addition to whiteness being disrupted on a global and national level, in asking these students to consider what it means to be white, I created "an element of trauma or bafflement [that needed] to be present to dislodge sedimented racial identity formations," as did the fall of apartheid, more dramatically and for a more extended period of time in the lives of Steyn's South African respondents.[40] Much was at stake for Steyn's respondents in the reworking of their identities, in all areas of their lives. Granted, the "trauma or bafflement" I created in the lives of my students was limited—it existed in only one area of their lives, my classroom, and only for the duration of the assignment. The worst that could happen should they fail to decipher their whiteness successfully was that they could do poorly on one assignment. Even this was not likely, as they had been assured that their autobiographies would not be graded on content so much as on technical merit and on whether they followed the directions of the assignment.

Still, asking students to consider what it meant to them to be white apparently did cause many a good deal of "bafflement," or was at least quite thought provoking. Although they could have written something quickly to meet the bare requirements of the assignment, I believe that I can say with some degree of certainty, after knowing at least half of the respondents for a semester, that they struggled over these autobiographies and sincerely tried to come to terms with something that most had never thought about before: what it means to be white.

As was evident in this book, the perception of whiteness as a liability is prevalent among respondents in this study. However, I believe this data shows that while Omi and others are correct in asserting that whites have become racialized, the *ways* in which these young people think of themselves as white are extremely complex and multidimensional. The primary aim of this book has been to explore and describe the ways in which these young whites think of themselves as white.

Conclusion: Toward an Antiracist Pedagogy [41]

These commentaries from younger white Americans outline themes of everyday whiteness. The views articulated here are of great consequence to those whites who express them, regardless of the fact that they may not have given conscious thought to whiteness before, and they are very consequential for the racial present and future of the United States. It is the views of "everyday whites" that motivate racist practices that in turn sustain institutionalized racism. Additionally, it is young whites who will be moving into positions in society (for example, in business, education, and the criminal justice system) that will allow them to make decisions that will have an impact on the racial status quo. Many have noted that white people lack consciousness about their racial identities. Lacking this consciousness, most fail to recognize white privilege or take responsibility for dismantling racism. My research shows that when whites are prompted to consider their racial identity as whites, in other words, when whiteness is brought to their consciousness, they perceive themselves as victimized as members of a racial group.

Not all whites experience being white in the same way in the United States. Class, gender, sexual preference, religion, and a number of other factors modify the extent to which whites benefit from white privilege. However, this study does not assume that whiteness is an essential characteristic complemented by other statuses. Instead, this research has explored whiteness as a symbolic resource that white people use in constructing their understandings of a racialized world. Whiteness in this sense is a discourse, a way of speaking of human experience and a way of seeing human relations. This way of seeing the world has material consequences in both white people's lives and the lives of people of other racial and ethnic groups.

As seen in the data, in constructing their racial identities, these respondents use a range of fictions of whiteness. Without the historical context with which to understand racism, and with a current crisis in their views of themselves as white, whites often construct themselves as passive recipients of racial knowledge and observers of racist actions. Their white identities have three commonplace elements: they are constructed as empty, socially/culturally stigmatized, and economically disadvantaged. Mirrored against the cultures of people of color, whiteness seems to lack content. Whiteness is explicitly perceived as being overwhelmed by other cultural intrusions. In part because of ignorance of history, socioeconomic privileges are usually omitted from white identity, leaving whites fictionalized as victims of racial disadvantages. Indeed, white identity is frequently seen as a liability. Further, because the white-dominated system is believed to be just and equal, whites perceive themselves as victimized by government policies such as affirmative action.

Given this set of beliefs, it is not surprising that whites often translate their views into action—or harmful inaction. Feagin and Vera note that whites not only vary in the degree of their racist attitudes but also in the level of their racist actions. White officiants are usually the most active in perpetrating discrimination as they make the key decisions and articulate the important racist attitudes. Other white actors act the part of acolytes, for they discriminate against African Americans or other people of color partly or mainly because they are told to do so by their employers. Yet other whites stand by and observe while the officiants and/or acolytes carry out overt discrimination against people of color. Passivity is a very important buttress of contemporary racism.[42] Many everyday whites take this passive role.

In their study of elite white men, Feagin and O'Brien found that whites as a racial group operate as a "dysfunctional family," often understanding and even acknowledging racial inequities and discrimination, but above all protecting other whites from recrimination.[43] White men in their study were likely to assume good intentions of other whites and were unlikely to intervene, particularly in all-white groups, against racial prejudice. In failing to confront bigotry, these elite white men zealously protect harmonious white spaces. The respondents were also overwhelmingly opposed to affirmative action policies.

Correspondingly, the young whites in this research for the most part do not express overt hostility and feelings of superiority toward people of color. However, the perception that they are losing out in a racial "game" that is stacked against them will certainly not predispose them to support policies designed to shift resources to people of color, making for a more equitable distribution and fair opportunities. Their belief that racism is a problem of the past also will likely dissuade this generation from antiracist action or from supporting policies to redress discrimination that goes on in the present.

The envy that young whites demonstrate of the culture and heritage of others, as well as a lack of connection with their own heritage, helps to maintain social distance and estrangement from people of color. Young whites,

lacking an understanding of how the cultures of people of color are meaningful to those people, are threatened by expressions of those cultures. Understanding that they can take part in cultural celebrations not just as "cultural
tourists," but *while engaging with* people of color themselves, could lead to
more meaningful interracial associations.

In addition, these autobiographies show the need for a sense of whiteness
that includes both an understanding of the past (that whites, too have an ethnic history and even some experiences with bigotry) with an understanding
of the present (that white ethnics were able to assimilate and progress and
now experience privileges based on whiteness). Some have suggested that
there may be some antiracist value in a revitalization of white ethnicity.[44]
This sense of whiteness as ethnicity could help to alleviate some of the perception of emptiness that young whites experience. In having their own sense
of ethnicity, young whites might feel less resentment toward people of color
for their connection to their cultures. They might also have a more meaningful sense of who they are aside from an identification as "white," with its
implications of domination and privilege. These new identities could also
help to create empathy that could be an impetus to orient themselves as allies
to people of color. To foster this allied behavior, it is also useful for instructors to help white students understand how racism can be used by the white
elite not only against people of color, but against working-class and middle-
class whites as well.

The exciting aspect of these findings is that many students have been moved
toward questioning at least some of the sincere fictions they have been taught.
Even one racial and ethnic relations course has moved many of them to reflect
on the views, attitudes, and images they hold about African Americans and
other people of color. These courses have helped many of them begin to see
structural racism, which this study suggests is a crucial element in motivating
antiracism. They are at least questioning, and some have gone to the point of
taking antiracist action. Many, indeed, seem to be more concerned than previously at least with being antiprejudiced, if not being antiracist in terms of
action. This is a hopeful finding.

This research has important implications for antiracist theory and practice.
Much reeducation is needed. As Feagin recently stated,

> A new cognitive framework will doubtless require a process of education
> or reeducation in which whites, as individuals and as groups, move
> toward understanding how the system of racial privilege was created and
> how they maintain it in everyday life. This reeducation will likely probe
> deeply into the character and composition of this society, including its
> extended racist history, and will require purposeful unlearning of the
> mythology and sincere fictions most whites use to paper over continu-
> ing racist realities. Systemic racism has persisted so well because its
> operation is often concealed and disguised.[45]

Racism as it extends into the twenty-first century is supported by the fictions of whiteness that have been exemplified in these autobiographies. As long as whiteness is viewed as a liability rather than a privilege, no serious work will be done by average whites to eradicate lingering racial inequality. To the extent that whites see themselves as culturally and economically disadvantaged as whites, they will not be moved to join with people of color as allies in antiracist efforts. Because most whites take a largely passive role in matters of race and do not think of themselves as having racialized identities, they do not engage in progressive movements for justice, but only react to what they sense as racial threats.

We must keep in mind that because this generation's view of everyday whiteness is different from that of previous generations, new antiracist strategies must be employed to confront everyday racism. If we continue to use models for combating racism devised for the parents and grandparents of young whites, we will not address the specific issues that lead the latter to actively endorse or passively support societal racism. Young white students will one day be the influential adults who may perpetrate everyday racism against African Americans and other people of color. Thus, particularly when speaking with students, for whom discussions of racism may be very new, instructors should carefully define their terms, making clear the distinctions between the key types of racism, such as covert, subtle, overt, and unintentional racism, or individual and institutional racism. Broader and narrower definitions of "racism" can be acknowledged in antiracist education.[46]

New discourses of antiracism must also make a distinction between race and ethnicity.[47] Part of young whites' racial resentment comes from a confounding of these terms. They believe themselves to be equally victimized, economically and culturally, as people of color. However, it is the *ethnicity*, not the "race," of people of color that is being protected by affirmative action policies and cultural clubs or festivals.[48] Thus, when whites question why there are no similar "white" clubs and festivals, part of the answer is because "white" is not an ethnic group. Further, it may indeed be the case that "whiteness" is for all practical *cultural* purposes "empty." However, it is quite "full" of practical purposes in terms of white privilege. A new antiracism might encourage whites who yearn for a group-based identity, in this time of a shifting sense of whiteness, to explore ethnicity, rather than continuing to look for "culture" in whiteness, which is a political identity based on domination and oppression of others.

In antiracist education we must counter the commonplace discourses of white privilege. The autobiographies suggest that many whites understand themselves to be privileged only in minor ways. For example, many students have read an article that includes a list of white privileges at all levels, both "micro-level" and structural.[49] Many refer to the article in their autobiographies, mentioning most that white people can buy "flesh"-colored bandages.

Although recognition of all levels of privilege is important, young whites should be reminded that white privileges not only make their everyday lives easier but also give them major economic resources and stability and enable them, on the average, to live six to seven years longer than African Americans.[50]

Researchers have suggested the need to explore the role of whiteness in pedagogy.[51] This study shows that one good venue for white re-education is the college classroom. The Latin American educator Paulo Freire once explained that the *true vocation* of human beings is not the dehumanization of others, in which they too often engage, but rather the humanization of the world. Teaching antiracism involves creating greatly expanded awareness, not only among the oppressed but also among the oppressors.[52] Many more college courses dealing with systemic racism in the United States are needed, with instructors who are as diverse as the society itself. Instructors teaching about the nation's racist history and current reality are in a position to disrupt or refute the many fictions of whiteness. For example, antiracist instructors are in a position to historically contextualize U.S. and global race relations in a way that can disrupt the fiction of whiteness as a liability. A first major step in dealing with white racism is to confront firmly its many myths and misconceptions. However, progressive educators must be certain not only to point out the seriousness of the problem of institutionalized racism, but also to suggest how whites may become antiracist activists in the field and allies to people of color. Instructors should suggest various antiracist activist groups, publications, and websites for their students to visit, and should be available for further conversations about racism when the course is over.

In addition, instructors can provide important information on how to counter racism in everyday practice and on how students can play a role in reducing prejudice and discrimination in their own spheres of interaction, such as family and friendship networks. Joe Feagin notes:

> Today the challenge for those seeking to expand the antiracist strategy seems to include the creation of conditions where more whites will have to confront the reality of the pain that their system of racism has caused African Americans and other Americans of color with whom they come into contact. A large-scale educational campaign—one that is candid and blunt about the past and present reality of racist ideas and practices—seems to be required if more than a handful of whites are ever to move into the stages of empathy. . . . Beyond that the building of more personal networks across the color line seems necessary. This idea may seem elementary, yet it is difficult and profound.[53]

Instructors can also bring in members of local organizations of color that are working against racial discrimination, in order to provide students with practical information on actions that are being taken against discrimination. By bringing in adults of color who have long suffered from racial discrimination and who are now taking action against it, instructors can not only better inform their students about racism in the "outside world" but also help students to build linkages to people of color outside the classroom. For many white students, particularly those who have grown up in rural settings, these may be some of the first relationships with people of color that they will begin to develop. The learning experiences with the greatest potential for disrupting sincerely held fictions of the white self are likely those that involve crossing racial boundaries and learning new racial attitudes while unlearning racist behaviors. Yet such interracial experiences must not be accepted as proof of the end of racism or conceived of as the final goal of antiracism.

Instructors who teach about racism must recognize one of the primary obstacles students cite to becoming active in antiracism: fears of social awkwardness or interpersonal discomfort and tension. Although some use this as an excuse, we as teachers of antiracism have a responsibility to try not to alienate white students who are part of our classrooms. Yet, we have an often conflicting responsibility to combat the denial of white privilege that is so evident in the words of young white people. Instructors should not try to remove all tension from discussions, because expression of these tensions can be enlightening for young people. Indeed, while being sympathetic to white students is very important, it is equally important to encourage them to take action in their own lives.

When speaking with students, for whom class discussions of racism are perhaps the first they have had away from their family dinner tables, we instructors must carefully define our terms. It is sometimes because of a confusion between individual and institutional racism that white students believe they personally are being "called racist" in race and ethnicity courses. Because they confound the terms "race" and "ethnicity," white students draw false parallels that cast whiteness as an apparent liability.[54]

In order to challenge structural racism, whites must relearn what it means to be white. Perhaps the best venue for this re-education is the college classroom. Antiracist instructors should place U.S. and global race relations in a historical context so that the fiction of whiteness as a liability is disrupted. We must be certain not only to point out the seriousness of the problem of racism but also to suggest how whites may become antiracist allies to people of color. It is crucial that young whites do not leave a course on racism believing either that there is nothing they *can* do or that, simply by taking the course, they have done all they *should* do to dismantle racism.

This study demonstrates that until white young people better understand the real position of whites in the racial hierarchy, they will not be moved toward antiracism. At best, they will adhere to a colorblind belief that because "everyone is equal," all groups have equal opportunities and access to institutional power. At worst, they will continue to insist that whites need *more* preferences and advantage, because they are unfairly penalized for their race. The challenge for antiracist scholars and instructors today is to show young people not only how racism has developed and been maintained in the United States but how they can actively resist it and renounce white power and privilege. Giving up racism means not only abandoning fictional beliefs about whiteness and racist attitudes but also relinquishing power and privilege. Until whiteness is recognized as a privilege by average whites, antiracism will not become important to most white people. It will take a shift in these everyday whites' views before the racial status quo can be changed to a more equitable system for the growing population of people of color in the United States.

Appendix A
Sample Validity

Beginning with the assumption that we live "storied lives,"[1] and drawing primarily on Norm Denzin's theory of interpretive biography and autobiography, I designed my research as an examination of how young whites construct whiteness in autobiographical accounts. Denzin asserts that a life is a text, and a moral, political, medical, technical, and economic production.[2] He suggests that studies of biographies and autobiographies should articulate how the author deals with certain issues, such as coherence, illusion, truth, epiphanies, and selves. The sociologist's task in examining autobiography should be to study how people produce "warrantable" stories relevant to their group's standards of truth.[3] Accordingly, this study investigates how whites produce "warrantable" stories of whiteness, which is a particular challenge, considering that most have not previously thought of themselves as white.

My work adheres to Denzin's critique of "objective" analyses of autobiographical texts. Citing Sartre, Denzin asserts that "if an author thinks something existed and believes in its existence, its effects are real. Since all writing is fictional, made-up out of things that could have happened or did happen, it is necessary to do away with the distinction between fact and fiction."[4] Thus, while assuming that the text is indeed a reflection of an author's "truth," I am not exclusively concerned with assessing whether the author's representations are indeed factually "True." If these authors believed these events to have occurred as they described, the effects of them in the construction of their identities are consistent with *that* perception of events.

In her guide to narrative analysis, Catherine Riessman discusses the dilemma posed by establishing the validity of a person's story:

> How are we to evaluate a narrative analysis? Can one tell a better one from a worse one? Prevailing concepts of verification and procedures for establishing validity . . . rely on realist assumptions. . . . A personal

narrative is not meant to be read as an exact record of what happened nor is it a mirror of a world 'out there.' Our readings of data are themselves located in discourses. . . . The historical truth of an individual's account is not the primary issue. Narrativization assumes point of view. . . . Telling about complex and troubling events *should* vary because the past is a selective reconstruction. Individuals exclude experiences that undermine the current identities they wish to claim. . . . Narratives are laced with social discourses and power relations, which do not remain constant over time. There is no reason to assume that an individual's narrative will, or should be, entirely consistent from one setting to the next. . . . In a word, traditional notions of reliability simply do not apply to narrative studies, and validity must be radically reconceptualized. . . . Trustworthiness' not 'truth' is a key semantic difference: The latter assumes an objective reality, whereas the former moves the process into the social world.[5]

Riessman goes on to suggest specific criteria under this general guideline of "trustworthiness" that researchers might use in assessing validity, two of which I will discuss shortly. Several things are important to note in her general statement. Throughout her text, Riessman points out that narrative analysis is particularly "suited to studies of subjectivity and identity," because it is a way to "systematically interpret [respondents'] interpretations."[6] In other words, personal narratives are *valued* for their subjectivity—it is not something to be overcome. Riessman includes this quote from the Personal Narratives Group:

When talking about their lives, people lie sometimes, forget a lot, exaggerate, become confused, and get things wrong. Yet they *are* revealing truths. These truths don't reveal the past 'as it actually was,' aspiring to a standard of objectivity. They give us instead the truths of our experiences. . . . Unlike the truth of the scientific ideal, the truths of personal narratives are neither open to proof nor self-evident.[7]

Still, although my data cannot be expected to be held to the same standards of validity that many other types of data would be, even for narrative data it poses some particular validation challenges. My data is unique, in that it was written by students, and whenever students are used as study participants, particular concerns about validity become more salient. Two facets of this study are especially important to note. First, because the data are written autobiographies turned in as a course assignment, respondents could conceivably edit their thoughts multiple times, hence, one could argue, the data I have is not reflective of their initial, uncensored response. Riessman mentions that adaptations would need to be made for the narrative analysis of written data, although she does not specifically mention issues of *validity* that would arise when life stories are written rather than spoken.[8] However, social science researchers know that respondents always edit themselves to some degree in any study. On written survey forms and questionnaires, respondents have varying degrees of time to think about their answers and even to go back and change them. Even in interviews, depending on the personality of the individual, most probably do not tell us *everything* they are thinking.[9] In fact, one could argue that a person might be *more* likely to report her or his "true" feelings in writing—that social desirability bias is less imposing when one is not face to face with an interviewer. Even aside from the issue of "bias" in the pejorative sense, an interview is, as Holstein and Gubrium point out, an interaction, in which both the interviewee and the interviewer are active participants—as such, the interviewer does affect the outcome of the interview.[10] All in all, a case could be made that allowing participants a chance to edit their written responses is no less "valid" and could even be preferable for research. The students were able to have time to reflect carefully back through their lives, talk to family members about their childhood experiences and family histories, and write in a narrative style, going through memories of their lives year by year.

A second, and more difficult, validity issue is raised by the fact that five of the nine subsamples, made up of 153 student respondents (or 79% of the total 193 autobiographies) were written by students in my own courses, and of these, 139 were initially submitted for graded course credit (14 were submitted only for extra credit). Consequently, of the total sample (193 autobiographies), 139 respondents, or 72% of the sample, may have felt some pressure to write what they thought might be agreeable to me, in order to receive a more favorable grade. The fourteen students (7% of the sample) who wrote papers for me for extra credit at the end of the course and with the number of words only as a standard, would likely find this to be less of a concern but would certainly still understand me to be their primary audience. Still, at least 21% of the sample wrote their papers knowing that their instructors would not see them at all and that they were not writing the paper to be submitted for part of their regular grade for the course.

Although concerns regarding social desirability bias raised by this point cannot be totally dismissed, I believe several factors support my belief that the students felt relatively free to express their thoughts honestly. I will discuss each of these in the following sections.

Diversity of the Sample

First, as I stated previously, 40 of the total 193 autobiographies were collected in colleagues' courses, for extra credit. Hence, approximately one-fifth (21%) of the sample, although still presumably interested in presenting themselves in the best light possible, as are any research participants, did not have any anxieties about impressing me as their instructor. Further, they had been assured that their course instructor would not see their autobiographies, because they were sent directly to me as email attachments.

Throughout the coding process, I compared the autobiographies of students who wrote knowing me as their primary audience with those of students who wrote their autobiographies for extra credit but did not know me. Based on this comparison, it does not seem that students in my courses censored themselves more than the students who knew that I would not be grading their autobiographies but would simply be telling their instructors whether or not they met the minimum word count (I will elaborate on this point subsequently). If anything, students in my colleagues' courses seemed to take a bit more of a distant and "polite" tone in their papers, as if they were speaking with a stranger. Students in both groups varied in the degree to which they accepted or rejected the general messages offered in the courses in which they were enrolled. Moreover, altogether this sample includes students from two distinct regions of the country and from four universities, in nine different courses. This variation itself lends strength to the validity to the data.

Continuing Course Dialogue

As previously discussed, it is difficult to categorize any of these students in terms of how "racist" or "antiracist" they are. After knowing many of them and reading their attempts to deal with these issues, I find labeling them in this way not only methodologically incorrect but also ethically distasteful. However, if I had to compare the papers written by "my" students to those written by my colleagues', I could generalize somewhat regarding their *style*. Students in my courses, rather than censoring themselves based on their knowledge that I would be reading their papers, seemed to become *more* candid. Compared to the autobiographies of students in other instructors' courses, the autobiographies by students in my classes have a tone of familiarity about them. Whatever their stance on race and racism, respondents who had been in my courses wrote papers that explicitly referred to me and the course content. These autobiographies were more "three-dimensional." I could understand better where the authors were "coming from" in the context of an ongoing dialogue. Some who never spoke in class found the paper a place to make points, sometimes insightful, sometimes angry, and sometimes just very personal, that they apparently had not been able to say in the classroom. Not only that, these students seem anything but afraid for their grades. Rather, many use the autobiography as a place to continue to clarify points of contention that were raised during the course of the semester. For example, in some semesters, the autobiography was submitted in two chapters. In the second chapter of several students' papers, there are statements about affirmative action, which we had discussed in class during the second part of the semester. Students used their own life experiences to contextualize their beliefs about the policy and explain to me why they held the opinions they did.

Far from succumbing to social desirability bias, some students actually stated outright that they disagreed with some things that we had discussed in the course, and were going to point them out in their autobiographies. For example, toward the beginning of the second chapter of his autobiography, Keith states:

> As far as Latinos, I thought they were poor and dirty. A city about five miles away from me . . . has a large population of Puerto Ricans. [This city] is quite poor, dirty, and has expansive drug and gang problems. So obviously what was I taught to affiliate with Puerto Ricans; I concluded that Puerto Ricans were the root of these problems. There were few Asians in my community. My beliefs of Asians followed the stereotypical beliefs; they were technically inclined and displayed superior intelligence. My only other significant contact with a minority group as thus far in my life is that of Arabian-Americans. . . . I cannot tell the difference [between] a native of one Arab nation from a native of a different Arab nation, but ever since Desert Storm, I find myself discriminating against Arabs.
>
> I would like to discuss my current beliefs and stereotypes of these minority groups as well as to provide insight on why I have concluded one idea or another. . . . I ask you to bear with me throughout my views. I understand that this course is meant to inform, open our minds, and ultimately to make a conscious effort to deter stereotypes and discrimination based on race or ethnicity. My beliefs do not always show the values that this course is intended to instill in our beliefs.
>
> The first minority group I focus on is African Americans; they are still the main focus of minority debate. I have to admit that I find myself stereotyping blacks on a regular basis. . . . As I interact with blacks on a regular basis now, I realize that there is a definite difference between blacks and whites. All the videos, lectures, and reading we do in class cannot convince me otherwise. That is textbook knowledge; the real education comes with experience. Blacks and whites have a totally different culture; I find that denying that cultural difference to be disturbing. We had a reading that denied the differences between blacks and whites, I disagree. There is a definite difference between blacks and whites. I cannot talk to most black people on the level that they talk to each other, and blacks cannot talk to most whites on the level that most whites talk to each other.

Keith informs the reader, who he assumes to be me, of what he understood the points of the course to be, not all of which he grasped in the way I intended to get across. Then he specifies what he disagreed with in the course, within the context of his life story. Obviously, Keith felt he could be candid with his opinions. He juxtaposes "textbook knowledge" against "real education [that] comes with experience."

In most social science research, the researcher tries, as much as possible, to keep her opinions about the topic under discussion out of the interaction with the respondent, in order to allow the respondent to feel free to give her or his "real" opinions. However, some have questioned whether those of us studying whiteness empirically with white people *should* try to keep our "values" hidden. For example, Charles Gallagher suggests that it is perhaps the responsibility of white researchers interviewing other whites to correct some of the misconceptions, in the course of our research, that allow white people to deny that white privilege exists.[11] Whether or not this is preferable, most of my respondents had been students in my courses, and in a course on race and ethnicity it is nearly impossible for a professor to be "value-free." Although such a course should impart some "factual" information, because it covers issues such as prejudice, discrimination, racism, and inequality, a professor's moral stance on these issue and beliefs regarding the best remedies for racial problems are reflected in course lectures and materials. Nonetheless, in their writing, several students expressed opinions and attitudes that were clearly in opposition to points that I had made in class. Students openly discussed their frustrations, anxieties, and even, sometimes, hostilities toward current debates and policies surrounding race and ethnicity. Another student, Victor, wrote:

> This semester has brought me to believe many different items racially. We have gone over many items that I didn't know and many that I didn't know existed. It also made me want to learn more about my family and myself. If I had one minor tiff about the semester it would be the way that you portrayed white culture. You based everything on white society and took the viewpoint of the different cultures instead of taking a completely neutral vantage point.

Many white students have a difficult time understanding why whites are used as the standard of comparison for other groups when discussing income, wealth, life expectancy, educational achievement, and political representation. They may use this as grounds to dispute statistics that were offered in class. For example, Ray writes:

> As far as the statistics concerning blacks and how they are at a disadvantage, I think it is sad that they are discriminated against in areas such as employment and housing. They are equal to us and should receive the same kind of treatment that white people do. I think it is unfair to limit their opportunities just because they are of another color. The only area which I think is blown way out of proportion is crime. This really disturbs me to hear that the law targets black people. The statistic that blacks make up roughly half of the prison population but approximately only 10–15% of the United States population, this is used as the excuse that there is racial profiling in the criminal justice system. I think this accusation is bogus, people are put in prison for a reason so obviously these people did something wrong to deserve imprisonment. Some blame is put on the area they live in and where they grow up, just because you live in the city does not mean you have to get involved with crime. . . . I don't like seeing white people and black people always being compared.

What is the point of comparing people, it makes no sense. . . . Comparing people of opposite races just pushes us further apart. Everybody is supposed to be created equal and treated equal so what do we have to compare?

As these young men's statements illustrate and many other examples in this book show, although they knew I would be grading their papers, the respondents felt reasonably reassured that they would not be penalized for articulating beliefs and values that might be in contrast to what they understood mine to be. Social desirability bias notwithstanding, there was a great deal of variation and candor in the students' stories.

Presentation in Stories

Another factor supporting the validity of this autobiographical data is that I asked the students to ground their writing, as much as possible, in their life experiences. Rather than simply writing an essay on "what I think about being white," or "what bothers me about race relations," I wanted them to tell *stories* about how race and racial identity had played a part in their life, from the earliest point they remembered to the present. In his discussion of the validity of student journals as data, Rabow asserts that reported behavior may be more valid than attitudes, because "[b]ehavior is much less reactive than expressed attitudes."[12] I believe that my data bear this out. While students were more often able to state their opinions in a manner that sounded racially "appropriate," their stories frequently revealed more nuances about their racial identities. Moreover, it was common for a respondent to be presented in a less than flattering, or at least more complex, way in her or his own story. This, I believe, is another testimony to the validity of the data—it seems that many respondents were being honest even at the risk of making themselves sometimes look deficient, uncertain, or inconsistent.

Difficulty of Studying Whiteness in a "Natural" Setting

Even though issues of validity undeniably do enter this research, they do so in any empirical study. Data gathered in any setting are, to varying degrees, generated by the researcher. People always speak from some position, and in this sense no empirical data are ever pristine or "natural" once we as researchers ask respondents for them. Granted, researchers impose themselves on the research setting, and in their participants' consciousness, less in some studies than in others.

I assert, nevertheless, that whiteness is exceptionally difficult to observe in "natural" settings and that, for researchers at this time, it is likely that white racial identity is a topic that has to be evoked more than many others. Since the inception of whiteness studies, perhaps the one theme common to nearly every piece of research on the topic is that whiteness, in a white-dominated society, most often remains "invisible" or "unmarked." As previously discussed, it has only been racially aware whites, those who have been awakened to the role of race in their lives by a dramatic event such as marrying a person of color, who have generally spoken or written about whiteness without being asked to do so. Consequently, I would agree that these autobiographies of whiteness were generated quite *un*naturally, for the purposes of this research. Yet, I maintain that they are nonetheless useful indications of the state of current whiteness amongst this generation in the United States.

"Correspondence" and "Pragmatic Use"

In addition to her discussion of general guidelines for establishing the validity of narrative data, Riessman goes on to suggest four specific criteria, following the general principle of "trustworthiness": persuasiveness, correspondence, coherence, and pragmatic use.[13] Two of these are especially applicable to this study: correspondence and pragmatic use. The criteria of correspondence, or "respondent validation," requires that an investigator take the findings of a study back to the respondents, to check with them to see whether the conclusions reached are consistent with their experience. Riessman does caution that there are limitations to this standard, however. First, human stories change over time, so what a respondent's narrative meant to her or him originally may differ from what it means to her or him when the researcher goes back to check the results of her study. Second, no one respondent can validate theorizing that is done by a researcher across multiple narratives. Applied to my data, any one of the students knows only his or her own life story and written autobiography intimately and cannot evaluate the conclusions I have reached based on an analysis of nearly 200 autobiographies over a four-year period of time.[14]

Still, with those limitations in mind, I believe I have been able to employ a type of correspondence to support the validity of this research further. Throughout the research process, I have presented the "work in progress" to students in various formal settings, such as the classroom and other presentations, and informal conversational settings. I have found this to be a valuable way to check to see whether the conclusions I was reaching make sense to whites in the generation and regions that are the focus of my exploration. One particularly effective instance of this type of validation occurred in the spring of 2002, when I was asked to present some of my research during a "Lunch with a Professor" gathering with a group of students. After my presentation, students asked questions, commented on my findings, and also gave me written comments. Their statements validated the conclusions I had reached at the time and also helped me to begin to push my theorizing ahead.

Another of Riessman's suggested criteria for validity—pragmatic use—also, I believe, applies to this study. Pragmatic use refers to the extent to which a study can be used by other researchers. Because the development of knowledge in social science assumes that we work within a "community of scientists," knowledge is validated in part by how useful it is within that community. Of course, this places the burden of establishing validity in the future, and Riessman admits that it is not particularly helpful for an individual researcher who needs to prove the validity of a given study. However, she points out,

> But we can provide information that will make it possible for others to determine the trustworthiness of our work by (a) describing how the interpretations were produced, (b) making visible what we did, . . . (d) making primary data available to other researchers. . . . We can, in addition, bring our 'foundational assumptions [and values] to the surface, not concealing them underneath the methodological artifice of science' (Agger, 1991, p. 120 [quoted in Riessman]).[15]

The principles just listed highlight the trustworthiness of this data. For each of the reasons I have discussed, I believe that the students' autobiographies are a valid tool that can tell us a great deal about whiteness in the late twentieth and early twenty-first century.

Appendix B
Sample Differences:
North/South or Rural/Urban?

Four years ago I moved from the South, where I had lived for my entire life, to rural Pennsylvania. Throughout my life in the South I have always lived in metropolitan areas of varying sizes. Never have I lived in a place as rural, or a town as small, as the one in which I live now. Since moving, I have been struck not only by the beauty of my physical surroundings but also by the lack of diversity of my cultural environment. According to the 2000 Census, the city in which I now live is 96 percent white.[16] This has been a new experience for me. In the same year, 2000, the city in which I grew up, Chattanooga, Tennessee, was about 60 percent white.[17] Of course, the larger surrounding area is more white than the city, at about 76.3 percent.[18] In the 1980s, when I was growing up in Chattanooga, the urban area was 78.4% white.[19] Thus, although until my move to the Northeast I've always lived in areas that are predominantly white, they have had enough diversity so that I encountered people of color on an everyday basis—on the streets, in stores, as colleagues, and as friends. Although the town in which I live has *some* diversity, it is very limited, and the people of color that I encounter are mostly involved with the campus where I teach. Other than these, I have only interacted with people who are not white as doctors in this town, and as the very few students of color I have in my classes. The diversity is so lacking that I am surprised to see an African American, Asian, or Latino person in the mall in town.

Not only was the town a surprise to me when I moved here, I seemed to be a surprise to the town. Students in my classes teased me for my use of the contraction "y'all" (which made as much sense to me as their equivalent term, "y'uns"). Although I'm told that it is beginning to fade, my southern accent used to cause heads to turn in public places. I have told people many times since that I never felt "Southern" until I moved up North.

What has surprised me the most have been the ideas that I confront about the South here in the North. Perhaps many people believe these things, but it is my students that voice them. Students consistently insist that the South is "more racist" or "more prejudiced" than the North, even today. Rarely do my students discuss racism in their own small hometowns, although they speak of racial isolation. Sometimes they ask me to tell them what it's like "down South," assuming that I will have tales to tell of dramatic racist incidents that I witnessed regularly. Some Southern respondents in this research are aware of perceptions of them based on their Southern heritage. Nathan writes:

> I am not white trash, which is what people think of many Southern whites. I was born and raised in a southern city and I think of myself as a cracker. This term is used to describe native Floridians like myself.

I am sometimes surprised by my feeling a need to defend my home region. But I don't think it comes so much from a sense of "Southern pride" as it does from a need to correct a fundamental misperception that students have about the nature of white racism today. This misperception allows them to use the South as a scapegoat for white racism and continue to ignore the prejudice in their own backyards. I do believe that there are differences in white attitudes that are based in part on the geographical space in which whites grow up. However, I believe that these differences are today no longer split as much along a North/South distinction but based on whether one has grown up in an urban or a rural setting. Even this distinction is not a "neat" one and may be true more in the North than in the South. In Southern states, even whites who grew up in rural areas have often had contact with people of color, specifically with African Americans, because of the agricultural nature of rural life and the historical involvement of African Americans with Southern agriculture. Whether or not this contact leads to a positive outcome differs, of course, for different white people. Still, at least the contact has been there, "messy" as it sometimes has been.

In the North, however, for rural whites, contact with people of color was and is less likely to occur. Thus, it seems that as prejudiced attitudes have abated in the country based at least in part on contact between whites and people of color, it is often whites who have had little contact with people of color who are left with attitudes that seem behind the rest of the country by several decades. I hypothesize that it is rural whites who are the least likely to have had contact with people of color and thus are the most unfamiliar with them. This can lead to essentialist beliefs, fears, and for some, outright prejudice and racism exhibited in their attitudes. It is ironic to me that while Northern students tell me how "racist" the South is, I have heard more overt racist statements, witnessed more hostile stares directed toward people of color, and toward me when I am with them, and seen more *Confederate flags* in proportion to the population since moving North than I did in the South. Some of the Northern students are aware of their lack of exposure to people of color. Victor insightfully writes,

You can go to any town or city in the United States and you will see some form of ethnic or racial formation, but there is a big difference in the diversity from an urban area and a rural area. I come from a small town of two thousand and some odd people and my perspectives are not that educated. In "educated" I mean that I have not had much to base my judgments on coming from a small rural town where you have 99.9% white American that have European descent. On occasion there would be an African-American, Latino, or Asian that would move into the area, but they were few and far between and most of the time when they would migrate to the area they would not stay for long. It is not a racist town, but maybe there were those few bigots that would give them a hard time and sway the minority out. Anyway you look at it my life has been pretty sheltered on the racial and ethnic front.

Similarly, Lisa understands that a town that is technically in the "North" can be very stereotypically "old South" in its attitudes:

I am white along with around 98% of my town. I grew up in Northern Virginia in a rural area. Most people there were farmers or descendents of farmers, and there was very little racial diversity. I remember seeing confederate flags and museums everywhere. It meant very little to me because I didn't understand what it all meant. If anyone asked, I would have said I was a northerner, but in fact my hometown had and still has a very "southern" attitude.

Lisa explicitly makes old-fashioned white racial attitudes more about a lack of exposure to people of color, a nostalgia for the traditions of the Confederacy, and a rural white lifestyle than about a living in the geographical area referred to as "The South."

When I began this project, I had only a Southern sample. Mentors advised me that I should also gather data in the North, because I would otherwise be criticized for having a regional bias. These same advisors hypothesized that I would not find much difference in whites' attitudes between my Southern and Northern samples, however. This hypothesis was correct in one way, but incorrect for a different reason. Although I did not find differences in my samples that I believe were based so much on "Southern" versus "Northern" white attitudes, I did find differences in the samples that were due to the fact that those whites born and raised in the South had different experiences than those born and raised in the North. They were likely to have had earlier and more frequent contact with people of color, regardless of whether they grew up in a rural or urban setting (although more of my Southern sample was from an urban setting). Those in the Northern sample were less likely to have had contact with people of color, because nearly all had grown up in a rural setting, where whites and people of color are relatively segregated. Thus, although I can describe differences in my samples, and the samples were from three southern universities and one northern university, I believe the differences were based more on the fact that the southern universities are located in more metropolitan, diverse areas, while the northern university is located in a small town surrounded by a very rural setting. Thus, when I refer to the "Southern" sample or the "Northern" sample, I do so not to imply that differences between the samples are based on that regional difference, since I believe them to be more due to differences in the population size and makeup of the towns, but simply as a shorthand way to reference the two samples.

The "Southern" Urban Sample

The Southern sample and Northern samples had many things in common, and except for in this section, throughout the remainder of the study, the results for both samples are discussed together. The primary way the samples differed was in the stories they tell about their early lives. Most of the ways that they perceive whiteness are similar, and where differences arise, I note them.

Two of the Southern subsamples were gathered from a very large state university, made up of some 47,000 students. Of these, 77 percent were white. Of the 23 percent who were of other racial groups, 9.6 percent were "Hispanic," 7.2 percent black, and 6.8 percent Asian or Pacific Islander.[20] The other two Southern subsamples were drawn from smaller branch campuses of this state university. The first subsample, who were students in my class, attended a university populated by approximately 12,000 students. Of these, 79 percent were white and 21 percent were "minority" students. The school's website did not break the students down any further by racial or ethnic group.[21] The second subsample had approximately 39,000 students. Of these, 69.7 percent were white.

A large number of the Southern respondents moved at various times in their youth, perhaps because the state in which this first stage of the research was conducted tends to be one of "transplants." Most grew up having very little contact with people of color until college. Still, most place their first regular interactions with people of color at a relatively young age, particularly compared to the Northern sample—while still in elementary or middle school. Although many speak of their hometowns as lacking in racial diversity, most of their towns were apparently more diverse than those of the Northern writers. Several of the Southern respondents had maids or nannies who were people of color, usually African American. I found this to be somewhat surprising, given that most of these young people were born in the 1980s.

The "Northern" Rural Sample

In contrast to the Southern sample, the Northern sample was drawn from a university that is a branch campus of a large state university. This campus is made up of 3,800 students, 89.93 percent of whom are white. Of the 10.07 percent who are of other racial groups, 5.25 percent are African American, 2.19 percent are Asian American, 1.65 percent are "Hispanic,".0.05 percent are Native American, and 0.93 percent are international students.[22] Although the campus obviously lacks the racial diversity of the Southern universities, it has increased in diversity in recent years. Additionally, it is interesting to note that relative to the surrounding area, the campus is more diverse. When many of these students wrote in their autobiographies or mentioned in class that they were "shocked" or "surprised" by all the diversity they encountered when they entered college, I was at first somewhat bemused, since I could tell by looking around campus that there were very few students of color in comparison to white students. However, when one considers that most of these students grew up in an area that is 96 percent white (or even more for many, because this figure refers to the city, and many students come from outlying areas), it is true from their perspective that college has brought them in contact with more people of color than ever before in their lives.

The town in which the Northern college is located has undergone economic hardship in the last few years, with factories and railroads closing and people being laid off from their jobs. Thus, students in the Northern sample sometimes seem more able to empathize with problems of inequality. Their sense of class inequality may enable these students to understand racial inequality in a way that more economically secure students have a difficult time doing.

Most of these students obviously grew up having very little contact with people of color. Compared to the Southern sample, their first regular interactions with people of color often did not come until high school, although a few remember brief encounters with a single student of color in elementary or middle school. Some had no ongoing contact with people of color until college. The autobiographies from the Southern respondents were full of stories and experiences they had with people of color; in fact, they often told their stories of whiteness by telling of each significant encounter with people of color they have had in their lives. Conversely, often the Northern respondents' autobiographies read more like position papers on matters of race—they did not tell about experiences with people of color as much but simply relayed their opinions about "racial" issues, such as prejudice and its causes, discrimination, crime, police brutality, and especially affirmative action. This could be because these students had so few interactions with people of color that they did not think of themselves as having any stories to tell of race, and particularly no stories of whiteness.

Also in contrast to the Southern samples, the respondents in the Northern sample tended to have more of a sense of their ethnic identity. Their autobiographies include more stories about ethnic traditions, heritage, and ancestry than do the Southern autobiographies. Interestingly, even when they state that they know very little about their ethnicity, often these respondents go on to give much more information than Southern respondents were able to provide. Although I did not gather demographic data on the ethnic background of every student, but simply allowed each student to self-report her or his identity in whatever way she or he chose (racially and/or ethnically), observation of those who did report their ethnicity shows that more in the Northern sample were of Italian, German, and Polish backgrounds while those in the Southern sample reported being of English, Scottish, and German backgrounds. Part of the reason, then, that those in the Northern sample may have had more ethnic information to report is because their ethnicity is less far removed in time from them, in terms of the immigration of their ancestors. Indeed, many in the Northern sample had grandparents or great-grandparents who had immigrated, while far fewer in the Southern sample told these stories. Thus those in the North may have had somewhat more of a sense of a "usable" ethnic past.

Despite these differences in the time of first contact with those of other groups and the knowledge of ethnic identity, the Northern and Southern respondents shared in common the major themes of whiteness reported in this study.

Appendix C
Autobiography Guide

This is an abbreviated version of the autobiography guide used over the various semesters I have been collecting data for this project. The description of the paper has changed slightly as I have modified the assignment for different classes. The list of guiding questions given here is a sampling of the total I have included in the assignment.

Description of the Paper

Everyone has some racial or ethnic heritage, though for some it may be less important than for others, both in how they see themselves, as well as in how others see them. This paper should focus on the racial/ethnic aspect of your identity.

Throughout your paper, try to use as many specific examples and tell about as many specific experiences, memories and stories as you can. Choose stories from your life when you were most aware of race and ethnicity. Use details to try to describe your thoughts and experiences as thoroughly as possible. This should read like a regular autobiography, but with a focus on issues of race/ethnicity. Tell things that have happened to you. This paper should NOT simply read as a long essay that could be titled "What I Think About Race," or "Current Racial Issues That Interest Me Most." Tell a story about something that has happened to you, and then you may add something that you learned from it. *Focus on things like change, stability, turning points, influences, stories, people, feelings, conflict, resolution, and recurring themes.*

Grading Criteria

Since you are writing about your life, you will not be graded so much on the *substance* of your autobiography as you will on whether you followed the directions for the assignment. So be sure to do these things: 1) Meet the word requirements, and the formatting requirements for the paper. 2) Proofread your paper flawlessly. 3) Write a grammatically correct paper. 4) Focus on stories and experiences, not opinions. 5) Show me that you gave this some careful thought, in the context of things we've been discussing this semester.

Guiding Questions

Remember to mention specific events that you remember as being significant to you in regards to your race or ethnicity. What I am looking for is the shifts, progression, or other development of your racial/ethnic consciousness. Be specific. Again, remember to work chronologically, from the first time you remember being aware of your or someone else's race/ethnicity to the present.

(For any questions with a blank, fill in the blank when reading it with the term you use to identify your race/ethnicity, whichever you identify with more.)

- What are some of your first memories of recognizing racial/ethnic differences and your place in a racial/ethnic group?
- To any extent that you can, write about "_____ness" *without* writing about any other groups who are not _____.
- Broadly speaking, what does it mean to be _____?
- If you were not being asked to discuss your race or ethnicity, could you tell your life story without mentioning race or ethnicity?
- Is your racial/ethnic identity one of the most important aspects of your personality? For example, if you had to describe yourself, is it one of the first things you would think of to say?
- If you identify more in racial terms, what do you know about your ethnic heritage (i.e., from what countries did your ancestors immigrate, or from what areas were they brought to the U.S.)?
- What, if any, messages did your family give you regarding your own race/ethnicity as you were growing up?
- Does/did your family have any specific traditions related to your racial/ethnic heritage? How do you think this compares with other families of your same race/ethnicity? How about with other families of other races/ethnicities?
- How, if at all, have your ideas about race/ethnicity changed through the years?
- What *specific* world events, personal incidents, relationships (with friends, classmates, etc.), environmental factors (the neighborhood you lived in, family situations, etc.), media images (books, toys, movies, television—-mention specific names/titles), etc. have had an effect on your ideas about race, ethnicity, and racism?
- What are some experiences that have made your race or ethnicity most visible to you?

- Throughout your life, have most of your friends and other people close to you been of your same racial/ethnic background? If so, why do you think this was the case? If not, what do you think led you to cross racial/ethnic lines in creating relationships?
- Have you been subject to discrimination based on your race or ethnicity? If so, what type(s)?
- Has your racial/ethnic identity brought you any privileges or benefits? If so, what type(s)?
- How do you think your racial/ethnic identity will be likely to affect your future, if at all?
- How do you think demographic changes that are currently underway will affect your experiences and attitudes relating to race, ethnicity, and racism?
- Do you think racism is becoming more of a problem, less of a problem, or not changing much in the U.S.? If you think it is a problem, what do you think the best solution(s) is/are?

Endnotes

Foreword

1. W. E. B. Du Bois, *Darkwater*, New York: Humanity Books, 2003 [1920].

Preface

1. C. Gallagher, "White Like Me?: Methods, Meaning and Manipulation in the Field of White Studies," in *Racing Research, Researching Race: Methodological Dilemmas in Critical Race Studies*, ed. F. Twine and J. Warren, New York: New York University Press, 2000, pp. 67–91.
2. A. McIntyre, *Making Meaning of Whiteness: Exploring White Identity with White Teachers*, New York: State University of New York Press, 1997.
3. R. Delgado, *The Coming Race War?: And Other Apocalyptic Tales of America after Affirmative Action and Welfare*, New York: New York University Press, 1996, pp. 34–36.
4. See, for example, L. Kenny, *Daughters of Suburbia: Growing up White, Middle Class, and Female*, New Brunswick: Rutgers University Press, p. 199; C. Stage, "We Celebrate 100 Years: An 'Indigenous' Analysis of the Metaphors That Shape the Cultural Identity of Small Town, U.S.A.," in *Whiteness: The Communication of Social Identity*, ed. T. K. Nakayama and J. N. Martin, Thousand Oaks, CA: Sage, 1999, pp. 69–83. Both are examples of researchers using an "insider" white perspective as a resource in a study of whiteness.
5. Charles Gallagher addresses this point, among others, in Gallagher, "White Like Me?"
6. This is quoted from an anonymous comment turned in by a student at the beginning of class that first summer I taught race and ethnicity, in 1998. Students that summer turned in questions or comments at the beginning of every class period. Since then, I have often heard similar comments and read them in the data presented in this book.
7. R. Frankenberg, *White Women, Race Matters: The Social Construction of Whiteness*, Minneapolis: University of Minnesota Press, 1993.

Chapter 1

1. All respondents' names have been changed to protect their privacy. Additionally, names of other people, names of places, and any other information that might identify them also have been changed to ensure them maximum confidentiality. In some of the quotes from the autobiographies, respondents' spelling and grammar have been corrected in minor ways to improve the clarity of their writing, but only in places where to leave the writing as is would render the narrative extremely confusing. No major changes have been made that would alter the tone and style of the students' prose, even if their grammar is incorrect.

2. This point is discussed more in the Preface.

3. In one of the Southern universities, there were two samples collected (from students in two different courses, with two different instructors), and in the other two, there was one sample from each (with different instructors at each). Thus, there were a total of four Southern subsamples. From the Northern university, there were four subsamples, from students in four semesters of the same course, with the same instructor.

4. Lyman and M. Scott, *A Sociology of the Absurd*, Dix Hills, NY: General Hall, Inc., 1989, pp. 112–113.

5. L. Lyons, "Is Tolerance a Non-issue for Teens?" The Gallup Organization, February 26, 2002. Available online at: http://www.gallup.com/poll/tb/educayouth/20020226b.asp (accessed January 28, 2004).

6. J. Robison, "Will Teen Tolerance Pass the Roommate Test?" The Gallup Organization, May 6, 2003. Available online at: http://www.gallup.com/poll/tb/religValue/20030506.asp (accessed January 28, 2004).

7. S. Crabtree, "How Well Integrated Are America's Teens?" The Gallup Organization, December 9, 2003. Available online at: http://www.gallup.com/poll/tb/educaYouth/20031209.asp (accessed January 28, 2004); S. Crabtree, "Do Teens 'Clique' with Diversity?" The Gallup Organization, December 16, 2003. Available online at: http://www.gallup.com/poll/tb/educayouth/20031216.asp (accessed January 28, 2004).

8. Because my interest is in the *collective* creation and presentation of whiteness, the unit of analysis is individual stories or examples of white "race talk," not individual white persons.

9. T. Morrison, *Playing in the Dark: Whiteness and the Literary Imagination*, Cambridge: Harvard University Press, 1992.

10. The recognition that whiteness takes much of its power from being able to be invisible has become one of the most oft-repeated themes in whiteness studies. Richard Dyer was one of the first to note it, in his article, "White," cited below, and Pamela Perry discusses it well in her article, P. Perry, "White Means Never Having to Say You're Ethnic: White Youth and the Construction of 'Cultureless' Identities," *Journal of Contemporary Ethnography* 30 (1), 2001, 56–91.

11. In order to indicate that they are not essential qualities, but are instead social constructions, words such as "white" and "race" are often placed in quotation marks when they appear in current theoretical writing on race. For the sake of convenience and readability, I will not place the words "white" and "race" in quotation marks at each occurrence, still, it is the assumption of this study that both are social constructions.

12. Some interesting work to consider here is that of Edward Said, particularly his work on Orientalism. Said was one of the first to articulate how Westerners maintained a vision of themselves as rational, objective, and reasonable by contrasting their culture with that of the irrational, subjective, unreasonable, Eastern "Other." See E. Said, *Orientalism*, New York: Vintage Books, 1978. In this same line of work, Marimba Ani's critique of Western culture similarly posits that its hegemonic power relies on a contrast of Western rationality against supposed African inferiority. See M. Ani, *Yurugu: A African-Centered Critique of European Cultural Thought and Behavior*, Trenton, NJ: African World Press, Inc., 1994. Others have applied this theory to empirical work. For example, in C. Lutz and J. Collins, *Reading National Geographic*, Chicago, University of Chicago Press, 1993, Lutz and Collins show how popular magazines, such as *National Geographic*, through the exoticization of non-Western bodies, constructs ideals of Western masculinity and femininity.

13. G. Lipsitz, *The Possessive Investment in Whiteness: How White People Profit from Identity Politics*, Philadelphia: Temple University Press, 1998, p. 22.

14. Richard Wright was one of the first to speak of racism as a white problem. Once, when asked what he thought of the "Negro problem" in America, he answered "There isn't any Negro problem; there is only a white problem." Reference to this story taken from Lipsitz, *The Possessive Investment in Whiteness*, p. 1.

15. See, for example, P. Essed, *Everyday Racism: Reports of Women of Two Cultures*, Alameda, CA: Hunter House, 1990; J. Feagin and M. Sikes, *Living With Racism: The Black Middle-Class Experience*, Boston: Beacon Press, 1994; J. Feagin, *Racist America: Roots, Current Realities, and Future Reparations*, New York: Routledge, 2000, p. 141.

16. J. Feagin and H. Vera, *White Racism: The Basics*, New York: Routledge, 1995, p. 173.

17. R. W. Emerson, "History," In *Essays: The First Series* (Boston, J. Munroe and Company, 1841). Available online at: http://www.jjnet.com/emerson/history.htm (accessed February 24, 2000).

18. C. K. Riessman, *Narrative Analysis*, Newbury Park, CA: Sage, 1993, p. 5. Riessman here cites G. Rosenwald and R. Ochberg, *Storied Lives: The Cultural Politics of Self-Understanding*, New Haven, CT: Yale University Press, 1992.

19. C. Barros, *Autobiography: Narrative of Transformation*, Ann Arbor: University of Michigan Press, 1998.

20. J. Ribbens, "Facts or Fictions? Aspects of the Use of Autobiographical Writing in Undergraduate Sociology," *Sociology*, 27 (1), 1993, 81–93.

21. R. Blauner, *Black Lives, White Lives: Three Decades of Race Relations in America* Berkeley: University of California Press, 1989, p. 4.

22. See, for example, M. Gergen and K. Gergen, "Narratives of the Gendered Body in Popular Autobiography," in *The Narrative Study of Lives*, (Vol. 1), ed. R. Josselson and A. Lieblich, Newbury Park: Sage, 1993, ch. 8. One example of a sociological study that does use written autobiography is M. Grimes and J. Morris, *Caught in the Middle: Contradictions in the Lives of Sociologists from Working-Class Backgrounds*, Westport, CT: Praeger, 1997.

23. See, for example, J. Okely, "Anthropology and Autobiography: Participatory Experience and Embodied Knowledge," in *Anthropology and Autobiography*, ed. J. Okely and H. Callaway, New York: Routledge, 1992, ch. 1.

24. Rosenwald and Ochberg, *Storied Lives*, p. 1.

25. See, for example, W. Harrington, *Crossings: A White Man's Journey into Black America*, New York: Harper Collins, 1992; J. Lazarre, *Beyond the Whiteness of Whiteness: Memoir of a White Mother of Black Sons*, Durham: Duke University Press, 1996; S. Rush, *Loving Across the Color Line: A White Adoptive Mother Learns About Race*, Lanham, MD: Rowman and Littlefield, 2000.

26. See, for example, E. Ball, *Slaves in the Family*, New York: Ballantine Books, 1998; H. Wiencek, *The Hairstons: An American Family in Black and White*, New York: St. Martin's Press, 1999; G. Williams, *Life on the Color Line: The True Story of a White Boy Who Discovered He Was Black*, New York: Plume, 1995.

27. See, for example, J. Griffin, *Black Like Me*, New York, Signet, 1960; M. Segrest, *Memoir of a Race Traitor*, Boston: South End Press, 1994.

28. See, for example, D. Conley, *Honky*. New York: Vintage Books, 2000; C. Ellis, "The Other Side of the Fence: Seeing Black and White in a Small Southern Town," *Qualitative Inquiry* 1 (2) 1995, 147–67; M. Halsey, *No Laughing Matter: The Autobiography of a WASP*, Philadelphia: J. B. Lippincott Company, 1977; J. Landsman, *A White Teacher Talks About Race*, Lanham, MD: The Scarecrow Press, 2001; L. Killian, *Black and White: Reflections of a White Southern Sociologist*, Dix Hills, NY: General Hall, Inc., 1994; C. Sartwell, *Act Like You Know: African American Autobiography and White Identity*, Chicago: The University of Chicago Press, 1998; L. Smith, *Killers of the Dream*, Garden City, NJ: Anchor Books, 1963; K. Watterson, *Not By the Sword: How a Cantor and His Family Transformed a Klansman*, Boston: Northeastern University Press, 1995.

29. See, for example, R. Blauner, *Black Lives, White Lives: Three Decades of Race Relations in America*, Berkeley: University of California Press, 1989; L. Funderburg, *Black, White, Other: Biracial Americans Talk About Race and Identity*, New York: William Morrow, 1994; M. Gillan and J. Gillan, *Identity Lessons: Contemporary Writing About Learning to Be American*, New York: Penguin Books, 1999; R. Takaki, *A Larger Memory: A History of Our Diversity, With Voices*, Boston: Little, Brown, and Company, 1998; S. Terkel, *Race: How Blacks and Whites Think and Feel About the American Obsession*, New York: The New Press, 1992; B. Thompson and S. Tyagi, *Names We Call Home: Autobiography on Racial Identity*, New York: Routledge, 1996.

30. J. Rabow, *Voices of Pain and Voices of Hope: Students Speak About Racism*, Dubuque, IA: Kendall Hunt Publishing, 2002; J. Waller, *Prejudice Across America: The Experiences of a Teacher and His Students on a Nationwide Trek Toward Racial Understanding*, Jackson: University of Mississippi Press, 2000.

31. T. Dublin (ed.), *Becoming American, Becoming Ethnic: College Students Explore Their Roots*, Philadelphia: Temple University Press, 1996.

32. M. Mazie, P. Palmer, M. Pimentel, S. Rogers, S. Ruderfer, and M. Sokolowski, "To Deconstruct Race, Deconstruct Whiteness," *American Quarterly*, 45 (2), 1993, 281–94.

33. See appendix A for a discussion of the validity issues raised by the use of student writing as data.

34. K. McKinney, "Affirmation, Transformation and Experimentation: Narrative Constructions of Interracial Dating," paper presented at the 1999 ASA Meetings in Chicago, Illinois.

35. On the idea of "epiphanies" in autobiography, see N. Denzin, *Interpretive Biography*, Newbury Park, CA: Sage, 1989. In this study, these turning points will be discussed in chapter 2.

36. Bob Blauner discusses the desire for "usable pasts" in R. Blauner, "Talking Past Each Other: Black and White Languages of Race," in *Race and Ethnic Conflict*, ed. H. J. Ehrlich and F. L. Pincus, Boulder, CO: Westview Press, 1994, pp. 27–34.

37. Here I borrow and modify West and Zimmerman's concept of "doing gender," to describe the set of daily processes by which gender is lived and created in individual people's lives, which then constructs and reconstructs gender on a structural level (this is my interpretation/ restatement of the concept). I believe the same can be said for how we as a culture "do race." A statement of the idea of "doing gender" can be found in C. West and D. Zimmerman, "Doing Gender," *Gender and Society* 1, 1987, 125–51. Another similarly useful idea is Omi and Winant's concept of "racial etiquette," which is "a set of interpretive codes and racial meanings which operate in the interactions of daily life." Through the everyday use of racial etiquette, race becomes "common sense." Racial etiquette could, perhaps, be seen as a product of "doing race" or, looked at in another way, could be conceptualized as the same process. This statement of the concept of "racial etiquette" was taken from M. Omi and H. Winant, "Racial Formations," in *Rethinking the Color Line*, ed. C. Gallagher, London: Mayfield Publishing Company, 1999, 12.

38. See appendix C for a composite list of the assignment that was given to students over the various semesters.

39. See appendix B.

40. B. Tatum, *"Why Are All the Black Kids Sitting Together in the Cafeteria?": And Other Conversations About Race*, New York: Basic Books, 1997.

41. Tatum, *"Why Are All the Black Kids Sitting Together in the Cafeteria?"*

42. J. Hartigan, Jr. *Racial Situations: Class Predicaments of Whiteness in Detroit*, Princeton, NJ: Princeton University Press, 1999.

43. S. D. McLemore and H. D. Romo, *Racial and Ethnic Relations in America*, 5th ed., Boston: Allyn and Bacon, 1998.

44. D. Roediger, ed. *Black on White: Black Writers on What It Means to Be White*, New York: Schocken Books, 1998.

45. Roediger, *Black on White*, p. 283.

46. David Roediger, *The Wages of Whiteness: Race and the Making of the American Working Class*, New York: Verso, 1991; Theodore W. Allen, *The Invention of the White Race*, New York: Verso, 1994; Michael Omi and Howard Winant, *Racial Formations in the United States: From the 1960s to the 1980s*, New York: Routledge, 1986.

47. Roediger, *Black on White*, p. 11.

48. Roediger, *Black on White*, p. 19.

49. Quoted in Roediger, *Black on White*, p. 178.

50. Quoted in Roediger, *Black on White*, p. 178.

51. W. E. B. Du Bois, *Black Reconstruction in the United States*, New York: Harcourt, Brace and Company, 1935. See also Oliver C. Cox, *Race Relations: Elements and Social Dynamics*, Detroit: Wayne State University Press, 1976.

52. Tatum, *"Why Are All the Black Kids Sitting Together in the Cafeteria?"*

53. J. Helms, *Black and White Racial Identity Development*, Westport, CT: Praeger, 1990.

54. J. Helms, *A Race is a Nice Thing to Have: A Guide to Being a White Person or Understanding the White Person in Your Life*, Topeka, KS: Content Communications, 1992.

55. See, for example, C. Block and R. Carter, "White Racial Identity Theories: A Rose by Any Other Name Is Still a Rose," *The Counseling Psychologist*, 24 (2), 1996, 326–35; D. Pope-Davis and T. Ottavi, "The Relationship Between Racism and Racial Identity Among White Americans: A Replication and Extension," *Journal of Counseling and Development*, 72 (3), 1994, 293–8; P. Ramsey, *Teaching and Learning in a Diverse World: Multicultural Education for Young Children*, New York: Teachers' College Press, 1998; W. Rowe, S. Bennett, and D. Atkinson, "White Racial Identity Models: A Critique and Proposal," *The Counseling Psychologist*, 22 (1), 1994, 129–47.

56. See David Roediger's analysis in *The Wages of Whiteness*.

57. J. Daniels, *White Lies: Race, Class, Gender and Sexuality in White Supremacist Discourse*, New York: Routledge, 1997; A. Ferber, *White Man Falling: Race, Gender and White Supremacy*, New York: Rowman and Littlefield Publishers, 1998; M. Novick, *White Lies, White Power: The Fight Against White Supremacy and Reactionary Violence*, Monroe, ME: Common Courage Press, 1995; J. Ridgeway, *Blood in the Face: The Ku Klux Klan, Aryan*

Nations, Nazi Skinheads, and the Rise of a New White Culture, New York: Thunder's Mouth Press, 1990.

58. T. W. Adorno, E. Frenkel-Brunswik, D. Levinson, and R. N. Sanford, *The Authoritarian Personality*, New York: Harper and Row, 1950; G. Allport, *The Nature of Prejudice*, Reading, MA: Addison Wesley, 1954; J. Kovel, *White Racism: A Psychohistory*, New York: Columbia University Press, 1984.

59. Merton postulated that there are four different personality types in regards to prejudiced attitudes and discriminatory behavior. These are the unprejudiced nondiscriminator, the unprejudiced discriminator, the prejudiced nondiscriminator, and the prejudiced discriminator. He discusses various reasons why a person my act in a manner inconsistent with her or his attitudes. See R. Merton, "Discrimination and the American Creed," in *Rethinking the Color Line: Readings in Race and Ethnicity*, ed. C. Gallagher, London: Mayfield Publishing Company, 1999, pp. 106–14.

60. Essed, *Everyday Racism*; Feagin and Sikes, *Living With Racism*.

61. M. Cohen, *Culture of Intolerance: Chauvinism, Class, and Racism in the United States*, New Haven: Yale University Press, 1998; D. Goldberg, *Racist Culture: Philosophy and the Politics of Meaning*, Oxford: Blackwell, 1993; Feagin and Vera, *White Racism*; D. Wellman, *Portraits of White Racism*, 2nd edition, Cambridge: Cambridge University Press, 1993.

62. B. Bowser and R. Hunt, *Impacts of Racism on White Americans*, Beverly Hills, CA: Sage, 1981; J. Feagin and K. McKinney, *The Many Costs of Racism*, Lanham, MD: Rowman and Littlefield, 2003; Feagin and Vera, *White Racism*.

63. Feagin and Vera, *White Racism*. See also H. Vera and A. Gordon, *Screen Saviors: Hollywood Fictions of Whiteness*, Lanham, MD: Rowman and Littlefield, 2003.

64. R. Frankenberg, *White Women, Race Matters: The Social Construction of Whiteness*, Minneapolis: University of Minnesota Press, 1993.

65. See, for example, L. Carr, *"Color-Blind" Racism*, Thousand Oaks, CA: Sage, 1997.

66. Feagin, *Racist America*, p. 123–5.

67. E. Bonilla-Silva, *Racism Without Racists: Color Blind Racism and the Persistence of Racial Inequality in the United States*, Boulder, CO: Rowman and Littlefield, 2003; Carr, *"Color-Blind" Racism*; Frankenberg, *White Women, Race Matters*.

68. J. Barndt, *Dismantling Racism: The Continuing Challenge to White America*, Minneapolis: Augsburg, 1991; J. Katz, *White Awareness: Handbook for Anti-Racism Training*, Norman: University of Oklahoma Press; P. Kivel, *Uprooting Racism: How White People Can Work for Racial Justice*, Gabriola Island, BC: New Society Publishers, 2002.

69. There are notable exceptions, for example, the work of Pamela Perry and Charles Gallagher. Their work will be discussed as it applies to specific findings of my research.

70. See, for example, Allen, *The Invention of the White Race*; S. Fishkin, "Interrogating Whiteness, Complicating Blackness, Remapping the American Culture," *American Quarterly* 47(3), 1995. 428–66; M. Hill, "Introduction: Vipers in Shangri-La: Whiteness, Writing, and Other Ordinary Terrors," in *Whiteness: A Critical Reader*, ed. M. Hill, New York: New York University Press, 1997, pp. 1–18; D. Roediger, *The Wages of Whiteness*; H. Winant, "Behind Blue Eyes: Whiteness and Contemporary U.S. Racial Policies," *New Left Review* 225, 1997, 73–87.

71. Morrison, *Playing in the Dark*.

72. R. Dyer, *White*, New York: Routledge, 1997.

73. R. Dyer, "White," *Screen*, 29, 1988, 44–64. p. 44.

74. Dyer, "White," pp. 45–46.

75. For examples of other discussions of the apparent "culturelessness" of whiteness, see Perry, "White Means Never Having to Say You're Ethnic"; J. Hitchcock, "Characteristics of Contemporary White American Culture," in his book *Unraveling the White Cocoon*, Dubuque, IA: Kendall Hunt Publishing, 2001, pp. 111–13.

76. A. Keating, "Interrogating Whiteness, (De)Constructing Race," *College English* 57 (8), 1995, 901–18.

77. Dyer, "White"; Dyer, *White*; D. Negra, "The Birth of Whiteness: Race and the Emergence of U.S. Cinema," *Film Quarterly*, 51 (4), 1998, 36–9.

78. L. Bloom, "Constructing Whiteness: *Popular Science* and *National Geographic* in the Age of Multiculturalism," *Configurations* 2 (1), 1994, 15–32.

79. H. Bhabha, "The White Stuff: Political Aspects of Whiteness," *Artforum* 36 (9), 1998, 21–4; C. Crenshaw, "Resisting Whiteness' Rhetorical Silence," *Western Journal of Communication* 61 (3), 1997, 253–78.

80. A. Bonnett, "Who Was White? The Disappearance of Non-European White Identities and the Formation of European Racial Whiteness," *Ethnic and Racial Studies*, 21 (6), 1998, 1029–55; M. Jacobson, *Whiteness of a Different Color: European Immigrants and the Alchemy of Race*, Cambridge, MA: Harvard University Press, 1998; Roediger, *The Wages of Whiteness.*

81. Allen, *The Invention of the White Race*; N. Ignatiev, *How the Irish Became White*, New York: Routledge, 1995.

82. A. Bonnett, "How the British Working Class Became White: The Symbolic (Re)formation of Racialized Capitalism," *Journal of Historical Sociology* 11 (3), 1998, 316–40.

83. K. Brodkin, *How Jews Became White Folks and What That Says About Race in America*, Rutgers, NY: Rutgers University Press, 1998.

84. C. Harris, "Whiteness as Property," *Harvard Law Review* 106 (8), 1993, 1709–91.

85. I. Lopez, *White By Law: The Legal Construction of Race*, New York: New York University Press, 1996.

86. B. Fair, "Foreword: Rethinking the Colorblindness Model," *National Black Law Journal* 13 (1–2), 1993, 1–82; B. Flagg, "Fashioning a Title VII Remedy for Transparently White Subjective Decisionmaking," *Yale Law Journal* 104 (8), 1995, 2009–51.

87. Flagg, "Fashioning a Title VII Remedy."

88. Lipsitz, *The Possessive Investment in Whiteness.*

89. T. Duggan, "Honky Blues," *Salon Magazine,*. Available online at: http://archive.salon.com/july9/white970702.html (accessed May 20, 2003). See M. Andersen, "Whitewashing Race: A Critical Perspective on Whiteness," in A. Doane and E. Bonilla-Silva (eds.) *White Out: The Continuing Significance of Racism*, New York: Routledge, 2003, pp. 21–34, for an excellent critique of the whiteness studies literature and a call for new studies more directed toward social change and against racism.

90. T. Duggan, "Honky Blues," *Salon Magazine*, Available online at: http://archive.salon.com/july9/white970702.html (accessed May 20, 2003).

91. Duggan, "Honky Blues."

92. R. Zeilberger, "Corporate American Learns: Diversity Is About White Men, Too," *Diversity, Inc.*, 3 (1), 2004, 16–20.

93. Essed, *Everyday Racism.*

94. I will discuss sociological studies of whiteness as they are relevant in later chapters.

95. K. Sheshardi-Crooks, *Desiring Whiteness: A Lacanian Analysis of Race*, London: Routledge, 2000, p. 4.

Chapter 2

1. J. Feagin and H. Vera, *White Racism: The Basics*, New York: Routledge, 1995, p. 139; J. Martin et al., "What Do White People Want to Be Called? A Study of Self-Labels for White Americans," in *Whiteness: The Communication of Social Identity*, ed. T. Nakayama and J. Martin, Thousand Oaks, CA: Sage, 1999, p. 28; B. Tatum, "*Why Are All the Black Kids Sitting Together in the Cafeteria?" And Other Conversations About Race*, New York: Basic, 1997, p. 93; R. Terry, "The Negative Impact on White Values," in *Impacts of Racism on White Americans*, ed. B. Bowser and R. Hunt, Beverly Hills, CA: Sage, 1981, p. 119.

2. B. Flagg, "'Was Blind, but Now I See:' White Race Consciousness and the Requirement of Discriminatory Intent," in *Critical White Studies: Looking Behind the Mirror*, ed. R. Delgado and J. Stefancic, Philadelphia: Temple University Press, 1997, p. 629.

3. A. Phoenix, "'I'm White! So What?': The Construction of Whiteness for Young Londoners," in *Off White: Readings on Race, Power, and Society*, ed. M. Fine et al., New York: Routledge, 1997, pp. 186–197.

4. Phoenix, "'I'm White! So What?'"

5. See, for example, Beverly Daniel Tatum's discussion in *Why Are All the Black Kids Sitting Together in the Cafeteria?* Tatum points out that racial identity is more salient for young African American students than for white students because they are constantly reminded of their racial identity by a hostile, racist society. Particularly for young black males, who see fear on the faces of whites that they pass on the streets, racial identity becomes important because society *makes* it important. This is a fundamental difference in racial identity between black and white students, and contributes to misunderstandings regarding racial segregation in schools.

6. F. Hobson, *But Now I See: The White Southern Racial Conversion Narrative*, Baton Rouge: Louisiana State University Press, 1999.
7. Hobson, *But Now I See*.
8. Hobson, *But Now I See*.
9. Hobson, *But Now I See*.
10. N. Denzin, *Interpretive Biography*, Newbury Park, CA: Sage, 1989, p. 69.
11. Denzin, *Interpretive Biography*, p. 71.
12. See the discussion in chapter 3 of "mirrored whiteness."
13. Rarely do authors write stories in which their parents are agents of epiphany, since they have usually been exposed to their parents' beliefs, or at least actions, in regard to race since birth, making them more aptly described as "influences." The data show that rarely are strangers agents of epiphanic stories, when a white person comes to a new or first understanding of her or his place in collective whiteness.
14. S. D. McLemore, H. Romo, and S. Baker, *Racial and Ethnic Relations in America*, 6th ed., Boston: Allyn and Bacon, 2001, p. 424.
15. D. Powers and C. Ellison, "Interracial Contact and Black Racial Attitudes: The Contact Hypothesis and Selectivity Bias," *Social Forces* 74 (1), 1995, 205–226.
16. K. Ihlandfeldt and B. Scafidi, "The Neighbourhood Contact Hypothesis: Evidence from the Multicity Study of Urban Inequality," *Urban Studies* 39 (4), 2002, 619–641.
17. L. Sigelman et al., "Making Contact?: Black-White Social Interaction in an Urban Setting," in *Race and Ethnic Relations in the United States: Readings for the 21st Century*, ed. C. Ellison and W. A. Martin, Los Angeles: Roxbury, 1999, pp. 285–292.
18. G. Allport, *The Nature of Prejudice*, Reading, MA: Addison-Wesley Publishing, 1954, p. 281; J. Farley, *Majority-Minority Relations*, 4th ed., Upper Saddle River, NJ: Prentice Hall, 2000, pp. 45–51; McLemore, Romo, and Baker, *Racial and Ethnic Relations*, pp. 424–425; N. St. John, *School Desegregation: Outcomes for Children*, New York: Wiley, 1975.
19. Ihlandfeldt and Scafidi, "The Neighbourhood Contact Hypothesis."
20. For an excellent discussion of this point, see B. DeMott, *The Trouble With Friendship: Why Americans Can't Think Straight About Race*, New Haven: Yale University Press, 1998.
21. M. Emerson, R. Kimbro, and G. Yancey, "Contact Theory Extended: The Effects of Prior Racial Contact on Current Social Ties," *Social Science Quarterly* 83 (3), 2002, 745–761.
22. Emerson, Kimbro, and Yancey, "Contact Theory Extended."
23. T. Towles-Schwen and R. Fazio, "On the Origins of Racial Attitudes: Correlates of Childhood Experiences," *Personality and Social Psychology Bulletin* 27 (2), 2001, 162–175.
24. Sigelman et al., "Making Contact?"
25. Powers and Ellison, "Interracial Contact and Black Attitudes."
26. Sigelman et al., "Making Contact?"
27. T. Pettigrew and L. Tropp, "Does Intergroup Contact Reduce Prejudice? Recent Meta-analytic Findings," in *Reducing Prejudice and Discrimination*, ed. S. Oskamp, Mahwah, NJ: Lawrence Erlbaum Associates, 2000, pp. 93–114.
28. Pettigrew and Tropp, "Does Intergroup Contact Reduce Prejudice?"
29. See also the discussion of "cultural tourism," described in chapter 3.
30. W. E. B. Du Bois, *Black Reconstruction in the United States*, New York: Harcourt, Brace and Company, 1935.
31. A. Lorde, *Sister Outsider*, Trumansburg, NY: The Crossing Press, 1984, pp. 114–115.
32. J. W. Johnson, quoted in *Black on White: Black Writers on What It Means to Be White*, ed. D. Roediger, New York: Schocken Books, 1998, p. 5.
33. R. Blauner, "Talking Past Each Other: Black and White Languages of Race," in *Race and Ethnic Conflict*, ed. H. J. Ehrlich and F. L. Pincus, Boulder, CO: Westview Press, 1994, pp. 27–34; B. Tatum, "*Why Are All the Black Kids Sitting Together in the Cafeteria?*" *And Other Conversations About Race*, New York: Basic, 1997; M. Waters, "Optional Ethnicities: For Whites Only?" in *Race, Class and Gender: An Anthology*, 5th Edition, ed. M. Andersen and P. Collins, Belmont, CA: Wadsworth, 2004, pp. 418–427.
34. G. Winter, "Schools Resegregate, Study Finds," *The New York Times*. Late Edition–Final, Section A, Page 14, Column 1. Available online at: http//www.nytimes.com/2003/01/21/education/ZIRACE.html (accessed January 27, 2003). This point will be discussed more in Chapter 5.
35. Annie M. Paul, "Where Bias Begins," in *Race, Class and Gender in the United States*, 6th Edition, ed. P. Rothenberg, New York: Worth, 2004, pp. 516–521.
36. See, for example, R. E. Park and E. W. Burgess, *Introduction to the Science of Sociology*, Chicago: University of Chicago Press, 1921, p. 440, for what is usually credited as the first

definition of "social distance" as the tendency to approach or withdraw from a racial group; see also E. Bogardus, "A Social Distance Scale," *Sociology and Social Research,* 17, 1933, 265–271, for the famous "Bogardus Scale" used to measure social distance.

37. Feagin and Vera, *White Racism.*
38. This will be discussed in depth in chapter 4.
39. I have come across these arguments in various texts; but I thank my father, Roy McKinney, Jr. (a member of the Army Reserves for most of my life) for discussions that brought these ideas together.
40. See "Consolidated brief of Lt. Gen. Julius W. Becton, et. al., as *amici curiae* in support of respondents," Amicus Brief filed in the *Grutter v. Bollinger* and *Gratz v. Bollinger* cases before the Supreme Court of the United States. Available online at: http://www.umich.edu/~urel/admissions/legal/gru_amicus-ussc/um/MilitaryL-both.pdf (accessed February 6, 2004).
41. A. Clymer, "Service Academies Defend Use of Race in Their Admissions," *New York Times,* Online, January 28, 2003. Available online at: http://www.nytimes.com/2003/01/28/education/28RECR.html?ex=1045049361&ei=1&en=951fa51b9aefc4e8 (accessed January 28, 2003).
42. See, for example, Blauner, "Talking Past Each Other." This will be discussed further in chapters 4 and 6.
43. Du Bois, *Black Reconstruction in the United States.*
44. See, for example, J. Feagin and K. McKinney, *The Many Costs of Racism,* Lanham, MD: Rowman and Littlefield, 2003, pp. 150–153.
45. C. Ellis, "The Other Side of the Fence: Seeing Black and White in a Small Southern Town," *Qualitative Inquiry* 1 (2), 1995, 147–167; K. McKinney, "Affirmation, Transformation, and Experimentation: Narrative Constructions of Interracial Dating," paper presented at the 1999 ASA Meetings in Chicago, Illinois.
46. M. Mazie et al., "To Deconstruct Race, Deconstruct Whiteness," *American Quarterly* 45 (2), 1993, 281–294.
47. M. Waters, "Optional Ethnicities: For Whites Only?" in *Race, Class and Gender: An Anthology,* ed. M. Andersen and P. Collins, Belmont, CA: Wadsworth, 1998, pp. 403–412.
48. Waters, "Optional Ethnicities?"

Chapter 3

1. M. Halter, *Shopping for Identity: The Marketing of Ethnicity,* New York: Schocken Books, 2000, pp. 4–6.
2. Halter, *Shopping for Identity,* p. 7.
3. G. Lipsitz, *The Possessive Investment in Whiteness: How White People Profit from Identity Politics,* Philadelphia: Temple University Press, 1998, p. 2.
4. Lipsitz, *The Possessive Investment in Whiteness,* p. 2.
5. Halter, *Shopping for Identity,* p. 9.
6. Halter, *Shopping for Identity,* p. 7.
7. It is interesting to note that although obviously Lacey has learned some of the terms used in the course, and is able to apply them to her own experiences, such as "symbolic ethnicity," and "marital assimilation," we had not discussed at all the idea of the commodification of ethnicity by corporate industries and the media—this was Lacey's own theorizing.
8. M. Waters, *Ethnic Options: Choosing Identities in America,* Berkeley: University of California Press, 1990.
9. P. Perry, "White Means Never Having to Say You're Ethnic: White Youth and the Construction of 'Cultureless' Identities," *Journal of Contemporary Ethnography* 30 (1), 2001, 56–91. Here Perry cites in support of her point R. Rosaldo, *Culture and Truth: The Remaking of Social Analysis,* Boston: Beacon, 1989.
10. C. Gallagher, "White Racial Formation: Into the Twenty-First Century," in *Critical White Studies: Looking Behind the Mirror,* ed. R. Delgado and J. Stefancic, Philadelphia: Temple University Press, pp. 6–11.
11. Gallagher, "White Racial Formation" in *Racial Formation in the United States: From the 1960s to the 1980s,* ed. M. Omi and H. Winant, New York: Routledge, 1986.
12. Perry, "White means never having to say you're ethnic."
13. Perry, "White Means Never Having to Say You're Ethnic."
14. Perry, "White Means Never Having to Say You're Ethnic," p. 67.

15. For example, Marimba Ani describes white Western European culture in many of the same terms that Perry does in M. Ani, *Yurugu: An African-Centered Critique of European Cultural Thought and Behavior*, Trenton, NJ: Africa World Press, 1994. Others have pointed out that the United States was founded on Anglo-Saxon hegemonic culture. For example, Adalberto Aguirre and Jonathan Turner, in *American Ethnicity: The Dynamics and Consequences of Discrimination*, 3rd Edition, Boston: McGraw Hill, 2001, discuss how the country's core cultural and institutional structures have been characterized by Anglo-Saxon hegemony, in law, economics, religion, education, values, and policies (pp. 48–53).

16. For a thorough discussion, see D. Roediger, *The Wages of Whiteness: Race and the Making of the American Working Class*, New York: Verso, 1991.

17. Although the correct spelling is "St. Paddy's" Day (with a *d* from *Pádraic* in the Gaelic), because I've chosen to edit the student's comments only very lightly for clarity in the most extreme cases, I left Fiona's spelling as is.

18. This point will be discussed more later in the chapter.

19. I use the term "American" here in the colloquial sense, as my respondents often use it—in other words, to mean U.S. culture—with the understanding of course, that the word "America" is often thus used incorrectly, and ethnocentrically, to refer to the United States, when the continents of North and South America are composed of multiple nations.

20. See, for example, P. Kivel, *Uprooting Racism: How White People Can Work for Racial Justice*, Garbriola Island, Canada: New Society Publishers, 2002, p. 47.

21. Perry, "White Means Never Having to Say You're Ethnic."

22. Gallagher, "White Racial Formation."

23. H. Gans, "Symbolic Ethnicity and Symbolic Religiosity: Towards a Comparison of Ethnic and Religious Acculturation," *Ethnic and Racial Studies* 17, 1994, 577–92. Although I believe that the ethnicity these respondents are utilizing is of the same type as what Alba, Gans, and others describe, I hesitate to describe it as "symbolic," because of the other connotations that term has within sociological literature and because of my belief that all types of ethnicity could, in a sense be called "symbolic." Instead, I call it "usable."

24. R. Alba, *Ethnic Identity: The Transformation of White America,* New Haven: Yale University Press, 1990.

25. Regarding the "ethnic revival," see A. Greeley, *Why Can't They Be Like Us?,* New York: E.P. Dutton and Company, 1971; M. Novak, *the Rise of the Unmeltable Ethnics*, New York: Macmillan, 1971.

26. Alba, *Ethnic Identity*; Gans, "Symbolic Ethnicity and Symbolic Religiosity;" Waters, *Ethnic Options*.

27. Some respondents did discuss that they see their religion, particularly Catholicism, as linked to their ethnicity. I do not include religion as a trait that is part of "usable ethnicity," because I believe that it is part of a kind of ethnicity that is more significant for some European Americans that does have an impact on their everyday lives and decision-making.

28. See S. Lyman and M. Scott, *A Sociology of the Absurd*, Dix Hills, NY: General Hall, Inc., 1989, pp. 113–117 on "excuses" as accounts.

29. This respondent's last name has been changed, of course, to protect his privacy. Previously, his last name created a slightly different nickname, but I attempted to stay as true as possible to the "spirit" of the nickname his team had given him.

30. See A. Marvasti, "Being Middle Eastern: Identity negotiation in the context of the war on terror," unpublished manuscript, submitted for publication, 2003.

31. Because I changed this last name to protect the privacy of the student, obviously the definition of the first part of his name no longer matches the description of what the name means in Celtic, which I also changed. Additionally, because I changed his name, it obviously does not sound as it should in keeping with the confusion regarding the Scottish-Irish or German origin, although I tried to stay as true as possible to the type of name he has.

32. C. Gallagher, "Playing the White Ethnic Card: Using Ethnic Identity to Deny Contemporary Racism," in *White Out: The Continuing Significance of Racism*, ed. A. Doane and E. Bonilla-Silva, New York: Routledge, 2003, pp. 145–158.

33. Gallagher, "Playing the White Ethnic Card."

34. b. hooks, "Eating the Other," in *Black Looks: Race and Representation*, Boston: South End Press, 1992.

35. Quoted in D. Roediger (ed.), *Black on White: Black Writers on What It Means to Be White*, New York: Schocken Books, 1998, p. 216.

36. Quoted in Roediger, *Black on White*, p. 240.
37. K. Holloway, *Codes of Conduct: Race, Ethics and the Color of Our Character*, New Brunswick, NJ: Rutgers University Press, 1995, p. 121.
38. The "black/white" paradigm, which shapes many of the ways in which race is discussed and conceptualized in popular culture in the United States, will be discussed more at the end of the chapter.
39. C. Aaron, "Black like Them," *Utne Reader*, March-April 1999 (2), 68–73; p. 69.
40. See, for example, Henry Giroux, quoted in Aaron, "Black like Them," 1999, p. 72.
41. Aaron, "Black like Them," p. 71.
42. My endorsing Eminem's *authenticity* as a rap artist are not to be taken as a comment regarding anything else about his artistry, particularly the politics implied in his lyrics.
43. I am writing this based on innumerable conversations with people of many different races and ethnicities, in many different parts of the country, from whom I have heard these things repeatedly.
44. Perry, "White Means Never Having to say You're Ethnic."
45. Quoted in Roediger, *Black on White*, p. 166.
46. W. E. B. Du Bois, *Black Reconstruction in the United States*, New York: Harcourt, Brace and Company, 1935; A. Lorde, *Sister Outsider*, Trumansburg, NY: The Crossing Press, 1984.
47. See J. Helms, *Black and White Racial Identity Development*, Westport, CT: Praeger, 1990. The data gathered for this study did include autobiographies of students of color. Although they were not analyzed systematically as were those by white students, the reading that I did of them revealed that students of color generally were able to discuss their ethnicity at more length without referencing other groups.
48. B. Tatum, *"Why Are All the Black Kids Sitting Together in the Cafeteria?": And Other Conversations About Race*, New York: Basic Books, 1997.
49. See, for example, Omi and Winant, *Racial Formation in the United States*.
50. See J. Feagin, *Racist America: Roots, Current Realities, and Future Reparations*, New York: Routledge, 2000, pp. 203–205 for a discussion of the black/white paradigm.
51. Feagin, *Racist America*.
52. Also, it could be argued that because of its grounding in the subordination of others, in a sense "whiteness" itself *is* cultureless except for in domination and oppression. However, others would argue that there is "white culture," and that a danger lies in failing to recognize it (see., e.g., Perry, "White Means Never Having to Say You're Ethnic"). Additionally, if whites knew more about their ethnic heritage, they would have a sense of "culture." It is their ethnicity, and not their race, that other groups are often celebrating, and whites might develop a clearer understanding of this as well (this point will be discussed in the next chapter).
53. The Southern sample consisted of more "transplanted" individuals and of those who grew up in slightly more diverse settings. Further, the areas in which the data was collected were more diverse themselves. The Northern sample, conversely, was made up of students who, for the most part, had grown up within the area where the college was located. This entire area is rural, with very little diversity and a low percentage of nonwhite residents. See Appendix B for more information.
54. Her last name has been changed, but was, like "Smith," a common U.S. surname.
55. J. Feagin and K. McKinney, *The Many Costs of Racism*, Lanham, MD: Rowman and Littlefield, 2003, p. 30.
56. Tatum, *"Why Are All the Black Kids Sitting Together in the Cafeteria?"*
57. J. Hartigan, Jr. *Racial Situations: Class Predicaments of Whiteness in Detroit*, Princeton, New Jersey: Princeton University Press, 1999, p. 52.
58. Hartigan, Racial Situations, p. 3.
59. F. Wu, "Yellow," in *Race, Class and Gender in the United States*, ed. P. Rothenberg, New York: Worth, 2004, p. 350.
60. A. Newitz and M. Wray, "Introduction," in *White Trash: Race and Class in America*, ed. M. Wray and A. Newitz, New York: Routledge, 1997, p. 2.
61. See, for example, J. Feagin and M. Sikes, *Living With Racism: The Black Middle-Class Experience*, Boston: Beacon Press, 1994.
62. Hartigan, *Racial Situations*, p. 46.
63. This is slightly more true for the Southern respondents than for the Northern, who tend to have a bit more of a sense of ethnic identity, perhaps because their families' immigration experiences were often more recent. However, it is interesting that even after many of these Northern respondents tell stories of their ethnic traditions and heritage, they

follow these up with a statement about how they really "don't know much" about their ethnic heritage, or "wish they knew about" their ethnic heritage. So, even when respondents *do* know a relatively large amount of information about their ethnicity, it is their *perception* that they do not, and it is perceptions on which identities are built.

Chapter 4

1. M. Frye, "Oppression," in *Feminist Frontiers*, 5th Edition, ed. L. Richardson, V. Taylor, N. Whittier, Boston: McGraw Hill, 2001, p. 6.
2. R. Kipling, "The White Man's Burden," McClure's Magazine 12, Feb. 1899.
3. E. Goffman, *Stigma: Notes on the Management of Spoiled Identity*. New York: Simon and Schuster. 1986.
4. In some portions of their autobiographies, respondents discussed feeling physically fearful or victimized as whites, though this is less common than comments regarding cultural victimization. In chapter 6, I will explain how, even when writing from an antiprejudiced or antiracist perspective, whites sometimes also fear social victimization through rejection.
5. This type of "supplanted" white identity was discussed in chapter 3.
6. This point was discussed in chapter 3. See C. Gallagher, "White Racial Formation: Into the Twenty-first Century," in *Critical White Studies: Looking Behind the Mirror*, ed. R. Delgado and J. Stefancic, Philadelphia: Temple University Press, pp. 6–11.
7. See, for example, the excellent essay by K. Hall, "My Father's Flag," in *Whiteness: Feminist Philosophical Reflections*, ed. C. Cuomo and K. Hall, Lanham, MD, 1999, 29–33; on the symbolism of the Confederate flag.
8. B. Jacobs, *Race Manners: Navigating the Minefield Between Black and White Americans*, New York: Arcade Publishing, pp. 130–131.
9. T. Wise, "Honky Wanna Cracker? A Look at the Myth of Reverse Racism," *ZNet Daily Commentaries*, June 24, 2002. Available online at: http://www.zmag.org/Sustainers/content/2002–06/24wise.cfm (accessed July 22, 2004).
10. See, for example, E. Bonilla-Silva, *Racism Without Racists: Color-Blind Racism and the Persistence of Racial Inequality in the United States*, Lanham, MD: Rowman and Littlefield, 2003; P. Perry, *Shades of White: White Kids and Racial Identities in High School*, Durham: Duke University Press, 2002.
11. J. Feagin and M. Sikes, *Living With Racism: The Black Middle-Class Experience*, Boston: Beacon Press, 1994, p. 24. Pages 56 through 64 also include many examples of the impact of the use of racial epithets. See also J. Feagin and K. McKinney, *The Many Costs of Racism*, Lanham, MD: Rowman and Littlefield, pp. 2–3.
12. Fighting Whites, "Official Homepage of the Fighting Whites." Available online at: http://www.fightingwhites.org/ (accessed July 22, 2004).
13. T. Wise, "Honky Wanna Cracker?"
14. Jacobs, *Race Manners*, pp. 98–103.
15. A. McIntyre, *Making Meaning of Whiteness: Exploring White Identity with White Teachers*, New York: State University of New York Press, pp. 108–115.
16. See P. Perry, "White Means Never Having to Say You're Ethnic: White Youth and the Construction of 'Cultureless' Identities," *Journal of Contemporary Ethnography* 30 (1), 2001, 80. Here Perry discusses this debate, noting that Charles Gallagher takes the former position, and she takes the latter.
17. See, for example, M. L. Oliver and T. M. Shapiro, *Black Wealth/White Wealth: A New Perspective on Racial Inequality*, New York: Routledge, 1995; D. Conley, "The Cost of Slavery," *The New York Times*, February 15, 2003. Available online at: http://www.nytimes.com/2003/02/15/opinion/15CONL.html (accessed February 15, 2003; registration required). This point will be discussed more in the next chapter.
18. See, for example, K. Sacks, "How Jews Became White." in *The Social Construction of Difference and Inequality: Race, Class, Gender and Sexuality*, ed. T. Ore, Boston: McGraw Hill, 2003, pp. 55–69; for a description of how African-American returning soldiers were kept out of the "boom" in college attendance for the middle class after World War II. The only alternative for most was to attend black colleges, which quickly became overcrowded.
19. Gallagher, "White Racial Formation."
20. For excellent books that proceed from this understanding and give alternative readings of U.S. history, see J. Loewn, *Lies My Teacher Told Me: Everything Your American History*

Textbook Got Wrong, New York: Simon and Schuster, 1995; and H. Zinn, *A People's History of the United States: 1492–Present*, New York: Harper Collins, 2003.

21. Study is summarized in "Marginalia," *Chronicle of Higher Education* 9, April 13, 1994, A-31, and cited in Roediger, *Black on White*, pp. 7–8.
22. B. Tatum, *"Why Are All the Black Kids Sitting Together in the Cafeteria?": And Other Conversations about Race*, New York: Basic Books, 1997, pp. 52–74.
23. R. Buttny, "Discursive Constructions of Racial Boundaries and Self-Segregation on Campus," *Journal of Language and Social Psychology*, 18 (3), 1999, 247–268.
24. P. Kivel, *Uprooting Racism: How White People Can Work for Racial Justice*. Revised Edition, Gabriola Island, Canada, 2002, p. 91.
25. R. Blauner, "Talking Past Each Other: Black and White Languages of Race," in *Race and Ethnic Conflict*, ed. H. J. Ehrlich and F. L. Pincus, Boulder, CO: Westview Press, 1994, pp. 27–34.
26. Blauner, "Talking Past Each Other."
27. Blauner, "Talking Past Each Other."
28. Perry, "White Means Never Having to Say You're Ethnic," pp. 83–84.
29. L. Rubin, "'Is This a White Country, or What?'" in *Race, Class and Gender: An Anthology*, 5th Edition., ed. M. Anderson and P. Collins, Belmont, CA: Thompson/Wadsworth, 2004, pp. 410–418.
30. Rubin, "'Is This a White Country, or What?'"
31. J. Feagin, *Racist America: Roots, Current Realities, and Future Reparations,* New York: Routledge, 2000, p. 117. Here Feagin cites P. Labovitz, "Just the Facts," *New York Times,* March 25, 1996, A2.
32. Feagin, *Racist America*, p. 117, citing a study by Charles Gallagher: C. Gallagher, "Living in Color: Perceptions of Racial Group Size," unpublished research paper, Georgia State University, 1999.
33. Rubin, "'Is this a white country, or what?,'"
34. Scientists have recently suggested that some languages may be more complex and require speakers to use more areas of their brains than do others. For example, apparently only the left temporal lobe of the brain is active for English speakers, whereas Mandarin speakers are utilizing both their left and right lobes ("Study: Some Languages Require More Brain Power," available online at: http://www.cnn.com/2003/HEALTH/06/30/brain.language.reut/index.html (accessed 1 July 2003)). This may be part of the reason that English speakers sometimes find it difficult to learn certain other languages that make more use of intonation, such as Mandarin. This new information makes students' derision of "foreign" professors' accents and languages particularly ironic.
35. M. Schwalbe, *The Sociologically Examined Life: Pieces of the Conversation*, London: Mayfield, 2001, 182.
36. Schwalbe applies the concept of "false parallels" to other relationships of unequal power, also, for example, to gender inequality.
37. Schwalbe, *The Sociologically Examined Life*, p. 184–185.
38. M. Waters, "Optional Ethnicities: For Whites Only?" *Race, Class and Gender: An Anthology*, 5th Edition, ed. M. Anderson and P. Collins, Belmont, CA: Thompson/Wadsworth, 2004, pp. 418–427.
39. B. Tatum, "Defining Racism: 'Can We Talk?'" in *Race, Class and Gender in the United States*, 6th Edition., ed. P. Rothenberg, New York: Worth, 2004, p. 129.
40. A. Ferber, "What White Supremacists Taught a Jewish Scholar About Identity," in *Race, Class and Gender: An Anthology*, 5th Edition, ed. M. Anderson and P. Collins, Belmont, CA: Thompson/Wadsworth, 2004, pp. 117–121.

Chapter 5

1. "New Scholarship Created for Whites Only," *CNN.com*, February 16, 2004. Available online at: http://www.cnn.com/2004/EDUCATION/02/15/whites.only.ap/index.html (accessed February 20, 2004); J. Styles, "Whites-Only Scholarship Generates Controversy," *CNN.com*. February 20, 2004. Available online at: http://www.cnn.com/2004/EDUCATION/02/18/whites.only.scholars/index.html (accessed February 20, 2004).
2. C. Gallagher, "White Racial Formation: Into the Twenty-First Century," in *Critical White Studies: Looking Behind the Mirror*, ed. R. Delgado and J. Stefancic, Philadelphia: Temple University Press, pp. 6–11.

3. For a summary of studies, see, for example, J. Feagin and C. Feagin, *Racial and Ethnic Relations*, Seventh Edition, Upper Saddle River, NJ: Prentice Hall, 2003, pp. 186–188; J. Feagin and B. McNair Barnett, "Success *and* Failure: How Systemic Racism Trumped the *Brown v. Board of Education* Decision," forthcoming in *University of Illinois Law Review*, 2004; J. Kozol, *Savage Inequalities: Children in America's Schools*, New York: HarperCollins, 1991.

4. P. Bourdieu, *The Logic of Practice*, Stanford, CA: Stanford University Press, 1980, pp. 124–125.

5. R. Delgado, *The Coming Race War? And Other Apocalyptic Tales of America After Affirmative Action and Welfare*, New York: New York University Press, 1996, pp. 72–73.

6. See, for example, Barbara Flagg's insightful legal concept of the "transparency phenomenon," which is the application of ostensibly neutral standards of evaluation and decision making that in effect reinforce white norms and in doing so discriminate against people of color. Although Flagg uses this concept in a discussion of the workplace, I think it could also be applied well to seemingly "neutral" standards of admission and evaluation in higher education, as well. B. Flagg, "Fashioning a Title VII Remedy for Transparently White Subjective Decisionmaking," *Yale Law Journal* 104, 1995, 2009–51.

7. See J. Farley, *Majority-Minority Relations*, 4th Edition, Upper Saddle River, NJ: Prentice Hall, 2000, pp. 404–10, for a useful summary of the debate and research regarding cultural test bias.

8. This point was made by Laura Purdy in L. Purdy, "Why Do We Need Affirmative Action?" in *Race, Gender and Sexuality: Philosophical Issues of Identity and Justice*, ed. J. Anderson, Upper Saddle River, NJ: Prentice Hall, 2003, pp. 404–11. Reading Purdy's article, and coming across this particular point, I was reminded of when, in college, I tutored young people who were juvenile offenders on "intensive probation." During the process, I often had long conversations with some of those I tutored. I remember after one conversation with a particular young man, an African-American sixteen-year-old who lived in the projects, I wrote in my journal something to the effect that he was more insightful and intelligent that I was—that he should be in college; he had a brilliant, philosophical and creative mind. The last I heard, however, he had not made it there. I agree with Purdy that if one looks at "qualifications" only in the conventional sense, the unconventional talents and abilities of those students of color who have not benefited from a conventional education may be overlooked.

9. Farley, *Majority-Minority Relations*, p. 495.

10. Farley, *Majority-Minority Relations*, p. 495.

11. D. Bok, "Expert Report of Derek Bok: *Grutter, et al. v. Bollinger, et al.* No. 97–75928 (E.D. Mich.)." Available Online at: http://www.umich.edu/~urel/admissions/legal/expert/bok.html (accessed June 25, 2003).

12. Farley, *Majority-Minority Relations*, p. 495.

13. Farely, *Majority-Minority Relations*, p. 495.

14. "Survey: Most Against Race-Based Admissions," Available online at: http//www.cnn.com/2003/EDUCATION/06/09/race.admissions.reut/index.html (accessed June 25, 2003).

15. D. Murray, "Race-Conscious Admissions Programs: The Court of Public Opinion" (a statement from the president of Marist College). Available online at: http://www.marist-poll.marist.edu/usapolls/030609MC.pdf (accessed June 25, 2003).

16. This "blind spot" has much to do with many of the ways that young whites think about whiteness. For example, it makes it difficult for them to understand the difference between "prejudice" and "racism"; it leads many to believe that when professors speak of "white racism," they are calling every individual white person a "racist," and it means that, even when white students are sympathetic to racial discrimination, that have difficulty envisioning its operation on a structural, rather than only an individual-interactional level.

17. See, for example, H. Hartmann, "Who Has Benefited from Affirmative Action in Employment?" in *The Affirmative Action Debate*, ed. G. Curry Reading, Massachusetts: Addison-Wesley, 1996, pp. 77–96, for a discussion of how white women, while having benefited more than women or men of color from affirmative action in some ways, still need to be considered an underrepresented group, deserving of affirmative action in the workplace.

18. Farley, *Majority-Minority Relations*, p. 495. Here Farley cites the General Accounting Office, 1994.

19. J. Larew, "Why Are Droves of Unqualified, Unprepared Kids Getting into Our Top Colleges? Because Their Dads Are Alumni," in *The Meaning of Difference: American Constructions of Race, Sex and Gender, Social Class and Sexual Orientation*, 3rd Edition, ed. K. Rosenblum and T. Travis, Boston: McGraw-Hill, 2003, pp. 300–305.

20. Larew, "Why Are Droves of Unqualified, Unprepared Kids Getting into Our Top Colleges?" p. 300.
21. Larew, "Why Are Droves of Unqualified, Unprepared Kids Getting into Our Top Colleges?" p. 300.
22. Larew, "Why Are Droves of Unqualified, Unprepared Kids Getting into Our Top Colleges?" p. 303.
23. Larew, "Why Are Droves of Unqualified, Unprepared Kids Getting into Our Top Colleges?" p. 303.
24. Larew, "Why Are Droves of Unqualified, Unprepared Kids Getting into Our Top Colleges?" p. 301.
25. L. Greenhouse, "Justices Back Affirmative Action by 5 to 4," *The New York Times.* Available online at: http://www.nytimes.com/2003/06/24/politics/24AFFI.html (accessed June 24, 2003).
26. "Supreme Court Hears Affirmative Action Arguments: Ruling Could Impact Job Hiring, Government Contracts," *CNN.com.* Available online at: http://www.cnn.com/2003/LAW/04/01/scotus.affirmative.action/index.html (accessed February 9, 2004).
27. Greenhouse, "Justices Back Affirmative Action."
28. "A Win for Affirmative Action," Editorial, *The New York Times.* Available online at: http://www.nytimes.com/2003/06/24/opinion/24TUE1.html? (accessed June 24, 2003).
29. Greenhouse, "Justices Back Affirmative Action."
30. "A Win for Affirmative Action."
31. News sources, civil rights groups, and education associations generally reported the decision as a victory for affirmative action. See, for example, "Joint Statement by National Higher Education Leaders on Today's Decision by the U.S. Supreme Court in *Gratz v. Bollinger* and *Grutter v. Bollinger*," American Council on Education. Available online at: http://acenet.edu/news/press_release/2003/06june/Supreme.html (accessed July 23, 2004). Some were cautiously optimistic, however, and pointed out that with such close decisions, affirmative action could be in peril in coming years, because some key justices, such as Sandra Day O'Connor, who was seen as the "swing vote," may be retiring. President George Bush was, at the time of this writing, in office, and had written against affirmative action specifically in the Michigan case, which is unusual for a President to do in office. Any Supreme Court appointments that he makes could have negative effects on affirmative action in the future.
32. "A Win for Affirmative Action."
33. S. Greenhouse and J. Glater, "Companies See Court Ruling as Support for Diversity," *The New York Times.* Available online at: http://www.nytimes.com/2003/06/24/national/24BUSI.html (accessed June 24, 2003).
34. "Amicus Briefs: Summary of Arguments, *Grutter v. Bollinger*," Available online at: http://www.umich.edu/~urel/admissions/legal/gru_amicus/summary.html (accessed June 25, 2003). Other studies have also found business leaders to be overwhelmingly in support of affirmative action. See, for example, B. Reskin, "The Effects of Affirmative Action on Other Stakeholders," in *The Social Construction of Difference and Inequality: Race, Class, Gender and Sexuality*, 2nd Edition, ed. T. Ore, Boston: McGraw-Hill, 2003, pp. 356–357.
35. Bok, "Expert Report of Derek Bok."
36. W. Bowen and D. Bok, "The Shape of the River: Long-Term Consequences of Considering Race in College and University Admissions," in *The Meaning of Difference: American Constructions of Race, Sex and Gender, Social Class and Sexual Orientation*, 3rd Edition, ed. K. Rosenblum and T. Travis Boston: McGraw-Hill, 2003, pp. 368–369.
37. "Reasons Why 'Percent Plans' Won't Work for College Admissions Nationwide," University of Michigan News Service. Available online at: http://www.umich.edu/~newsinfo/Releases/2003/Jan03/r012903.html (accessed June 25, 2003).
38. G. Winter, "Schools Resegregate, Study Finds," *The New York Times.* Late Edition—Final , Section A , Page 14, Column 1. Available online at: http://www.nytimes.com/2003/01/21/education/21RACE.html (accessed January 26, 2003).
39. "Fighting School Resegregation," *The New York Times.* Late Edition—Final, Section A, Page 24, Column 1. Available online at: http://www.nytimes.com/2003/01/27/opinion/27MON1.html? (accessed January 27, 2003).
40. Winter, "Schools Resegregate."
41. Winter, "Schools Resegregate."
42. Winter, "Schools Resegregate." See also the brilliant work of Kozol in *Savage Inequalities.*
43. Winter, "Schools Resegregate;" "Fighting School Resegregation."

44. Winter, "Schools Resegregate."
45. "Reasons Why 'Percent Plans' Won't Work."
46. Winter, "Schools Resegregate." Although stereotypical depictions of the South cast it as more "racist" than the North, as these data show, that is a rather simplistic view of circumstances as they are today. Both regions of the country have their own types of racial problems, but it does seem to be the case that white students in the sample gathered in the Southeast have had more contact with nonwhite students prior to their arrival at college than had the students in the Northeast who wrote autobiographies, and the recent study by the Harvard Civil Rights Project supports this finding.
47. Bok, "Expert Report of Derek Bok."
48. W. Bowen and D. Bok, *The Shape of the River: Long-Term Consequences of Considering Race in College and University Admissions*, Princeton, NJ: Princeton University Press, 1998.
49. For a thorough discussion of this phenomenon, see J. Feagin and K. McKinney, *The Many Costs of Racism*, Lanham, MD: Rowman and Littlefield, 2003, pp. 203–207.
50. Feagin and McKinney, *The Many Costs of Racism*, p. 205, here citing the Eleventh Circuit Court of Appeals in *Faragher v. City of Boca Raton*.
51. Feagin and McKinney, *The Many Costs of Racism*, p. 206.
52. Feagin and McKinney, *The Many Costs of Racism*, pp. 206–207.
53. M. Marable, "Staying on the right path to racial equality," in G. Curry (ed.) *The Affirmative Action Debate*, Reading, MA: Addison Wesley, 1996, p. 12.
54. See Reskin, "The Effects of Affirmative Action," pp. 352–53, for a review of this literature.
55. B. Reskin, "The Effects of Affirmative Action," p. 352.
56. B. Reskin, "The Effects of Affirmative Action," p. 353, citing a study conducted by Alfred Blumrosen, reported in 1996, in a statement submitted to the Supreme Court of California responding to Proposition 209 on September 26, 1996.
57. B. Reskin, "The Effects of Affirmative Action," p. 353.
58. B. Reskin, "The Effects of Affirmative Action," p. 354.
59. Of course, some white men benefit more than others from "old boys' networks." White men that are born into the upper class and into elite social circles are much more able to utilize the most valuable of these networks. Still, simply because white men are more often in hiring and other power positions, it is more likely that any white man will have social networks connecting him to social advantages than it is for white women or people of color.
60. P. Kivel, *Uprooting Racism: How White People Can Work for Racial Justice*, Revised Edition, Gabriola Island, British Columbia: New Society Publishers: 2002, p.189.
61. The phrase "affirmative action" was first used in an executive order signed by President Johnson in 1967 that simply stated that government contractors must not discriminate against employees but rather should take "affirmative action" to ensure they are treated fairly, with no regard to race, religion, national origin, sex, or color. In other executive orders requirements were added for "goals and timetables" toward which contractors should direct their "good faith efforts" to make up for past inequities in utilizing white women and people of color in their businesses if deficiencies existed. These requirements have been mandatory only for companies doing businesses with the government, which includes most colleges and universities, but most other companies have put affirmative action practices into place voluntarily. Parts of this summary were drawn from Farley, *Majority-Minority Relations*, p. 490–91.
62. Kivel, *Uprooting Racism*, p. 190.
63. Marable, "Staying on the Right Path to Racial Equality," p. 13.
64. Kivel, *Uprooting Racism*, p. 190.
65. Marable, "Staying on the Right Path to Racial Equality," p. 13.
66. R. Jensen, "White Privilege Shapes the U.S.: Affirmative Action for Whites is a Fact of Life," in *The Social Construction of Difference and Inequality: Race, Class, Gender and Sexuality*, ed. T. Ore, Boston: McGraw-Hill, 2003, p. 515.
67. A. Aguirre and J. Turner, *American Ethnicity: The Dynamics and Consequences of Discrimination*, 3rd Edition, Boston: McGraw-Hill, p. 58–59.
68. Marable, "Staying on the Right Path to Racial Equality," p. 13.
69. D. Conley, "The Cost of Slavery," *The New York Times*. Available online at: http://www.nytimes.com/2003/02/15/opinion/15CONL.html? (accessed February 15, 2003).
70. K. Sacks, "How Jews Became White," in *The Social Construction of Difference and Inequality: Race, Class, Gender and Sexuality*, 2nd Edition, ed. T. Ore, Boston: McGraw-Hill, 2003, pp. 61–63.

71. K. Brodkin, *How Jews Became White Folks: And What That Says about Race in America*, New Brunswick: Rutgers University Press, 1998, p. 47.

72. I am indebted to Dr. Barbara Weins-Tuers for her assistance with this point, through personal conversations and the excellent presentations she has done for my race and ethnicity courses each semester.

73. Sacks, "How Jews Became White," p. 64; Kivel, *Uprooting Racism*, pp. 28–30.

74. Brodkin, *How Jews Became White Folks*, p. 49.

75. See Joe Feagin's discussion of how some whites, while not engaging in discrimination themselves, serve as bystanders, providing support for those who do, in J. Feagin, *Racist America: Roots, Current Realities, and Future Reparations*, New York: Routledge, 2000, pp. 140–41.

76. See, for example, T. Sowell, *Preferential Policies*, New York: Morrow, 1990; S. Steele, *The Content of Our Character: A New Vision of Race in America*, New York: St. Martin's Press, 1990.

77. Farley, *Majority-Minority Relations*, p. 496.

78. Farley, *Majority-Minority Relations*, pp. 496–97.

79. Farley, *Majority-Minority Relations*, p. 496.

80. A. Krueger, "Economic Scene: Sticks and Stones Can Break Bones, but the Wrong Name Can Make a Job Hard to Find." *The New York Times*, Thursday, December 12, 2002, p. C2. See also J. Feagin, *Racist America*, pp. 160–62, for a discussion of studies of discrimination in hiring.

81. Krueger, "Economic Scene," p. 226; K. Subach, "Study: 'White-Sounding' Names Help in Job Search," Available online at: http://www.collegian.psu.edu/archive/2003/01/01-31-03tdc/01-31-03dnews-01.asp>; "'White' Names Give Job Seekers an Edge," in *Race, Class and Gender in the United States,* 6th Edition, ed. P. Rothenberg, New York: Worth Publishers, 2004, p. 226.

82. Krueger, "Economic Scene."

83. Krueger, "Economic Scene;" K. Subach, "Study: 'White-Sounding' Names Help."

84. Krueger, "Economic scene."

85. B. Reskin, "The Effects of Affirmative Action," p. 354.

86. B. Reskin, "The Effects of Affirmative Action," p. 355. Here Reskin cites a study by Leesa Kern, conducted in 1996 at Ohio State University.

87. B. Reskin, "The Effects of Affirmative Action," p. 355. Here Reskin cites a study conducted by Harry Holzer and David Neumark in 1998.

88. B. Reskin, "The Effects of Affirmative Action," p. 355.

89. B. Reskin, "The Effects of Affirmative Action," p. 355.

90. B. Reskin, "The Effects of Affirmative Action," p. 355. Here Reskins cites a study by the Glass Ceiling Commission of the U.S. Department of Labor, conducted in 1995.

91. B. Tatum, *"Why Are All the Black Kids Sitting Together in the Cafeteria?": and Other Conversations about Race,* New York: Basic Books, 1997.

92. B. Reskin, "The Effects of Affirmative Action," p. 359.

93. B. Reskin, "The Effects of Affirmative Action," p. 357.

94. B. Reskin, "The Effects of Affirmative Action," p. 358.

95. B. Reskin, "The Effects of Affirmative Action," p. 358.

96. B. Reskin, "The Effects of Affirmative Action," p. 358.

97. B. Reskin, "The Effects of Affirmative Action," p. 359.

98. L. Carr, *"Color-Blind" Racism*, Thousand Oaks, CA: Sage, 1997; R. Frankenberg, *White Women, Race Matters: The Social Construction of Whiteness*, Minneapolis: University of Minnesota Press, 1993.

99. See, for example, E. Bonilla-Silva, *Racism Without Racists: Color-Blind Racism and the Persistence of Racial Inequality in the United States*, Lanham, MD: Rowman and Littlefield, 2003; Frankenberg, *White Women, Race Matters.*

100. Frankenberg, *White Women, Race Matters.*

101. G. Myrdal, *An American Dilemma*, New York: Harper and Brothers, 1944.

102. See, for example, M. Ani, *Yurugu: An African-Centered Critique of European Cultural Thought and Behavior,* Trenton, NJ: Africa World Press, 1994.

103. D. Carbaugh, *Talking American: Cultural Discourses on DONAHUE*, Norwood, NJ: Ablex Publishing Company, 1988.

104. Delgado, *The Coming Race War?* pp. 39–40.

105. See R. Blauner, "Talking Past Each Other: Black and White Languages of Race," in *Race and Ethnic Conflict*, ed. H. J. Ehrlich and F. L. Pincus, Boulder, CO: Westview Press, 1994, pp. 27–34.

106. D. Roediger, *The Wages of Whiteness: Race and the Making of the American Working Class*, London: Verso, 1991.

107. Lillian Smith, *Killers of the Dream*, Garden City, New York: Anchor Books, 1963, pp. 164–65.
108. Kivel, *Uprooting Racism*, p. 35.
109. Langston, "Tired of Playing Monopoly?" p. 149.
110. Farley, *Majority-Minority Relations*, p. 498.
111. U.S. Department of Justice, "Hate Crimes on Campus: The Problem and Efforts to Confront It," Bureau of Justice Assistance Monograph, October 2001. Available online at: http://www.cphv.usm.maine.edu/monograph.pdf (accessed February 9, 2004).
112. Estimates from the FBI and U.S. Department of Education suggest that more than a half a million college students are the targets of hate-motivated slurs or assaults each year, and that at least one hate crime per day happens on a college campus somewhere in the United States. This is according to "New Center Project Fights Hate on Campus," *Southern Poverty Law Center Report*, 33 (3), September 2003. Available online at: http://www.splcenter.org/center/splcreport/article.jsp?aid=47 (accessed July 23, 2004).
113. M. Waters, "Optional Ethnicities: For Whites Only?" in *Race, Class and Gender: An Anthology*, 5th Edition, ed. M. Anderson and P. Collins, Belmont, CA: Thompson/Wadsworth, pp. 418–27.
114. Aguirre and Turner, *American Ethnicity*, p. 195.

Chapter 6

1. Portions of this chapter are adapted from K. McKinney and J. Feagin, "Diverse Perspectives on Doing Antiracism: The Younger Generation," in *White Out: The Continuing Significance of Racism*, ed. A. Doane and E. Bonilla-Silva, New York: Routledge, pp. 233–251.
2. J. Feagin, *Racist America: Roots, Current Realities, and Future Reparations*, New York: Routledge, 2000, p. 105–136.
3. P. McIntosh, "White Privilege: Unpacking the Invisible Knapsack," in *Race, Class and Gender: An Anthology*, 5th Edition, ed. M. Andersen and P. Collins, Belmont, CA: Thompson/Wadsworth, 2004, pp. 103–108.
4. B. Tatum, *"Why Are All the Black Kids Sitting Together in the Cafeteria?": And Other Conversations About Race*, New York: Basic Books, 1997.
5. Feagin, *Racist America*, p. 204.
6. J. Helms, *A Race is a Nice Thing to Have: A Guide to Being a White Person or Understanding the White Persons in Your Life*, Topeka, KS: Content Communications, 1992.
7. G. Yamato, "Something about the Subject Makes It Hard to Name," in *Race, Class and Gender: An Anthology*, 3rd Edition, ed. M. Andersen and P. Collins, Belmont, CA: Wadsworth Publishing Company.
8. See, for example, E. Bonilla-Silva, *Racism Without Racists: Color Blind Racism and the Persistence of Racial Inequality in the United States*, Boulder, CO: Rowman and Littlefield, 2003; L. Carr, *"Color-Blind" Racism*, Thousand Oaks, CA: Sage, 1997; R. Frankenberg, *White Women, Race Matters: The Social Construction of Whiteness*, Minneapolis: University of Minnesota Press, 1993.
9. J. Helms, *Black and White Racial Identity Development*, Westport, CT: Praeger, 1990.
10. McIntosh, "White Privilege."
11. P. Kivel, *Uprooting Racism: How White People Can Work for Racial Justice*, Gabriola Island, BC: New Society Publishers, 2002, pp. 96–106.
12. Although various theorists discuss this point, here I draw on the work of Jay Gubrium and Jim Holstein, particularly in their 1998 work, J. Gubrim and J. Holstein, "Narrative Practice and the Coherence of Personal Stories," *The Sociological Quarterly* 39 (1), 1998, 163–188.
13. S. Lyman and M. Scott, *A Sociology of the Absurd*, Dix Hills, NY: General Hall, Inc., 1989, pp. 151–152.
14. Here I borrow Omi's term "emerging crisis of white identity," which I will discuss and cite in the ensuing discussion.
15. H. Winant, *Racial Condtions: Politics, Theory, Comparisons*, Minneapolis: University of Minnesota Press, 1994, p. 111.
16. Melissa Steyn. 2001. *"Whiteness Just Isn't What It Used To Be": White Identity In a Changing South Africa*. Albany: SUNY Press. p. xxiii.

17. Winant, *Racial Conditions*, p. 111.
18. M. Omi, "Racialization in the Post-Civil Rights Era," in *Mapping Multiculturalism*, ed. A. Gordon and C. Newfield, Minneapolis: University of Minnesota Press, 1996, pp. 178–186.
19. M. Halter, *Shopping for Identity: The Marketing of Ethnicity*, New York: Schocken Books, 2000.
20. Omi, "Racialization in the Post-Civil Rights Era."
21. J. Hitchcock, *Unraveling the White Cocoon*, Dubuque, Iowa: Kendall Hunt Publishing, 2001, p. 19.
22. Feagin, *Racist America*, p. 237.
23. J. Feagin, "The Future of U.S. Society in an Era of Racism, Group Segregation and Demographic Revolution," in *Sociology for the Twenty-First Century*, ed. J. Abu-Lughod, Chicago: The University of Chicago Press, 1999, pp. 199–212.
24. Hitchcock, *Unraveling the White Cocoon*, pp. 19–20.
25. For example, studies have shown that to be effective in ending prejudices, interracial contact must be equal-status contact, it must be noncompetitive and nonthreatening, it must be in a situation in which the parties are required to be cooperative and interdependent, and it must be more than superficial. (This summary of intergroup contact research draws on the excellent review by John E. Farley, in J. Farley, *Majority-Minority Relations*, 4th Edition, Upper Saddle River, New Jersey: Prentice Hall, 2000: pp. 46–51.) See also the discussion of the contact hypothesis in chapter 2.
26. J. Rabow, *Voices of Pain and Voices of Hope: Students Speak About Racism*, Dubuque, Iowa: Kendall Hunt Publishing, 2002, p. xvi. Here Rabow discusses a study conducted by Troy Duster at the University of California, Berkeley.
27. Omi, "Racialization in the Post-Civil Rights Era," p. 182.
28. Omi, "Racialization in the Post-Civil Rights Era," p. 183–185.
29. Lillian Rubin, "Is This a White Country, or What?" in *Experiencing Race, Class and Gender in the United States*, 2nd Edition, ed. V. Cyrus, London, Mayfield Publishing, 1996, p. 410–418.
30. C. Gallagher, 1997. "White Racial Formation: Into the Twenty-first Century," in *Critical White Studies: Looking Behind the Mirror*, ed. R. Delgado and J. Stefancic, Philadelphia: Temple University Press, 1997, p. 7.
31. See, for example, D. Conley, "The Cost of Slavery," 2003. *The New York Times*. Available online at: http://www.nytimes.com/2003/02/15/opinion/15CONL.html? (accessed February 15, 2003); M. Oliver and T. Shapiro, *Black Wealth/White Wealth: A New Perspective on Racial Inequality*, New York: Routledge, 1995.
32. Kivel, *Uprooting Racism*, p. 190.
33. M. Marable, "Staying on the Right Path to Racial Equality," in *The Affirmative Action Debate*, ed. G. Curry, Reading, MA: Addison Wesley, 1995, p. 13.
34. Feagin, "The Future of U.S. Society."
35. Feagin, "The future of U.S. society in an era of racism, group segregation and demographic revolution."
36. G. Lipsitz, *The Possessive Investment in Whiteness: How White People Profit from Identity Politics.* Philadelphia: Temple University Press, 1998.
37. Omi, "Racialization in the Post-Civil Rights Era."
38. M. Waters, *Ethnic Options: Choosing Identities in America*. Berkeley, CA: University of California Press, 1990.
39. Gallagher, "White Racial Formation: Into the Twenty-first Century."
40. See note 12.
41. These remarks are adapted from K. McKinney and J. Feagin, "Diverse Perspectives on Doing Antiracism: The Younger Generation," in *White Out: The Continuing Significance of Racism*, ed. A. Doane and E. Bonilla-Silva, New York: Routledge, pp. 233–251.
42. J. Feagin and H. Vera, *White Racism: The Basics*, New York: Routledge, 1995, pp. 9–10.
43. J. Feagin and E. O'Brien, *White Men on Race: Power, Privilege, and the Shaping of Cultural Consciousness*, Boston: Beacon Press, 2003.
44. R. Blauner, "Talking Past Each Other: Black and White Languages of Race," in *Race and Ethnic Conflict*, ed. H. J. Ehrlich and F. L. Pincus, Boulder, CO: Westview Press, 1994, pp. 27–34.
45. Feagin, *Racist America*, p. 254.
46. Blauner, "Talking Past Each Other."

47. See Blauner, "Talking Past Each Other;" C. Sleeter, "White Silence, White Solidarity," in *Race Traitor*, ed. N. Ignatiev and J. Garvey, New York: Routledge, 1996, pp. 257–265. Sleeter asserts that "equating ethnicity with race is a related strategy for evading racism," p. 260.
48. Blauner, "Talking Past Each Other."
49. McIntosh, "White Privilege."
50. For an in-depth discussion of the health costs of racism, see J. Feagin and K. McKinney, *The Many Costs of Racism*, Lanham, MD: Rowman and Littlefield, 2003.
51. See, for example, H. Giroux, "Racial Politics and the Pedagogy of Whiteness," in *Whiteness: A Critical Reader*, ed. M. Hill, New York: New York University Press, 1998, pp. 294–316.
52. P. Freire, *Pedagogy of the Oppressed*, New York: Continuum, 1995, p. 17. See also J. Feagin and H. Vera, *Liberation Sociology*, Boulder, CO: Westview, 2001, pp. 21–22.
53. Feagin, *Racist America*, p. 255.
54. Blauner, "Talking Past Each Other."

Appendix A

1. From the title of the 1992 volume edited by G. Rosenwald and R. Ochberg, *Storied Lives: The Cultural Politics of Self-Understanding*, New Haven: Yale University Press, 1992.
2. N. Denzin, *Interpretive Biography*, Newbury Park, CA: Sage, 1989.
3. Denzin, *Interpretive Biography*.
4. Denzin, *Interpretive Biography*, p. 25.
5. C. Riessman, *Narrative Analysis*, Newbury Park, CA: Sage, 1993, pp. 64–65.
6. Riessman, *Narrative Analysis*, p. 5.
7. Personal Narratives Group, "Truths," in Personal Narratives Group (Eds.) *Interpreting Women's Lives: Feminist Theory and Personal Narratives* (pp. 261–264). p. 261. Indianapolis: Indiana University Press; quoted in Riessman, *Narrative Analysis*, p. 22.
8. Riessman, *Narrative Analysis*, p. 69.
9. Some recent work has even begun to look at not only how respondents edit *themselves* in interview situations but, particularly in institutional interview contexts, how the interviewer may engage in an interactional editing process with the interviewee/client. See, for example, A. Marvasti, "Constructing the Service-Worthy Homeless Through Narrative Editing," *Journal of Contemporary Ethnography* 31 (5), 2002, 615–51.
10. J. Holstein and J. Gubrium, *The Active Interview*, Thousand Oaks, CA: Sage, 1995.
11. C. Gallagher, "White Like Me?: Methods, Meaning, and Manipulation in the Field of White Studies," in *Racing Research, Researching Race: Methodological Dilemmas in Critical Race Studies*, ed. F. Twine and J. Warren, New York: New York University Press, 2000, pp. 67–92.
12. Jerome Rabow, *Voices of Pain and Voices of Hope*, Dubuque, Iowa: Kendall Hunt, p. xxiv.
13. Riessman, *Narrative Analysis*, p. 68.
14. Riessman, *Narrative Analysis*, p. 66.
15. Riessman, *Narrative Analysis*, p. 68.

Appendix B

16. U.S. Census Bureau, "Geographic Comparison Table, Race and Hispanic or Latino: 2000: Geographic Area: Pennsylvania—Place and County Subdivision." Available online at: http://factfinder.census.gov/servlet/BasicFactsTable?_lang=en&_vt_name=DEC_2000_PL_U_GCTPL_ST7&_geo_id=04000US42.
17. U.S. Census Bureau, "Geographic Comparison Table, Race and Hispanic or Latino: 2000: Geographic Area: Tennessee–Place." Available online at: http://factfinder.census.gov/servlet/BasicFactsTable?_lang=en&_vt_name=DEC_2000_PL_U_GCTPL_ST7&_geo_id=04000US47.
18. Calculated percentage from U.S. Census Bureau, *County and City Data Book*, 2000, Table B-2.

19. Calculated percentage from U.S. Census Bureau, "General Population Characteristics—Tennessee," 1980, Table 14.

20. These data was gathered from the school's website and reflect the population in 2001. In order not to disclose the name of the school, I cannot disclose the website address.

21. This university's webpage gave data from past years, so I was able to use data from the year that I gathered data at this school, 1998.

22. This data was gathered by Eric Liddick from the Office of Admissions on this college campus.

Index